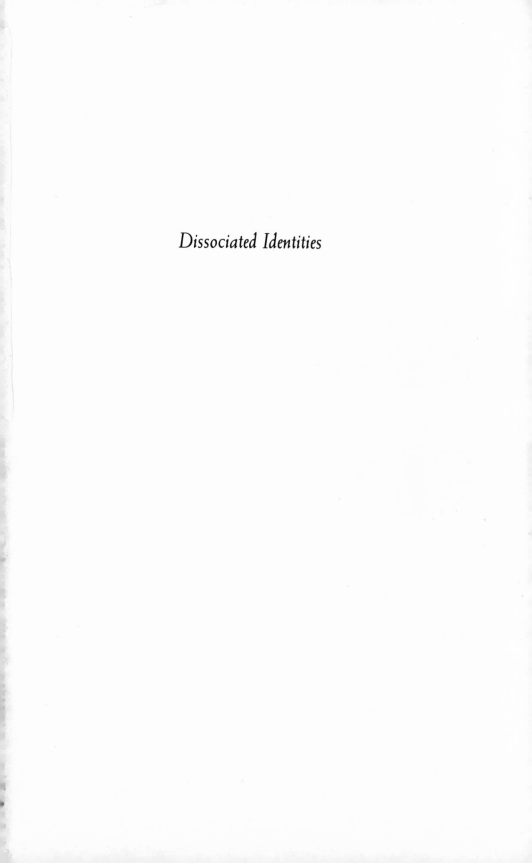

Dissociated Identities

Dissociated Identities

Ethnicity, Religion, and Class in an Indonesian Society

Rita Smith Kipp

Ann Arbor

THE UNIVERSITY OF MICHIGAN PRESS

1996   1995   1994   1993   4   3   2   1

A CIP catalogue record for this book is available from the British Library.

Library of Congress Cataloging-in-Publication Data

Kipp, Rita Smith.
    Dissociated identities : ethnicity, religion, and class in an
Indonesian society / Rita Smith Kipp.
        p.   cm.
    Includes bibliographical references and index.
    ISBN 0-472-10412-8 (alk. paper)
    1. Karo-Barak (Indonesian people)—Ethnic identity. 2. Karo-Batak
(Indonesian people)—Religion. 3. Indonesia—Ethnic relations.
4. Social classes—Indonesia.   I. Title.
DS632.K3K56   1993
305.89'922—dc20   93-19776
                                                              CIP

For Sarah and Jesse

Acknowledgments

This book draws on research undertaken over a period of almost two decades, some of it prompted by questions different from those pursued here. The list of people who have helped me along the way is correspondingly long.

Data gathered in 1972–74 over a period of eighteen months for a Ph.D. dissertation are the baseline of my knowledge of Karo society and culture. I had envisioned a dissertation on the subject of religious conversion but wrote one instead about two secular rituals—weddings and funerals—and the kinship ideology these express. During this time I lived in Payung Village and made frequent trips to neighboring villages. My husband and I lived with a Christian family and attended church and other Christian activities with them. My generalizations about Karo village life are primarily about Payung and my experiences there, ignoring the regional variations of custom and economy within Karoland. Payung is an accessible village, located on a major bus route, and it rests within a relatively densely populated, wet rice region. Virtually all the households in this relatively prosperous village engage in farming, some men and women are brokers of farm produce at wholesale markets, and others are teachers. The majority of Payung's 1,300 inhabitants are Christian.

During 1980–81 I worked in the Netherlands gathering materials for a historical study of the missionaries to the Karo. Using missionary and government archives as well as library sources, I gained a new sense of historical depth of what I had seen in Karoland during my dissertation research, and a new appreciation for the regional dynamics of which Karo society was one part. Some of those historical materials are put to use in this book. Correspondence to and from the Board of the Dutch Missionary Society (Nederlands Zendelinggenootschap, or NZG), extracts of the minutes of NZG meetings (Extract Acten), and other publications by the NZG were used especially in reconstructing the history of Karoland and the foothills region of the East Coast of Sumatra during the colonial period.

I returned to Indonesia for three months in the summer of 1983 collecting oral histories for the missionary project. During 1986 I spent three months at the Institute of Southeast Asian Studies in Singapore working on the theoretical and historical sections of this book, especially those sections having to do with the history and politics of Indonesia. From Singapore I went to Indonesia for three months where I lived in Kabanjahe, the district capital of Karoland. I lived with a Muslim family during this visit and participated in Muslim study groups and other events, attempting to rectify the fact that, until then, my contacts and interaction had been primarily with Christian or Perbegu Karo. I also began to explore the migrant experience on this trip with brief visits to Banda Aceh and Jakarta, and I began to attend more to the Karo scene in Medan where I had spent some time on and off for many years, always staying with a Karo family when in that city.

Finally, I spent several weeks in Jakarta in the summer of 1989. I lived with a Karo family during this period, attended church with them or other Karo friends, went to weddings, and interviewed leaders in the Karo community. I spent several days in Bandung as well, staying with members of my extended Karo family there and interviewing clergy and other leaders. In 1990 I returned for another brief visit to Indonesia, spending a week in Jakarta and two in Sumatra, touching bases again with friends and family in Payung Village, Medan, Kabanjahe, and Jakarta. Through these recent trips, I gained an understanding of how Karo society now spans both urban and village settings, and what differences of wealth mean for this society. While in Jakarta I stayed with a wealthy family and interviewed many community leaders, but I also spent a great deal of time with two working-class women, tagging along with them on a visit to a friend in the hospital, to the beach on an outing with their relatives from Sumatra, to a credit association meeting, and to a prewedding negotiation ceremony. My methods throughout have been resoundingly qualitative rather than quantitative, relying on participant observation, interviews, and written sources such as newspapers. Most of my interviews and interaction have taken place through the Karo language, in which I am more fluent than in Indonesian, although life in the cities and even in Kabanjahe required a great deal of interaction through Indonesian as well.

Granting agencies that have funded this research include the National Endowment for the Humanities and the Wenner-Gren Foundation for Anthropological Research (for the year in Holland), and the Fulbright Foundation (for the time at the Institute of Southeast Asian Studies and three months in Indonesia). The Program for Inter-Institutional Collaboration in Area Studies (PICAS) enabled me to spend a semester at the University of Michigan in

1989, during which time I carried out library research for this project. The Kenyon College Faculty Development program has also provided two small grants supporting summer trips to Indonesia. I am grateful for all these sources of financial support.

The list of those who have helped me or cooperated with me in Indonesia is long indeed. In citing interview or fieldnote materials I attempt to guard the anonymity of my sources, but here I would like to thank the following people: Roberto Bangun, Nd. Rosdinawati br. Bangun, Suci br. Bangun, Teridah Bangun, Kuasa Bukit, Bapa Helen Ginting, Juara Rimantha Ginting, Lemba Ginting, Nalinta Ginting, Mahmut Ginting, Meneth Ginting MADE, Sada Kata Ginting, Selamat Ginting, Tambarta Ginting, Christian Gintings, A. Ginting-Suka, Mbune Karo-karo, Haji Selama Kita Lingga, Martadi E., Masa Manik, S. M. Meliala, T. G. Munte, Pak Murni, Nd. Eva br. Purba, Damaris br. Purba, Gemok Purba, Kuasa Purba, Sartika br. Purba, Amran Rohany, Tine Ruiter, Anna br. Sebayang, Kita Sebayang, Marfin Sebayang, E. P. Sembiring, Jamin Sembiring, Nd. Lema br. Sembiring, Terbit Sembiring, Tanggu Sembiring, J. P. Sibero, Musa Sinulingga, Sampaten Sinulingga, Seh Malem br. Sinulingga, Saridin Siregar, Syabudin Siregar, Budi Sitepu, Kompeni Sitepu, Bapa Ros Sitepu, Abdul Salam Tarigan, Nd. Bahtera br. Tarigan, Ibu Haji br. Tarigan, Nd. Grace br. Tarigan, Henry Guntur Tarigan, Jamaluddin Tarigan, Juan Tarigan, Koman Tarigan, Neken Tarigan, Ridho Tarigan.

A special thanks goes to families with whom I have lived: Rosma br. Bangun in Payung; Payung Bangun and Esther Siregar in Medan; David and Jodi Randall in Medan; Haji Sebayak, R. S. Ginting Suka, and Bibi Biring in Kabanjahe; and Terkelin Surbakti and Nd. Eka br. Sembiring in Jakarta. The Bangun family is my Karo family, the link through which other Karo construct kinship with me.

A number of people read chapters and returned critical comments: Katherine Bowie, Don Emmerson, and R. William Liddle. John Bowen offered useful criticisms about the whole manuscript. Erica Spaid worked on the photographs, and George Markakis on the maps. As usual, Richard Kipp has read, edited, and commented on the whole manuscript in its various stages, and I am especially grateful for his help.

Contents

Chapter 1

Conceptualizing Identities

This book is about an Indonesian people, the Karo, and their modern predicament. The Karo heartland lies three degrees north of the equator on Sumatra, beginning just at the northern edge of the spectacular crater lake Toba and extending north over some 5,000 square kilometers (fig. 1). This heartland, a cool highland plateau surrounded by mountain peaks, is coextensive with a government district, Kabupaten Karo, but when the Karo speak of this place they call it Taneh Karo, Karoland. Karo speakers spill over into a number of adjacent districts to the northeast, occupying the rugged foothills that ripple toward Sumatra's East Coast. Since Indonesia does not take census data on ethnicity, it is difficult to say precisely how many Karo there are, but the population of Kabupaten Karo in 1985 was 236,780,[1] and at least that many Karo live outside Karoland in adjacent districts and in the urban centers of Indonesia. Karo is one of the Batak languages, and several other Batak peoples live along the mountains extending south of Karoland.

House styles and ceremonial clothing are among the prominent signifiers whenever Indonesians depict ethnicity in museums, on postcards, and in tourist arts. Looking for such markers in Karoland from the vantage of a tour bus, a person would find the view barely distinguishable from the lowlands and from other Batak areas. The traditional Karo house, a large multifamily structure with a massive dormered roof, is increasingly rare, having given way almost everywhere to single-family dwellings with a standard Sumatran look. The maroon or deep red cloths that women wrap around their heads as *tudung* and wear as shawls around their shoulders do give Taneh Karo a slightly different visage.[2] A woman wearing a maroon tudung anywhere is recognizable (to other Karo) as a Karo, but most women, especially the younger ones, don this headwrap only on ceremonial occasions. Otherwise the dress of men and of younger women resembles that of other Indonesians.

Karo most often recognize each other, however, through intangible rather than tangible markers, specifically through linguistic symbols. A person's clan or subclan name is one such marker (although there are a few Karo

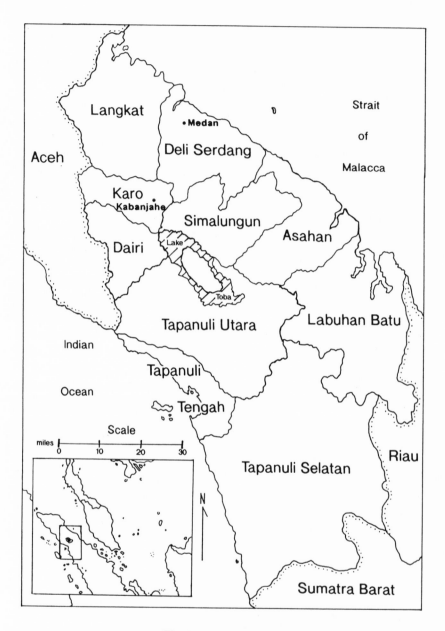

Fig. 1. North Sumatra

subclan names that appear in other Batak clan systems as well). Overhearing a person speak Karo—in a bus or a market in the city—is another sure index by which Karo recognize each other. Other Indonesians, especially non-Batak Indonesians, would not be able to recognize either the clan names or the spoken language as marking specifically Karo identity. In fact, both strangers and the close neighbors of urban Karo are more likely to label them Batak than Karo, as I found wandering around Jakarta neighborhoods looking for the addresses of Karo friends or informants, or looking for Karo churches. The intangible markers signify Karo only to insiders; to outsiders, these people are Batak.

The main forces today shaping people's sense of themselves as Karo are migration out of Karoland, greater communication between Karoland and areas outside it, and the Karo's incorporation into an ethnically diverse nation striving for economic development. A family I know in Jakarta exemplifies the effects of these forces.

Bapa Mina (a pseudonym) has lived in a Jakarta working-class neighborhood for at least fifteen years. In the past he has worked as a driver and construction worker, but now carries two printed business cards indicating that he is a building contractor. In fact, he does not work regularly, but gets by on payments from a Chinese construction company for which he is an indigenous front man. Raised on the Karo Plateau by his mother's father who was a traditional bonesetter (*patah tulan*), Bapa Mina learned to treat broken limbs and to make medicines for kidney stones and high blood pressure. He treats patients occasionally in his house. Also an expert traditional dancer, he was once picked to tour France with a performing group, but the abortive coup of 1965 interfered with those plans. (He never mentions his own political involvements, only that in that era his father sheltered PKI [Indonesian Communist Party] suspects who feared for their lives.) He and Nande Mina first met when she was in a group of young people that he was teaching to dance. He was living in Medan then, where he played and sang in a pop band. It was there that he first started going to the movies regularly, as he continues to do with enthusiasm.

[28 August 1990. Jakarta.] Bapa Mina has seen *The Gods Must Be Crazy* more than once. He recounted the whole story and acted out his favorite scenes for a cousin, the cousin's Sundanese wife, a neighbor woman, and me. Nande Mina (his wife), who was also familiar with the movie, embellished his telling from the side. Bapa Mina rose out of his chair now and then to portray the Stone Age Bushman adventurer astounded and baffled by what he finds in the modern world. His favorite scene still brought tears of laughter to his eyes: the Bushman sees a woman taking off her jacket and thinks she has removed her skin. After the story and the laughing were over, Nande Mina reflected that what had happened to the primitive traveler was for the good. His eyes had been opened, and he had learned that there are many kinds of people in the world, there are churches, and other things he had not imagined. He was all the wiser for his experiences, she assessed.

The Gods Must Be Crazy aptly allegorizes the life story of Bapa Mina and of thousands of other Karo who were born and raised in village settings and have since migrated to urban centers throughout Indonesia. The Karo, unlike some of their Sumatran neighbors, did not have a tradition of *merantau,* in which young men are expected to leave home for religious education or to seek their fortunes. Significant migration outside of Karoland (or its contiguous areas where Karo live) did not take place until after 1950 and has increased significantly since 1970. People recall that when students or other young people left for Jakarta in the 1950s families took them to the port at Belawan for a tearful farewell, presuming that the separation would be long. Today going away for education is routine, and the traffic between Karoland, Medan, and Jakarta is constant enough to deflect much of the separation anxiety.

This book is about Karo identities, and about what it means to be Karo in a plural world. The pluralities of Karo life are not merely cultural and geographic, as the vignette about Bapa Mina describes, but also religious. Most Karo claim to be Christian, their affiliations divided among Catholicism and a variety of Protestant denominations. In addition, there are small minorities of Karo Muslims, Hindus, and Perbegu. Wealth differences, too, create different life-styles and tastes, with the wealthiest Karo able to travel and educate their children abroad and the poorest rooted in a daily struggle to survive. To some extent the wealth differences parallel the urban/rural divide as well; Karo of middle and upper means are preponderantly urban.

Sketching the ethnic, religious, and class dimensions of Karo life does not exhaust "what it means to be Karo in a plural world." I do not, for example, consider gender identities, which are indeed as central to Karo lives as they are to the lives of men and women everywhere. In addition, some Karo identify themselves, like Bapa Mina, as bonesetters; others as professional musicians, teachers, vendors, and on through a variety of specific skills and occupations. Clan and village origin identities, as well as age, are also very important in most Karo's sense of who they are. Any identity coordinates we select to analyze are invariably incomplete, a "horizontal trajectory of adjectives" ending with an "exasperated 'etc.'" (Butler 1990, 143). To know about ethnicity, religion, and class in contemporary Karo society is to know a great deal about many persons' identities, although it will never take us to the limits of even one person's sense of self.

I have selected ethnicity, religion, and class among the possible dimensions of identity because I wish to explore here the links between identity and state power. The Karo, citizens of Indonesia, exist in a polity in which controlling ethnicity, religion, and class have been especially important to the country's leaders. Indonesia manages religion, for example, through a unique bureaucratic structure unlike any other in Southeast Asia or the Muslim world. Its policies on ethnicity, too, are quite different from those of its closest neighbors. The Indonesian state responds to class politics in ways similar to other states, that is, both by officially ignoring class in public discourse and by strongly repressing political expressions of class interests. The state also controls class indirectly by bureaucratically legitimating cultural and religious identities. The government's policies on culture and religion aim foremost to control the disruptive potential of cultural and religious differences, but consequently shape the terms in which people think about other kinds of identities, in particular their class interests.

The "exasperated 'etc.'" that occurs at the end of any list purporting to specify identity politics hints too that the unfinished business of identity formation always stretches from a past into a future. What follows is as much a historical as an ethnographic exercise. I want to argue that, through time, some important aspects of Karo identities have pulled apart from each other, becoming conceptually dissociated. At one point in the Karo past religious conversion almost inevitably entailed the crossing of an ethnic boundary. By becoming a Muslim one stopped being a Karo and became a Malay. Today, Karo Muslims are a growing minority. Furthermore, history reveals the emergence of "Karo" as an identity from within a larger category, "Batak," a process that continues today as some urban Karo have begun a movement to de-Batak themselves. This movement asserts (so far, with only limited success) that the Karo are not, and have never been, Batak. A Karo Muslim association exists to reaffirm and reassure its membership that they are Karo; a letter and publication campaign asserts that the Karo are *not* Batak: these hint at some outlines of identity politics in contemporary Karo life, but also at historical traces of old struggles between Batak and Malay, Karo and Toba Batak, periphery and center.

Identities of any kind (gender, sexual orientation, race, ethnicity) take form through a conceptual process of contrast (Norton 1988). In many cases the contrasts mark not merely differences, but hierarchies of value and power. Identity politics are thus a contest to retain power, or else an assertion of value against the grain. Karo have come to rethink their ethnic identities through time as a result of greater contact with people who do not identify themselves as Karo or as Batak, and who see themselves as morally and culturally superior. These assertions of moral or cultural superiority might have made little difference to the Karo had their relative isolation remained intact or had the assertions not sometimes had the teeth of militaristic, technological, and organizational force behind them. Since identities are so often constructed around differences of power, the state—a structure of centralized, concentrated power—constitutes a significant site of that construction. For example, laws and policies on marriage and inheritance shape citizens' expectations about gender, and access to leadership (or merely jobs in the bureaucracy) may be officially or informally constrained by ethnicity or religious affiliation.

The Karo's cultural and religious identities have emerged historically through repositionings in relation to centers of state power, even states of which Karo were not citizens. The Karo heartland in precolonial times was outside of, yet linked to, surrounding Muslim polities that were themselves nodes in an international trade network. Starting at the end of the nineteenth century the Karo were incorporated into a colonial state and, in the 1940s, found themselves in the midst of a revolution to forge a new nation. Since independence they have joined other Indonesians as citizens of the largest polity in the region. These shifting power centers have created new contexts in which Karo persons came to think about ethnicity, religion, and nationalism, and about themselves.

The parsing of Karo identities is rooted in the precolonial past, but it continues in the present under the so-called New Order that has controlled Indonesia since 1965. One of my goals will be to show how the modern Indonesian state capitalizes (pun intended) on the dissociation of people's identities, a process for which it is only partly responsible. The state's bureaucratization of religion and culture encourages that process of dissociation, with functional consequences for state stability.

At an ethnographic level this book attempts to link the compartmentalization of Karo life with an understanding of ideological domination, but the subjects of this analysis do not easily yield to my view of them as subjected. Unlike the Karo spirit mediums, storytellers, and healers Mary Steedly (1989) eloquently depicts "hanging without a rope" between the past and the present, the village and the city, most of the people in this book are literate and self-consciously Christian or Muslim men and women. My closest Karo friendships have been with a poor rural woman, an urban middle-class family, and two poor women in Jakarta, but I have interviewed and spent a great deal of time with people who span the range from very wealthy to very poor—vendors, entrepreneurs, farmers, clergy, academics, journalists, teachers, and other government employees. My lasting impression of most of these acquaintances is not one of anomie, disempowerment, and loss, but of people who know who they are and what they want. They want, for the most part, material security, the respect of their kin and neighbors, and health and success for themselves and their children.

One question animating this analysis, then, is how the pluralities of Karo lives work *for* some men and women. The goal is to understand how the compartmentalization of modern life enhances the ability of the state to exert its control, but also how some persons benefit from and embrace this compartmentalization for their own ends. These analytical goals require some orientation in relation to concepts such as identity and the self and, later, the state and ethnicity, all of which have come under analytical scrutiny and may not be taken as self-evident conceptual tools.

Selves and Identities

The Western conception of the person as a bounded, unique, more or less integrated motivational and cognitive universe, a dynamic center of awareness, emotion, judgment and action organized into a distinctive whole and set contrastively both against other such wholes and against a social and natural background, is, however incorrigible it may seem to us, a rather peculiar idea within the context of the world's cultures. (Geertz [1974] 1983, 62)

This commonsense view of the autonomous, bounded person can be found throughout social science scholarship up to the present, and much standard psychological theory still posits the self as a "pristine unity" (Gregory 1987, 198). Classical social theory presumed, furthermore, that this kind of self would evolve elsewhere with the spread of modernization. In *The Division of Labor in Society* ([1933] 1964), for example, Durkheim posited an inverse relationship between the "collective conscience" of simple societies organized through mechanical solidarity and the "personality" that characterizes those who live in complex societies. Primitive peoples exhibit less individuality, Durkheim thought (ibid., 128ff.). Self-consciousness is a by-product of modern, heterogenous societies with specialized divisions of labor.[3]

Many observers agree, furthermore, that the Western emphasis on an autonomous self emerged in connection with the "abstract domination" of capitalism (e.g., Barnett and Silverman 1979, 68). Durkheim had admitted the dark possibility of anomie in modern societies under "abnormal" conditions of hierarchy and coercion, but Marx regarded hierarchy and coercion as intrinsic to modern capitalism, and alienation inevitable. More than simply greater diversity and "personality," modernity entails inequalities. Persons alienated from the means of production are separated from the products of their own labor. The recent emphasis on self-realization and self-fulfillment (e.g., Taylor 1989, 506–13) answers the marketing requirements of advanced capitalism (Giddens 1991, 917; Lasch 1979). "For us, our very notions of self and self-identity are tied to production and market processes designed to sell us a range of products" (Barnett and Silverman 1979, 34).[4]

Scholars have also been busy analytically taking apart the Western self for some time. The view of selves as "partible" has thus appeared gradually in scholarly literature (Comaroff and Comaroff 1991). Sociologists began to see selves as divided, split between a subjective, experiencing "I" and an awareness of "me" as one supposes one appears to others (Mead 1934). The psyche characterized by "multiplicity, disunity, and self-deception" that Freud envisioned (Rosenau 1992, 45) has been reworked and incorporated into modern social theory (e.g., Giddens 1984). Like the commonsense view of the autonomous, bounded self, the scholarly vision of the partible self has also been historicized in the rise of capitalism, and specifically in the requirement for appropriating persons' time and labor. The germ of a divided self predates capitalism in our intellectual heritage, perhaps, but it resonated especially with the inner-directed self of the Reformation, and finally "colonized the popular consciousness" during the Victorian era through the vehicles of literacy and literature (Comaroff and Comaroff 1991, 62).

Perceiving that the Western self was invented,[5] one part of a whole sociocultural system, anthropologists have documented how other peoples, occupying different socioeconomic worlds, have invented themselves differently. Partly inspired by Clifford Geertz's work in Indonesia and elsewhere (1983, 1973a), anthropological studies of the self and personhood proliferated.[6] Selves in such diverse places as Bali, New Guinea, and India appeared to be divisible, relational, multiple, and situationally specific in contrast to the autonomous and unitary Western self (Shweder and Bourne 1984). Japanese women's selves (Kondo 1990) could be added to that gross comparison of the West versus the rest, except that the commonsense view of the Western self seems increasingly to be an illusion that ignores the "webs of interlocution" enmeshing each of us with others (Taylor 1989, 39).

Quite beyond seeing the self as autonomous but divided in various ways, postmodernist theory in the humanities and social sciences deconstructs the "subject" almost entirely. The postmodern subject is, at the very least, "either divided inside himself or divided from others" (Dreyfus and Rabinow 1983, 208) and, at most, elided entirely in theory. Some postmodernists explain away the rational, meaning-seeking agent as a linguistic fiction, a relic of modernism and humanism, and a disguise for various forms of domination.[7] Unexamined assumptions about "the individual" and a presumed antinomy between the individual and society underlie Marx as surely as Durkheim, Marilyn Strathern charges, skeptical that we will find "society" and "the individual" wherever we go. "The internal critique of Western capitalism that draws attention to alienation—to the separation of a person from his/her work—rests ultimately on the notion that persons somehow have a natural right to the products of their own work, since they are the authors of their acts" (Strathern 1988, 142).

Postmodern gender theory has been leading away from essentialized conceptions of being, reconceptualizing identities as multiple and, always, "constructed" through repetition and discourse (e.g., Briskin 1990). Judith Butler, a philosopher, de-essentializes gender identities with implications for identities of any kind, questioning whether one can be said to *have* or even *be* a gender. For her, there is no essential gender identity behind or aside from the *expression* of gender in our speech and action (Butler 1990, 25). The self Butler envisions is thus closer to what anthropologists have written about selves in New Guinea, India, or Bali. "There is no self that is prior to the convergence [of demands made of it] or who maintains 'integrity' prior to its entrance into this conflicted cultural field" (ibid., 145).

Why does the postmodern self in the late twentieth century—divided, context dependent, and relational—look strangely like the selves anthropologists have been seeking and finding in all kinds of places once thought barely modern? This congruence of the postmodern understanding of the self with the data of ethnography may have occurred because postmodern anthropologists see themselves in their subjects, or because anthropology's relativism, and especially the discipline's linguistic element, makes up a large part of the very mirror through which the postmodern self has become visible to other scholars. The florescence of self-and-person studies in anthropology no doubt both indexes and influences the postmodernist climate in which the "pristine unity" of the Western self seems more and more chimerical (or ideological). "Identity is conjunctural, not essential" (Clifford 1988, 11).

To suggest, as I do, that key aspects of Karo identity have become conceptually distinct fits classical social theory about an ineluctable and apparently universal social evolution. Both Durkheim and Marx envisioned others becoming more and more like us as they are swept into capitalism and modernization, a truth now mooted by the realization that who we are is neither uniform, fixed, nor certain. There is never an "I" apart from an internalized "other," and selves are linguistically constructed and partitioned everywhere. Where classical theorists led us to imagine encroaching homogeneity in the march of history, we are finding instead the proliferation of differences (Marcus and Fischer 1986).

Karo Identities: Modern Dissociation or an Indigenous Dissembledness?

Perhaps, then, Karo identities were *always* dissociated and contextual, and what this book documents is less social change than a change in theoretical conceptions allowing us to see that dissociation. Perhaps what I am seeing as newly compartmentalized identities and attributing to modern societies (and especially to the exercise of modern forms of power) is actually a self that has been there all along, an indigenous variety that differs in kind from Western selves. In the tradition of finding different kinds of selves in different cultural settings, Ward Keeler (1987) speaks of the Javanese self in terms of a "dissembled center," meaning a self-effacement that opens one as a conduit of supernatural power.[8] He finds evidence of this displaced or disguised self in the inactive silence of ritual sponsors, the use of indirect quotations, and above all, in the figure of the *dhalang* (puppeteer). I could marshall similar information about Karo self-effacement: the invisibility of ritual sponsors thanks to the use of layered intermediaries in all formal speaking (Kipp 1979); the rarity of names as opposed to kin terms in address and reference; and an etiquette of kin-term usage that requires a speaker to describe his or her close kin as the addressee's close kin, and, conversely, to speak of the addressee's close kin as if they were the speaker's (Kipp 1984b, 913–14).

One thing cannot be gainsaid: the contexts and conditions of Karo lives have changed markedly in the last one hundred years. This book looks to specify some of those changes and their consequences for selfhood and identity. For example, the complex language of kinship through which Karo speakers politely dissemble themselves is increasingly lost to the children of urban migrants who grow up speaking Indonesian; and at the lavish weddings of the urban middle class, the principle sponsors and the bridal couple are now plainly displayed. The latter tendency especially suggests a new focus on the individual, but we cannot expect Karo individuals to be "bounded, unique, more or less integrated . . . etc." any more than we now expect Western versions to fit this model.

I will view the dissociation of Karo identities as an indication of social change, aware that my viewing cannot be separated from who and where I am. Arguing the fragmentation of Karo lives and granting that Karo identities, like mine, are contextual and built up from the repeated use of signs and symbols, I find Karo men and women more modern than postmodern. A description of the hypothetical postmodern individual, concerned with instant gratification, and "shying away from collective affiliation and communal responsibility , . . . a floating individual with no distinct reference points or parameters" (Rosenau 1992, 52), does not fit most of the Karo I know.[9] For that matter, most Americans seem not very postmodern in those terms, either. As Geertz once said, contemplating the bugbear of anthropological relativism, "There may be some genuine nihilists out there, along Rodeo Drive or around Times Square, but . . . at least most of the people I meet, read, and read about, and indeed I myself, are all-too-committed to something or other, usually parochial" (1984, 265). Likewise, the persons who appear in this account are, on the whole, movers, doers, and joiners, incorrigibly hopeful and busy—organizing ethnic associations and publishing ethnic newspapers, studying Arabic recitation or Christian hymns, looking for success with a little print shop or a truckload of cabbages. The somewhat separate spheres of ethnic and religious identities create for them a "free space," to borrow a phrase from David Martin (1990), in which they can maneuver toward their goals and find satisfaction in their lives, a series of nonisomorphic boundaries across which they move. To be sure, the middle and upper classes command the resources to move most adroitly among the dissociated identities of modern life.

One of the oldest chestnuts of Asian/Western comparisons, whether proffered by Asians or by Westerners, is that Westerners are individualistic, Asians communalistic and group oriented. Discussions with my Karo friends and other Indonesians confirm again and again that they, too, have learned this contrast to be "true," and that they do not like to think of themselves becoming more like the West on this score.[10] I suggest, nonetheless, that the changes characterizing Karo selves *are* similar to some of the changes documented in Western history, and that the causes for these changes—wage labor, urbanization, the growth and bureaucratization of the state—are also similar. Unlike Durkheim, however, I do not presume that Karo of a century ago had less personality or individuality than those of today. Unlike Marx, I do not presume that those Karo who work for wages are any more or less alienated than those who continue to work on their own land producing at least part of their subsistence needs.

Karo life has, nonetheless, become partitioned in new ways that compare to the processes sociologists describe as secularization (Martin 1978).

[T]he individual has been taken out of a rich community life and now enters instead into a series of mobile, changing, revocable associations, often designed merely for highly specific ends. We end up relating to each other through a series of partial roles. (Taylor 1989, 502)

Religion, for example, has become a delineated sphere that lends itself to a degree of choice. Karo families and urban ethnic communities try to insulate kinship solidarity and ethnic identity from religious divisiveness. Contemporary Karo express both religious affiliation and an ethnic identity more self-consciously than in the past, too, and through new sets of contrasting possibilities. Wealth differences and different life-styles separate Karo from each other to a greater degree than in the past, but, unlike ethnicity and religion, these have not generated organized collectivities. This compartmentalized, secularized society in which middle-class people see religion and ethnicity as more essential than class strikes me as more than coincidentally similar to my own where the "myth of classlessness" dies hard (Ehrenreich 1989; Parker 1972). Scholars have readily appropriated ethnicity and religious differences, aspects of Indonesian "peasant ideology," as analytical categories (Kahn 1982). For Indonesians and scholars alike, an image of society divided by culture and religion obscures the politics of class.

Before examining contemporary Karo identities and how the policies of the Indonesian state influence them, we will look at the formation of Karo ethnic and religious identities historically to seek the beginnings of their dissociation. Some theories of ethnic identity have stressed the top-down forces of colonial administrations that divided in order to conquer and control, categorizing "tribes" in order to administer them. Other theoretical arguments point to bottom-up forces: subjugated or despised peoples protect their dignity by asserting their positive differences from those around them.

Still other explanations stress the competitive struggle for power, influence, and resources that prompts ambitious men to rally a following by fanning ethnic antagonism. All of these forces shaped the emergence of Karo ethnic identities, although they came into being at different times and varied through time in their relative importance. Once operant, they have all continued in some measure to affect Karo ethnicity.

The earliest of these forces was a top-down labeling by powerful others such as Malay chiefs and foreign traders with whom "Batak" peoples interacted. State policies represent a second, successive top-down influence: first those policies of the colonial state, especially those governing missionaries and delimiting administrative partitions and, later, policies of the Indonesian nation-state aiming to contain class and communal fragmentation. A third force, competition between Karo and other ethnic groups for economic and political spoils, gained importance in the colonial period. While ethnic rivalry continues in the present, it must be greatly muted in accord with government policies and national values that castigate *sukuisme* (tribalism).

Notes

1. Buku Pintar Kabupatan Daerah, Tingkat II Karo. 1985. Kabanjahe: Bappeda.

2. The ubiquity of the maroon color is comparatively recent; the color of women's clothing prior to the 1930s was uniformly indigo.

3. Mary Douglas (1969) contrasts primitive and modern consciousness in similar terms. In the words of another classical theorist, context specific relations based on "contract" supersede those based on ascribed "status" (Maine 1970).

4. See also Sennett and Cobb 1972.

5. Barnett and Silverman 1979; Foucault 1977, 194; Wagner 1975.

6. See Harris 1989, Mines 1988, and Shweder and Bourne 1984 for some conceptual writings on the topic; see also J. Errington 1984, S. Errington 1983, and Keeler 1987 for some studies from Indonesian settings.

7. See Rosenau 1992, 42–61 for a review of this discussion.

8. This is related to mystical practices seeking God within the self, e.g., Errington 1984, 279.

9. See also Sturrock 1979, 13–15 for references to postmodernism's war on "ego-philosophies."

10. See also Heider 1991, 30–34.

Chapter 2

Precolonial Conversations about the Batak

The chief symbolic marker is a name, and names exist in a system of names. (Nash 1989, 8–9)

The culture history of the Karo Batak is obscure, but speculations abound. One researcher hopes to place the ultimate Batak origins in Mesopotamia, suggesting that Oceanic peoples migrated east from there around 1500 B.C. (Hostetter 1988). Others have sought connections with a Hindic past, finding cognates in Sanskrit and Karo and suggesting that Karo society incorporated Tamil traders who married Karo women (McKinnon 1987). The Sembiring clan (literally, the dark ones) contains a number of subclans with Indian-derived names, such as Berahmana. There is also no mistaking the Sanskrit source of many deities, calendrical and astrological labels, and so on, but the same can be said for many Indonesian peoples (Gonda 1973; Kern 1903; Parkin 1978).

Certainly the majority of the Karo's cultural roots are indigenous. The Batak languages, like most Indonesian languages, are of the Austronesian group, and Batak social organization based on patrilineal descent and the ideal of asymmetrical cross-cousin marriage has parallels throughout the archipelago. J. H. Neumann, a missionary who worked in Sumatra for fifty years, judged from the Karo's linguistic uniformity that they had occupied their present homeland perhaps only since A.D. 1600. Attempting to trace the origins of each of the five clans that constitute this society, Neumann concluded that these clans and subclans had had diverse sources and that their predecessors had converged in the Karo region at different moments (Neumann 1926). His origin model, which has influenced Masri Singarimbun (1975, xx, 72) as well as other scholars of Karo culture history, suggests that Karo society is a linguistically convergent amalgam of groups who moved into the region relatively recently from surrounding areas.

15

Some speculate that the Karo are the remnants of Haru or Aru, a coastal Sumatran chiefdom from the twelfth to the fourteenth century which is named in a wide variety of early sources and appears also on early maps of the region (Schadee 1918). Kota Cina, an extensive archaeological site eight kilometers inland from the present port of Belawan, may have been a major city of Aru (Milner, McKinnon, and Sinar 1978; Wolters 1970, 1975). The discovery at Kota Cina of two Buddha figures of South Indian or Sinhalese origin suggests this was an "Indianized" polity, although historical sources describe Aru as Muslim. Edmund McKinnon's archaeological research led him to conclude that, beginning in the second century, Kota Cina, at which a significant community of Indians existed, was an emporium on the China-to-India trade route. Chinese settlers came later, in the twelfth century, at about the time of Aru's initial and imperfect Islamization (Milner, McKinnon, and Sinar 1978). Aru became a military and marine force powerful enough to force enormous concessions from the Sultan of Banten (Malacca) but, after continual confrontations with Aceh, finally came to a fiery demise in 1539 under the forces of Aceh's Iskandar Muda, who supposedly besieged the city with a hundred elephants. At that time Iskandar Muda deported a large part of the population and, in his effort to crush Aru, may have crushed even its name, for after this the region is called Deli, a small sultancy that was subject to Aceh at least periodically thereafter. The site of Kota Cina was abandoned at this time. When Alexander Hamilton (1930) passed this area sometime between 1688 and 1723 nothing was being exported through Deli. All trace of Aru's splendor was gone, and Hamilton feared to land because of rumors of cannibals.

So extensive is Kota Cina that those who have analyzed the site wonder why Aru does not appear even earlier than it does in historical sources. Kota Cina lies a little farther south than people had supposed Aru to be located, and is identical in locale to the area known after the fifteenth century as Deli (Tibbits 1971, 494), but Aru may have specified a whole region of coastline rather than a single settlement (Miksic 1979, 47). Perhaps Aru was the P'ata of earlier sources: "It is not impossible that an Islamized P'ata assumed the name 'Aru,' and P'ata (Batta) came to be used in a more general sense in reference to the pagan people of the interior" (Milner, McKinnon, and Sinar 1978, 37). In this sequential name shifting, P'ata, a Hindic polity of the East Coast, was reincarnated as Aru, an Islamic kingdom, and then, when subjugated by Aceh, became known as Deli. In the process, *Batak* shifted to delineate the interior, pagan peoples. Although this neat linkage of names with political and religious changes is certainly possible, it remains only an interesting conjecture about the historical connection between those "pagan people of the interior" to which the names Karo and Batak later became attached, and the coastal kingdoms of Aru and P'ata mentioned by the earliest travelers.

The question here, however, is not really culture history, but ethnic consciousness; not how and when did the culture and language called Karo Batak emerge from their ancestral sources and incorporate other influences, but how did this culture and language come to be used self-consciously as identity markers. The two words, *Karo* and *Batak*, indicate a nested relationship, with Batak the more general category and Karo a kind of Batak. What were the forces that shaped people's understanding of *Batak* and *Karo*, and led people to apply these labels to certain cultural traditions? And, since we understand ethnic consciousness as something that has relevance only in culturally plural settings, who were the Others against which *Batak* and *Karo* were cast? These questions presuppose a synthetic view of ethnicity as a form of identity politics.

Conceptualizing Ethnicity: A Synthetic Approach

Studies of ethnicity multiplied apace in the 1970s and 1980s. Aside from edited collections and monographs, a number of new journals also appeared. Sociologists and political scientists wanted to understand the emergence of ethnic based interest groups and the grassroots celebration of ethnicity in the United States at a time when ethnicity had been all but written off as an anachronism (Enloe 1973; Glazer and Moynihan 1975; Nielson 1985). Theories of assimilation and national integration had assumed that ethnicity would gradually lose its significance in modern societies, and, to the extent that it remained significant in some, it signaled a retarded political development. What, then, did this "new" ethnicity mean? The dramatic and unexpected results of ethnic politics in the former Soviet Union and Eastern Europe have rekindled the question (e.g., Emmerson 1991; Laitin 1991).

Anthropological studies of ethnicity began to proliferate in roughly the same period, although their impetus differed slightly from those in sociology and political science. In the late 1960s anthropologists came to worry over the nature of the entities they had traditionally taken unthinkingly as their units of description and comparison. This "problem of the tribe" seemed especially acute in highland Southeast Asia where persons sometimes changed tribes at will or stated a tribal identity that varied according to context (Leach 1954). The question had special relevance to cross-cultural approaches in which accurate statistical interpretation of the comparison of hundreds of units rested on the assumption that such units were real and more or less bounded (Helm 1967).

Anthropological studies in urban Africa were further undermining the concept of the tribe and pointing instead to issues of ethnicity.[1] It became clear that first the colonial period and now urban life in independent nations were heightening if not creating "tribal" consciousness. Abner Cohen (1969) spoke of the "retribalization" of Africans in the cities, but others came increasingly to speak of this phenomenon as ethnicity rather than tribalism. The term *tribe* connoted some kind of pristine isolation that no longer existed, if indeed it ever had, and *tribalism* implied a decidedly primitive form of political bonding. In other cases "tribes" were shown to be fictitious entities that colonial governments had created for purposes of administrative convenience. One scholar of Africa announced that he had expunged the word *tribe* from his professional vocabulary (Southall 1976), and like him, others spoke less and less of tribes and more and more of ethnicity (e.g., Wallerstein 1960).

Ethnicity took the tribes out of anthropology, detribalized it, so to speak. The concern with ethnicity, more than simply a new trend (Drummond 1983) or a shift in jargon, signaled a change in anthropology's view of its subject matter. Some romantic delusions were lost there as anthropologists came to acknowledge their subjects' historicity and to describe the competition for resources in fully urban contexts and modern states. The peoples anthropologists studied were thus implicitly comparable to the ethnic groups sociologists and political scientists described in the industrial West.[2]

As anthropologists began to conceptualize their subject as ethnicity and ethnic groups, it seemed important to define ethnicity and distill its essence. "Ethnicity has already become the subject of such an extensive literature," said Cohen in 1981, "that there can hardly be any conceptual formulation about it not made by someone before" (307). Several good reviews have taken stock of the disagreements and arguments.[3] Weber, in an early but brief discussion of the concept of ethnicity, doubted its analytic utility, preferring instead to speak of the more straightforwardly political concepts of nation and nationalism (1961, 1978). Emically taken, people perceive ethnicity as an everyday commonplace, but, despite the explosion of writing about ethnicity, Judith Nagata bemoaned "the weak status of 'ethnicity' as an 'etic,' or social scientific concept" (1981, 91). Here I will use an old, straightforward definition, one that leaves open the extent to which ethnicity is a basis of political action, "an ethnic group consists of those who conceive of themselves as being alike by virtue of their common ancestry, real or fictitious, and who are so regarded by others" (Shibutani and Kwan 1965, 47). This definition has both subjective and objective components.

The current slipperiness of ethnicity as a heuristic tool stems partly from a shift from objective to subjective criteria used in discussions of the topic. Fredrik Barth's *Ethnic Groups and Boundaries* (1969) ushered in this subjective emphasis. After Barth we could never be sure from the outside and the outset which of the objective differences we see—language, dress, religion—will be salient ethnic markers. Ethnicity is not so much something we determine by noting the differences between people, much like a naturalist categorizing kinds of insects, but rather something we discover by finding out which differences, if any, matter to people. In fact, the relevant differences for insiders may be hardly perceptible to outsiders (Blu 1980). Edmund Leach's *Political Systems of Highland Burma* (1954) could be read retrospectively to make a similar argument. The categories "Kachin" and "Shan" were comprehensible only as subjective contrasts of each other and, within Kachin, there were still more specific levels of contrast. Leach also averred that these identities were mutable for individuals and groups, as persons became Shan and whole villages altered identity over time. A cognitive impulse to make and mark the contrasts between "us" and "them" underlay the plethora of headwraps and modes of dress by which the Burman highlanders distinguish their identities. This structural, contrastive feature continues to inform interpretations of ethnicity in Southeast Asia and elsewhere.[4] "If There were No Malays, Who Would the Semai Be?" Robert Dentan wondered rhetorically (1975).

The main theoretical division in the ethnicity literature has been cast rather unfortunately as the primordialists versus the circumstantialists (Glazer and Moynihan 1975). Geertz borrowed the phrase "primordial sentiments" from Edward Shils (1957) to name "an attachment that stems from the assumed givens of social existence," for example, kinship, place, culture, race, or language, noting that such sentiments were "rooted in the nonrational foundations of personality" (Geertz 1963, 128). As primordialist approaches developed further, the discussion increasingly turned around questions of identity, and A. L. Epstein's later essays took on a frankly psychological cast as he sought to understand "the expression of a degree of affect, all the more powerful because it is rooted in the unconscious" (Epstein 1978, 94).

The circumstantialists consider the interesting issues to be *Ethnopolitics,* to use the title of a book on that subject (Rothschild 1981). In this view, ethnicity is "basically a political and not a cultural phenomenon" (Cohen 1969, 190).[5] Circumstantialists see ethnic groups as interest groups that emerge as people vie with each other for control of important resources and positions (Despres 1975a; Jiobu 1988). While this occurs frequently in urban settings, there have been attempts to see ethnic differentiation in the hinterlands also as a response to distributing people in different ecological niches (Boyd and Richerson 1987; Rambo, Gillogly, and Hutterer 1988). This circumstantialist tradition portrays leaders and intellectuals as cultivating ethnicity in order to build a power base (Hutchinson 1987). The extent to which ethnicity is politicized varies, and Cohen (1981) speaks of *degrees* of ethnicity, the strongest degree being when ethnicity shapes violent confrontations.[6] Countering the notion that ethnicity springs from nonrational sources, circumstantialists also like to show the rationality of cultivating ethnic identities and the calculating choices people make when activating or asserting them (Banton 1977; Laitin 1986).

Since we cannot always see ethnic groups as interest groups in any obvious material sense, primordialists come back to the idea of cultural identity, not simply as a reactive or dependent variable, but as "emanating out of a corpus of basic elemental and irreducible 'primordial' loyalties, with a power and determinism uniquely their own" (Nagata 1981, 98).[7] In a study of a Javanese enclave of political exiles persisting in northern Sulawesi, Tim Babcock decided, for example, that "Identities do not have to serve any particular function (unless providing a meaning is a function)" (1989, 218). Many scholars point to people's assertion or assumption of common origins that gives ethnic bonding a kinlike quality,[8] and some have pushed this observation into a sociobiological interpretation based on kin selection (Boyd and Richerson 1987; van den Berghe 1981).

Missing from this primordialist perspective at times is a way to conceptualize why ethnic loyalties are sometimes important and strong, and sometimes not (Fenton 1987). James Eder (1987) argues for the survival value of ethnic identities, but makes us wonder why the Philippine Batak, for example, did *not* take the route to ethnic pride rather than the route to demographic and cultural extinction. Even when it exists in a strong form, ethnic identity is situationally contingent, one of a series of nested identities that people call into play as appropriate (Bennett 1975; Vincent 1974). "Ethnicity cannot explain action. It is itself a form of action to be explained" (Norton 1983, 191).

Like the proverbial blind men describing the elephant, those who have talked about ethnicity have often laid hands on only one part of the beast at a time. If political approaches have often been blind to issues of affect and identity, primordialist approaches have sometimes been blind to issues of choice and power. However, the trend is increasingly toward synthetic approaches.[9] The assumptions guiding my interpretation of Karo ethnicity are similarly synthetic.

Donald Horowitz's work, among the most comprehensive of these synthetic efforts, systematically draws out the psychological and symbolic dimensions of ethnic politics. Starting from the position that ethnic identity is, in most cases, "relatively difficult for an individual to change," Horowitz downplays the view that ethnicity stems narrowly from competition for material prizes (1985, 52, 131). Aware, too, that leaders may fan the flames of ethnic consciousness to advance their own interests, he assumes that these leaders would not be successful unless their followers also see something to be gained for themselves by ethnic unity. That "something" amounts in many cases, perhaps most cases, to what Horowitz terms *entitlement,* an affirmation of personal power and worth that is an end in itself. From the literature on experimental social psychology, he describes the propensity of humans to contrast their group with others, and how enhancing the worth of the group to which one belongs redounds to a person's sense of individual worth. Ethnic loyalty implies a moral evaluation of one's background, values, and practices, especially as these appear "backward" or "advanced" relative to those of other people. This explains why ethnic antagonists may hotly contest symbolic spoils that often appear trivial to outsiders (ibid., 144, 167).

Ethnic Adaptation and Identity, a collection of papers focusing on the Karen of the Burma-Thailand border, suggests through its title that both the survival aspect of ethnicity and its subjective aspects are significant (Keyes 1979). In this synthetic mode, one of the contributors suggested

> Ethnic categories are the conceptual means by which people adapt to their social and natural environment. . . . In fact, it can be argued that one of the very reasons for an historical and continued Karen identity is that peoples in relatively poor areas are better off in their own eyes if they maintain cultural styles and aspirations distinct from those of their richer neighbors. (Lehman 1979, 249)

And perhaps more than merely in their own eyes, as Eder argues that ethnic identities help minorities "resist marginalization to wider social systems," with consequences for biological as well as cultural fitness (1987, 221).

Nagata's treatment of Malay identity in Malaysia is similarly synthetic (1981). She asks questions that flip between the primordialist and circumstantialist sides of the ethnicity coin. The way Nagata uses the term *primordial* does not suggest "characteristics programmed into individuals" nor behavior irrationally detached from political interest. Primordiality is, in her terms, simply a matter of *usage*.[10] Only through the circumstances of usage in particular oppositional contexts can we discern why some cultural features are *primordialized,* or central to a sense of identity, and others are not. She would agree that an ethnic identity must be comprehended "not as an archaic survival but as an ongoing process, politically contested and historically unfinished" (Clifford 1988, 9). Regardless of how recently its defining features were invented, discovered, or revived, an identity and its diacritical markers often appear unchangingly eternal to those who embrace them (Blu 1980, 210).

Identity as self-ascription or self-definition is, of course, only one side of ethnic categorization (Despres 1984, 9). A label may also be other-ascribed, a phenomenon that severely limits the element of choice.[11] For this reason, Anya Royce (1982) speaks of a "double boundary" for ethnic groups: one defined from the inside, and one recognized or assigned from without. With more than one group interacting, the boundaries could well be multiple. If the others ascribing labels and features to us are more powerful than we, their ascriptions may have as much impact on us as those we embrace for ourselves (Despres 1975b). The power dimension is perhaps the most important one in ethnicity (Royce 1982). Generally, those within a group have a more subtle or elaborate sense of what features mark their boundary from outsiders and of differences marking subcategories within the group, whereas the boundary outsiders see will be more grossly marked. Even so, that outer boundary may be all the more impervious.

Above all, persons in positions of power may have the opportunity to reify their ethnic categories by allocating residential space and jobs according to these categories. The colonial governance of Penang was predicated on ethnoreligious blocs, each of which was represented by a *kapitan* (Nagata 1981). Similarly, Stamford Raffles laid out Singapore as a collection of ethnic wards, locating the Chinese near the business quarter because he expected them to excel there, and the Malays far from the centers of commerce and government because he envisioned them as fishers and farmers (Buckley 1984; Turnbull 1977). Raffles's expectations were not idiosyncratic; the Chinese were already known in the region for their energy and business acumen, and the Malays, contrastively, as "lazy" rural peasants. But with the very physical shape of Singapore, Raffles embodied the

Chinese/Malay difference in space, giving the Chinese an early advantage over the other Asian peoples there (Benjamin 1976).

While those in power have greatly superior capacities to make reality accord with their ethnic stereotypes, power is a two-way relationship. "All forms of dependence offer some resources whereby those who are subordinate can influence the activities of their superiors" (Giddens 1984, 16). Subordinates can resist and balk in a thousand small ways and can also inculcate guilt, to name some of the sources of their power (Royce 1982, 3; Scott 1985). Because the ethnoreligious blocs sculpted by the British in Penang, for example, did not fit popular views of the significant ethnic divisions, these blocs did not work for long. Local Arabs protested their inclusion with the Malays in the single category Muslim. Similarly, in recent decades the Malaysian government tried to introduce a new category, Bumiputera, lumping Malays and scattered indigenous peoples together as "sons of the soil" to give these a slim numerical majority over persons of Chinese and Indian origins. The idea never really caught on. "Administrative definitions, from colonial times on, have always been subject to rearrangement and reshaping at the local level," Nagata concludes (1981, 110).

The power dimension, thus conceptualized as cutting both ways, needs more careful attention in studies of ethnicity than it has received. Colonial powers may have created ethnic divisions for administrative purposes, or nurtured tribal divisions as a divide-and-rule strategy, but how successful were these efforts? Just as ethnicity cannot always be legislated from the top down, so it cannot always be erased by fiat. The new African states have viewed tribalism as "enemy number one," but have not been able to suppress fully the bases of communal organization through which people choose to interact (Cohen 1981).

Karo ethnicity comes into sharper focus through these theoretical lenses. In the pages that follow, we will look at Karo relations with powerful outsiders and with state centers. Relations with Malay sultanates, then with a colonial bureaucracy and its allied missionaries, and finally with a new, indigenous nation have proved definitive for Karo ethnicity. The contemporary state context, that is, the history and politics of modern Indonesia, will be examined later. The point of focusing on the state is not just to suggest that states intentionally create ethnicity (although that does happen sometimes), but that states must also react to and manage grassroots ethnic responses to their assertions of power. Karo ethnicity seldom reaches the degree of political action, owing partly to the way the government manages culture and defines ethnicity as noncontroversial. When political action has erupted around Karo ethnicity, however, it has as much to do with symbolic as material spoils in most instances. The issue is pride, and the historical roots of the Karo's need to prove themselves reach far back into the precolonial past.

Precolonial Understandings of "Batak"

In the precolonial period, Sumatran Malays and international traders (Indians, Arabs, Chinese) perceived the Batak as politically and culturally inferior to themselves, and thus set the terms of a "conversation" between themselves and the Batak.[12] As with all conversations, this one shaped and validated the sense of self each party held. We act partly as we suppose others expect us to act and partly to project an image of ourselves. While interaction molds both parties to a conversation, if there is a power difference between them, the one with the upper hand enjoys more freedom to set the terms of the conversation and to shape it in a way that compliments his or her "face" (Goffman 1956, 1974). Societies as wholes do not converse and interact, of course, but individuals do, in countless encounters, and these face-to-face situations have society-wide and historically significant structural consequences (Giddens 1984). The identity Batak first emerged through the myriad interactions between subordinates and superiors in the cultural plurality of precolonial and colonial Sumatra. When used to designate Karo, Batak is still used more often by outsiders than by Karo themselves.

The first European to visit Sumatra was Marco Polo in 1292 (Loeb [1935] 1972). By this time, some of the coastal towns of Java Minor, or Java the Less, as he termed Sumatra, had converted to Islam, but the people of the interior still lived, "for all the world like beasts, and eat human flesh, as well as all other kind of flesh, clean or unclean" (Polo 1929). Polo did not name the "hill-people" of the interior, nor did *Relations,* a ninth-century Arab source, that spoke of the "man-eaters" of Al-Ramni, the latter thought to be Sumatra.[13] An early Chinese traveler, Chau Ju-Kua, speaks of a coastal kingdom of East Sumatra in 1292 called Pa-t'a, which could be a rendering of Batak.[14] Another Chinese traveler, Cheng Ho, visited Sumatra several times over a period from 1405 to 1433, and on two of these trips refers to a place called Na-Ku-erh, which supposedly translates as Batak (Su 1967), or perhaps more precisely as either Gayoland or Karoland (Taneh Karo = [Ta] na-ku-erh) (Gerini 1909).

Historical geographies based on ancient Chinese and Arabic toponyms are prey to many slips of translation and transliteration. Often, it is unclear whether a name refers to a town, a region, or a polity. More confidently, we can recognize the name Batak, or some cognate of that word, in works by Portuguese travelers who visited Sumatra in the sixteenth century. Tome Pires refers to an area called Bata in the vicinity of Aru (Cortesao 1944, 146). William Marsden's history of Sumatra, written in the late 1700s, lists in a footnote several references to "Batta" by European travelers from the fifteenth to the seventeenth centuries:

> Mention is made of the Battas and their peculiar customs by the following early writers: Nicoli di Conti, 1449, "In a certain part of this island (Sumatra) called *Batech,* the people eat human flesh. They are continually at war with their neighbors, preserve the skulls of their enemies as treasures, dispose of them as money, and he is accounted the richest man who has most of them in his house." Odoarus Barbosa, 1516, "There is another kingdom to the southward, which is the principle source of gold; and another inland, called Aaru (contiguous to the Batta country) where the inhabitants are pagans who eat human flesh and chiefly of those they have slain in war." Be Barros, 1563, "The natives of that part of the island which is opposite to Malacca, who are called Batas, eat human flesh, and are the most savage and warlike of all the land." Beaulieu, 1622, "The inland people are independent and speak a language different from the Malayan. Are idolaters and eat human flesh; never ransom prisoners, but eat them with pepper and salt. Have no religion, but some polity." (Marsden 1966, n.390–91)

European travelers were particularly fascinated by Batak cannibalism. This was perhaps the trait that most dramatically marked for them the wide gulf between civilization and the primitive (Arens 1979). Comments on Batak bellicosity and idolatry simply embellish the cannibal image. Marc Dion translates the sentence by De Barros about the Batak somewhat differently than Marsden, raising the hyperbole: "the most savage and warlike people in the whole world; they eat human flesh" (Dion 1970, 143). In 1701 someone in Batavia talked with a Chinese merchant who had lived ten years in Deli where he had married a "Bata" woman. The merchant described the Batak as "virtually wild people who hold up in the mountains and forests," but they were also capable farmers who produced a surplus of rice. "With Malay in the lowlands they have no solidarity since they are not Muhammedans; for they love pork as a delicacy.... They also eat human flesh...." The report writer continued in some detail on this last point (de Haan 1897).

Some of the accounts above contrast Batak specifically with Malay. There is little sense, by European observers at any rate, of distinctions among the various kinds of Batak at this time, except for De Barros, who begins his account with the contrast between Moors and heathens and then acknowledges that the heathen Batak "differ from one another in language" (Dion 1970). Did the separate but related Batak-speaking peoples of Sumatra have a sense of themselves as any kind of entity, or of the cultural and linguistic differences that separated them? Along some linguistic boundaries people would have realized that their neighbors were different from themselves. But linguistic boundaries were gradual in some cases rather than abrupt, as is the case today between Simalungun and Karo.

Trade routes in the highlands oriented predominantly to the coasts (e.g., McKinnon 1987; Marsden 1966, 379). This prevailing direction of traffic and interaction suggests that the contrasts between highland and lowland, glossed culturally as Batak and Malay, were probably more obvious to Batak peoples themselves than were the contrasts along the mountain range among Batak peoples. From either coast travel to the interior was arduous, but the escarpment of the Karo Plateau on the east was (and is) murderously steep. There were seven passes through which one could reach the Plateau from the East Coast, but only one of these could accommodate horse caravans. Thus, trade goods carried into and through Karoland were most often carried on human backs and heads, which limited trade primarily to high-profit luxury goods. Salt, which was both imported and manufactured on the West Coast (Dobbin 1983), was a consumable luxury and a common standard of value in precolonial Batak areas (Sherman 1990, 37–38). Other imported items were metal products (wire and other hardware), Chinese porcelains, Indian cotton and other textiles, guns and gunpowder, and opium. The products coming out of, or at least transported through, Karoland were camphor, benzoin, gambir, pepper, dye woods, wax, ivory, horses, and slaves. These were exported from the coasts. The Dutch bought horses in Sumatra in the days of the Dutch East Indies Company, and many female slaves exported from Sumatra became wives for immigrant Chinese in Malaysia (Anderson 1971; Milner, McKinnon, and Sinar 1978).

There is no need to overstate the case about the highland-to-lowland trade arteries. Some north-south traffic was necessary in order to reach coastal ports.[15] Barus, on the West Coast, was an important early port specializing in camphor export (Drakard 1986), but Alas traders from the interior of Singkel on the West Coast came also to the East Coast (Anderson 1971, 83). Because of the pattern of monsoons, East Coast ports might have been preferred over West Coast ports at some times of the year (McKinnon 1987). Obviously, highland Batak did not live in total isolation from each other; economic and cultural exchanges did take place within the highlands. Today, all of the Karo's handwoven cloths come from Toba, and this trade in textiles probably goes back very far (Sherman 1990, 30, 282). Arcane ritual and medical esoterica, another example of trans-Batak ties, were recorded in bark books in a common syllabic script despite the spoken differences among Batak languages (Voorhoeven 1961), and the experts who created these books often lived and taught outside their home regions. Today the reputations of Batak healers still span linguistic and cultural boundaries (Yoshida 1992). It is impossible to say exactly how much and what kind of inter-Batak commerce there might have been, but it was surely overshadowed by trade links that went to the coast. This traffic pattern persists today. Although roads traverse the length of the highlands, travel is heaviest to the lowland cities such as Medan and Sibolga (Ginting and Daroesman 1982). The prevailing traffic patterns of the past would thus have heightened, in Batak perception, the contrast between Malay and Batak, while the contrasts among the various Batak peoples would have remained blurred.

The origins of "Batak" as a form of *self*-ascription are elusive in the precolonial period. We know the term only as it is used by Europeans, who learned it no doubt from the Malays with whom they had the most contact. The term may well be an epithet in origin, applied by outsiders who regarded themselves as morally and culturally superior to those who lived, as Marco Polo supposed, "for all the world like beasts." The peoples to whom it referred no doubt had other names for themselves, perhaps quite locally specific names, although with outsiders, they may have referred to themselves as Batak to be understood in the others' terms.

The etymology of the term *Batak* provides few clues. A Sanskrit term, *bhata* or *bhrta,* meaning "mercenary, soldier, warrior; hireling, servant," was incorporated into Old Javanese (Macdonell 1954; Zoetmulder 1982), and this certainly fits the roles Batak sometimes played in Sumatran lowland kingdoms. But perhaps focusing too narrowly on Sumatra or even Indonesia is misleading. A highland Philippine people of Pelawan are also called the Batak and are apparently unrelated to the Sumatran Batak, being of a different racial stock (Eder 1987, 22). Further, one of the Negrito peoples of Malaysia is termed *Batek.* Unless merely a coincidence that these scattered and unrelated highland peoples of insular Southeast Asia are called something like "batak," it may be that the term was once used widely throughout the region as a general term for "savage," or perhaps "bumpkin."[16] Loeb suggested long ago that the term probably began as "an abusive nickname given by the Mohammedans and signifying pig-eater" ([1935] 1972, 20). Whether the term *Batak* first began as pejorative, it certainly became so. Djajadiningrat's 1934 dictionary of Acehnese remarked that people regarded the Karo as "first-class savages," and that the way to insult someone was to call them a Batak.

Malay and European Perspectives on the Batak/Malay Contrast

When John Anderson visited the coast of Sumatra in 1823, scouting the area's commercial potential for British interests, he found a narrow coastal band of Malay villages under chiefs with a variety of titles. He was especially interested in forging links with area sultans, but he also traveled up the rivers as far as he could to learn about the region's economy and natural resources. The majority of the population were "Batta" or people of Batta extraction. In some cases, Batta men contracted to plant pepper for the sultan, who provided capital, tools, and some living expenses. Three years later, the sultan would buy two-thirds of the produce for a price below the market value. Essentially itinerant farmers, these Batta, of the tribe "Karau Karau," left their families in the highlands and went home for periodic visits. For payments in opium and other commodities, some Batta men hired out to serve as soldiers for the sultans or those contending with the sultans for power (Anderson 1971). In fact, these mercenaries constituted the majority of the sultans' forces.

The sultanates of this region rose and fell through a constant struggle to control trade and piracy, activities not clearly differentiated at this time (Hall 1985; Milner 1977). The territorial edges of these sultanates or rajadoms were not well defined either, since territory was not significant for power (Bronson 1977). Sultans fought to maintain their prerogative to tax the movement of goods and used their wealth to win followers and to demonstrate their power and prestige. Sultans, and probably lesser figures as well, extracted taxes and duties from traders who moved between the coast and the interior carrying salt, opium, wax, horses, and pepper. The traders were, apparently, Batta. In addition to mercantile and military relationships, or perhaps as an adjunct to them, intermarriages sometimes occurred. Especially, Batak women appear to have been married off to sultans or rajas by families hoping to gain from the connection.

The Batak/Malay distinction was not racial but cultural, and by converting to Islam and taking on Malay dress and culture, Batak could become Malay (Milner 1977). The term *Malay* denoted a wide-spread cultural type that was found throughout the Straits region and well beyond (Milner 1986). Anderson found the dress, language, and etiquette of the Sumatra sultans predictable based on his familiarity with rulers on the Malay Peninsula. Interested in the market for British textiles, Anderson was a keen observer of local fashions and the sources of cloth. He remarked on the different styles of dress that separated Malay and Batak, and on the presence of mosques in many villages near the coast. Islam was perhaps the most definitive Malay marker. Marsden had noted the linguistic convention on the West Coast of describing conversion to Islam as *menjadi Melayu* (to become Malay) (Marsden 1966, 42). On the East Coast, people termed such conversion *masuk Melayu,* or *masuk Jawi* (the Karo say *Jawiken*). Religious conversion implied an ethnic switch. By virtue of this religious-ethnic conversion, Malayization was advancing slowly inland. By the time the Dutch assumed control of Sumatra's East Coast in the late nineteenth century, the coastal band of Malays had widened considerably from Anderson's time.

Anderson's meeting with a certain young Sultan Ahmet of Bulu Cina provides a sample "conversation" that is quite revealing of Batak/Malay ethnicity and the permeability between these types. The Sultan was not at home, so Anderson sought him in Kullumpang, where some two hundred Batta of the tribe Karau Karau, as well as others who were Malay, cultivated pepper for him. When Anderson fired shots warning of his approach, people thought it was an attack and came running. It was "a motley assemblage, and an extremely wild and savage looking group," too. Anderson writes:

The sultan came out to meet me; but being little acquainted with diplomatic ceremonies and receiving European visitors (for he had never beheld a white face before), he was a good deal embarrassed, which appeared in an affectation of excessive civility and compliment. On my pulling off my hat therefore in saluting him, he pulled his handkerchief right off his head, and made a similar profound salutation, which is quite contrary to all rule of Malayan etiquette. They salute by bending, and nearly touching each other's heads twice, clasping each others hands lengthways, that is, the inferior putting his two clasped hands into the superior's, who gives them a gentle pressure. In presenting seree [betel] they are very ceremonious. Sultan Ahmet is a fine, sensible, good humoured lad, however, and became quite frank and unreserved. (1971, 58–59)

Anthony Milner suggests that this young man was probably a Batak aspiring to become a Malay sultan (Milner 1982, 88). In his company was a "tutor, a Javanese priest, who had been on a pilgrimage to Mecca, and who has been teaching him to read the Koran, and instructing him in the mysteries of his religion" (Anderson 1971, 59). Milner guesses that a manuscript called the "Hikayat Deli" served as a primer on the etiquette of state. Redundantly explicating courtly dress and protocol, it primed aspirant rajas whose backgrounds did not provide sufficient knowledge on such matters. The incentive for a young Batak man to become a Malay raja probably lay in the fact that the rajas, as tenuous and limited as their power may have been, were still far more prestigious than any Karo headman.

Another vignette from Anderson describes his meeting a second, oddly rude young man of a chiefly family. While most sultans and chiefs Anderson met gave him a gracious reception, this one was frankly hostile. Hoping to meet the chief (Orang Kaya) of Soonghal [Sunggal], Anderson's party met instead 100 armed men led by "the Orang Kaya's nephew, Datu Malela, a dissolute, opium-smoking young man of twenty." Violently gesturing with a sword in one hand, the young *datu* gruffly demanded that Anderson and all his men put on sarongs before entering the village, and also remove the flints from their muskets. Anderson called his bluff. He had come on a peaceful mission, he said, and should have been warned ahead of time if there was any objection.

> I informed him also, that it was quite contrary to all our rules of good breeding to wear a petticoat; and that I should bring disgrace upon myself and my employers, by complying with so ridiculous a custom; and I assured him, that when he favored me with a visit at Pinang, he should be at liberty to wear any dress he pleased. (1971, 66)

The young man began to smile at Anderson's "jocose manner," and soon agreed to let him enter unconditionally. When the Sultan of Soonghal returned, he received Anderson immediately and dismissed his nephew's rudeness: "Ah! This young man is quite beyond my control; if I tell him to go to the right, he goes left" (ibid., 67).

Anderson does not say that this *datu* is a Batak, but most of those who used the title *datu* on the East Coast were (see the following). This young man's brusque threats, his ignorance of etiquette, and his name all suggest that he was Batak. Malela could well be Anderson's rendering of Milala, a Karo subclan name, and as "nephew" to the sultan he could have been a brother's child of one of the sultan's Karo wives. If so, and following Karo kinship, he would be the sultan's *kalimbubu,* the ritually superior "wife-giver," a status that might explain his contrariness toward an uncle who was his elder and political superior.

The figure of the raja embodies the starkest contrast with Batak, for, as Milner describes them, the rajas represented the highest ideals of Malay culture. The "Hikayat Deli" lists the virtues of a raja: sweetness, softness, refinement, gracefulness, and gentleness (Milner 1977, 103). They placed great store by genteel manner, public decorum, and courtly pomp. Malay rajas also belonged to a literate elite. The holy book in Arabic, and also epics, poetry, and didactic literature in Malay (written in Arabic script) were read aloud to audiences. Anderson mentions seeing books in the villages of coastal Deli, among them the stories of Alexander the Great, who is called Iskandar in Malay. In short, to become Malay meant adopting the values of a literate civilization that nourished a sense of its connection to world history. It meant also adopting Islam and a refined sense of gentility.

Batak manners contrasted sharply (and no doubt intentionally) with Malay manners. Whereas Malay valued ceremony and a smoothness in social inter-course, Batak tended to express themselves forthrightly if not crudely (recall Anderson's final judgment of the Sultan Ahmet). Malay subjects acknowl-edged the legitimacy of the raja as a spiritual and moral exemplar, but the Batak were inspired by an egalitarian ethos. There are few formal marks of subservience between Batak such as the hand position in the Malay greeting.

The dietary differences between Malay and Batak were especially salient markers, judging from the comments of precolonial observers. Aside from eating humans, Batak also ate other dubious foods—rats, grubs, dogs, and pigs—a fact that impressed Anderson. The dietary markers, especially pork-eating, were surely among the most significant ethnic signs, as they continue to be. None of the other peoples surrounding the Batak—Malay, Acehnese, or Minangkabau—all of whom were Muslim by the nineteenth century, ate pork. Pork eating seemed so definitively Batak that the Karo did not at first know how to classify the Christian Minahassa teachers who arrived with a Dutch mission at the end of the nineteenth century. The Minahassa Christians looked Indonesian but ate pork, an anomaly so confounding to one Karo man that he deduced to one of these teachers, "You, too, are a Batak" (Tampe-nawas 1894).

Cannibalism was the most dramatic dietary distinction, of course, and the subject sparked dramatic displays from Bataks who interacted with Anderson and Marsden. Anderson seems to have asked every Batak he met if he or she had ever eaten human flesh, and some of those who said yes obviously delighted in telling their experiences. One professional soldier, a Batak from "Seantar" [Siantar] and thus probably a Toba or Simalungun Batak, related precisely which parts of the body were tastiest and how he loved devouring his enemies. Another described drinking blood from the severed head of a man who had seduced his wife. "He pointed to a spot of blood on the kris [knife], which he requested me to remark, which he said was the blood of his victim, and which he put to his nose, smelling it with a zest difficult to describe, and his features assuming at the same time a ferocity of expression which would not have been very agreeable, had not my safety been guaranteed by my watchful sepoy guard" (1971, 35). Anderson had surely witnessed there not simply an account of revenge but a performance. Raffles, traveling in southern Batak regions in the same general period, fully shared Anderson's preoccupation with cannibalism. He, too, found showmen willing to indulge his worst fantasies with grisly confessions (e.g., Raffles 1830, 426–27).[17]

Through the conversations between Batak and Europeans in the early days of their contact, the Batak received very clear messages that Europeans wanted to hear about cannibalism. This does not mean that the cannibalism of the Batak was purely a fictional product of braggadocios on the one side and gullible travelers on the other, although it was apparently a much more restricted practice than Europeans and Malays thought. Considering, too, that Batak men frequently sought employment as hired soldiers, it was in their interests sometimes to portray themselves as bloodthirsty and ruthless.

Karo Perspectives on the Batak/Malay Contrast: Incest and Marriage

Karo, at least those who are not Muslim, persistently say that people convert to Islam when they have committed "incest." Many Karo think that this was *the* prevailing incentive for conversions to Islam in the past. I have always found this opinion curious because I suspect that "incest" accounts for only a small percentage of conversion to Islam, and that political, religious, economic, or other circumstantial motives are the more frequent incentives. The widespread perception or rumor of the incest incentive for Islamic conversion confronts us as itself a social fact worth exploring. Why does a conceptual link stand in Karo minds between Islam and incest? The answer, I believe, requires understanding the different ways Karo and Malay define incest. In understanding this puzzle we come to see something important about what it means to be Karo.

The identities labeled Malay (Muslim) and Batak were once mutually exclusive, at least on Sumatra's East Coast. If Batak there converted to Islam, they ceased being Batak and became Malay.[18] Marsden (1966) mentions, referring to the West Coast, that becoming Malay was marked by three things: learning to read Arabic (by which he probably meant learning to sound out words written in Arabic, if not to comprehend them), circumcision, and practicing the ceremonies of the (Muslim) religion. Becoming a Muslim required, too, that one delete certain Batak practices, such as eating pigs and dogs. These no doubt applied on the East Coast as well where the loss of Batak clan names was another important marker of the religious-ethnic shift. Milner reports a Malay noble lamenting that many of his people had recently begun citing clan names again when asked to identify themselves, implying that they had recrossed the Batak/Malay rubicon to become Batak again (1977, n.186).

Clan identities are today essential markers of Karo ethnicity. The first thing Karo explain about their culture to any outsider or novice is that there are five clans (Kipp 1976, 3–4; Kipp 1979, 65). Clan membership is assigned unequivocally and automatically through patrilineal descent into one of these five clans: Karo-karo, Peranginangin, Sembiring, Ginting, or Tarigan. A requirement for clan exogamy ensures, furthermore, that clan membership can be traced unambiguously through fathers only. Clans never function together as groups but remain merely conceptual categories. The requirement for clan exogamy keeps these imagined units conceptually discrete and exclusive.

The Karo, as well as other Batak, express a preference for matrilateral cross-cousin marriage, that is, for a man to marry his mother's brother's daughter, or some close classificatory equivalent (Singarimbun 1975). This pattern is sometimes termed *asymmetrical connubium* or *asymmetrical alliance,* and it typically involves a ritual status difference, with wife-givers superior to wife-receivers (Leach 1961; Lévi-Strauss 1969). In this social ideal, a man's wife and mother come from the same group, and thus marital alliance (like patrilineal clanship) acquires generational continuity. Patrilineal groups receive brides from the same group through the generations and give brides in turn to another group. This structural ideal links a patrilineal line to other patrilineal lines through the generations in one-way marital alliances (fig. 2). Furthermore, marriage to all other kinds of cousins, who should be regarded like siblings, is strictly prohibited. Women cannot marry

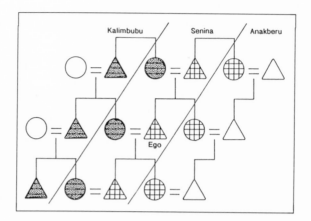

Fig. 2. Ideal model of affinal relations

into families from which their brothers have obtained brides. Yet, few Karo marriages conform to the positive ideal that those getting married should be related as mother's brother's daughter and father's sister's son. In fact, marriages less often repeat alliances of previous generations than create new marital alliances, so the reality is that a family has multiple wife-giving groups and multiple wife-receiving groups as well. The overwhelming majority of Karo marriages do conform to the negative rule that the parties to a marriage must not be related as sibling-like cousins nor be members of the same clan.

Clans and an ideal of unidirectional marriages are the minimal requirements for a social model that permits any two Karo to calculate a metaphoric kin relationship with each other, a model enveloping the whole society into a single "kinship" system (Kipp 1984b). Since few marriages accord with the positive ideal and since the clans are probably as often the products of assimilating migrants as they are of descent and branching, the significance of clanship and asymmetrical marriage is precisely and primarily conceptual. Furthermore, unlike the Toba Batak who imagine themselves descended from a common mythical patriarch (Sherman 1990; Situmorang 1987), Karo see the bonds between the five clans as marital bonds. Clanship and exogamy are the very heart of this imagined order, which is why "incest" between even distant classificatory "siblings" prompted banishment. If people married their clan "siblings," the five clans would no longer be conceptually discrete; if people married their "sibling" cousins, marital alliances could not be conceptualized as hierarchical.

Restrictions on the interaction between males and females of the same clan, and between those cousins of the opposite sex who are like siblings, reinforce these marriage rules. Opposite sex "siblings" (i.e., persons with the same clan name or related as nonmarriageable cousins) treat each other with respect and reserve.[19] Romance being what it is, such "sibling" marriages, especially between people with the same clan name or cousins of the "wrong kind," actually occur now and then, often at great cost to the parties. Karo aver that persons who marry against the "incest" rules sever ties with their families, move outside the Karo world, and begin a new life as Malays. One euphemism for this was that they had "gone to Sunggal," a location in the lowlands near the current town of Medan. "There's still a lot of room in Sunggal!" highland boys joke today when flirting with girls claiming coyly to be their "siblings."

Incest might well provoke banishment, but why would it necessarily impel conversion to Islam? As we have seen already, being Malay was the most readily available alternative to being Batak in the past, and Islam partly defined the package of Malay traits. But the cultural logic of the religious conversion in this case goes even beyond that. According to Karo standards, Muslim marital law actually permits "incest."

Karo are aware that their five-clan social system distinguishes them from Malay, who have no clans at all.[20] Malay kinship is bilateral or cognatic, and thus discrete clan identities are impossible. As in other bilateral systems, a Malay's kinship networks are not conceptually bounded groups. Egocentrically radiating outward, bilateral kindreds overlap with other persons' kin networks. Incest, too, is simply egocentrically defined (as it is for Westerners) with reference to some degree of closeness between persons. Finally, Malay notions of incest and marriage draw from Muslim law.

Muslim law in Indonesia, following the Sjafi'i school, conceives of marriage as a contract between two persons, specifically between two men, one of whom is the guardian of the bride, and the other the groom (Spies 1961, 314). The wedding rite focuses on the man and woman getting married, however, and their obligations to each other. This contrasts with Batak conceptions of marriage, that emphasize a relationship between collectivities of kin. In traditional Karo weddings, the bride and groom played an almost tangential role (Bodaan 1910; Kipp 1976). Weddings dramatize an ideal union of two descent lines, a union that precedes and outlasts the particular marriage at hand. The different forms of bride-price in Muslim law compared to Karo law index these different ways of understanding marriage. For Karo and other Batak, the groom's family gives a payment to the bride's family; under Islam, the groom gives a present to the bride.[21]

Unlike Karo marital norms, Sjafi'i rules state no preferred category of kin with whom marriage should occur, but rather list only the proscriptions (and these only for males). Basically, Muslim incest rules say that men may not marry mother, sister, daughter, aunt, or niece. These rules extend to step, foster, and in-law relations as well (Juynboll 1925, 185). Cousins of any variety, however, are permissible partners in Muslim law. In fact the marriage of parallel cousins is preferred practice in some parts of the Muslim world, a practice that counts as incest for Karo. Marriage between persons of the same clan (also incest, in Karo terms) would not violate Islam's rules, as long as the persons were not closely related by "blood" or, in the case of foster relations, by having shared the same breast milk (Jaylani 1959). Defining incest and marriage in ego-oriented terms, Muslim marital law differs fundamentally from Karo marriage law, which draws the boundaries of incest in reference to social categories such as clan but also asymmetrical alliance categories. Karo idealize marriage as a bond spanning the generations and linking discrete descent groups. Muslims conceive of marriage as a bond between persons and of incest as egocentrically defined.

No so long ago, Muslim/Malay and Karo were exclusive identities, the defining markers of which were assumed to adhere in holistic packages. Renouncing pork, practicing Muslim rituals, and dressing in Malay style were the visible or tangible signals of conversion to a new identity. Dropping one's clan name was less visible but no less significant, for it meant that a person had abandoned one of the criterial social standards that, in Karo eyes, marked Batak from Malay. Karo who became Muslim/Malay were people who, having given up their clan identities, would no longer be able to tell if they or their children were committing "incest." Analogously, for those Karo who committed "incest" by marrying, say, a distant clan mate, conversion to Islam would have appeared a foregone conclusion: their behavior was already like that of a Muslim.

Where there are rigid oppositions, there are likely to be mediating institutions. On the East Coast of Sumatra in the precolonial period, the figure of the *datuk* (*datu*) was such a mediator between Malay and Batak. The term *datuk* means various things in the Malay world, sometimes denoting a ritual practitioner, and sometimes a political chief. In the ancient Sumatran kingdom of Srivijaya, *datuk* were apparently district-level chiefs who allied themselves with the king (Hall 1985, 95–96). Sources from the nineteenth century reveal that on Sumatra's East Coast, the office or status of *datuk* had some additional associations. Leaders in their own right, *datuk* linked sultans and their subjects, some of whom were Batak. *Datuk* were mediators, not merely as go-betweens for the sultan, the villagers, and their headmen, but also in a cultural sense, blending features of Batak and Malay. *Datuk* were invariably Muslim, but unlike other Batak Muslims, they kept their clan names. This facilitated their interaction with other Karo in the idiom of kinship that shapes all social intercourse in that society (Halewijn 1876), while their adherence to Islam signaled their participation in the political hierarchy that culminated in the sultan.

In much of the Malay world, the ruler's Muslim religion defined the religious identity of his subjects, defining his realm as *dar al-Islam*. Some Karo did become Malay, but the majority of lowland Karo did not. Dutch missionaries encountered stiff resistance from pagan headmen in the lowlands who feared that converting to Christianity would preclude their being village leaders under the sultan. Headmen could be Batak (pagan) with impunity, but becoming a Christian would have openly repudiated the sultanate and obviated the need for the *datuk*'s mediation. While Karo lived in the lowland sultanates, they did not fully identify themselves as subjects of the sultan, a negative status that was probably marked by resisting Islam. The mediating institution of the *datuk* was the point of articulation between the sultans and the nearby Batak who resisted subjection to them. The "Batak War" that broke out on the East Coast in the 1870s also indicates that the lowland Batak did not see themselves fully as subjects of the sultan. This rebellion protested the large amounts of land the sultans were conceding to European plantations. The war did not seek to prevent these concessions so much as to claim a share of the rents paid for them. Batak leaders asserted that the lands under concession were Batak lands, not the sultans', and finally persuaded the Dutch to apportion some of the rents to them (Pelzer 1978).

Marriages that occurred between Karo women and Malay leaders also mediated the Batak/Malay divide. Additionally, these marriages gave the proudly egalitarian Batak a way to maintain their dignity at the bottom of a power hierarchy. Batak marriages are asymmetrical, not simply in the direction people can marry, but also in the roles and rights of affines. The family group that gives brides (*kalimbubu*) is of superior moral and ritual status to the family group receiving brides (*anakberu*). This means that the Malay chiefs and sultans who married Karo women were in a ritually inferior position to their Karo inlaws who, as *kalimbubu,* held a supernatural power over their fertility and well-being.

Did the Malay chiefs and rajas who married Karo women accept the Karo's affinal roles, and their own symbolic inferiority, or did these marriages follow Malay family protocols? Like the figure of the *datuk,* these mixed marriages may have combined features of both Malay and Batak traditions. Perhaps Batak marital statuses applied in some situations, while at other times the Karo wife and her family were expected to act according to Malay kinship etiquette. In any case, from the Karo perspective, the pride of being *kalimbubu* to the sultan or a *datuk,* of standing as the moral and social pinnacle in a system that relegated them to political and material inferiority must have mitigated somewhat the humiliation of being called heathen savages and man-eaters.[22]

The Others against which we define ourselves help us test and rethink the limits of the really human, however we construe that. For the Europeans and Malays, Batak cannibalism hinted at the outer limit between savage nature and human civility. From the Karo's perspective, the Malay's cavalier disregard for "incest" pointed toward another uneasy boundary between the beastly and the really human. Otherness was not negotiated here in a conversation between equals, however. Malay were linked into networks of trade and power—through literacy and Islam, through access to ocean routes, and, later, through European recognition and rents—that far transcended the local scene. Thus, Malay construal of the Batak has had more weight and influence in the long run of history than the Karo's construal of the Malay. Today, the Sumatran Malays do not feel they must live down a reputation for incest, but Batak (and those who study them) are still responding to allegations about their cannibalistic past.

Notes

1. Cohen 1969; Epstein 1967; Little 1957; Mitchell 1956, 1960.

2. The blurring of subject matter can go the other way as well. Weatherford's book on the American Congress, *Tribes on the Hill* (1981), used the word *tribe* with studied effect, implying that we gain insight by regarding our esteemed legislators from the same angle of vision once reserved for exotic primitives.

3. Cohen 1978; Despres 1984; Horowitz 1985; McKay 1982; Royce 1982.

4. Bruner 1974; Handelman 1977, 191; Horowitz 1985, 143ff.; Jayawardena 1980; Thomas 1992, 213; Vincent 1974.

5. See also Davis 1979, Despres 1975a, and Patterson 1977.

6. See also Thompson 1983.

7. See also Blu 1980, 228–29; Epstein 1978; Norton 1984.

8. Horowitz 1985; Keyes 1981; Nagata 1981; Norton 1984; Weber 1961.

9. Horowitz 1985; Keyes 1976; Royce 1982; van den Berghe 1975, 72.

10. "The social category or group that is salient for a given interest will be identified by those primordial(ized) characteristics that most effectively differentiate them from the significant oppositional categories in connection with that particular issue" (Nagata 1981, 95).

11. Blu 1980; Cohen 1981; Williams 1989, 420; Worsley 1984, 246.

12. The Comaroffs (1991) also use the metonym of a conversation to describe Tswana-European interaction.

13. Harris 1764, vol. 1, 523; Marsden 1966, 4; Polo 1929, 288.

14. Hirth and Rockhill 1911; Milner, McKinnon, and Sinar 1978; cf., Gerini 1909, 627.

15. McKinnon 1984, 23; Miksic 1979, 105; See especially McKinnon 1984, figs. 7, 137, 138.

16. A cursory and selective look at some languages of insular Southeast Asia reveals that words sounding like "batak" often have negative meanings. Among Philippine languages, *batak* means bad smell or stinking in Bikol (Mintz 1971); in Tausug, child (Hassan 1975); and in Cebuano, *batak-batak,* a kind of frog with a loud croak, also describes a loquacious person (Wolff 1972). In Indonesian, *batak* is a vagabond or hobo, and *membatak* means to rob or plunder (Echols and Shadily 1961; Poerwadarminta 1976). Some Karo who are sensitive about the appellation Batak point to its negative associations in Bahasa Indonesia.

17. My interpretation compares with Obeyesekere's (1992) tales of cannibalism in the Pacific.

18. This was not the case for the Mandailing Batak and Angkola Batak, many of whom converted to Islam during the nineteenth century. Mandailing Muslims did not like being called Batak, but did they wish to be termed Mandailing (Keuning 1953–54, 156; Wijngaarden 1894). For them, Islamic conversion entailed movement away from the Batak label, but it did not mean adopting some other ethnic identity, as it did on the East Coast. Mandailingers, oriented more to Sumatra's West Coast than East Coast, may have had an early model for maintaining their name in the Rejang, whom Marsden (1966, 42) described as Muslim but not Malay.

19. Symbolically flaunting these ideals and restrictions, however, couples perversely express their romantic love for each other in the tantalizing idiom of brother-sister incest (Kipp 1986a).

20. They are also aware that it distinguishes them from other Batak, whose clans are more numerous (Singarimbun 1975, 71).

21. This is *mahr,* often translated incorrectly as dowry.

22. George (1989) describes a similar phenomenon for an upland Sulawesi people who conceive of themselves metaphorically and spiritually as the benevolent senior sibling to the coastal peoples for whom they work as seasonal migrant laborers.

Chapter 3

Emergent Ethnicity: Karo

Did the term *Karo* also arise as a label applied by outsiders? Karo political organization stopped effectively at the village level, each village having its own headman (and sometimes more than one). Loose, named federations of villages existed, but these were not effective at preventing intervillage warfare even within the federations. Certainly there was no indigenous institution of raja, and Karo were never united into a kingdom. When, and under what circumstances, then, did these people come to see themselves as a cultural or social entity? Limited again to the historical record left by outsiders, we can glean only the traces there of a self-conscious ethnicity.

The Dutch missionaries who came to the lowlands of Deli in 1898 generally referred to the Karo Batak as Batak, both in their publications and their private documents. As we will see, the missionary territory was specifically Karo delineated, yet the missionaries continued to use the term Batak to refer to the people they served. Judging from the missionaries' quoting of Karo speakers, furthermore, Karo also referred to *themselves* as Batak around the turn of the century. For example, one village headman tried to dissuade an early missionary from opening a school in his village, saying that "we Batak" were too dumb to learn. Were they only calling themselves Batak knowing what these outsiders understood and expected?[1] The persistent self-referencing as Batak that appears in the early missionary literature rings oddly to anyone who knows the contemporary Karo. While most Karo today would not deny that they are Batak, and if necessary will specify the compound term *Batak Karo,* only rarely do they call themselves by the single term *Batak* (Kipp and Kipp 1983, 4; Singarimbun 1975, 3). Some, going even further, repudiate the Batak label altogether: they are Karo, period.

Finding Sumatra's Tribes

The Batak peoples named most often on ethnic maps today are (from north to south) Karo, Pakpak, Simalungen, Toba, Angkola, and Mandailing (fig. 3). These do not designate ancient peoples and cultures of timeless existence, but rather precipitates of a political process through which some names became inscribed in "history," a history written by Europeans.

Anderson was not consistent in his distinctions (nor in his orthography) of different kinds of Batta he saw in Sumatra in 1823. Those he found in the lowlands of Deli and Serdang, he termed most often *Karau Karau*. He wrote of the Tubba or Tuba Batta around the great lake in the interior, and listed several subdivisions of Tubba (Anderson 1971, 325). Elsewhere he mentions the Kataran tribe, whose "principal state" was Simalungun, and a Perdimbanan group, named from the dialect of the Asahan area. He also names the Pappah and Kappak (Pakpak?), people whom he knew only secondhand (ibid., 251). Anderson does not make explicit his criteria in this naming, but, like Marsden, he probably relied on the knowledge and categories of local informants, predominantly Malays one must suppose. He did attend to language as a marker, providing at one point a comparative word list for Karau Karau and Perdimbanan dialects (ibid., 326–27). Another of Anderson's ethnic sifters was cannibalism, for he found that not all Batak were equally anthropophageous.

The Karau Karau were, in Anderson's scheme, one of the Batta "tribes" who did not practice cannibalism. They kept their pepper plots beautifully free of weeds and resembled the Chinese in their frugality. As Anderson was the first European to characterize this specific tribe, his views are noteworthy.

> The Karau Karau and other tribes which are not addicted to cannibalism, are extremely avaricious; and in proportion as they have had dealings with the Malays, they become cunning. They are extremely fond of amassing money, which makes them industrious, notwithstanding they are addicted to gambling, opium-smoking, and other vicious propensities. They are proud and independent, and cannot bear any restraint on their inclinations, becoming in this case furious and desperate. (1971, 222)

Today, the double term *Karo-karo* signifies one of the five major Karo clans. This clan predominates in the Deli lowlands and on the side of the Plateau that abuts those lowlands. Anderson had thus entered an area where the clan Karo-karo predominates as village founders. Members of other clans would have resided in these lowland villages as well, but founders' descendants are the titular "owners" of the surrounding land, and village headmanship devolves in that family line. Anderson was not looking for clans, but

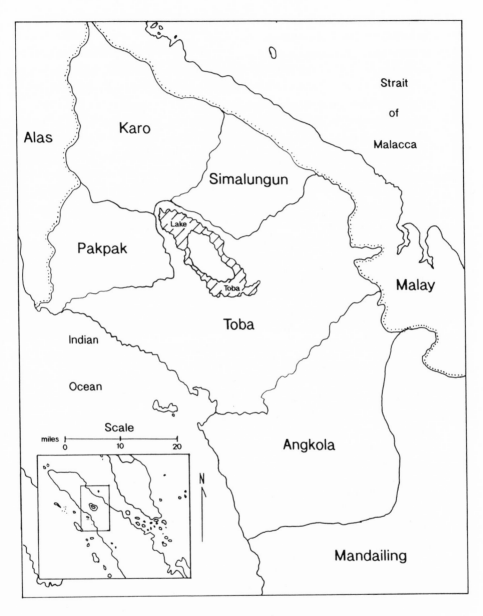

Fig. 3. Batak regions

rather for "tribes" and "states." Using Malay as his medium of communication, moreover, he would have had difficulty differentiating tribe and clan, both of which can be termed *suku*. What Anderson took to be a tribal label for the Batak could have been the result of people identifying themselves or their village domain by a clan label that he mistranslated as an ethnic label.[2] Did other Europeans of this era make a similar mistake? The numerical strength of the Karo-karo clan in the lowlands and on the eastern edge of the Plateau, and their political prominence as village headmen in this region, would have given this clan greater visibility to outsiders than other clans. At least one other early European visitor who reached the Karo Plateau designated the inhabitants as Karo-karo (de Haan 1870).[3]

This raises the possibility that the single term *Karo,* like the Batak label, might have come from outsiders, not as an epithet this time, but as a misunderstanding and an abbreviation of a clan name, but this conjecture ignores a few early usages of the single term. Marsden's usage is, to my knowledge, the earliest recorded use of the single word *Karo* as an ethnic label (original 1811). Familiar primarily with the West Coast, Marsden does not enumerate the Karo in his subdivisions of the Batak. He mentions them, rather, as an interior people of Aceh who "resemble the Battas, from whom they are divided by a range of mountains" (Marsden 1966, 366, 396). Only once does Anderson use the single term *Karau* in the way Marsden did (Anderson 1971, 69). Neumann assumed that the single term *Karo* had some antiquity, naming originally a small, localized descent grouping on the Plateau. These original Karo, in his speculation, were ancestors of the present subclan Sekali of the Karo-karo clan, who term themselves *Karo Sekali.* Neumann's reasoning was etymological: *Sekali* means literally "once," and Neumann conjectures that other groups moving into the area were thus called Karo-karo, the doubling of the term indicating that these newcomers were assimilated as "something like Karo," i.e., not the real thing (1926, 2–3, 32–33). How the tiny and insignificant subclan Karo Sekali (in Neumann's time restricted to one ward of a single village) could establish legitimacy as the real or original Karo is not clear from Neumann's explanation.

The Karo's sense of themselves as a *suku,* an ethnic group, rests today on an imagined kinship order, the boundaries of which could hardly be more precise. Karo see their five-clan order as the constitutive and definitive basis of their ethnic identity. Recall that when "incest" or conversion prompted the change to Malay identity, persons dropped their clan names to signify the change. When speaking poetically and rhetorically of themselves as a people, Karo speakers often call themselves *Merga si Lima* (The Five Clans). This ubiquitous phrase also denotes Karo voluntary organizations and Karo-owned enterprises. It is probably the most popular name for Karo ethnic associations in urban and university settings and has for decades been the masthead of one ethnic newspaper after another. These modern usages of *Merga si Lima*, like the single term *Karo* of which it is a conceptual equivalent, cannot be extracted from a context of heightened ethnic consciousness in urban settings. How long have the Karo thought of themselves as a separate *suku*? At least as long as Karo have conceptualized a five-clan system, they must have had a sense of themselves as a bounded society, distinct from Malays, and distinct from other kinds of Batak. Europeans, thus, did not fabricate the Karo "tribe," but their choice of nomenclature was probably behind the ascendancy of the term *Karo* to denote that entity, rather than the more complex but literally descriptive term *Merga si Lima*. Europeans, at least since Marsden's time, have sometimes used the single term *Karo* when needing to distinguish the different kinds of Batak. If the term *Karo* did originate endogenously, its currency and legitimacy grew as Europeans increasingly came to reify it, especially in printed sources.

The term *Karo* appears more and more during the late colonial era, although outsiders continued to speak of these people as Batak in many contexts. Indeed, Karo themselves sometimes used (and rarely still use) Batak as a self-referential term, at least when they were talking with outsiders. The ascendancy of *Karo* was gradual, I suspect, and resulted from two interconnected processes: first, the territorial delineating of missionaries and colonial administrators and, second, a heightened competition between Karo and other Batak peoples.

Today separate churches shore up ethnic distinctions among Batak. Different kinds of Christian Batak have come to use somewhat different liturgies, hymns, doctrines, and ecclesiastical forms. In particular, a Toba-Karo ethnic distinction came to be one of the vested interests of the two missions (later the two churches) that served these peoples. The sources of this ethnic denominationalism deserve some consideration.

Dutch Colonial Rule and the Politics of Missions

The Dutch established rule over the East Coast of Sumatra in the 1870s. Reports and publications from the East Coast throughout the entire colonial period overwhelmingly use the umbrella term *Batak* without making any differentiations. For example, an early civil servant's report enumerates all the villages in Deli and estimates the number of their households (Halewijn 1876). The population was composed of about 20,000 Batak, 12,000 Malay, 4,000 Chinese, and 70 Europeans, according to this count, and the Batak lived in villages separate from the Malay. In 1911 an official letter from two civil servants in the region spoke only of the "Bataks" and about legal procedures in "Batakland." In the beginning the Karo were virtually the only kind of Batak on the East Coast, so there was not much need to be precise.

Increasingly, the term *Karo* appears in Dutch discourse. The first civil servant appointed as Controleur of the Batak on the East Coast (Carel Westenberg) wrote in 1892 that only recently had Dutch ethnologists come to realize that there were several varieties of Batak in the Sumatran high-lands, and he complained that most people did not appreciate the differences within the category Batak. Westenberg was married to a Karo woman and was a student of Batak ethnology, both of which must have sharpened his sense of Batak cultural differences. Still, even he used the generic term *Batak* when speaking informally of the Karo,[4] but used the term *Karo-Batak* in his scholarly publications. Engelbert Bevervoorde (1892), who made a trip into the highlands in the 1890s, writes also of the "Karo territory," while others continue long afterward to refer to the region as Batakland.

European tobacco planters had begun experimenting in the Deli region of the East Coast in the 1860s, and by the 1890s vast tracts of land had been conceded to European planters in long-term leases. The Deli region became one of the most lucrative in the Dutch colony. Tobacco cultivation reached its peak in the 1890s and then declined in response to market conditions (Pelzer 1978, 107–8), but rubber, oil palm, and other plantation crops sprouted as tobacco acreage retracted.

Tobacco culture and processing were highly labor-intensive at this time. Neither the Malays nor the Batak wanted to become plantation coolies, and in any case this region was very thinly populated. The plantations were thus forced to import a labor force, at first predominantly Chinese through Pe-nang, and later Javanese (Reid 1970; Stoler 1985). Soon the East Coast of Sumatra was one of the most ethnically heterogenous parts of the Indies, and the Batak, the majority grouping in 1875, eventually became a minority. By the 1930s the population of the East Coast was 43 percent Javanese, 15 percent Malay, 10 percent Chinese, and 9 percent Batak. Medan, the major city of the region, became a boomtown, attracting other kinds of Batak (Cunningham 1958). Some of these were Christian Toba with mission educa-tions who moved rapidly to fill the clerical, medical, and teaching positions open to indigenous peoples in the colonial realm.

The florescence of Deli's tobacco industry corresponded in time with the Aceh War, the longest of Holland's colonial wars. Fervently Islamic, the Acehnese fought that war as a *jihad* (holy war) against infidels. Men making their fortunes in the neighboring Deli region were nervous about the proximity of the Acehnese resistance, fearing that if the pagan Batak converted to Islam, the *jihad* would be at their back door. Throughout the plantations' existence, Karo raiding parties had carried out barn-burnings and other vandalism, and it was no secret that the Karo regarded the plantations with loathing. Fearing a Karo-Acehnese alliance under the banner of Islam, J. T. Cremer, the leader of Deli's largest company and, at that time, a member of the Second Chamber in Holland, lobbied in 1888 for a two-pronged defensive response. First, he wanted the government to establish control over the independent Batak highlands and, second, he wanted to make the Batak into a Christian buffer. Since there were no obvious sources of income to be gained in the highlands, the government resisted annexing the area for the next fifteen years, but Cremer proceeded with the second half of his program, soliciting contributions from planters and other men with business interests in the East Coast to support a Christian mission post (Kipp 1990).

Although Cremer's speech to the Dutch Parliament on this issue and the circular he composed canvassing for money named only the generic "Batak," Cremer was explicit enough in his negotiations with the Dutch Missionary Society: the mission was to target the area north of Lake Toba, specifically the Karo Batak.[5] The Toba were already Christian for the most part. In fact, the earlier and spectacular success of the Rheinischen (German Lutheran) Mission there had inspired Cremer to envision something similar for the Karo. Although he hoped to replicate the success of the German missionaries, Cremer was adamant that he would not support any German-run mission in the Deli or Karo region. Cremer and other Dutchmen with interests in Sumatra hoped to limit the German presence there as much as possible.[6]

Several times in the later history of the mission to the Karo, financial crises led the mission leadership in Holland to consider turning over the field to the German Lutherans, but the Dutch missionaries in the field always objected vigorously. In official and public ways the two missions cooperated, even to the point of exchanging personnel, but when Dutch missionaries worked in the German mission they often complained that the organization was too authoritarian for them. Others found the Lutherans doctrinaire. The Hervormde Kerk, the church of most of the missionaries to the Karo, was staid and reserved in its liturgical and oratorical tone, but also doctrinally liberal. The cultural division between Toba and Karo has thus been amplified or overlaid by the ethnic animosities and church cultures that divided German Lutheran and Dutch Reformed missionaries who brought these two Batak peoples the Gospel.

Mission territories were among the most influential inscribers of Karo identity.[7] Protestants held a virtual monopoly over missionary activity in Sumatra until the 1930s and agreed among themselves to observe distinct domains of operation.[8] In the spirit of Protestant missionary cooperation, the Dutch Missionary Society was quick to inform the Rheinischen Mission of its intentions and to delineate these so as not to impinge on the field the Germans had staked out. The new field would target only the *Karo* Batak. Through the years, the precise boundaries of each mission's purview had to be rediscussed and renegotiated. The primary ethnic marker used in these deliberations was always language, but peripheral areas, where languages sometimes shaded into each other, were cause for minor disputes. Also ambiguous was the case of the Simalungun Batak. Geographically between Toba and Karo, the Simalungun fell between the cracks of the two missions, receiving little attention from the Germans; yet the Germans continued to object if Dutch mission activities spilled over into the Simalungun area. More difficult still was keeping mission territories intact under the swell of Batak migration and urbanization. As the major towns and cities of the region grew increasingly heterogenous in the colonial period, so did pastoral flocks, confounding the neat geopolitics of missions based on linguistic or "tribal" units.

The missionaries to the Karo seized on a perception of linguistic homogeneity from which to argue the very existence of a Karo Batak society (Steedly 1989, 282–88). The Dutch Missionary Society always stressed that its people learn the local language of their setting. Further, it invested in linguistic scholarship, producing dictionaries, translating scripture, and composing school texts as well as religious literature in local languages. The two missionaries most responsible for the pioneering work on the Karo language—Meint Joustra and Neumann—were intelligent, reflective men who understood both the cognitive subtlety and political implications of translation. The missionaries' wish to present themselves and Christianity in the local language stemmed first from the fact that most Karo, especially those in the highlands, did not know Malay, the coastal lingua franca. Also, speaking Karo, even brokenly, proved indispensable to the missionaries' gaining rapport. Finally, deeper knowledge of the language brought insights about Karo culture that were essential to the effective translation of Christianity.

Beyond the practical motives of translation, being understood and winning rapport, the missionaries' language policy also aimed to insulate the Karo from Malay influence. The missionaries feared that if people spoke or even dressed like Malays, they would be susceptible to Muslim propaganda. Primary school classes and church services were thus conducted in the Karo language, and children were taught to read and write in this language. Translating the Bible, Neumann generally tried to find Karo glosses rather than borrow words from Malay, even if it meant retrieving archaic Karo terms and giving them new twists of meaning.[9] He wanted to enrich and preserve the distinctiveness and vitality of the language against the constant seepage from Malay.[10] Intending that linguistic distinctiveness would protect the Karo from Muslim influence, the missionaries unintentionally sowed the seeds, too, of ethnic denominationalism, separating Batak Christians from each other and from other scattered Christian congregations throughout the archipelago that worship the same God in a variety of local tongues.

In the earliest years of the mission, before any literature in Karo existed, children used Malay texts, and later the mission introduced the study of Malay into its teacher training and other advanced schools. Still, the missionaries' resistance to teaching Malay was a complaint Karo frequently leveled against mission schools, for facility in Malay was a prerequisite to many jobs within and outside Karoland. The missionaries did not want Karo to use their education to migrate to the Muslim dominated lowland cities. Instead, they envisioned an educated rural peasantry, farmers who used their literacy primarily to read the Bible and for personal enlightenment (Neumann 1922, 64).

The Karo who greeted the first missionaries in 1890 did not have a clear notion of what a missionary was, nor did they yet see religious and ethnic identities as separable things. Many Karo villagers in the lowlands, where the missionaries were limited to working at first, expected the missionaries to start planting tobacco or to adjudicate their quarrels, attributing roles to them that they had seen planters and civil servants play. Having no indigenous category of religion, the Karo could not understand these men who made religion their full-time work, and who sought from them a specifically religious response. They did not understand what "becoming a Christian" would entail. When the first six converts underwent the rite of baptism, people suspected that it was a charm of some kind, quite literally a brainwashing, that would result in the converts being conscripted to fight with the Dutch against Aceh or taken away to some other, distant place. Some imagined that the new Christians would receive a salary, becoming coolies of the missionaries. Would the new converts continue to come under the authority of their village headmen? Could a Christian be eligible himself for headmanship? The baptismal rite that for the missionaries symbolized a change of heart, mind, and religious identity symbolized to many Karo observers a change in ethnic identity, political loyalty, and/or occupation (Kipp 1990, 133–35). These confusions had a firm basis, of course, in the traditional equation in this region of Malay ethnicity, the Muslim faith, and political fealty to a sultan. As Karo began to understand the differences among civil servants, planters, and missionaries, they learned to situate themselves in relation to new divisions of experience—religious, political, ethnic, and economic.

Ethnopolitics in Karoland, 1920–1940: Karo versus Toba

The Dutch East Indies colonial government established control over the Karo Plateau in 1904 through a military expedition that used a missionary as guide and interpreter. Until that time, the period from 1889 to 1904, the mission's activities had been limited to Karo living in the Deli foothills, since the government refused to grant missionaries permission to work under the uncertain conditions of endemic intervillage warfare on the Plateau. With the *pax neerlandica* the missionaries looked forward to moving to what they saw as the heart of Karo society, the highland plateau. The missionaries lobbied with the government to place all of the Karo-speaking people in a single administrative district. This all-Karo district would have come under the rules termed the Short Declaration (Korte Verklaring), in which a colonial officer would have been appointed its head, relieving the missionaries of having to negotiate with the sultans over property rights and building permits, a continuing source of frustration. Since an administrative unit encompassing all Karo would have taken great chunks out of the sultanates of Deli, Serdang, and Langkat, the sultans would certainly have objected. The government hardly considered the missionaries' proposal. Thus, the new government district called Landschap Karo did not match linguistic, cultural, and missionary boundaries, being much smaller than the actual extent of Karo distribution. That colonial district became Kabupaten Karo under the independent republic and remains today the organizational and cultural heartland of Karo society. The mission's administrative center of gravity shifted to Kabanjahe, the district capital on the Plateau, where the central offices of the Karo church are located today. Karo who live in adjacent districts, however, sometimes feel slighted by the arbitrary authority of these administrative boundaries that imply that Karo who live in the district by that name are somehow more genuinely Karo.

After the Dutch annexed the Karo highlands, new kinds of jobs opened on the Plateau. Kabanjahe, the district capital, became Karoland's educational and medical center, an important market, and the transportational nexus of the Plateau. A network of new roads greatly increased traffic between Karoland and the world outside. Karo began to migrate to Medan and other cities, and diverse peoples—Chinese, Minangkabau, Toba, and Europeans—migrated to the two major Karo towns. Berastagi, the second largest town, became a resort where rich lowlanders could escape the tropical heat. It was also a center for agricultural experimentation and the development of modern cash cropping. Toba, whose access to mission schools predated the Karo's by decades, filled many of the first teaching, medical, and clerical positions in Karoland.

The first schools available to Karo were mission schools. The missionaries imported Christian teachers, initially Minahassa from the Celebes (now Sulawesi). In 1899 the first Toba teacher came to work in a Karo school, and in 1901 two more arrived. One of these, Martin Siregar, remained for decades in service to the mission, but his colleague left after a short time, in what would become a familiar pattern of rapid turnover among these Toba teachers. The Toba so frequently ran into difficulties with the Karo pupils that the missionaries were ambivalent about using them. The missionaries would have preferred Karo teachers from the start, but Karo were not attracted to the schools in large numbers at first, so the shortage of local teachers persisted for a long time. The mission continued to use Toba teachers when it expanded its operations to the Plateau in 1904. In 1908 a missionary on the Plateau wrote that he was forced to fire the few Toba teachers working under him because "they look down on the Karo" (van den Berg 1908). The mission set up a teacher's training school on the Plateau in 1910 and hired a Toba teacher to help the European director and a Minahassa teacher. Again, the Toba teacher had to be dismissed. According to the missionary's report, the Toba man had used words in conversation that Karo consider taboo, persisting in this even when he was corrected, and his demeanor was coarse and rude. "The Karo cannot tolerate rudeness," wrote the school director (Smit 1911).

By 1920 enrollments at the mission's primary schools had dwindled almost to nothing, so the mission suddenly closed all its schools. The missionaries hoped this dramatic gesture would shock people into seeing the value of education, at which point they would beg the missionaries to reopen the schools. The missionaries were half right. Many parents wanted schools for their children, but few wanted *mission* schools. In many villages, parents set up their own independent schools, sometimes using the same facilities and teachers that the mission had used. The survival of these private, indigenous schools surprised the missionaries and other Europeans. The district government assumed the management and financing of primary education after several years. Toba teachers continued to work in these village schools, although Karo began gradually to displace them. Many Toba still lived in Kabanjahe and Berastagi, however, where they taught in the advanced schools, worked as school inspectors or in other government offices, or practiced as veterinarians and paramedics.

During this period the mission continued to have little success in making Karo converts. In fact, the large Toba community in Kabanjahe kept the mission congregation there alive. The immigrant Christian Toba sought pastoral care and spiritual support from the missionaries, and at first participated enthusiastically in the mission congregations in Kabanjahe and Berastagi. Toba constituted a majority of those who regularly attended church, and their financial contributions supported an impressive new building in the 1920s. One missionary wrote that he considered these Toba, who knew "to come on time, to sit down . . . well-dressed with a clean shirt," a good example for the Karo.[11] The songs and service were, of course, in the Karo language, so when the mission celebrated its twenty-fifth anniversary in 1916, one missionary said that he could not blame the Toba for not having attended the celebration in large numbers. But, he noted, the Toba community had sent a generous contribution (Talens 1916).

The Toba in Karoland began to ask for their own churches in the 1920s, that is, to be permitted to establish separate Toba congregations. Aside from the language issue, Toba were unhappy with some differences of practice between the (Lutheran) Toba and (Reformed) Karo missions. Toba, for example, were used to having critically ill babies baptized at home as a precaution, a practice the Dutch missionaries prohibited as "magical." These efforts to separate the Toba church in Karoland from the Karo mission went against an agreement between the Germans and the Dutch that they would each take care of the other's people in their respective territories. Reciprocally, Karo who had migrated to Siantar or other towns to the south were supposed to go to the Toba churches and seek pastoral help from the local ministry.

The private correspondence of the Dutch missionaries on these issues displays a marked "my people" syndrome and an ambivalence toward the

Toba who kept their congregations alive but also out-competed the Karo in so many ways. The Toba parishioners in Karoland could not have helped but discern these mixed feelings, and this, too, may have been part of their desire to secede from the mission church. In 1926 the missionary van den Berg composed a report called "On the Care of the Toba Christians in our Territory and the Application of the Toba Adat and Rites." He argued there against allowing the Toba to break away, fearing this would undercut the mission's base of support. He described further the rivalry between the Karo and Toba and the head start the latter had gained both in the church and in secular life. Van den Berg judged that the Toba's Christianity was, nevertheless, often superficial. "The stronger the position of the Toba here, the weaker will be that of the Karo. . . . What I fear is that permitting the Toba to be independent in the religious arena will have its consequences in the social and political arenas."[12] The head of the Toba mission, Johannes Warneck, agreed at this time that Toba and Karo in Karoland should remain "one congregation."[13]

The year 1927 was a low point in the Karo mission's history. Conversions had slowed to a standstill. The church rolls were actually diminishing. The mission had no schools, and the missionaries bickered and blamed each other for the field's failure. During this crisis, the ethnic tensions between Karo and Toba were used to rationalize the continued separation of the two missions. A departing missionary, a German by birth who was serving in the Dutch mission to the Karo, suggested that some form of closer cooperation between the German mission and the mission to the Karo could well benefit the latter. Toward this end, the German mission director, Warneck, came to meet with the missionaries at Kabanjahe. The Dutch missionaries suspected that Warneck's visit was the first stage of his taking over the field for his organization. Before the meeting even began, one of the Dutch missionaries read an impassioned protest, then walked out, leaving everyone shaken. Added as an appendix to the minutes of this meeting, the statement said in part, "Every interference from the Toba side, even if slight, will alienate our Karo from Christendom." Warneck concluded that it was still "premature" to try to unite the two missions. Soon after, a visiting director of the Dutch Missionary Society concluded likewise: Toba and Karo did not get along well enough to consider putting them together in one mission. While the protest against the merger was thus framed "out of sympathy for the Karo people," and on the rationale that Toba and Karo could not get along, no one admitted publicly that the Dutch missionaries would have had great difficulty taking on the Germans as colleagues, not to mention as superiors.[14]

The ethnic competition between Karo and Toba to which the missionaries appealed was, nonetheless, a reality, and one that existed also outside the Christian sphere. Karo leaders felt sharply the competition from the educated and successful newcomers who owed them no loyalty. These leaders kindled a sense of Karo identity and solidarity against other kinds of Batak, but against Toba especially. From these ethnopolitics grew a new, emphatic sense of *Karo* identity. By the 1930s certain Karo leaders outside the church had come to appropriate a rhetoric of ethnic pride and separateness, becoming vocal in their anti-Toba sentiments. These leaders also tended to view the mission as a competitor in the power game. Since Toba were so closely associated with mission congregations and schools, these two competitors—the missionaries and the Toba—became the common Other against which some began to speak of their Karo identity. Education was a primary arena for this conflict.

The mission, once again in the business of education by 1930, opened a high school in Kabanjahe and a set of hostels to accommodate students from out of town who attended it. Most of the Toba families on the Plateau sent their children to this school, which employed some Toba teachers as well. There was also a secular private high school in Kabanjahe, the board of which consisted of several pagan Karo headmen. The foremost of these, the most powerful Karo leader of his day, was Pa Sendi, the Sibayak (chief) of Lingga. He had founded his alternative secular school as an explicitly Karo institution. Speaking of the Christian high school, Pa Sendi told people, "That is not truly a Karo school, but more of a Toba school." At the same time, he set the fees of his institution below that of his competitor. Many Karo students decided to switch schools (although none of the Toba students did), and the mission had to lower its fees to keep its students.[15]

Whenever the missionaries encountered this rising sense of ethnicity among the Karo, they used the word *nationalism* for it. When the missionaries spoke of increasing nationalism in the 1920s and 1930s, they were not referring to pan-Indonesian consciousness, of which there was apparently very little in Karoland of this era, but rather of the people's growing sense of ethnic identity. For example, the famous missionary-ethnologist Albertus C. Kruyt visited the Karo mission in 1924 on an inspection tour and commented: "Speaking generally, the Karo put little price on being Christian. In this respect, they differ from the Toba, who regard their being Christian as part of their nationality."[16]

By the late 1930s Karo had begun to displace Toba in the civil service positions on the Plateau, and Karo constituted a majority in the church in Kabanjahe, with 280 Karo on the church role compared to 160 Toba.[17]

Interestingly, the missionary Hendrik Vuurmans began to use a different label, Tapanuli Bataks, inserting beneath this still finer differentiations: "We speak here of Tapanuli Bataks and not, as is so often done, of Toba Bataks, for the simple reason that it has long been not just Toba Bataks. The Tapanuli Bataks . . . must again be subdivided in four groups as follows: Sipirok-Angkola, Silindung-Sihumbang, Toba, and Samosir Bataks." Of these groups, Vuurmans found the Sipirok Batak most like the Karo in their personal characteristics. For political reasons, all of these groups had to be separately represented in the church's governing council.[18]

The 1930s were years of growth in the Karo mission, and as the numbers of Karo in the church mounted, the Toba increasingly pressed for the right to establish their own congregations. "The number of Karo Christians increased," Neumann recorded in 1939, "and the Toba become a minority. The Toba character can bear that only with difficulty, so they want to make themselves independent."[19] In 1940 a joint meeting between Dutch and German missionaries decided to let Toba in Karoland set up their own churches and the Karo in Toba-dominated towns do likewise. By this time, there was already a rebel group of Toba at Berastagi that had formed their own congregation, saying they wanted "a 100 percent Toba church service." Likewise, Karo in the Toba-dominated town of Siantar vowed they would join the Methodists if the Dutch Missionary Society would not send them a Karo pastor. There was some disagreement at this meeting in 1940 over whether the Karo or Toba churches would take care of Simalungun Batak who lived in Karo towns.[20]

On the eve of World War II, ethnic "nationalism" was a ground swell that the missionaries had to recognize. In retrospect, it is clear that the ethnically delimited missions had helped cultivate this phenomenon. Nationalism in the pan-Indonesian sense finally flowered in Karoland, too, during the Japanese period. In the chaos of the Japanese occupation, when the missionaries were interned, the Karo leaders in the mission proclaimed the birth of the independent Gereja Batak Karo Protestan (GBKP, the Karo Batak Protestant Church).

Some Contours of Living in the Karo Heartland

Increased migration outside of Karoland, ethnic heterogeneity within Karo towns, and improved transportation between Karoland and other areas continue to stoke ethnic consciousness. The economic contours of life in Karoland make clearer the impetus for migration to the cities. Migration to urban areas stems from "pull" factors that include the attraction to education and the hope for upward mobility. The wealthiest and most influential Karo today are those who do not live in Karoland. Those who aspire more modestly simply to join the middle class know, too, that their chances are better in urban areas than rural. The positive pull of the city's bustle and amenities, and the higher prestige of clerical or professional jobs over the manual labor of farming are considerable, but population growth and poverty, the classic "push" factors of urbanization operate, too. Kabupaten Karo does not have enough land for all those who would like to make their living farming, and many young people leave as a consequence. Families with relatively generous landholdings are also the more likely to afford the education for their children that will take them off the land, and off the Karo Plateau.

The population of the Karo Plateau in 1984 numbered about 235,000 and the growth rate for the decade 1974–84 was 2.1 percent annually (Ginting and Daroesman 1982). In the decade before growth was 2.8 percent, and two decades before was 2.12 percent. Annual increases since 1984 have apparently been well under 2 percent. This marked pattern of decline reflects, no doubt, the national campaign for family planning, as well as people's increasing desire to limit the size of their families. There are twenty-eight family planning clinics on the Plateau (although nineteen of these are in the Kabanjahe-Berastagi area), and the rate of women who use birth control is quite high in Kabupaten Karo compared to other districts in North Sumatra.[21] Despite the organized campaign for family planning in the past decade, I still encounter women in rural Karoland who feel they cannot sufficiently control their reproduction. In 1990, as in my previous visits to Karoland, women complained to me that they could not tolerate contraceptive pills. Barrier contraceptives, IUDs, and sterilization were the other available solutions, and these, too, were not always satisfactory to many women. According to Kabupaten Karo statistics in 1986, the rhythm method remains by far the most popular method of family planning. The average size of households in Karoland is 4.5 persons.

The two largest towns are Kabanjahe, with about 27,000 people, and Berastagi, about half that size (fig. 4). Most of the population lives outside these two towns in nucleated villages or in scattered houses. Traditional Karo villages were often quite large, consisting of a few thousand people, and village sizes are still large compared to other areas of rural Sumatra.[22] Several of the villages in populous Kecematan Payung give some indication: Batukarang, over 4,000 inhabitants; Gurukenayan, 2,374; Tiganderket, 1,554; and

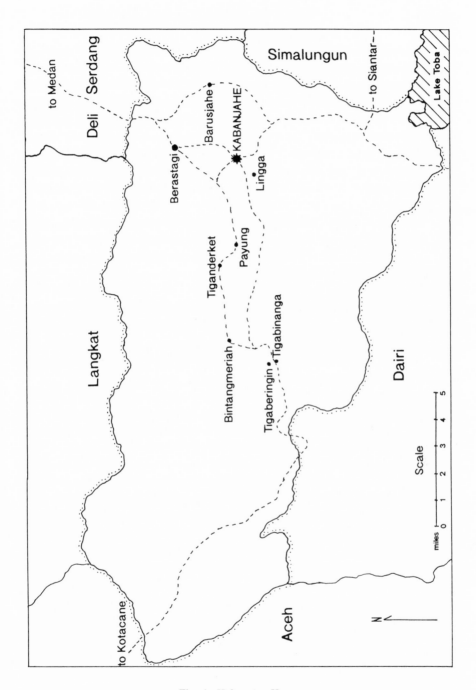

Fig. 4. Kabupaten Karo

Payung, 1,375. The overall population density of Karoland was about 111 persons per square kilometer in 1985. The most densely populated county on the Plateau outside Kabanjahe, Kecematan Payung, my original field location, had a population density of 170 persons per square kilometer (and also more extensive wet rice cultivation than most others). In contrast, one of the least populous counties, Mardinding, had about 53 persons per square kilometer.

Life on the Karo Plateau is overwhelmingly rural and agricultural; even in Kabanjahe County, which includes both Kabanjahe and Berastagi, 40 percent of the households still farm. Many people who live in Kabanjahe walk or ride public transport to farm fields. Truck gardens of cabbages and other cool-weather vegetables surround Berastagi. Elsewhere on the Plateau over 90 percent of the households engage in agriculture. Karoland is one of the richest agricultural areas in Sumatra and is self-sufficient in rice, a goal that Indonesia as a whole proudly achieved in 1984. Karoland, in fact, has produced from ten to twelve tons of surplus rice each year for the past several years. Slightly more than half of this rice comes from dry fields, the rest from irrigated fields. Most of the dry rice cultivation is accomplished through chemical fertilizing rather than shifting cultivation.

In 1967, Penny and Singarimbun compared Karo farmers to those of four other ethnic groups in North Sumatra. They found the Karo remarkable for their innovativeness, energy, and frugality. Karo farmers were responsive to new crops and new methods of cultivation and avid users of fertilizers and pesticides. They had a higher income than farmers of the other three ethnic groups, and were more capable of accumulating capital because of a tradition of asceticism, thrift, and pressures against conspicuous consumption. (Recall Anderson's remarking in 1823 on the Karo's fondness for amassing money, and their industriousness.) Many contemporary rural Karo who occupy rather simple if not drab-looking houses can nonetheless amass considerable amounts of money when necessary for investment, education, and feasts.

Human energy and hand tools still accomplish most cultivation, but water buffalo and cattle prepare the irrigated fields, and tractors can be hired to plow the largest dry fields. Some Karo, particularly young women, perform agricultural work for wages, especially tilling and weeding. In 1990 the daily wage for women field workers in Payung, a typical rural village, was 3,500 rupiah, and 4,000 for men.[23] Young men could earn 3,000 rupiah a day picking cloves in 1986, a wage that compared well with what government employees earned. Most rice is machine milled these days rather than pounded by hand, but harvesting and other processing take place through human labor. The labor of children—guarding a rice field against marauding birds, or processing cash crops such as corn or shallots—is often of considerable value to a family.

Rice can always be turned into cash. Exactly which other crops families raise for the market depends on complex considerations of the capital, labor, and marketing projections of price, as well as some concern for crop rotation. Around the village of Payung in 1972–74 the predominant annual cash crops were corn, tomatoes, and chilies; in 1986 tomatoes and chilies were rather rare, and, in fact, produced poorly when planted. Instead people were cultivating shallots (green onions). Cash crop choices shift with the market, but because persistent cultivation of certain crops tends to produce high disease levels over time, people also change to something new to avoid those diseases or pests. In 1986 corn was the largest "second crop" after rice, according to the district's Department of Agriculture.

Over time, large-scale trends in crops emerge and then fade from locale to locale. For example, one of Karoland's primary cash crops in the past was citrus fruit, but the trees began to die some twenty-five years ago as a result of disease, and replanting has not been successful. Aside from some scattered areas where citrus will still grow, other perennial crops, such as coffee or cloves, have partly replaced it. In the late 1970s and early 1980s a veritable craze of clove planting occurred, spurred by the demand created in Indonesia's clove cigarette industry. In addition to planting cloves on steep hillsides and other places where orange trees had previously grown, people began to turn large cultivable fields into clove orchards—fields that once produced corn, dry rice, or other crops (Kipp 1984a). The high prices in the clove market created a momentary boom effect in the local economy in 1983, but by 1990 many of these clove orchards had been devastated by disease just as they were reaching maturity. Speculators were trying a new crop—asparagus—but this labor-intensive field crop was no substitute for the tree crops that had generated extra income from otherwise unusable land. The boom had busted.

In the past women did virtually all the agricultural labor except clearing and plowing. Men's energies went into warfare, gambling, crafts, and child care. Today, women still perform the bulk of the field labor, but men also are active farmers. Ideally, a married couple acquires land through the husband's inheritance and lives in his village. In fact, people live wherever they can obtain land to use, and not infrequently families loan or give land to daughters (Slaats and Portier 1981; Portier and Slaats 1987). Families whose own land is insufficient, especially newly married couples, will also share-crop, often with a relative, splitting the harvest with the field owner. Land can be alienated through mortgaging, but transfers of land through sales, while increasingly possible, are still comparatively rare. A family's landholdings and land-in-use are typically of various kinds—wet and dry fields, kitchen gardens, clove or fruit orchards—scattered around a nucleated village.

Families in Payung aim to produce at least enough rice for their own subsistence needs, but must sometimes sell rice to meet cash needs. In some areas of the Plateau people grow only cash crops and purchase all their rice. Even those who produce all their own rice depend on many commercial products—cooking oil, dried fish and other foods, and clothing, to name some of the most persistent necessities. Successful farming increasingly requires cash inputs as well for seeds, pesticides, and fertilizers. All families must also pay taxes, and if they have children, school fees. Transportation and medicine also require cash.

Running small tea shops and general stores, teaching, and other government jobs provide other sources of income in the rural villages of Karoland. Those who live within an hour or so of Kabanjahe can commute there to work either by bus or motorcycle, and the buses provide reduced fares for government employees as well as school children. As elsewhere in Indonesia, the government is the biggest employer, with over 4,600 on the payroll in Karoland, including public school teachers. Teachers' salaries were about 45,000 rupiah monthly in 1986. Other sources of employment on the Plateau are extremely limited. Tailoring provides work for about 300 people; there are some 150 carpenters, some fruit drink factories near Berastagi that employ about 100 people, and there is a guitar factory that employs about the same number. A chopsticks factory that employed over 200 people for some years has closed. Official estimates calculate about forty tourists per day are on the Plateau, but tourist attractions are still underdeveloped. Although there are some tourist-class hotels in Berastagi, most tourists to Karoland merely pass through in tour buses and spend very little money there. Small numbers of people make their living driving or servicing vehicles (bus drivers earned 5,000 rupiah daily in 1986). Agriculture-related processes such as rice milling employ some people. Figures are not available on commerce, but a myriad of market stalls and shops provide income for many Karo families. Some of the larger shops in Berastagi and Kabanjahe are Chinese-owned, but Karo have maintained control of the wholesale agricultural trade, unlike many places in Indonesia where Chinese middlemen constitute the links to larger markets. Those who buy produce in Karoland and then transport it to

Medan for sale are as likely to be women as men. Transport is effected either in trucks or on the tops of passenger buses.

North Sumatra's per capita income in 1982 was substantially greater than the national average (118,092 rupiah compared to the national average of 74,268), and although figures on this were not available, the income of Karo households is probably among the highest in North Sumatra's rural areas, and probably has been for some time (Ginting and Daroesman 1982; Penny and Singarimbun 1967; Reid 1979). Figures comparing Kabupaten Karo's Gross Regional Domestic Product per capita in 1984 showed it to be greater than any of the Kabupaten surrounding it.[24] There are other indexes of wealth as well. Motorcycles, trucks, and small pickup trucks are much more common in the villages today than they were a decade ago. The number of privately owned vehicles registered in Kabupaten Karo and engaged in public transportation of goods or passengers grew from 364 to 2,231 in the decade 1974–84. In 1984 seventy-five villages were served by the government electric service, and sixty-three others by privately owned generators. A massive hydroelectric project was aiming to illuminate many more villages in 1987. The number of radios, tape players, and televisions has expanded accordingly. The number of telephones went from 302 in 1974 to 761 a decade later. These phones and instruments of mass media not only evidence greater material accumulation, but also greater awareness of national and international news and an expanded awareness of the world outside the Plateau.

Traditional Karo villages consisted of large communal houses in which several families lived together in a partitionless space organized around open cooking hearths and a central walkway.[25] Most of these large houses, constructed without nails and roofed with thatch, were burned during the revolution and were not replaced. Like traditional houses elsewhere in the Indonesian archipelago, Karo houses carved up space according to cosmic and social categories, but safety appears to have been a practical incentive for these multifamily structures. There were other practical advantages, for example, in minding children and having a large place available for ceremonies and other gatherings. Additional patterns of communal behavior disappeared with these big houses, such as the fact that young men used to sleep in a men's house rather than in their family compartments, and teenage girls often slept together in the compartment of some house rather than with their families. During the early 1950s, some multifamily houses with the traditional floor plan were still being constructed, although they were generally larger than the original houses and made with modern materials; for example, metal roofs rather than thatch. At that time, the early years of the Republic, order was still tenuous in rural areas, and the large houses afforded some defense against groups of men who came around asking for "contributions." There seems to be little regret that the old style houses have given way to private dwellings. One of the six men who had constructed one of these modified traditional houses in 1955 admitted to me the difficulties of living where one's life was constantly displayed in view of several other families. People have different ideas about cleanliness, he pointed out, and are able to afford different qualities of food.

The traditional house is one of the most ubiquitous symbols of Karo ethnicity, copied on the official rubber stamps of many Karo voluntary associations and foundations, gracing the covers of books about *adat* (customary law) and newspaper mastheads. A few villages where these houses are still standing and are convenient to the roads (Lingga and Dokum) have become tourist stops, and this has prompted government officials only recently to consider the merits of preservation (Warsani, Ginting, and Purba 1989; Ginting 1989a, 1989b). But the villagers who live in and near these houses are usually more keen on the idea of selling off salvageable bits of them to antique dealers than they are on living in or preserving them (Beatriz Primselaar, personal communication).

The first "private" houses built after the war tended to be row houses or longhouse configurations, with small family compartments separated from their neighbors only by a thin plank wall. (The partitions are often removable to afford large spaces for gatherings or special events.) Such closely packed houses still make up the core of many contemporary villages. The newest houses tend to be of brick and cement construction, often two-storied, and set off with some surrounding yard. Isolated homesteads located in fields or along the roadside appear to have increased in popularity in recent decades. In sum, there has been a tendency to move from dense settlement to a more open pattern.

Rural villages do not have water and sewer facilities, and even in Kabanjahe these are rudimentary to nonexistent in many neighborhoods. Kabanjahe, chronically short of water, must ration this basic necessity. The houses with piped water receive it only for a limited period each day, during which people fill barrels and bathtubs for their daily use. Many households in the town use public spigots, from which they tote water to their houses, or they purchase water in large plastic drums. The inhabitants of rural villages usually use a common water supply—a river, irrigation canal, or spring—and locales for laundry, bathing, toilet, and drinking water are often in close proximity of each other.

Health figures for the Plateau show prevalent Third World diseases—high rates of tuberculosis and other respiratory problems, also worms, diarrhea, and much "stomach" illness. There were over 9,000 cases of malaria in 1984. In addition, certain diseases of modernity are present as well. Hypertension is fairly common (6,701 cases treated in 1984), and there were 1,358 cases of heart disease. Cancer certainly occurs but does not appear in the statistics as such.

Primary schools are located in all villages of substantial size to serve a surrounding radius of smaller villages. According to the 1980 census, 95 percent of children aged 7–12 were attending school. This compared with 87 percent in neighboring Simalungun district, and was significantly better than many other rural areas in Indonesia. The Province of North Sumatra as a whole "leads all other provinces in the proportion of its school aged children actually attending school, and in the low proportion of dropouts" (Ginting and Daroesman 1982). Secondary schools are located in county seats or other larger villages. There are twenty "continuing schools" of various kinds; seventeen of these are located in Kabanjahe. Students can thus complete a technical or high school education in Karoland, but have to move to Kabanjahe and board with families there. Some elect instead to move to an urban area and live with a married sibling or other relative while attending school.

In 1986 the Bupati (district head), Meneth Ginting, established a university in Kabanjahe, Universitas Karo Area (UKA). Ginting, himself an academic, helped recruit teachers from Medan universities to commute periodically for lectures. UKA aims to attract not only new high school graduates, but also adults who want to work toward a degree while maintaining their jobs. By 1990 enrollments had reached about 1,400, with an entering class of 300. UKA moved into its own campus in 1990, a simple, U-shaped complex of plank buildings that looks little different from a secondary school. The law school was attracting the most students (317); the technical school had the least with only 62 students. Twice as many men as women attend UKA, and almost half the women students are in the school of education.

Education is one of the main avenues linking highland Karo to the larger world, both for those who stay in Karoland as well as those who migrate to the cities. Tridah Bangun (1986c) suggested that education, rather than land scarcity or poverty, was the initial impetus for the Karo's postwar migration. Most young Karo who went outside Sumatra in the 1950s did so to study for higher degrees. Only since the 1970s, he says, have the young migrants gone to Java looking for jobs as bus drivers or other manual laborers. Education remains a passion, Bangun notes, citing the sacrifices families have to make to provide for children away at school, and how frugally those students must live. Even at UKA, for example, the tuition was 275,000 rupiah a year for students entering in 1990, payable in two installments. Room and board and other expenses are added to tuition costs. Bangun estimates, nonetheless, that college graduates number well over 1,500, and that they increase by about 200 per year (personal communication). He estimates that there is one graduate for every 400 Karo, a remarkable achievement, considering that in 1950 there were hardly any, and that in Indonesia as a whole less than 2 percent have a tertiary education (Vatikiotis 1991). As is the case throughout the country, many new graduates remain unemployed.

Well educated or not, Karo who live in urban, ethnically mixed environments remember constantly that they *are* Karo, and, obviously, even rural Karoland is not an ethnically isolated setting. Newspapers and other media bring the Indonesian language and the national, multiethnic context into awareness daily, as do the scattered Chinese or Javanese families who live in Karoland as shopkeepers or farm workers. But these reminders do not heighten the ethnic consciousness of Karo in Karo-speaking, rural villages to the same degree as the experience of being a minority in predominantly Javanese, Sundanese, or Acehnese environments. There, Karo move back and forth constantly between linguistically segmented settings, code-switching between public (Indonesian or other) language and a private (Karo) language.

Notes

1. Volkman (1985, 2–3) suggests a similar historical interpretation of the term Toraja in Sulawesi, and Howell (1989) of the term Chewong in Malaysia.

2. The predominance of the Karo-karo clan in the lowlands may account for the fact that highlanders assert that the Karo-karo clan is especially prone to commit "incest." Because of its geographical distribution, this clan would have had extensive contact with Malays. Karo-karo couples who wanted to marry would have had a ready alternative at hand, so the threat of societal banishment would have had less sting. They were living in the proverbial Sunggal already!

3. The same source designated the Toba people with the double term *Teba-teba* (de Haan 1870). Interestingly, "Teba" is the Karo pronunciation of Toba.

4. I gather this from reports of conversations with him in missionary letters, e.g., Joustra to Board, 6 June 1897.

5. Extract Acten (NZG) 14 November 1889, 188–89.

6. For example, when a German started exploring for gold in the Karo highlands in the 1890s and spoke of getting a mining concession for that region, the head of the colonial government in Medan, Resident Michielson, worked behind the scenes to prevent it (Kipp 1990, 75–76).

7. Missionaries were also important formulators of ethnic consciousness in Southern Africa. See Crais 1992 and Vail 1989.

8. The Pentecostal and Roman Catholic missions that came in during the 1930s did not agree to territorial partitioning with the Protestants.

9. J.H. Neumann, Jaarverslag 1933, Ressort Kabanjahe. Most of the other information in this section comes from my unpublished manuscript covering the mission from 1905 to 1942, a sequel to the first book that covered only the initial fifteen years of the mission's existence (Kipp 1990).

10. In the 1980s the Karo church that derives from the mission revised Neumann's original translation of the Bible: too many archaic words in it, obscure even in Neumann's time, are now incomprehensible.

11. Laurens Bodaan to Board, 19 October 1912. Jaarverslag 1916, Ressort Kabanjahe.

12. E. J. van den Berg, Jaarverslag 1929, Ressort Kabanjahe.

13. Extract Acten 1928, NZG.

14. Both of the quotations here are from an unpublished report, Notes of a Conference of the Deli Zending, 24–25 January 1928.

15. Hendrik Vuurmans, Jaarverslag 1932, Ressort Kabanjahe.

16. Albertus C. Kruyt to Board, 27 March 1942. A linguistic shift has marked this changed sense of nationalism. In prerevolutionary documents, and in the memory of Karo adults I know, the word *bangsa* was once used to delineate ethnic groups (e.g., *bangsa* Batak or *bangsa* Karo), as well as Indonesian nationhood. Similarly, in colonial era documents from Sumatra's West Coast, the term *bangsa* designated, at times, a multiethnic entity, the rajadom and, at other times, specific ethnic groups within the rajadom (Drakard 1990, 77, 135, 182). Today, Indonesians use the word *bangsa* almost exclusively to name the nation-state, and the term *suku* (less commonly, *suku bangsa*) denotes an ethnic group. The term *sukuisme* denotes tribalism, implying a charge of disloyalty to the nation.

17. Hendrik Vuurmans, Jaarverslag 1938, Ressort Kabanjahe.

18. Hendrik Vuurmans, Jaarverslag 1938, Ressort Kabanjahe.

19. J. H. Neumann, Jaarverslag 1939, Ressort Kabanjahe.

20. Notes of a Conference 1940, Deli Zending, NZG.

21. Keluarga Berancana (Family planning) Rally, Kabanjahe 1986.

22. One of the early European travelers on the Plateau mentioned that the village of Sibraya had fifty large houses, and he estimated that if each held seven or eight families at an average of five persons per family, the population of the village was about 3,000 people (Bevervoorde 1892). Another traveler from the same era estimated that Kabanjahe had six hundred families, Berastagi and Barusjahe two hundred families (de Haan 1897).

23. At this time, the exchange rate was over 1,600 rupiah to the dollar.
24. Buku Statistik Tahunan 1984, Kantor Statistik, Kabupaten Karo.
25. Singarimbun (1975, 58) provides a diagram.

Chapter 4

Capitalism and the Management of Diversity

The Karo's placement in a modern nation-state, Indonesia, influences identity construction in a number of ways (fig. 5). This chapter establishes some theoretical understanding of how modern states manage diversity, the better to comprehend Indonesia's current policies and its recent history. Indonesia's cultural composition, its problems, resources, and history are unique, but its current policies and its history also exemplify general processes through which modern states dependent upon capitalism protect that economic system via programs of cultural management.

Pluralities of religion, class, and ethnicity characterize most modern states. Ethnicity has become one way groups assert their claims "over or against the state" (Despres 1984), and separatist movements based on ethnicity threaten empires with fragmentation. Modern states also exist increasingly in relation to supralocal forces—transnational corporations, international markets of goods and labor, and electronic and satellite communication—that sometimes enhance and sometimes challenge state control in subtle ways. One of the oldest cultural forces of a supralocal character are the universalistic religions. Blind in principle to ethnicity, these religions promise the possibility of transcending ethnic and national differences, but in practice have often spawned new communalistic discord within polities. Class differences, too, undermine the integration of states (but also erode ethnic solidarity and communities of faith), and in this postimperialist era, class also appears increasingly supralocal or world-systemic. Capital has become transnational, raising the question of whether labor or other forms of resistance will soon emerge in like manner (Becker et al. 1987; Wallerstein 1974).

Scholarship from the Left has long assumed ethnicity, nationalism, and religion to be competitive with class consciousness. Later I examine how

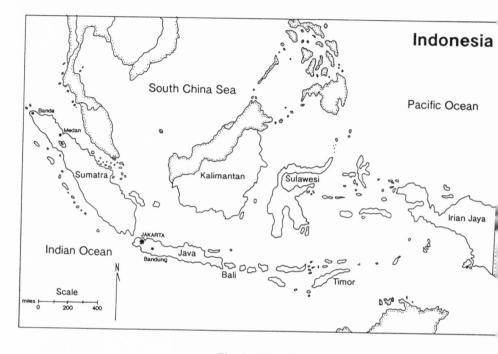

Fig. 5. Indonesia

Indonesia, cultivating religion and ethnicity as useful adjuncts of nationalism, diverts attention from the unevenness of development, and consequently benefits from the fact that these cultural elements countervail each other. Here, as elsewhere, ethnopolitics sometimes threaten to disrupt communities and challenge the regime, but I will suggest that ethnic divisions at times prove useful to those in power. Research has tended to highlight cases where religion exacerbates ethnic conflict, sharpening the boundary between groups and heightening attachment within by sacralizing ethnic identity, but religious affiliations frequently transect ethnic groups in modern states. My argument is that the transection of cultural and religious elements mitigates the political impact of both, while each diminishes the impact of class.

Like other Indonesians, most Karo tend to "see" ethnicity and religion more readily than class, whether looking internally at their ethnic group, or outward to the nation of which they are proud citizens. Class blindness is a safe affliction to have in a polity that imprisons and banishes suspected

Communists. The government encourages such blindness, too, through ignoring class while bureaucratically reifying communal identities. Class blindness fits, nonetheless, with many Karo's own perceived self-interests, especially with their hopes for upward mobility and progress. Within social life
as Karo, most people hold fast to an ideal that kinship solidarity (which
underlies ethnic consciousness in this case) should be impervious to distinctions of wealth and power. Most Karo also carefully compartmentalize religious life from issues of kinship and ethnicity, guarding these core aspects
of identity from the potentially divisive issues of faith. That is, class blindness protects valued identities that the Karo construct for themselves along
communal lines. First, I want to step back from the particulars of the Karo
case, however, and from Indonesia, to build a framework through which to
understand the general connections at the state level between cultural and
religious diversity, nationalism, and capitalism in the developing world.

Communalism and the Autonomous State

Theoretical assessments of the relationship between ethnicity and state are
ambiguous, stemming partly from the substantive variability of states,[1] but
also, as I will argue here, stemming from a logical tension between the uses
and dangers of ethnicity to states and to the capitalism on which they depend.
The ethnicity-state relationship is not ambiguous at all when ethnic separatism threatens the viability of the state.[2] If one group dominates control of
the state, ethnic assertiveness can be a reactive response to subordination
(Nielson 1985; O'Brien 1986). The relationship of the state to ethnicity is
not necessarily inimical, however (e.g., Young 1983). There can be multiple
levels of identity and integration (Madan 1984, 140; also Smith 1983, 69)
such that ethnic and national identities do not conflict, an argument that
William Liddle once made specifically about Indonesia (1970, 230).[3] Where
ethnic divisions coexist in a segmental rather than hierarchical order of "units
of equivalent and/or complementary status," the state often mediates and
regulates their coexistence (Smith 1984, 154).

The state's regulation of religious and cultural expression and the extent
to which ethnic categories receive legal recognition significantly shape ethnicity (Nash 1989; Williams 1989, 416). Ethnic groups may, for example,
form convenient administrative units, an argument heard most often in relation to ethnogenesis in colonial states; even so, ethnic groups remain admin-

istratively significant both in Singapore and Malaysia, two of Indonesia's closest neighbors. In Singapore, ethnic identity is "bureaucratically ascertained" and thoroughly institutionalized via identity cards and educational tracks sorted according to language. Mutually exclusive and obligatory identity labels inhibit people from thinking of themselves as "mixed" or simply Singaporean (Siddique 1990).

Some theories suggest that ethnic politics emerge in the context of the state because the state serves as the "direct arbiter of economic well-being," and claims by larger and more amorphous interest groups (e.g., workers) are so general as to be unwieldy (Glazer and Moynihan 1975). Interest groups based on ethnicity, in contrast, "make claims for groups large enough to make significant concessions possible and small enough to produce some gains from the concessions made" (ibid., 9). In postcolonial societies, too, "the state over-shadows the market as the controller and distributor of economic opportunities in ways constrained by its cooperation with transnational capitalism," a situation that encourages ethnic patronage and ethnic politics (Norton 1984, 430).[4] Conversely, some writers suggest that it is less the powers and resources of states that prompt ethnic politics than the implicit limits of those powers and resources. Ethnic resurgence in the West has occurred precisely during a period of supranational politics and a postindustrial global economy. As power shifts away from the locus of the nation-state, "a vacuum is created into which the emerging ethnic elites can move" (Richmond 1984, 5).[5] The explosion of ethnic politics in Eastern Europe and Central Asia is widely understood both as cause and consequence of the Soviet Union's demise (Laitin 1991).

The relationship of ethnicity to the state is, therefore, theoretically ambiguous—sometimes in conflict, sometimes complementary; now a product of the state's patronage and power, now a response to a power vacuum. This ambiguity, I suggest, stems partly from the state's "autonomous" relation to capital.

Traditionally, Marxists viewed the state as a product of capitalism and as the protector of property, acting almost inevitably on behalf of capital (Carnoy 1984; Engels 1972).[6] Marxist revisions now accord the state a relative autonomy, meaning that state bureaucracies work somewhat independently of capital's needs and toward their own interests of preservation and aggrandizement. Although states do monitor and help maintain the capitalism on which they depend, they must at times go against or check the actions of particular capitalists or firms in order to do so.[7] The state's partial autonomy stems also from the internal differentiation of elements that operate at some higher level as if unitary. The military, executive, legislative, and other elements that constitute the state's unity break down into competitive factions at times. (As Robert Hefner phrased it, speaking of Indonesia, "no state is a single agent, and despite the best efforts of some despots, none is ever wholly monolithic [1990, 219].) Likewise the propertied class that states protect is internally divided and competitive, requiring the state's mediation in its internal conflicts (Alavi 1972).

Although acting somewhat autonomously of capital, states still attempt to mediate or repress the class conflict that would threaten their stability, and ethnicity is widely recognized as a muffler of class consciousness. Whether we see ethnic divisiveness as a top-down imposition from the powerful, or a grass-roots response to humiliations and frustrations, it muffles class consciousness.[8] Some have tried to understand the conditions under which ethnicity assumes a saliency over class.[9] Horowitz (1985) supposes that class is not salient in many Third World countries because some degree of occupational mobility mitigates class politics. Ethnic origin, relatively more ascriptive than class, appears the more compellingly urgent.

If ethnicity sometimes disguises class interests, then we might expect postcolonial states to nourish ethnicity as self-preservation in much the way colonial states were said to protect themselves through divide-and-rule tactics. Anthony Smith, for one, does suggest that "ethnicism" reinforces the power and stability of African states (1983, 70–71). The interests of capital and regime are not enough to insure ethnic politics an easy ride. Indeed, modern states often regard ethnicity warily, fearing communalistic discord and regional separatism at least as much as class warfare. Here the "relative autonomy" of the state from the interests of capital is obvious. Despite its benefit of deflecting class politics, ethnicity may threaten the very existence of the state that protects business as usual. The state, ethnicity, and the interests of capital exist in a triangular tension, thus precluding any singular determination of the relationship between ethnicity and class or between ethnicity and the state. Contradictory forces are at work. If class tensions appear great, states may permit or promote ethnic expression as a diversion; if that diversion itself becomes a threat, then the tolerance and patronage of cultural diversity gives way to repression.

Culture and Religion in Service to the Nation-State

Traditional Marxist visions of the state emphasized coercion as the basis of state power, but again revisions of recent decades modify that by suggesting that state control entails ideological as well as coercive mechanisms. Schools, churches, trade unions, and political parties, what Louis Althusser called Ideological State Apparatuses, promulgate values and behaviors that maintain the sovereignty of the state and the ruling classes (Callinicos 1976, 64). The values and assumptions of the dominant class become hegemonic, although subordinate classes continually contest and counter these in a variety of ways (Gramsci 1957, 1971, 333; Williams 1977). Especially pertinent to the issue of identity formation, states "reify people as individuals," isolating individuals both through competition in capitalist relations and through the practice of democracy (Carnoy 1984, 100–101). The nation, an imagined community, to use Benedict Anderson's now famous phrase (1983), appears to reunify these separate individuals in institutions in which "everything takes place as if the class 'struggle' did not exist" (Poulantzas 1974, 188).[10]

All systems of domination seek legitimacy (Weber 1964, 325). Even the military regimes that characterize Indonesia and so many developing countries, or a polity such as South Africa where the state's control rests so obviously on force, do not neglect the effort to legitimate their rule ideologically.[11] Because military regimes are generally unstable (Fryer and Jackson 1977, 241), they may invest all the more in such efforts. Political legitimation becomes more and more difficult in advanced capitalist states because governments become increasingly embroiled in the administration of the economy; economic crises engender crises of legitimation (Habermas 1975). The state takes an increasingly interventionist stance in advanced capitalism (e.g., Block 1987; O'Connor 1973, 1974) but also in the bureaucratic-authoritarian regimes in the Third World and in the newly industrializing countries of the Pacific Rim. These regimes in developing countries rationalize their resort to force and their limitations on democracy by the necessity of giving experts free rein to engineer economic expansion.[12] In these regimes, too, continual crises of "meaning" arise as legitimacy becomes tied to the rhetoric about development, and development slips always into the future.[13]

"Nationalism and the nation attract the greatest allegiance in the modern world," much more than communities based on class or on political and religious doctrines (Thompson 1986, 48–49).[14] Nationalism is partly an issue of allegiance and community, but is, above all, a form of *politics,* related to the goal of obtaining or using state power (Breuilly 1982). States utilize their considerable resources and powers to shape the imagined national community (ibid., 374; Foltz 1963), and policies on culture, education, and religion are the tools through which states accomplish this, hoping to preempt conflict and challenge. The mass media and the schools at the disposal of modern states have become powerful means to forge nationalistic loyalties and identities over and above ethnic, religious, and class divisions, and to define and depict cultural pluralism in nonthreatening ways (Gusfield 1962, 29). One nonthreatening way is to encourage cultural and religious pluralism as a value. In the absence of primary ends on which everyone agrees, people might be persuaded to accept the "secondary virtues," such as tolerance, compromise, and fair play (MacIntyre 1967, 24). Pluralism can be depicted as a source of strength, as it frequently is in the United States in the familiar imagery of the melting pot, and also as it is in Indonesia, although the imagery is not the same (Liddle 1988b, 4).[15]

The state context is perhaps the most significant variable in explaining the extent to which culture is self-consciously "objectified" for political and psychological ends.[16] Forging a national identity often relies on claims of historical and cultural commonalties that unite the disparate subjects of the state and also set them apart contrastively from other countries (Gellner 1983). Toward this end, states may protect and provide a place for ethnic differences as the fonts of a distinctive heritage (e.g., Kligman 1988, 257–58). Leaders discover or invent "traditions" from the religious and ethnic streams available to them (Hobsbawm and Ranger 1983). Rather than harshly repressing ethnic expression entirely, leaders may opt to "ride the tiger of exacerbated pluralism and possible internal strife" (Foltz 1963, 128), attempting to turn pluralism to the nation's benefit.

States' manipulation of religion and culture occurs in the context of transnational political and economic processes, not merely in response to internal fault lines of religion, class, and ethnicity.[17] The "managerial bourgeoisie" that is the ruling class in most of the Third World must rely on transnational capital to achieve development, and development is a goal without the passion, romance, and political potency of the independence movements and revolutions that brought the postcolonial states into being and first ignited their populist nationalism (Foltz 1963). The leaders of new states are also nationalists, fiercely concerned about political and cultural autonomy and sensitive about dependence, neocolonialism, and cultural imperialism (Sklar 1987, 28). Linguistic and aesthetic diffusions challenge the nationalist's claim to a unique identity. The political and economic concessions tied to loans or aid are only the most blatant challenges to independence. Ideologies of various kinds, whether pan-Islam, secular humanism, feminism, or communism, may also appear to leaders as threatening, foreign importations. A state's policies on ethnicity, culture, and religion must be seen against such an external, transnational background as well as the internal political situation. Effective cultural management requires using cultural and religious sources to promote and sacralize an indigenous nationalism, while controlling the divisive potential of ethnic and sectarian identities.

Some polities, Indonesia for one, officially ignore cultural differences as far as possible in the interests of national unity; others, Malaysia, for example, blatantly link economic and political privileges to ethnic membership; still others, such as Singapore, tout and use cultural diversity for the end of nation building. In Singapore, where a large Chinese majority reigns securely, "multiracialism" was a founding myth or charter of the young nation. Suspecting that Singapore has no distinctive culture of its own (English is the medium of all public and interethnic communication), and that the "multi" cultures of the Republic are losing ground to Western influences, the government sponsors and promotes a calendar of cultural shows and events in Tamil, Malay, and Chinese media. The cultural shows are "projective fantasies" that the timeless traditions still live (Benjamin 1976).

State-endorsed ethnicity, as performance and exhibit, is an increasingly visible strategy as the new states attempt to manage both the heterogeneity within their boundaries and the homogenizing threat of consumer goods and popular culture deriving from the West (e.g., Goulet 1983, 53–54 on Mexico). The invention of tradition responds to this also.[18] Layne (1989) describes how elements from Bedouin tribal cultures have been selected to represent a unique Jordanian national identity. Reducing culture to performance and exhibit in heterogeneous societies comes to terms with ethnicity by appearing to embrace cultural differences as a source of national strength, while actually delimiting carefully the public arenas (tourist shows, parades, museums, airline stewardess costumes) where "feathers and flourishes" are appropriate (Williams 1989, 435).

In Malaysia, where Chinese constitute a strong one-third of the populace and Malays about one-half, Malay leaders worry as much about internal balances as the threat of external, cultural inundation. "Ethnicity in Malaysia is . . . a tool of the state for resource allocation and political control" (Ackerman and Lee 1988, 4). Policies attempt to counter the economic power of urban Chinese and Indians by giving Malays a monopoly on government positions and the rural economy. In rural areas, Malays have access to government development programs by virtue of ethnicity and ethnic party membership (Osman-Rani 1990; Rogers 1982), while Chinese are prohibited from buying land (Winzeler 1988). Ethnicity regulates educational opportunity, too, again favoring Malays (Basham 1983). Superimposed over ethnicity, furthermore, is a great religious divide. Malayness is so tightly bound up with Islam that defending Malay identity is often expressed as a defense of Islam against Christian proselytizing or expansion (Ackerman and Lee 1988). Conflict between Muslims and non-Muslims, or Malays and non-Malays, disguises the class divisions among Malays themselves as well as their disagreements about religion (Lee 1988; Scott 1985). Wealth differences have increased *within* each of Malaysia's three main ethnic groups, but in this atmosphere of heightened ethnic and religious division, class conflict has not emerged (Osman-Rani 1990).

Religion, too, holds both uses and dangers for national leaders. Where possible, states draw on religion to sacralize national identities and legitimate the government's goals. The universal religions based on sacred texts are among the "cultural roots" of modern nationalism (Anderson 1983; Gellner 1983, 56–57). Secular ideologies appealed to the popular imagination partly because religious and cultural pluralism and the rationalism of the Enlightenment undermined the sacred and unitary certainties of the great textual religions. The "secular transformation" of a transcendent nation, looming out of an immemorial past and gliding into a limitless future, to paraphrase Anderson, took place in this meaning gap (1983, 19). Some writers have interpreted nationalist ideologies, especially socialist ones, as partly replacing religions (Lessa and Vogt 1965, ix; Nottingham 1971), but religion continues to play a prominent role in national identities, even in socialist polities and others that are constitutionally and explicitly secular.[19] States incorporate religion into state ceremonies, constitutions, coins, and so forth as "social cement" for the body politic (Thompson 1986, 41ff.). The notion of civil religion, a construct used by Robert Bellah and others to describe the integration of U.S. society in the 1950s and 1960s, equated nationalism with religion. Writers analyzed the sacred trappings of U.S. nationalism, its icons, ceremonies, commemorative holidays, and confession-like pledges of allegiance.[20] This "religion" unified the United States more thoroughly during some periods of history than others, critics of the concept later pointed out.

The civil-religion concept initially glossed over power differences and conflicts within the polity. A single "dominant ideology" of a powerful ruling class never entirely squelches alternate and resistant ideologies: "It is more fruitful to think of the ideological terrain as a complex of discourses which have ideological effects, and the balance of forces in that field as being always in a flux and the site of contestation over meanings" (Thompson 1986, 48). Although control of the schools and electronic media frequently provides states enormous advantages in propagating nationalism over counterideologies (cf., Breuilly 1982, 241), there is always room for that slippage James Scott describes as the fate of all great traditions, political or religious. Speaking primarily of the religious traditions of Southeast Asia, Scott notes that "any moral order is bound to engender its own antithesis, at least ritually, in folk culture" (1977, 33), and that the farther one goes from core to periphery of Southeast Asian states, or the farther one moves down the ladder of stratification, the more one sees the "steady erosion of faith in the normative order of ruling elites" (ibid.). Nation building is not a foregone conclusion, even with all the ideological apparatuses of the state. The very ethnic and religious traditions on which nationalism draws may become the sources, too, of its contestation (Smith 1983, 127). Alternate allegiances, whether based on religion or ethnicity or both, constitute alternative vantages from which hegemony may be questioned.

States attempt to harness religion to their service, but at times religion also poses a threat to states, especially in its millenarian or utopian aspect. This echoes the familiar church/sect distinction. A church that "accepts the basic structure of a society, that has compromised with the secular powers, is likely to be the group that is supported by those who have fared relatively well in the distribution of goods and power in their society." In contrast, a sect that is "based on the conviction that there are basic evils in society with which one must not compromise, is most likely to be supported by the least privileged groups" (Yinger 1957, 142). It follows that states will be most comfortable with the churchly forms of the great religions, and most wary of schismatic variants. Although sects are often apolitical, aiming at personal salvation and/or to solve the concrete problems of existence (Ackerman and Lee 1988; Shibutani and Kwan 1965, 307–11), they may evince political heresy by espousing pacifism or by resisting the state's incursions into personal decisions about family life, education, or medical care. In an article reviewing ten recent books on politics and religion, many of them treating resistance movements, Daniel Levine notes religion's "continuing creative link to politics at all levels," and less secularization in the modern situation than a restructuring of religion's place in society (1986, 96).

Crosscutting Identities: Pluralism Reconsidered

Surprisingly little has been written about the effects of religious pluralism on ethnic identity.[21] In many cases, religious differences coincide with ethnic differences, and most discussions of ethnicity either assume this as natural or, if ethnic groups *are* internally differentiated by religion, do not place any importance on this fact. In a recent discussion, for instance, Nash describes religion and ethnicity as "a single recursive metaphor" (1989, 11). Similarly, theories of religion have not sufficiently addressed ethnic divisiveness, perhaps an effect of the Durkheimian legacy in theories of religion. Anthropologists have most often described religious beliefs and practices as if universal within a community or society and then demonstrated religion's consequences as fostering social solidarity. Some virtually equate social identity with religion (e.g., Mol 1976, 1978).

Religion may provide sources of identity that are sometimes competitive with and sometimes complementary to ethnicity (Kayal 1973; Smith 1978), and religion and ethnic identity are often dissociated in the modern world. In some cases (Lebanon to name a dramatic example), sectarian strife cuts across ethnic affiliation. In other cases, different religious communities co-exist peacefully within an ethnic enclave (Rodgers 1981). Religion is, in fact, central to some ethnic identities, and not at all to others. Observers often contrast the Malay and Chinese in Malaysia in these terms: Islam partly *constitutes* Malay identity, but religion is irrelevant to being Chinese.[22] The Chinese/Malay contrast is worth pursuing briefly, for both these ethnic groups are historically important in Indonesia.

China has no single unified religious tradition. Buddhism, Confucianism, and Taoism competed and blended with each other and with elements of folk religions for centuries.[23] Although the Han forced changes in land tenure, law, dress, taxation, and leadership in their early conquest of northern Vietnam (Higham 1989, 290–91), they did not apparently require religious conversion. Centralized empires in China thus encompassed many cultural and religious differences.

In contrast, Malay sultanates were not territorially defined at all. Many of them were based on the control of ocean trade and traffic, relying on the allegiance of scattered subjects (Milner 1977), but political loyalty and religion were so of a piece that stories of the coming of Islam to the Malay world frequently equate the conversion of the populace with the conversion of a chief or ruler (Mukhlis and Robinson 1985, v). Islam enjoyed virtual hegemony in the Malay world, and while ancestor recognition and animism existed too, they were subsumed in "Islam." Furthermore, Islam's view of community and polity does not compartmentalize sacred and secular, church and state. Loyalties to religion, ethnic group, and polity were not as easily dissociated in the Malay world as they were for the Chinese.[24] This comparison suggests that ethnic identity and religious faith may be dissociated more readily in the context of a long history of imperialism and religious pluralism than where one religion is hegemonic and states have not been strongly territorial.

Where we do find religious identity and ethnic identity conceptually separable, religious pluralism within ethnic groups sometimes has little political import. Assuming that religious pluralism would undermine ethnic solidarity, David Laitin (1986) examined religious pluralism within Yoruba society. He wondered, specifically, why Yoruba Muslims and Christians did not operate as sectarian political blocs. Laitin found instead that Yorubaness, and subdivisions of Yoruba based on ancestral cities of origin, continue to be the salient identities, a situation he attributed to the British legacy of indirect rule based on tribal divisions. Looking for "neo-Benthamite" motivations, Laitin missed seeing why Yoruba identity and its origin-city subdivisions remain central to people's sense of pride and, perhaps, what uses ethnic diversity might have to the modern Nigerian state. Although historical residues from the colonial period surely continue to exert some influence in societies such as Nigeria and Indonesia, ethnicity and religion are probably even more influenced by contemporary political and economic conditions. The Yoruba case is not unusual, moreover, when compared to similar cases from Indonesia, where people pointedly assert the precedence of ethnic unity over sectarian divisiveness (e.g., Rodgers 1981).

It becomes increasingly important to recognize ethnic diversity in generalizations about religious solidarity, and, likewise, to include discussion of religious variations in studies of ethnic identity, because ethnic differences and religious differences correspond less and less in modern societies. Like the Chinese, the Yoruba, and the Karo, ethnic groups will less and less frequently constitute unitary religious congregations. Two conditions promote this dissociation. First, national constitutions make religious affiliation irrelevant to citizenship, and usually express the protection of religious freedom. The universalistic religions benefit from this official tolerance and protection and from proselytizing with electronic and print media. Competing with each other, sometimes within the same communities, universalistic religions continue to displace tribal religions in which the "church" was once coterminous with the society, and which cannot compete with the organization and vast resources of these universalistic religions. The latter exhibit, all the same, their own internal problems of fracturing and sectarian secession (Niebuhr 1954). A cafeteria model, "the religion of your choice," comes to characterize the condition of religion in secular societies (Wilson 1976, 96), implying that religious affiliation is a private matter, irrelevant to nationalistic or ethnic loyalty.

Second, the claim of national identities to transcend local identities also encourages the conceptual compartmentalization of national, religious, and ethnic identities (Gellner 1983). If the imagined community of the nation does not rely on religious and ethnic homogeneity, the religious congregation is likely to see its membership similarly unbounded by nation and ethnicity, and the ethnic group to conceptualize its identity apart from citizenship and faith. The likelihood of religious differentiation within polities, and within ethnic groups, thus increases.

Viewed positively, the pulling apart of ethnicity and religion increasingly evident in today's complex societies produces an integrative boon. To the extent that ethnic and religious identities crosscut each other, the chances decrease that either can be effectively divisive of state sovereignty. As Marxist theorists would suggest, both religious and ethnic identities decrease the saliency of class, mitigating its divisive potential (Smith 1983, 70). Religious pluralism tempers ethnic separatism and ethnicity tempers sectarian strife, while both these highly visible, communalistic loyalties deflect class consciousness.

Viewed negatively, the dissociation of ethnicity and religion allows the centralized polities of stratified societies to contain and control their impoverished, heterogeneous citizenry. This idea resembles, in a perverse form, theories of pluralism. Henry Kariel traces the historical roots of the theory of pluralism to an early twentieth-century political ideal. He terms pluralism still "the heart of the liberal ideology of the Western world" (1968, 164). It also became a social scientific theory about how power works in democratic polities. Class, ethnicity, or religion can each alone become divisive, and the coincidence of any two of these, what Ralf Dahrendorf called superimposition, enhances the potential for conflict (1959, 213–18). Where these form "crosscutting" differentiations, however, a kind of "balancing mechanism" comes into play.[25] Arend Lijphart's classic study of the politics of religion in the Netherlands proceeded from and illustrated this assumption (1968), and he went on to prescribe how "consociational" policies might prevent conflict in other polities as well (1977).

Pluralistic political theory presumes democratic polities (e.g., Dahl 1956, 1982, 1986). It posits a state openly neutral with regard to society's divisions, a state serving as the arena in which the various segments of society meet, contest for political spoils, and compromise (Carnoy 1984, 37). Descriptions of pluralistic democracies imply that the political balancing act occurs on its own and uncoordinated, merely a function of the open competition between more or less equal interest groups. Idealistic views of pluralism tend, therefore, to gloss over the differences of power and resources that interest groups command when it comes to influencing the political process.

While most Third World countries are pluralistic in a simple cultural sense, they are not generally described as pluralistic in this specifically political sense. Quite the reverse, political analysts often describe Third World polities as the antithesis of pluralistic democracies (e.g., Andrain 1988; Hirschman 1979, 94–96). Third World authoritarian states often rely more on military support than popular legitimacy and have no reliable mechanisms of succession. Yet Juan Linz, analyzing and differentiating kinds of totalitarian and authoritarian regimes, suggested that some of these exhibit a "limited political pluralism" (1975, 264). This pluralism may be in a highly regulated or coordinated form such as corporatism, meaning that the state tries to eliminate spontaneous interest group formation by establishing a limited number of authoritatively recognized groups over which it maintains control (Malloy 1977, 4). Only the formal (usually elite) leaders represent their groups' interests before the state in a kind of orchestrated pluralism (O'Donnell 1977, 49). The corporatistic polities of the developing world and the democratic, pluralistic polities of the West function differently but sometimes produce similar outcomes (Schmitter 1974, 107).

Even without formal corporatist structures, interest groups not created by nor directly dependent on the state may exercise influence in authoritarian polities (Linz 1975, 264). Political participation, meaning the activity of private citizens designed to influence governmental decision making, can take different forms (Huntington and Nelson 1976, 4, 12). In Indonesia, as in other authoritarian regimes, electoral politics are relatively meaningless. Elections only channel the participation of the masses into safe expressions, and legitimate the regime as a "democracy" (e.g., Klesner 1990, 11–12 on Mexico), but other forms of political participation—lobbying, contacting government officials, demonstrations, and violence—remain options for groups attempting to turn government decisions toward their favor. Liddle (1987) discusses how "anticipated participation," that is, the fear that certain groups or constituencies will resort to protest, and other informal processes in Indonesia may bring concessions from those in power.

To the extent that a regime stays in power by balancing the demands of different social segments, it exhibits what Linz would call a "limited pluralism." Donald Emmerson (1983) has used this phrase to describe Indonesia. While Linz and Emmerson used the limited pluralism concept to clarify the extent to which authoritarian regimes approach democracy, I will use it instead to explore the consequences for integration and stability. That is, I will consider the possibility that concessions granted to one segment dampen its potential for resistance and, at the same time, strengthen it as counterweight relative to other segments.

Why do authoritarian, and presumably coercive, regimes have to respond to demands from any popular segment? States in the developing world increasingly "serve the interests of postimperialist international capital, but being relatively autonomous, cannot ignore the interests of subordinate classes either" (Becker 1987a, 53). The state's powers are thus limited by the threat of class struggle, even if all the contending classes are not physically represented in the state structure (Becker 1987b, 208). The state's response to popular demands will seldom take the form of class politics, and few policy debates will engage class issues directly. "Most often the interests immediately engaged are parochial ones belonging to functional groups or institutions controlled by them, regardless of whether the outcome has an impact in class terms" (ibid., 211) The state is constrained by the demands and pressures of subordinate groups and classes, and some concessions to these groups are necessary for legitimacy. "But to the extent that the state acts in the interests of the dominant class . . . it will seek to destroy the cohesion and consciousness of subordinate groups, i.e., to 'disorganize' them" (Hamilton 1982, 14). "Subordinate groups," for my purposes, include ethnic, regional, or religious movements as well as the poor, any of which may destabilize a regime.

Taken together these observations about the politics of authoritarian regimes in developing countries suggest, first, that these politics take place against a background of class divisions.[26] Second, that the stuff of public political struggle will be between "functional" groupings instead, and that in the modern world two important sorts of groupings, ethnic and religious, are increasingly differentiated from each other. Finally, concessions to the different functional groupings deflect and "disorganize" class interests. Horowitz briefly alluded to the possibility of deliberately counterbalanced concessions, but he felt it unlikely that cleavages based on social class or territory could be effectively manipulated to displace ethnicity (1985, 599). I believe that ideological manipulation of this kind does occur, although in a form opposite to what Horowitz imagines. Nation-states may not purposefully manipulate social class and territory to forestall ethnic conflict, but they do quite openly manipulate ethnicity and religion.

Class operates somewhat differently than either ethnicity or religion, both in the consciousness and identity of subjects and in the way states respond to class politics compared to religion and ethnicity. People ceremonially embrace ethnicity and religious affiliation in ritual or other public moments, but outside the events of organized labor (and perhaps debutante balls), they do not ceremonially acknowledge a class position. Sociologists count class among the strongest predictors of people's behavior and attitudes, yet also find, especially among middle- and upper-class U.S. citizens, people persistently denying its relevance.[27] Notice that while theorists of ethnicity frequently describe their subject in terms of identity, theorists of class speak more commonly of *consciousness*.[28] There can be no identity with something that one does not recognize. Recognition or consciousness comes in degrees and, even if conscious of a class position, actors may not translate this into political identities and organized action for a variety of reasons that have to do with their survival interests and safety (Scott 1985).

Although religion and culture sometimes threaten state stability, states also capitalize on these sources to build the nation's sense of community. Class differences do not share the saving graces of these cultural differences, and thus states manage class differently. Leaders construe the public realm as if class issues were irrelevant there (Poulantzas 1974, 187–89). Class conflict, which is only an implicit threat most of the time, can be greatly contained by an apparent indifference. The "indifference" of the state to class quickly disappears when moving to control Communist organizations, labor movements, or even religious protests with overtly utopian or populist overtones. In such instances, both the coercive as well as ideological defenses of the state will be raised against class politics. In between the occasional, necessary show of force, class politics can be controlled quite indirectly, by throwing north and hitting south, as one Javanese saying has it. State-sponsored celebrations promulgate national values and tout the nation's cultural and religious roots. States may also build bureaucratic structures to manage cultural and religious diversity, giving this diversity an organized visibility while providing channels of corporatistic control.

States attempt to control class, ethnicity, and religion through raw repression only if necessary, preferring to manipulate these forces ideologically. Particularly, states treat class as a nonissue, construing political life in terms of ethnicity, religion, or other functional groupings. Revisions of state theory give new room to imagine that states may permit or endorse ethnicity in some forms, even if they must at other times suppress ethnic separatism. Regime stability and economic development may benefit from communalistic loyalties that divide a nation against the grain of socioeconomic classes, so the ruling elite may welcome a limited or ceremonially disciplined communalism as a distraction from the poverty and inequities that betray populist dreams. (These same inequities, of course, also mock religious ideals and diminish ethnic solidarity.) Ethnic and sectarian divisions are useful to state sovereignty until they spread beyond artistic or ceremonial limits and begin to outweigh the threat of class conflict, at which point states will take coercive measures. Whether class or communalism constitutes the larger threat may shift through time, eliciting changing responses from the state.

State monopoly of power, therefore, always rests on a delicate balance of the various forces of order, any of which may also be a source of disruption and challenge (Foltz 1963). Ethnic and religious identities ballast each other, and together diminish the threat of class politics, but the resulting stalemate is probably a consequence rather than a socially engineered goal. That is, I cannot argue that those who hold power in Indonesia attempt to manipulate culture and religion toward the goal of an orchestrated pluralism, only that this is the *effect* of other "independent" ends they do pursue, namely, forestalling class conflict, sectarian domination, and regional secessions while cultivating and sacralizing a national identity. Managing the various forces of order and disorder requires an ever "dynamic compromise" (Foltz 1963) that, in the context of a centralized, authoritarian state such as Indonesia, may have the appearance of an orchestrated pluralism.

Notes

1. Recent theorists of the state agree that "the" state and theories about it are ultimately illusory. Generalizations about feudal states will not hold for those of early capitalism, and generalizations about the latter will differ again from conclusions about the state under advanced capitalism or in the developing Third World. Theory does not substitute for the requirement to understand the historical and cultural realities of particular states (Carnoy 1984, 255; Skocpol 1985, 28).

2. Deutsch and Foltz 1963; Geertz 1963; Maybury-Lewis 1984b; Shils 1957, 144; Tambiah 1989.

3. Even more positively, sociologists have found that immigrant participation in ethnic associations actually facilitates upward mobility and integration into U.S. society (Lal 1983).

4. See also Despres 1984, 17; cf., Bentley 1987.

5. See also Bell 1975; Boulding 1979; Nash 1989, 58–59.

6. Theories of the state were underdeveloped in traditional Marxist thought because the state was seen as an epiphenomenon, soon to disappear with the demise of capitalism (Poulantzas 1972, 239).

7. Becker 1987b, 208; Block 1987; Carnoy 1984; Jessop 1985; Miliband 1969, 1972.

8. See also Norton 1984; Wee 1988; Wolf 1982, 18; Worsley 1984.

9. E.g., Bell 1975; Goyder 1983; Light 1981; Norton 1984; Smith 1984, 170; Thompson 1983; van den Berghe 1975; Yengoyan 1988.

10. See also Becker 1987b, 211–12; Poggi 1978, 95.

11. E.g., Greenberg 1987; Hamilton 1982, 14; Tainter 1988, 27.

12. Alavi 1972; Collier 1979; Krause, Tee, and Yuan 1987; O'Donnell 1977, 54.

13. E.g., Hamilton 1982; Seligson 1987, 5.

14. See also Anderson 1983, 11–14.

15. A. Jakubowics (1984) describes multiculturalism as an ideology that attempts to recast Australian class divisions.

16. Linnekin and Poyer 1990; Rambo, Gillogly, and Hutterer 1988; Williams 1989.

17. Barth 1984, 84; Hamilton 1982, 16; Poggi 1978.

18. Hobsbawm and Ranger 1983; Keesing and Tonkinson 1982; Philibert 1986.

19. Apter 1968; Markoff and Regan 1986; Weissbrod 1983.

20. See Mazrui (1969) for a comparison of the United States with Britain and Nigeria.

21. Smith lists religion among several factors that may produce a "social structure characterized by fundamental discontinuities and cleavages" (1969, 27).

22. Ackerman and Lee 1988; Enloe 1973, 20; Gellner 1983, 141; Ismail 1987; Tamney and Hassan 1987.

23. This process has not always been free of struggle. Buddhism's reception into China, for example, was marked by extensive critique of its "Barbarian" origins (Chan 1963; Ch'en 1964).

24. Only now, with some Chinese Malaysians converting to Islam and becoming fluent in Malay, are Malays coming to rethink the linguistic and religious markers of their identity (Long 1986; Nagata 1984, 130; Nash 1989, 38).

25. Coleman 1956; Gusfield 1962; Kuper 1969, 478–79. Lijphart 1968, 8–9.

26. Class divisions are increasingly transnational phenomena (Becker et al. 1987).

27. Bottomore 1966; Giddens 1982; Marwick 1980.

28. For identity approaches to class, see Centers 1949; Jackman and Jackman 1984.

Chapter 5

The Politics of Religion and Class in Indonesia

Indonesia has enjoyed relative stability and continuity when compared to many other formerly colonial countries. Since 1949 there have been only two heads of state, and the current one, Soeharto, has been in office twenty-five years. This continuity is all the more impressive considering the diversity that is the country's hallmark: the national motto, *Bhinneka Tunggal Ika* (Sanskrit), is usually translated as Unity in Diversity. Peoples speaking hundreds of different languages and occupying thousands of different islands have managed to operate as an "imagined community" for the last four decades. Statistics on religion show that nearly 90 percent of the country is Muslim, giving a deceptive impression of near uniform Islamization. In fact, the religious dimension is another important source of diversity—and dissent (Kipp and Rodgers 1987). Issues of religion have been politically significant in Indonesia from its inception as a nation, beginning with the framing of its constitution and continuing into the present, but rebellions for regional autonomy and a communist movement have actually occasioned the most violent threats to national unity. The politics of religion are often deeply intertwined with these other conflicts.

Scholars have frequently noted that religion and ethnicity, as noncoincident, crosscutting bases of diversity, counterbalance each other and stabilize the Indonesian polity (e.g., Drake 1989, 13–14; Peacock 1973, 149). Emmerson put it this way:

> Had ethnic and religious distinctions coincided, Indonesia could not possibly have survived as one nation; the struggle for power and other resources would have blown her apart. Instead, the abangan-santri [i.e., statistical/devout Muslim] contrast divided the Javanese and prevented their presence in politics from becoming monolithic, while the ethnic contrast between Javanese and non-Javanese mitigated religious conflict by cutting through core and periphery in the community of Islam.

85

The impact of Islam was further vitiated by competition within, notably between that fundamentalist minority of reformers in the cities who would return to the Koran and the sayings of the Prophet and the easier-going custodians of evolved Muslim custom in the countryside. (1976, 23)

The policies of the Indonesian government on culture and religion have, at the least, maintained this set of crosscutting cleavages, and these policies have consequences, too, for class mobilization.

For the last twenty-five years, Indonesia has made development its overriding concern, with the predictable result that income disparities have widened (Drake 1989, 169–70). While the government has used its oil revenues to increase industrialization and achieve self-sufficiency in rice production, and while real economic growth has occurred, widespread poverty continues, especially in the rural areas, along with a growing urban middle class and a small elite that enjoys great wealth (Robison 1986; Booth and McCawley 1981). It is not coincidental, either, that during this same period the state has penetrated Indonesian society more deeply and pervasively. "No other noncommunist state in Southeast Asia has anything like such a prominent state sector as Indonesia" (Mackie 1990a). The military remains firmly in control of the country, and political participation is strictly limited, but the ideological apparatus of the state has grown along with the coercive one. Through control of public education and the mass media, Indonesia propagates religion, a national ideology termed *Pancasila,* and a view of culture as artistic performance.

The government monopolized television transmission until the last few years, which is still the case for all but Jakarta and one or two other cities. The one private television network in Jakarta does not have its own news program but has to broadcast only the news prepared by the government network. National news broadcasts never contain stories about political issues or debates, although such stories do appear in newspapers and news magazines, nor is there any television reporting of criminal acts or actions by the police and military. Natural tragedies such as floods make the news, but for the most part the national "news" depicts ceremonial moments—stone layings or stone inscriptions by the president, arrivals of foreign dignitaries, ribbon cuttings and inaugurations—many of these in connection with development projects or industrial expansion. While the press is independent and enjoys more freedom than radio and television in its selection of news and through its editorials and essays, more than one newspaper has been banned for being too critical of the government (Emmerson 1987–88).

Democracy is an avowed principle in Indonesian political life, but political practice does not measure up to the term, at least by Western standards. A Parliament consisting of a two-tiered assembly operates, as set out in the constitution, but it is powerless.[1] The press reports debates of the assemblies, providing a loose (if one-way) channel between representatives and their constituencies. Technically not a political party, although it functions as such, Golongan Karya (Golkar) organizes some 200 different "functional groups" such as women, students, workers, and businesspeople. Civil servants and the military are the two largest and most powerful of Golkar's components. Two "opposition" parties exist also, but neither these nor Golkar have much significance. The Parliament, parties, and elections are the trappings of democracy that help legitimate the regime (McVey 1982), but real power rests with the president, the ministers of the major governmental departments, and the military.

What is "the state" in Indonesia's case? Political theorists have spent as much time on "the state" in the abstract as anthropologists have spent defining and redefining the culture concept, and scholars use the term inconsistently, depending on their theoretical perspective. In the discussion that follows I will use the term *state* to aggregate the president, the other structures of government, Golkar, and the military.[2] These different elements do not always act in unison, of course, and political analysts spend a great deal of effort assessing their relative strengths and the power struggles *within* the state as I term it. While Soeharto's power and political acumen are great, and while state control rests on military might, considerable jockeying for influence occurs between Soeharto and the military.[3] The different government ministries, in particular the Department of Religion and Department of Education and Culture, follow deliberately contradictory charges on the issue of traditional religions. Indeed, this is one of the best examples of Indonesia's centrally directed pluralism. At the local level, furthermore, the contradictory charges of these two departments on issues of religion permit groups and persons a degree of maneuverability.

This chapter focuses on the national level as a context for understanding the forces shaping Karo religious identities. Indonesia's unusual policies on religion have emerged to forestall the possibility of an Islamic state and to contain sectarian divisiveness among Muslims as well as between Muslims and non-Muslims. Islam and other religions serve to sacralize the nation and the actions of the state, and religious politics, as destabilizing as they may be, draw attention away from other dimensions along which political fissures might form, namely, class and ethnicity.

The Politics of Islam

Scholars still dispute the dates of Islam's arrival in the archipelago and the processes by which it spread.[4] Although it spread virtually throughout the region, it did so unevenly, saturating the culture of certain areas (western Java and the North Java coast, the coastal areas of southern Sulawesi, Aceh, and West Sumatra), while in other places, especially the interior of Java, becoming only a nominal or "statistical" reality (cf., Woodward 1989). In much of the interior of Sumatra and other large islands, and on small islands off the major sea routes, Islam did not penetrate at all. In those island interiors, Christian missionaries in the colonial period enjoyed some of their greatest success. Bali, too, remained relatively impervious to Islam and later to Christianity. These broad areal patterns disguise the divisions that exist within locales. Geertz's (1960) classic study of the religion of Java explored the differences between devout Muslims (*santri*) and statistical Muslims (*abangan*) in a single town. A similar distinction, variously named, probably operates in Muslim areas elsewhere in Indonesia (e.g., Cederoth 1981; Mudzhar 1985).[5]

The politics of Islam in Indonesia up to 1970 have been well covered by Western social scientists.[6] According to one recent figure, 87.6 percent of Indonesians claim Islam as their religion.[7] With the world's fifth largest population, Indonesia can boast a larger number of Muslims than any other country, but both of the country's regimes have resisted the idea of an Islamic state.

The Republic of Indonesia came into being after the end of World War II. There had been some nationalist movements before the war, of which the one with the widest appeal was a Muslim organization, Sarekat Islam. The Dutch had long regarded Islam as one of the greatest threats to their colonial designs; the two worst of their colonial wars were against Muslim forces. The Japanese occupied the Dutch East Indies in 1942 and, during the years of their occupation, cultivated the country's Muslim leaders, the *ulama* (religious scholars), to oppose Dutch domination and to support Japan's vision of Asian unity (Pluvier 1978; van Nieuwenhuijze 1958). Under the Japanese, Islam received the benefit of being organized and institutionalized in new ways. The Japanese created the Office of Religious Affairs, for example, concentrating mainly on Islam, and also a new council of Muslims, called Masyumi, which later assumed the form of a political party (Benda 1958).

The Japanese had created a study committee in 1945 to prepare the country for eventual independence. The committee's deliberations had turned around the issue of whether the new nation would be an Islamic state. Exactly what kind of Islamic state was not spelled out in great detail, but some proposals required the president to be a Muslim, for Islam to be the state religion, and for all Muslims to be subject to Islamic law. Sukarno's formulation of the Pancasila was developed as an alternative to that possibility. The Republic was to be founded on five principles or "pillars" called the Pancasila. These are, in the *current* formulation: Belief in the Almighty God, Nationalism, Humanitarianism, Democracy, and Social Justice. In the first formulation of these principles, nationalism was in first place. What is now the first pillar and is viewed as underlying the rest, belief in the Almighty God, was listed last (Pluvier 1978, 202; van Nieuwenhuijze 1958, 188). This revised placement hints at the compromises that shaped the new nation.

Indonesia's official commitment to "the Almighty God" in its philosophy of state represents a compromise between Muslims who feared a totally secular government and those who feared a specifically Muslim one. The official stance remains, as the Minister of Religion, Munawir Sjadzali, expressed it in a speech in 1986, that Indonesia is neither a religious nation, in the sense of having an official religion of state, but neither is it a secular nation, meaning one that rejects the government's involvement in matters of religion.[8] The state actively promotes Islam along with several other selected religions. Indonesian Christians readily express the idea that the Pancasila protects their minority interests in a Muslim country, and they worry that Soeharto's successor will not keep to these ideals.

The order of the Pancasila's pillars was not the end of the compromises. A department of religion, the Departemen Agama, representing some continuity with the Japanese period's Office of Religious Affairs, also helped make the new government palatable to Muslims who had been hoping for an Islamic state (Boland [1971] 1982; van Dijk 1981, 62). The Departemen Agama, "as it is organized in Indonesia, is probably a unique phenomenon in our world . . ." (Boland [1971] 1982, 105).[9] It is divided into sections representing the interests of Muslims, Catholics, Protestants, and Hindu/ Buddhists, although the Muslim section naturally far outweighs the others. The department's most important work is organizing religious instruction in the schools. Such instruction is now compulsory through the second year of university, so has engendered new colleges to train the necessary number of religious teachers. Other charges include giving material support to restore and maintain places of worship and to supervise the registration of Muslim marriages and divorces. Offices of this department extend down to the district and *camat* (county) level. Personnel from the Departemen Agama provide opening prayers at all sorts of public government gatherings and ceremonies and, conversely, they attend the anniversaries, ground breakings, or other celebrations of private religious groups, there to represent the government. The rank of the attending official corresponds to the size or level of the meeting or ceremony. Soeharto himself attended an anniversary celebration in 1986 of the Huria Kristen Batak Protestan (HKBP), the largest Christian body in Indonesia, and in 1989 he presented the opening address at the national congress of the Nahdlatul Ulama, the country's largest Muslim organization (Vatikiotis 1989b).

The constitution guarantees freedom of religion, but in Indonesia "freedom of religion nowadays does not include the freedom to be non-religious, let alone anti-religious" (Boland [1971] 1982, 189).[10] While official identification cards do not list a person's ethnicity, they do list the person's religion. Persons who aspire to work as teachers or in any other civil service job, including the military, must have an *agama,* an officially sanctioned religion.[11] One Muslim woman I knew who was a candidate for the Karo district assembly (DPR) described the six-hour screening that covered facts about national history and law as well as the candidates' religion. Candidates had to say when they joined the religion they had claimed, and then cite its "pillars" by memory. She sympathized with the Christian candidates who had to remember all the Ten Commandments. Furthermore, local ministers or other religious leaders are sometimes asked to verify, for employment or other application purposes, that someone is, in fact, a member in good standing of the *agama* he or she claims.

As various groups through the years lobbied to have their religions legitimated under the *agama* rubric, the criteria of an *agama* have been the subject of much discussion. The official understanding of the concept is now rather firm (e.g., Naim 1983). *Agama* includes only certain organized, world religions, five of which are officially recognized by the government. These are usually described as monotheistic, and as having a prophet and a "book," although Buddhism does not fit these criteria very well (Brown 1987). The category does not include most sects, even one as large as the Sikhs, nor the organizationally amorphous Kejawen (Javanism) and other mystical traditions that are now categorized as belief (*kepercayaan*) rather than *agama.* Peoples who practice their traditional, usually animistic, religions do not have an *agama,* or do not *yet* have one, as Indonesians say (Kipp and Rodgers 1987).

One sense of religious freedom in Indonesia means that those who already have an *agama* should be free of proselytizing by others. Since 1978 it has been illegal to try to convert someone who is a member of an *agama*. Christian groups such as Jehovah's Witnesses, which aggressively seek converts among Muslims, have been banned along with some other sects. While protecting people in the certified *agama* from unwanted proselytizing, the government encourages those people who do not yet have an *agama* to embrace one. Where children in isolated areas of Irian Jaya, Kalimantan, or Sulawesi have access to government schools, they are required, like all Indonesian children, to take religious education in an *agama* of their choice, even if they do not "yet" have one. They learn from their lessons on Pancasila philosophy, too, that an *agama* identity marks one as a modern Indonesian citizen.

Indonesians have been part of the worldwide resurgence of Islam. Popular study groups sprang up around mosques and universities bringing Indonesian Muslims into closer contact with the universal community of believers through translations of works by Muslim intellectuals from other countries. The Indonesian revival seems to be carried along largely by the energy of young people who meet for study groups around university area mosques and, when necessary, show their force in street rallies and public speeches (Awanohara 1985). As elsewhere, the international resurgence of Islam is propelled partly by the resistance to cultural inundation from the West. Islam presents itself as a cultural and moral alternative to Western domination. The Iranian revolution provides a model of a people who vigorously threw off Western domination (Jones 1980), although some Muslims speak also of the excesses and "deviation" (*penyelewengan*) from that revolution as well (Rais 1983, 11).

Islam in Indonesia has been propelled by the political dynamics of resistance against colonial rule; it can serve similarly against the present government (McVey 1983, 205; Utrecht 1978). As in Malaysia, where the populist opposition party, PAS, is an Islamic party, Muslim opposition provides Indonesians with one of the few *legitimate* bases of popular protest against government policies (Dick 1990, 68). In September 1984 approximately thirty people were killed in Tanjong Priok, Jakarta's working-class port city, protesting the police entry of a mosque (Awanohara 1984). Some time later the national monument of Borobudur was bombed, apparently in protest of trials connected to the Tanjong Priok riots. Another bombing, at the Bank of Central Asia, was linked to similar motives, and the government detained for trial several "radical" Islamic teachers (Weatherbee 1986). In more recent years the government has broken up the settlement of a militant sect called Mujahidin Fisbilillah in Lampung, an isolated region at the southern tip of Sumatra, and has faced continuing guerrilla actions of other "extremists" in

Aceh, especially around the giant gas liquefaction plant at Lhokseumawe.[12] Reports surfaced that one thousand deaths occurred over an eighteen-month period in 1991–92 in connection with the Free Aceh movement (Aznam 1992).

It is not clear to what extent these events should be read as signs of an increased militancy in Indonesia's Islamic opposition, or whether frustrated groups of various sorts are using the Islamic banner "to give moral justification to their anger" (Awanohara 1984), or whether the government is looking for its opposition only in the simplest terms. Muslim leaders suspect that the government makes more of the radical Muslim threat than it deserves (Vatikiotis 1991). "It can also be argued that the violence of the radicals provides the Malaysian and Indonesian governments with useful tools to contain undesirable nonradical Islamic groups" (von der Mehden 1986, 225).

The government has sought to control all political or religious organizations, even the legitimate parties. Islamic parties are especially an anathema (Liddle 1988a). Party politics in the last twenty-five years have been given a secular face, but more than that, parties have been depoliticized altogether. The Christian parties have been combined into a coalition party with the nationalists called the Indonesian Democracy Party (PDI), and the Muslim parties have been fused into the Unity and Development Party (PPP). Both of these ostensibly "opposition" party coalitions have had all reference to religion extracted from their labels, and the PPP flag was not allowed to have a representation of the *ka'ba* (Mecca's holy black stone) on it. Soeharto appointed the first general chairman of the PPP "over the opposition of several Muslim spokesmen who disdained the new party as an artificial creation of the regime" (Emmerson 1976, 237). Nahdlatul Ulama (NU), once the party of traditionalist Muslims, felt it could not pursue its policies in the partisan arena, so removed itself from the PPP in 1984 (Liddle 1988a).[13]

Even in the absence of effective Muslim political parties, Muslim issues remain in the public forefront, and Muslims have gained significant concessions in recent years. Abdurrahman Wahid, the leader of NU, has argued that the organization will have greater political weight *outside* the party structure than in it. The solicitous courting of the NU by Soeharto and other leaders seems to have proven Wahid right (Vatikiotis 1989b). Newspapers and news magazines of 1989 were full of stories about the Parliament's debate of legislation (which eventually passed) strengthening the Islamic courts relative to state courts. Christian groups opposed the measure, fearing that non-Muslims might be subject to Muslim laws of inheritance and divorce, and many Muslims wanted to insure that Muslims, too, would not lose the option of using the state courts (Vatikiotis 1989a). As important as these legal concessions are, some symbolic ones, such as the use of Arabic phrases in speeches by Soeharto and other officials, a practice that has become standard, and Soeharto's pilgrimage to Mecca, may also have great influence in the long run (Emmerson 1991).[14]

While some observers have noted a growing frustration among Muslims as a response to the New Order's restrictions on political expression, others have suggested that Muslims are in any case obligated to put the law in practice in their lives. Rather than speaking of an Islamic state, some speak instead of working for an Islamic society. This means in effect trying to turn statistical Muslims into practicing Muslims, and thus a revitalization process called *dakwah* has been mounted. The Departemen Agama has coordinated some *dakwah* efforts, and student groups have been an important spontaneous force. Movements for renewal and reform, usually entwined with political and economic issues, have been part of the Islamization process in Indonesia for centuries (e.g., Dobbin 1974, 1977, 1983). "*Dakwah* has acquired a new sense of urgency not only because it represents a new opportunity to make amends for past negligence but also because it is an area of Islamic action in which there appears to be room for autonomous Muslim creativity outside the area of politics" (Kamal 1982, 279–80).

There are signs that Indonesia, while no closer to being an Islamic state than it ever was, is becoming a more thoroughgoing Muslim society. Exactly what percentage of the population shares the purist *santri* outlook has never been clear, but in 1980 Jones estimated 20 percent. Recent estimates range from 30 to 50 percent (e.g., Liddle 1988b). The question is whether that figure is increasing, and the answer is apparently yes, based on impressionistic data.[15] New mosques, most of them built with government money, have appeared throughout the country. The number of mosques in Jakarta has increased 400 percent since 1965, and attendance at mosques across Indonesia is reported to be high.

Exactly what should be the relationship between Islam and the state has been the theme of much thinking and writing among Muslim intellectuals in Indonesia in recent years. Nurcholish Madjid, leader of the most important Muslim university student group in the early 1970s, came to articulate a theme of renewal (*pembaharuan*).[16] Madjid's slogan was, "Islam, yes; Islamic Parties, no," arguing for a secularization of politics. Elsewhere, he denied that this meant he was arguing for the secularization of society and for a division of the secular and the religious similar to that of Western societies (Madjid 1979, 1989), but that is how Muslim critics understood his position. Reaction from the older, established Muslim leadership was sharp. In the press and other publications, Muslims have reasserted the position that such a division is not possible for them (e.g., Rais 1983).

Muslim political parties, such as they remain, must take an accommodationist position (Jones 1980, 1984). This fits rather well the position Madjid takes. One form of accommodation argues that, since the principles of the Pancasila are consonant with Islamic ethics, Indonesia is finding its own way toward the creation of an Islamic state, a way that need not necessarily resemble Middle Eastern and other models.[17] This has become the new goal for which many Muslims are striving (Mahasin 1990). Some see the old dichotomy between *santri* and *abangan* being progressively closed by the process in which state-supported Islam has become more and more visible in Indonesian villages and schools (Hefner 1987). There may be important intellectual and theological changes as a consequence. As the statistical/ devout distinction loses some of its sharpness, and as Islam becomes in truth the majority faith, Muslim intellectuals apparently feel freer to suggest reforms and reinterpretations that once would have been heretical.[18]

Accommodation and compromise are also expectable results of the fact that the government has become a major protector and patron of Islam, providing thousands of new jobs for teachers of Islam in the public schools, and employing thousands of managers and clerical workers who staff the Departemen Agama offices throughout the country. One survey of *ulama* and *mubalig* (Muslim authorities) in the Yogya area found that 50 percent of them were government employees.[19] "The government builds mosques by the tens of thousands, sponsors an official biennial national Koran reading competition, gives assistance to Muslim schools, teaches religion in the public schools, and consults regularly with Muslim leaders in the corporatist *Majelis Ulama Indonesia* (Indonesian Islamic Teachers' Assembly), state-sponsored national and regional councils of respected Islamic leaders" (Liddle 1988b, 30–31). The interests of Muslims and of Islam have become institutionally interwoven within state structures. While thus supporting Islam, the Departemen Agama also permits the government a corporatistic control of this potentially disruptive religious force. The Departemen Agama has grown faster than any segment of the government. By 1963 it was the fourth largest of twenty-five government ministries (excluding defense). Now it is second only to the giant Department of Education and Culture.[20]

The state's patronage of Islam deflects much organized Muslim opposition to the government, but not all Muslim opposition. The barest hint of guerrilla activities or street protests with Muslim overtones quickly elicits a forceful response. The irony is inescapable. The state has been the country's biggest patron of Islam, and this partly explains the deepening Islamization of Java that has occurred in the 1980s (Hefner 1985, 1987, 1990), but this new level of Muslim strength has prompted, in turn, the government's closer surveillance and control of Islamic politics.

What is not yet clear from this history of the politics of religion is *why* the state has been such a patron of Islam and of the other organized religions. For that we must examine still more history and, also, the politics of class. While Islam has generated its share of worries among Indonesia's leaders, it has also been of great value. Religious identities, in particular the Muslim identity, have served to counter class-based identities. This is not merely an abstract conflict of loyalties and principles, either: Muslims and Communists have fought each other to the death.

The Democratic Experiment and the Politics of Class

Indonesia declared its independence on 17 August 1945 and, in the next five tumultuous years, struggled to make the declaration a reality. Two rebellions against the new Republic broke out during this period, one communist, the Madiun Rebellion in East Java, which was rather quickly subdued, and one religious, the Darul Islam, which was more intractable. Coming when they did, during the time when the future of the new Republic was still tenuous, these rebellions seemed especially traitorous, drawing the lines of opposition between the new nation and two of its primary internal threats: class politics and Islamic politics. Significantly, the lines of opposition also lay *between* these two threats: "Muslims opposed communists . . . on the grounds that the communists were atheists. . . . The communists . . . regarded the Muslims as hypocritical Arabs who exploited labor through capitalism and women through polygyny" (Peacock 1973, 86). During the Madiun Rebellion, for example, mosques were burned and local *santri* persecuted.[21]

The Darul Islam began with conflicts between the Republican army and irregular groups of guerrillas in West Java. The Republican armies were not able to suppress this rebellion fully until 1962, and Darul Islam became a kind of "banner," to use van Dijk's term, under which several scattered dissident movements coalesced. Uprisings in Central Java in the early 1950s, South Sulawesi (1950–65), South Kalimantan (1950–63), and Aceh (1953–62) each claimed some legitimacy through a nominal link with the Darul Islam.

Many Muslims who sympathized with the aims of the Darul Islam hoped to achieve the same ends through peaceful political action via parties. In the first years of the new Republic, several political parties took shape, some based on religious identity. The first Islamic party was Masyumi, actually an umbrella organization for many Islamic organizations. In 1952 one of its most important constituents, the NU, withdrew, leaving Masyumi to represent "modernist" Islam, while NU represented the more traditional Muslims, appealing especially to the Javanese, who regarded Masyumi as " 'too fanatical,' that is to say, too rigorously Islamic" (Boland [1971] 1982, 50). Implicated in a rebellion in West Sumatra in 1958, Masyumi has been banned. There were, in addition, two smaller Muslim parties (Perti and PSII). Catholics and Protestants had separate parties, too, and all the religious parties competed for membership with a strong nationalist party (PNI) and a Communist party (PKI) (Feith and Castles 1970).

Ricklefs (1981) terms the years 1950–57 "the democratic experiment." A total of six coalition governments ruled the country during this period, the longest of which held power for two years. Great anticipation accompanied the country's first national elections in 1955, but the results were disappointing both to those who hoped the election would clarify and simplify the lines of power and, also, to the Muslim parties who had hoped to work toward an Islamic state through the mechanism of parliamentary democracy. The four Islamic parties together obtained 43.5 percent of the total votes, but only four parties had more than eight seats. The result was a stalemate (Boland [1971] 1982, 53; Ricklefs 1981, 53) and, ultimately, the experiment failed (Feith 1962).

Abrogating the constitution, and dissolving Parliament and the elected cabinet, President Sukarno declared a new centralized authoritarian system he called Guided Democracy. The period of Guided Democracy, 1959–65, were years of phenomenal growth of the Indonesian Communist party (PKI). The PKI was not simply a class-based organization (Hefner 1990, 208; Mortimer 1974, 15; Mortimer 1982), but it represented the interests of the poor, and its strength in this era reflected and intensified class antagonism, contributing to a climate in which rural workers enjoyed relatively more bargaining power with landowners than they do now (Hart 1986, 37). Sukarno sympathized increasingly with the PKI and strengthened Indonesia's links with socialist countries, developments that disturbed Muslims. He termed his own ideology *Marhaenism,* apparently a blend of socialism and elite-led populism (McVey 1970).

In the early 1960s Indonesia was on the edge of crisis. The economy was in shambles, with inflation extremely high. Sukarno appeared to be in ill health, and people wondered what would happen in the power vacuum that his death would create. General Abdul Nasution, leading the army, was regarded as a friend of the Islamic community against the growing communist strength (Boland [1971] 1982, 86). It was in this context that the so-called September 30th Movement (G30S) took place, the details of which are still muddy. Certain officers in the palace guard ordered the capture and execution of several generals, seven of whom were murdered. Order within the army and the palace was quickly restored by General Soeharto and others in the army, who depicted the coup as primarily a PKI plot. The consequences of the coup followed from that depiction (Mortimer 1974).

With the encouragement of the army, Communists "became targets of attack in the worst episode of domestic slaughter in Indonesia's history" (Ricklefs 1981, 272). Exactly how many died is not certain, but estimates are in the hundreds of thousands, and at least as many more were imprisoned. Muslim circles tended to view the events surrounding the attempted coup as a struggle between Islam and Communism, and Islamic groups played a role in naming and searching out PKI sympathizers, "being firmly convinced they would have been the victims themselves if the PKI had come to power" (ibid.).

The postcoup killings and incarcerations effectively erased Communists from the political arena. Twenty-five years later, however, the New Order government still regards communism as "public enemy number one" (Abdullah 1981). Golkar published in 1988 an album of newspaper clippings, pictures, and other records of its twenty-four years of "hard work." The book begins with a picture of Soeharto signing what is shortened nowadays as *Super Semar* (in full, *Surat Perintah Sebelas Maret,* the order to exterminate the PKI movement). Golkar celebrates this event annually. Economic sanctions against suspected communist sympathizers continue. Those once incarcerated as communists cannot work as civil employees, and civil employees who merely have some suspected trace of PKI connection in their background are "retired" as early as possible. Screening of DPR candidates entails extensive investigation of their background to determine if there is any connection with the PKI.[22]

The *Super Semar* catchword encodes the New Order's sense of what is still potentially the greatest threat to national security. But what really is the nature of this threat? There is no sign of a Communist party revival (Liddle 1985, 1987), nor would it be permitted. Only because the strength of anticommunist sentiment is so high at a popular level can charges of communist taint be effective weapons in factional power plays within the government, even at the very top (Vatikiotis 1988; Vatikiotis and Fonte 1990). But observers agree that today there is "a clearer trend towards the formation of social classes" or a "growing gap between the 'haves' and the majority of the 'have-nots'" (Abdullah 1981, 68, 72). Golkar's defensive posturing against a ghost organization makes little sense except as exorcism of a specter with quite real dimensions—class politics. Observers have noted the tendency to mark any criticism of the widening gap between rich and poor as communist inspired (van der Kroef 1976, 1985; Vatikiotis and Fonte 1990). When student protests in 1974 took the lives of eleven persons and injured more than a hundred (the so-called Malari incident), the government claimed PKI instigation. The students were protesting the widening gap between rich and poor and the relationship with foreign countries, in particular Japan, which they felt exacerbated Indonesia's poverty (van der Kroef 1976). Emmerson suggests that the government used the PKI as a scapegoat in this instance, rather than accept what were in fact complex sources of blame (1976, 250).

The government does not openly express a fear of class mobilization, and, perhaps outside of urban journalists and intellectuals, Indonesians do not often speak directly about class either. Class issues surface, nonetheless, in discourse about the separation between the elites and the masses (e.g., Sjamsuddin 1989, 13) or about the gulf between leaders and "the people" (*pemimpin dan rakyat*), as well as talk about communism.[23] A proliferation of nongovernmental organizations (NGOs) dealing with human rights, the environment, development, and labor—organizations often funded by foreign or international sources—are another venue for class issues, one that the government now watches closely. Discussion about class is also implicit and increasingly evident, too, in forecasts that democracy and social justice will be among the most pressing problems of the near future.[24] Those who constitute the state in Indonesia, as well as the middle and upper classes whose interests it serves, exhibit in their fear of communism a generalized anxiety about the political volatility of the country's impoverished masses.

Robison (1986, 98) suggests that the abortive coup of 1965 and the rationale of a communist threat gave the New Order its license for authoritarianism. Like the bureaucratic-authoritarian regimes of Latin America in the 1960s and 1970s (Seligson 1987, 5), the Indonesian state presents itself as operating above politics in the interests of the society, as the executor of scientifically conceived strategies for development (Robison 1986, 108). Part of these economic strategies have entailed greater scope for the free market, including a greater influx of international capital and international aid than Sukarno's regime permitted, and an emphasis on high tech industries such as aircraft manufacture (Nasir 1987). In the early years of the New Order, Indonesia benefited enormously from oil revenues, but growth continued even in the 1980s when the price of oil remained low. Economic growth in 1989 was 6.2 percent, and was expected to be between 6 and 7 percent in 1990 (Goldstein 1990).

While there has been a general improvement in the standard of living throughout the country, landlessness has increased in some rural areas (Hart 1986, 70), and overall calorie consumption has declined for the very poorest citizens (Booth and Sundrum 1981; Vatikiotis 1990b). Inequalities have increased between different rural areas and between rural and urban areas; Jakarta claims the benefits of development at the expense of the rest of the country (Drake 1989, 247, 260–61). While there has not been a rapid increase in income disparities and in the number living in absolute poverty *everywhere* in the country, "the number of people in Indonesia, and particularly Java, living below any acceptable level of material well-being is still extremely large, and if it is declining at all the rate of decline is very slow" (Booth and McCawley 1981, 214).

Still, many observers conclude that the government operates from a broad base of legitimacy. "More support has been bought with distribution than . . . through coercion," Liddle judges (1989b, 58; see also Emmerson 1987–88), and he sees a wide acceptance of repressive institutions and, in 1985, few demands for democratic participation (Liddle 1985). Speaking of the New Order, Robison also decided that it rules with the general acquiescence of most people and in the general interests of the middle and upper classes and has provided the conditions for economic growth and social stability (1986, 120). In fact, the state protects the interests of the middle and upper classes, quite directly at times, against the interests of the poorest. The press frequently recounts, for example, land disputes between large developers or corporations and small owners, squatters, or others with unwritten claims to land.[25]

If the power of the state in Indonesia rests on a broadly felt legitimacy among the middle and upper classes, it rests, too, on a powerful army. Coercion is used only sparingly to maintain order in Indonesia, but it is, nonetheless, always in the background (Liddle 1988a). Physical repression has been used most frequently against Communists, radical Muslims, students, and lower-class urban groups (Liddle 1989b; Robison 1988, 159–66). The army has consistently portrayed itself as mediating the extremes of the communist Left and the Islamic Right in order to guarantee the stability necessary for the government to implement its development plans.[26] Not exactly "above" or outside politics, as they are in most bureaucratic-authoritarian regimes, the armed forces have assumed a so-called dual function (*dwi-fungsi*) of administration and defense. Military officers involve themselves directly in the work of governing. This means, partly, that army personnel occupy some leadership positions in most of the major government ministries and a large block of the seats in Parliament (Crouch 1978; Emmerson 1983). The military is the most powerful political faction of the New Order.

The military's coercive powers complement rather than replace ideological manipulation, and this is especially clear in the government's promotion of religion to control the politics of class. In the months of terror following the September 30th Movement, membership in one of the recognized *agama* became a badge of protection against reprisal, as people sought to show their innocence of PKI involvement by a display of religious devotion. Partly because of an opposition logic that had pitted Muslims against Communists, many of these new devotees chose to align themselves with Christianity rather than Islam. A Baptist missionary in Java estimated that two million baptisms occurred in Indonesia in the years 1965–71 (Willis 1977). Reports of mass conversions to Christianity surfaced widely, especially in four areas: East and Central Java, East and West Kalimantan, Timor, and Karoland. In Java, the PKI's following had been mainly in East and Central Java among that sector of society termed *abangan,* roughly the peasantry or working class, and specifically those in the working class who had been only statistical Muslims. The Karo area was also a PKI stronghold before 1965. The sudden conversions in these areas were not entirely spontaneous. Members of the military and government officials often accompanied teams of evangelists, brass bands, and choirs, "on the theory that the making of believers was the unmaking of Communists" (Thomson 1968, 8). Literally thousands at a time were added to the church rolls in this way (Beyer 1982, 42; Pederson 1970, 190–92). The military also mounted *dakwah* drives in several areas (e.g., Mudzhar 1985). Suspected Communists detained in jails in this period were given the "opportunity" to convert, and some did.

This postcoup rush to religion heightened Muslim-Christian tensions, as well as tensions between Javanist and purist Muslims. Islamic leaders, considering the victory over the PKI as in some sense their victory, expected that in the new regime Islam would gain a new political legitimacy. In particular, they hoped for the reinstatement of the Masyumi party, which had been outlawed since 1960, but this hope was disappointed. At the very moment when the Muslim parties were being frustrated anew in their struggle to shape the Indonesian polity toward an Islamic state, they watched with dismay as the government and military encouraged the ranks of other religions to swell. Many felt "threatened and offended by the growth of other religions" (Ricklefs 1981, 273). Kamal (1975) speaks of the "defensive psychology" that emerged in the postcoup Islamic community.[27] A defensive psychology, and the fact that Christianity continues to expand, accounts for the fact that Muslim objections sometimes do supersede Pancasila ideals, resulting in restrictions placed around Christian activities. These restrictions can be material ones, commonly the difficulty of gaining building permits (e.g., Latuihamallo 1968), or symbolic ones, such as when the World Council of Churches was denied permission to meet in Indonesia and the Pope was denied permission to visit the country.

These defensive responses index "deep-seated fears of Christianization and secularization" (Cohen 1992, 28). The Central Bureau of Statistics has not released the 1985 and 1990 census figures on the country's religious makeup. "In 1980, Muslims comprised 87.1% of the population, down from 95% in 1955" (Cohen 1992). If Islam has lost some percentage share of nominal adherents, it has, at the same time, gained depth and strength as a religion, and its influence in the polity has never been greater. The numbers would probably show that Christianity has a growing percentage share as well, for the general impression is that Christianity, especially the Pentecostal varieties, is expanding rapidly.

Wanting to sacralize nationalism and to counter communism, the Indonesian government supports *agama* in general and Islam, the majority religion, in particular. The Departemen Agama propagates Islam while providing some degree of corporatist control over this social force, especially since so many Muslim teachers and leaders have become state employees. Partly as a result of state patronage, Islam has gained breadth and depth in the society. But those in power are not willing to turn the country into an Islamic state, nor even to give Muslim forces enough influence to risk thwarting the trajectory of economic development. The state has thus placed greater strictures on political participation and above all on Muslim politics.

The class factor is as important for understanding Indonesia's unique proreligion ideology as the religious pluralism that this ideology aims to placate. In the absence of organized communism or even much popular sentiment for it, the government's preoccupation with this "enemy" veils a generalized anxiety about class mobilization during a period when a small number have grown very wealthy, and middle-class Indonesians are increasingly visible while most Indonesians remain mired in poverty. Islam can be counted as a traditional foe of communism, so although Islam, on its own, remains potentially threatening to the current political order, it is also, when it comes to communism, the state's proverbial "enemy of my enemy." Under the New Order the Islamization of Indonesia has deepened. The bureaucratization of *agama* in a government ministry and the veneration of religious pluralism in the Pancasila benefit both Islam and Christianity, strengthening their hands against the small or just amorphous minority religious groups. At the same time, Islam and Christianity have grown all the stronger in facing each other. The state's policies have thus sharpened *agama* identities all the more, probably deflecting class identities in all socioeconomic strata (e.g., Hefner 1990, 207).

Notes

1. For a useful outline of government structures and of where power rests in the Indonesian polity see Rinn-Sup Shinn 1983. Political scientists fond of classifying polities are not sure how to typify Indonesia. (See Wood 1990, 23 n. 3.) Some have called it neopatrimonial, stressing the personal power of the president and of patron-client ties throughout the system; others have termed it bureaucratic (Jackson and Pye 1978); Dwight King (1978) has interpreted it as a bureaucratic-authoritarian regime that uses corporatist strategies. Emmerson decided it was a hybrid type, at once patrimonial, corporatist, and bureaucratic-authoritarian, a regime, "more complex and more legitimate . . . than many observers have acknowledged" (1983, 1223). Emmerson's label for this hybrid was "bureaucratic pluralism."

2. Liddle (1989b), for example, speaks of the military as if it were not part of the state.

3. These internal struggles are not very significant externally, however, either when viewed from the international level, where Indonesia must function as a unitary player for many purposes, or from the local level where anthropologists usually work (and from where all the powerful players appear equally remote and inaccessible).

4. See the readings in Ibrahim, Siddique, and Hussain (1985) for the classic papers in the debate. See also Hall 1977.

5. The term *abangan* carries a pejorative connotation now and is used less frequently than other terms such as *Kejawen* (Javanism) to denote the syncretic religion that combines elements of Hinduism, Buddhism, and Animism along with Islam (Hefner 1987).

6. Among them Benda (1958), Boland ([1971] 1982), Emmerson (1976), and Jay (1963).

7. Biro Pusat Statistik 1984, 210.

8. *Sinar Indonesia Baru*, 17 October 1986. Published in Medan.

9. See van Nieuwenhuijze 1958, 217ff. for a description and critical view of this ministry. See also Noer 1978.

10. Van Nieuwenhuijze suggested that the better translation of freedom of religion in the Indonesian setting is "freedom for religion" (1958, 82). Naim 1983 sets out a government view of the issue.

11. The recognized *agama* identities are Muslim, Protestant, Catholic, Hindu, and Buddhist.

12. "Asia Watch," 16 March 1989; *Tempo*, 18 February 1989; Vatikiotis 1990c.

13. Since party membership no longer indexes one's commitment to Islam nor one's opinions on the issues that currently divide Muslims, there is more focus on outward symbols that establish Muslim identity, in particular headgear and dress codes for women, than party affiliation (Jones 1984).

14. Analysts see these symbolic gestures as Soeharto's attempt to gain Muslim support in opposition to the army (e.g., Chalmers 1991).

15. *Christian Science Monitor* (1986) quoting Geertz; *Tempo*, 14 June 1986; Vatikiotis 1989a, 1990b.

16. Kamal (1982) provides translations of some of Madjid's papers.

17. *Tempo*, 29 December 1984.

18. *Tempo*, 14 June 1986.

19. *Tempo*, 15 July 1989.

20. *Islamic Herald* 9, 21–25, 1985; Lev 1972.

21. Cf., Swift (1989), who suggests that the masses were not mobilized along the syncretic-devout divide in this revolt.

22. One candidate was removed, for example, when it was revealed that his father-in-law had been killed as a suspected communist in 1965, even though the candidate was not yet married at that time (*Tempo*, 11 October 1986).

23. See also Liddle 1988b, 9–10, 21–22.

24. *Kompas*, 12 September 1990.

25. To facilitate its burgeoning automobile traffic, and perhaps to enhance a modern image, Jakarta eliminated pedicabs in all but its most fringe areas in 1990, despite the vociferous protest of the pedicab drivers.

26. Emmerson 1976; Liddle 1988b, 21; Rogers 1988.

27. See also Vatikiotis 1990d.

Chapter 6

The Politics of Culture in Indonesia

The Indonesian government attempts both to control ethnicity and to use it. That it requires control almost goes without saying: ethnic or regional secession recurrently threatens modern states; short of that, ethnic animosities can flare into violence, destroying lives and property. On the other hand, indigenous cultures provide a repository of traditions and symbols that leaders can use to forge national identity and foster a sense of community. The tourist industry provides another important incentive for the government to take a hand in the preservation and cultivation of traditions. Finally, ethnic differences, and even ethnic animosities, around which "primordial" loyalties emerge, complicate and mitigate other kinds of differences and animosities. Were reformist Muslims to generate a movement to transform the polity, or more modestly, just to change economic policies on matters such as banking and advertising, they would succeed only by getting past the ethnic and regional interests that separate Javanese from Acehnese and both of these from Minangkabau. Were farmers or laborers to coalesce around their common interests, they would need to surmount the same kinds of ethnic divisions.

Indonesia's policies on culture and ethnicity must be seen in terms of these contradictory demands to minimize the destabilizing potential of ethnicity, and also to use traditional cultures for economic and integrative ends. Two related levels of cultural politics at the national level will concern me here. First, Indonesian intellectuals still wonder whether they have a national culture, and if so, what it is (e.g., Darmaputera 1988; Suryohidiprojo 1990). Constructing nationalist ideals, a nationalist sense of history, and a transcendent loyalty to the nation have been goals of both Old Order and New Order governments. Second, Indonesia has had to come to terms with ethnic diversity. The fact that there are so very many different cultures and languages matters less, I will argue, than the fact that two peoples among all these stand out, although in different ways. The Javanese constitute two-thirds of the population, and they predominate in the leadership elite. The Chinese, numerically a small minority, dominate the international business circles and the retail sector in Jakarta and other cities throughout the archipelago. The policies of the state encourage traditional cultures partly to mask these imbalances. An ideology celebrating cultural (artistic) diversity addresses the problem of the national culture and supports the lucrative tourism industry; and a blindness to ethnic affiliation for all official or political purposes obliquely addresses the two imbalances in the diversity quotient, Javanese dominance and Chinese wealth.

Inventing a National Culture

"What is Modern Indonesian Culture?" was once the theme of a summer conference on Indonesian Studies. The epilogue to the publication from that conference concluded ruefully that, whatever Indonesian culture once *was*, it was fast disappearing under the bulldozer of a homogenizing modernization (Davis 1979). A decade later, Karl Heider (1991) is confident that there is a national culture, one that an indigenous film industry both captures and constructs. Cinematic themes wrestling with order versus disorder and individual autonomy versus responsibility to the group reveal its outlines. In an essay on politics and culture in Indonesia, Liddle argues that national culture is built on a desire to blend the indigenous with the modern: "Most Indonesians want Western education and a modern life-style, but deplore many of modernization's social and cultural consequences" (1988b, 1). The government's push to modernize has thus been cloaked in an indigenous national style. The phrase *gotong royong* provides an example (Bowen 1989). Originally a Javanese term that denoted forms of mutual aid, it comes up in almost every discussion of an authentically Indonesian national culture (e.g., Suryohidiprojo 1990). In practice, it usually designates the mobilization of corvee labor for collective projects of the state or local government.[1]

Scholars agree that whatever else the national culture may be, the national language is central to it and to the nation's successful integration (e.g., Heider 1991; Errington 1985, 60). Bahasa Indonesia (Indonesian) was born of the Malay lingua franca that had been a language of trade and other public activities for centuries. Now the medium of education, the press, other mass media, public offices, and all formal occasions, Indonesian is "perhaps the most important single ingredient in the shaping of the modern culture" (Liddle 1988b, 1). Although most Indonesians continue to grow up learning Javanese, Sundanese, Acehnese, or one of the literally hundreds of other different local languages as their mother tongue, instruction in primary school shifts gradually from their local language to Indonesian in the first three grades. An increasing number of children learn to speak Indonesian first. A recent Ph.D. dissertation in linguistics determined that Indonesian was more likely to be the language of the home in ethnically mixed (Javanese-Sundanese) marriages than ethnically homogeneous ones.[2] My experience with Karo families suggests that urban children usually learn Indonesian first even when both parents are Karo, and if they know a second language, it is more likely to be the local language of their peers rather than Karo. The success of Bahasa Indonesia has saved Indonesia from the divisive politics of language that are so common in formerly colonial countries (Drake 1989, 62; Feith and Castles 1970, 318).

The Department of Education and Culture is the state's main instrument for preserving, inventing, and transmitting both national and local cultures. As this ministry's name suggests, it is divided into two branches, one for education and one for culture (*kebudayaan*). The education side of the ministry supervises schools at all levels, and Indonesia has invested heavily in education in recent decades. The number of primary schools increased by 65 percent between 1970 and 1980, junior high schools by 62 percent, and senior high schools by 53 percent. According to official statistics, 97 percent of Indonesian children between the ages of seven and twelve were attending school in 1983–84 (Drake 1989). As in any country, the public schools are the primary arena where children learn the standard language, history, and symbols of their nation and participate routinely in rituals of allegiance.[3]

Crowning the national culture is the Pancasila (Sutrisno 1983). Pancasila is presented as a philosophy and an ethical position transcending religious and ethnic parochialism. Courses on Pancasila philosophy are required from primary school through university, and refresher courses in it are also mandated for all public and civil servants. Now with academic legitimacy, Pancasila philosophy spawns a scholarly literature of theses, dissertations, and books crossing several disciplines. Pancasila increasingly resembles a full-fledged ideology, that is, a system of thought "more or less intellectually elaborated and organized, often in written form . . ." (Linz 1975, 266–67; cf., King 1982, 111 n.17). It also resembles a religion.

A national holiday, *Hari Kesaktian Pancasila,* the day of Pancasila Sacred Power, commemorates on October 1 each year the 1965 defeat of the Communist party by the army under the leadership of then Major-General Soeharto.

To devout Muslims, whether favorably or unfavorably disposed to Pancasila in general, the doctrine cannot possibly be *sakti* (holy, possessing sacred power). Describing Pancasila in this way comes close, they say, to giving it the status of a religion, despite the President's frequent denials of such an intention. (Liddle 1988b, 16)

To outsiders, certainly, Pancasila has all the appearance of a classic civil religion (Purdy 1982).

The government requires that the Pancasila be the "sole foundation" of all organizations, including religious organizations. The Political Parties Bill, passed in February 1985, required all parties to espouse only the Pancasila as their motivating principle. A similar bill was passed in June of the same year for "mass organizations" of whatever kind (Weatherbee 1986), and Christians as well as Muslims questioned what this meant for their religious organizations (Awanohara 1985). These steps suggested to several observers of the Indonesian scene that the New Order was attempting to tighten its ideological control of the country.[4] Emmerson (1983) attributed this enhanced control to the government's nervousness about the elections that were approaching in 1987 (although the controls have not abated since then) and to the fact that as Soeharto and other leaders of his generation age, they must ensure the continuity of the programs and institutions they have created. The New Order's dual anxieties about inequities of wealth and about deepening Islamization also explain the enhanced propaganda, since the Pancasila is used "for both anti-Islamic and anti-communist purposes" (Liddle 1988b, 16).

Ethnic Blindness and Showcase Cultures

The Pancasila and the national language ride atop a wide array of local cultures and languages, but inequities of power and wealth roughly overlay and accentuate two groups—Javanese and Chinese—within that array. Among the major threats to the country's disintegration Christine Drake lists "the growing Javanization in government" (1989, 257–58, 269). She points out that the economic center of the country is not Java as a whole but specifically Jakarta, which enjoys a disproportionate share of the country's wealth, while the Javanese countryside remains among the poorest regions (Drake 1989). Still, Jakarta is situated on Java, and from the perspective of peoples who live in other regions, Jakarta's wealth and the Javanese predominance in the government seem to go together. The Javanese have long dominated the military leadership as well (*Indonesia* Editors 1992). As for the Chinese, they are found disproportionately in the middle class and among the country's wealthiest ranks (Schwarz 1991a).

The associations with wealth and power that overlay the categories "Javanese" and "Chinese," not the sheer magnitude of the country's cultural diversity, present the real challenges to national integration and explain the government's "know-nothing" attitude about ethnicity.[5] In the early days of the Republic, appeals to ethnicity were regarded suspiciously as *sukuisme* (tribalism), a divide-and-conquer tactic of the colonial past (Feith and Castles 1970, 317). The several secessionist rebellions that the Republic faced in the 1950s gave further reason to downplay the ethnic factor. Indonesia thus officially ignores ethnicity altogether in the kind of settings where its neighbors have institutionalized it. Vivienne Wee, a Singaporean anthropologist, was struck by Indonesia's "laissez-faire" approach to ethnic labeling compared to Singapore (1985, 8). Identification cards list religion but not ethnicity. Indeed, census takers do not collect data on ethnicity. The schools and government are ethnically blind, at least in principle.

The ideal of ethnic blindness is so sacred that pointing out its infractions or exceptions is almost traitorous. In the 1970s the press popularized the acronym SARA as a shorthand for factors that could overwhelm national unity. Still used with some frequency, the initials stand for *suku* (ethnicity), *agama* (religion), *ras* (race), and *antar golongan* (groups or classes). The discussion of these issues was getting so heated that the government prohibited any discussion of SARA in public forums (Emmerson 1976, 274). Two conditions suggest that ethnicity surely constrains opportunities more than people can or want to admit.[6] First, *korupsi* (corruption) exists at every level, a bane that people discuss openly, and, second, officials from a particular region or ethnic group tend to hire others from that region or ethnic group (Bruner 1974; Liddle 1988b). Young people with or without college degrees have their best chance of finding work in a business or office where they know someone. I heard the term *korupsi* most often when the conversation was about the necessity of paying for entry level positions. To the extent, then, that jobs are in scarce supply and are allocated on the basis of payments and personal connections, and that the Javanese dominate the political bureaucracy (Drake 1989, 263–64), and the Chinese predominate in businesses, ethnicity constrains opportunities.

The laissez-faire approach to ethnicity is a tolerant approach, however, at least for non-Chinese Indonesians. Americans should not read melting pot imagery into Indonesia's motto, Bhinneka Tunggal Ika, which is rendered

Various, yet One more accurately than Unity in Diversity (Darmaputera 1988). "Both semantically and in political practice . . . the Indonesian version reflects more the idea of coexistence or of a permanent balance between the many and the one, each legitimate in its own way, while the American conception—for most of our history, anyway—has stressed the absorption of the many into the one" (Liddle 1988b, 4). Indigenous languages and cultures are not repressed, they are merely relegated to private life where they continue to flourish (Kartomihardjo 1979; Liddle 1988b).

More than tolerantly laissez-faire, in fact, the government actively promotes the showcase aspects of culture or tradition—dance and music, the plastic and textile arts, rituals, costumes, and indigenous architecture. Cultural performances and displays target two audiences: first, Indonesians themselves, for whom these arts exhibit in their totality the indigenous heritage that makes Indonesia distinctive; and, second, the burgeoning numbers of tourists who come to Indonesia every year (Volkman 1990). Tourism is projected soon to be the world's largest "industry," and developing countries are vying to capture as much of its profits as they can. The primary form of tourism in Indonesia, the so-called cultural or anthropological tourism, attracts people who want to experience the arts and temples of Bali, or the houses and funerals of Toraja Land (Adams 1990; Volkman 1990). An article in *Kompas* reported that 20,000 foreign tourists had visited Toraja in 1984, 37,000 in 1989, and the goal for 1990 was 42,000.[7] In a cooperative effort to boost tourism, the Association of Southeast Asian Nations (ASEAN) designated 1991 "Visit Indonesia" year. In that year, over 2.5 million visitors arrived, spending more than two billion dollars in the process (Schwarz 1992b).

Viewing performances and museum displays in Indonesia, one cannot escape the sense that these are crafted as much for Indonesians as for the foreign tourists (Volkman 1984, 1990). The number of Indonesian visitors to Toraja Land, for example, was 160,000 in 1989, four times as many as foreign tourists.[8] Taman Mini Indonesia Indah (Beautiful Indonesia in Miniature), a gigantic theme park just outside Jakarta, celebrates Indonesia's diversity. While there are displays of birds and other fauna, orchids, houses of worship representing each of the official *agama*, amusement park rides, several museums, an Irex theater, and a Disney-like play castle, the core of the park consists of replicas of traditional houses, grouped according to province. Far taller and far larger than the traditional houses actually are, the Taman Mini exemplars sometimes have authentic floor plans and furnishings in place, but more frequently they contain display cases of tools and other artifacts or historical dioramas. Handicraft exhibitions and sales take place in some. Theatrical or musical groups perform on the grounds around the houses on weekends. Indonesians, who go there to learn about and take pride in the multicultural heritage of their country and in their particular regional and ethnic roots, far exceed the numbers of foreign tourists.[9]

Archaeological treasures play a similar role, but because many of these are temples the politics of religion blend ambiguously with the politics of culture and tourism in their preservation and use. The temples of Java, dating from the eighth to the fifteenth centuries, have been rescued from decay through extensive restoration projects that include the construction of paved paths leading to and around the sites, rest room facilities, and licensed hawker stalls. A large concrete amphitheater with elaborate lighting sits just behind the Prambanan temple complex where a four-night ballet of the Ramayana epic takes place monthly, "DeMille-like spectacles," as one guidebook describes it (Dalton 1977, 121).

At one level, these monuments and the Ramayana spectacles of Prambanan represent a national heritage, but at another level they bespeak a definitively Javanese past and, yet again in other terms, a non-Islamic religious variant. The enhanced access to these once crumbling sites has made them more accessible also for Indonesians, many of whom come as tourists of a national heritage, but some of whom come as devotees. Foreign tourists and Indonesian teenagers climbing the steep and narrow steps of Prambanan move out of the way to let small family groups of Javanese carrying incense and pedestaled platters pass by, and at all the small temples on their itinerary, tourists will see the rose petals and ashes of recent offerings. I heard a well-educated Javanese guide at Prambanan explain to his group of American tourists that while Indonesia was a Muslim country, it was not an Islamic state, and the government did different things to please different groups. The restoration of Prambanan, he suggested, was a concession to the Hindu element of Indonesian society. The tourist "objects" of Toraja Land and Bali are equally ambiguous, embodying multiple significances as national treasures, ethnic emblems, and religious rituals or artifacts.

The government deliberately cultivates and preserves, not the whole circle of what anthropologists term culture, but only a small part of the arc—especially houses, ritual costumes, handicrafts, and dances. These can be marketed as tourist "objects" (Adams 1990; Volkman 1990). Arts such as oratory or poetry do not translate well for tourists, even domestic tourists, although these arts are intensely important in many Indonesian cultures. Nor is it easy to display and market intangibles such as kinship structures, land laws, or the etiquette of interpersonal interaction.

Some of the cultures of Indonesia are more easily objectified than others. Where the local traditions have not included elaborate dances and costumes, enthusiastic officials have sometimes invented them (Acciaioli 1985). Air transit passengers entering the country in Biak, Irian Jaya, are treated to songs and dances by locals dressed in "traditional" costumes that look newly minted. I watched a television documentary in Jakarta in 1989 about a Javanese ethnochoreographer. Moving in with a group of Dayak for awhile, he dressed in local style, observed their everyday life and dances, and then composed and taught them two new dances incorporating some of their traditional movements. Similar processes of inventing, enhancing, and streamlining the dances once done for rituals or local entertainment have occurred throughout the country in response to the requirements of stage and television, the new performative contexts of the age.

In many cases the government seeks to identify a single cultural type for each province, and to play down the extent and breadth of the country's actual ethnic diversity (Bowen 1989).[10] Each of the country's twenty-seven provinces is usually represented at Taman Mini by only one house, although the North Sumatra section contains both a Karo and a Toba house. Aceh is represented with an Acehnese house, but the artifacts within it are an amalgam of Gayo and Acehnese. The fillers on national television displaying traditional dances often label them according to *province* without specifying the ethnic tradition from which they come.

The government's attempt to stimulate *regional* arts without stimulating ethnic consciousness is only partly successful. People proceed to split what the government would lump, constructing and defining ethnic identities at the grass roots. Gayo oral artistry, for example, springs to new life among urban migrants in Jakarta (Bowen 1991). Susan Rodgers has traced the objectification of Angkola Batak tradition in local newspaper articles about kinship and *adat* and in cassette tape dramas (1984, 1986, 1987, 1991). She is quick to point out that "local ethnic groups are not allowed any significant political power," Angkola rajadoms being merely a ceremonial shell of the polities they once were. In that context, she supposes, family drama "is a relatively safe area of activity and symbolic maneuver" in comparison to equally traditional themes of hierarchy and alliance. As Rodgers's work makes clear, the objectification impulse comes also from within Angkola society, not just from the state. Angkola themselves alight on dance, music, textiles, and folktales to represent themselves to other Indonesians and for "strategically defending Angkola Batak culture vis-à-vis the national state," for they cannot use the distinctive oratorical traditions Rodgers has described elsewhere (1979, 1981, 1983).

The Old Order talked about *kepribadian nasional* (national personality); the New Order catchphrase became *kelestarian kebudayaan nasional* (the preservation of national culture) (Abdullah 1981). The earlier phrase encoded only a defensive stance toward foreign contaminants, while the new term has come into use along with positive financial support for art centers and traditional arts groups. "For several reasons, including tourism, appeasement of provincial middle and upper class cultural pretensions, and its own Javanist inclinations, the government has encouraged the maintenance or restoration of traditional customs and ceremonies, which creates the appearance of local cultural, if not political autonomy" (Liddle 1988b, 19). Government-supported institutes study *Javanologi* or *Baliologi.* "Every governor's office now sponsors a traditional (actually very 'nationalized' in style and content) dance troupe which entertains official guests" (ibid., 30). The government's cultivation of artistic, ethnic pluralism surely deflects attention, not simply from the concentration of power at the center, as Liddle suggests, but from the specifically *Javanese* domination of that center.

More recently still, the catchword in discussions of national culture has become *kreativitas* (creativity), meaning the attempt to redefine, revise, and translate traditions for increasingly urban and foreign audiences (Abdullah 1981). Television provides a major arena for the new *kreativitas.* Government television regularly depicts dances or music from each of Indonesia's twenty-seven provinces, but these are usually fairly simple, low-cost productions using local people. A program on a private network newly available in Jakarta prompted this entry in my field notebook on 28 August 1990:

I just saw an amazing ballet on RTCI following the English language news. Billed by an announcer as "traditional dance" from Kalimantan, it was in fact a modern choreographed spectacle involving scores of dancers and singers on a modern, multilevel stage. The dance depicts, first, Kalimantan's ethnic diversity (with people dressed in a variety of "traditional" costumes including some striking ones with feathers and masks), and then the richness of Kalimantan's forest. (Some dancers and singers, representing the forest, simply stand in the background waving schematic stick-trees; others prance through in bird and animal costumes.) Enter five men and women dressed in pith helmets and khakis. These scientists or engineers knowingly assess the untapped resources of the forest and then direct the natives to begin felling trees, planting crops, and using fertilizer. An industrial city grows up, and all of this progress (explains a narrator) started when people put their many differences aside in the interests of national unity. In the finale, as the chorus swells, scores of dancers carrying large Indonesian flags weave through each other, encircling the stage.

This artistic creation condensed messages about the subordinate place of ethnic diversity under a modern and transcendent nationalism, the authority of science, and the ideals of development, messages that typify the content of most government television programming, whether artistic or informational.

The concern with artistic preservation responds as well to a genuine apprehension of Western cultural domination general among the urban middle class. A new, private television network (RTCI), first available only by subscription, but since 1990 available to anyone in Jakarta with a color TV set, broadcasts almost entirely in English and without subtitles. Most of its programs come from American television. Adventure cartoons, sitcoms, and police thrillers beam into Jakarta living rooms all day, with frequent fillers of MTV-style rock videos and interruptions for commercials. The Jakarta press in the summer of 1990 contained many articles and essays about the potential cultural and moral impact of these programs and of the advertisements that support them. Advertisements had been banned on the government station after 1981, partly at the behest of Muslim groups who worried about consumerism and Western influences (Schwarz 1990). "Masters of the Universe" and "The Golden Girls," Madonna and M. C. Hammer—what will be the effect of these alien but riveting sounds and images on Jakarta's youth, people wondered. Outside Jakarta and one or two other large cities with private TV stations, similar influences come mainly from cassette tapes, foreign movies, and videos. Middle-class intellectuals and Muslim leaders alike decry these corrupting influences, to which the preservation of indigenous traditions appears as an antidote.

From the point of view of the strictest Muslim revisionists, however, some of the indigenous costumes and dances also betray Muslim standards of modesty and sexual decorum. The government's promotion of the indigenous aesthetic might thus be read as an effort to counter a Middle Eastern aesthetic or what some Muslims recognize as the Arabic cultural hegemony within Islam. All this suggests that the government-supported traditional arts serve multiple uses: fodder for an indigenous national identity, tourist attractions, an ethnic diversion from class interests, and as reinforcement for an indigenous aesthetic against foreign diffusions from East and West.

The Limits of Cultural Laissez-Faire

The government's know-nothing stance on ethnic identity and its positive cultivation of showcase diversity reach their limits in three types of peoples who resist easy incorporation into the nation: secessionists, such as those of the East Timor movement; primitive peoples, in particular those of Irian Jaya; and Indonesians of Chinese descent. For over two decades, Indonesia has battled secessionist guerrilla forces that would like to unite Irian Jaya with the rest of independent Papua New Guinea. Irian Jaya, culturally and historically separated from the rest of Indonesia, has received over two hundred thousand Javanese transmigrants as part of a plan to send one million there, at which point the indigenous Irian Jaya peoples would become a minority in their own region (Drake 1989, 57). At a handicrafts promotion conference sponsored by Sarinah, one of the country's largest department stores and a large purveyor of traditional handicrafts, a government official assured the audience that the government's development goals and the transmigration program are not aiming to replace local cultures with Javanese culture.[11] In fact, the transmigration program has long been rationalized not merely to relieve overpopulation on the core islands, but also as "a vehicle to promote national stability and integration" (Gietzelt 1989, 209). Efforts to "Indonesianize" the people of Irian Jaya (e.g., discouraging penis gourds in favor of Western pants) continue through the schools and through village campaigns (Premdas 1985).

East Timor's attempt to claim its political autonomy has invoked less cultural engineering than sheer physical force, with perhaps a third of its population lost to fighting, starvation, or disease since 1975 (Drake 1989, 58–59). In a speech in Bogor in 1990, Defense Minister L. B. Murdani admitted that Indonesia faced little threat from external sources. He pointed, instead, to the recent heightened political valence of ethnicity in other parts of the world, and said that it must not happen in Indonesia. There had been separatist movements in Indonesia's past, and Indonesia had learned from each of them, Murdani assured his audience.[12] The army put these lessons to use in November 1991 in a massacre of perhaps 180 people gathered at a memorial for a slain activist, an event that drew world attention once more to the case of those in East Timor who wish to resist incorporation into Indonesia (Aznam 1992)

Any *suku terasing,* literally "isolated ethnic group," is expected to accept education, *agama,* and other markers of progress.[13] The phrase *suku terasing* connotes cultural backwardness. On Sumba, the feasts of the Weyewa, events central to local politics and religion have been outlawed as wasteful, although local officials of the Department of Education and Culture are keen to preserve (as folklore) the oratorical traditions that went with feasting (Kuipers 1991). Only now and then will someone question the rightness of modernization. An extensive center feature in *Tempo* on the Badui, perhaps Java's last *suku terasing*, described not a lost remnant of aborigines so much as a renegade village isolating itself from Islam, public schools, and other modern contaminants (such as coffee) to pursue a simple life. *Tempo* essayists, and no doubt *Tempo*'s urbane middle-class readership, used this story about the Badui like readers in the United States use *National Geographic* accounts of exotic peoples—to reflect on the pros and cons of retreat versus engagement, and of a romanticized rural past versus a stressful open-ended urbanity.[14]

Ethnic tensions between Chinese Indonesians and other Indonesians are fairly general and have deep historic roots (Feith and Castles 1970; Mackie 1976). An estimated five million Chinese Indonesians live scattered throughout the country (Suryadinata 1986), but the Chinese have never been included in discussions of "preserving culture," nor *kreativitas*. Chinese music and dance do not appear on television spots showing the archipelago's artistic diversity, and the Chinese heritage is absent from the Taman Mini complex. Rather, a newspaper article prompted by Indonesia's normalization of diplomatic relations with the People's Republic of China used the English loan words *asimilasi* (assimilation) and *akulturasi* (acculturation) to describe the goals for Indonesia's Chinese population.[15] No obvious cultural gulf exists between the Indonesian Chinese and the indigenous peoples of Indonesia. Most can no longer speak Chinese, and their everyday life is much influenced by Western and Indonesian culture. Many are either Catholic or Protestant, although many are also Buddhist and Confucian (Suryadinata 1986). At the encouragement of the government, many have adopted Indonesian names (Suryadinata 1984, 171–73). Some Indonesian Chinese have accepted the goal of assimilation; others have argued against total cultural annihilation (Feith and Castles 1970; Mackie 1976).

The cultural differences that do exist between the Indonesian Chinese and other Indonesians are not readily visible, but these intangible differences have had quite tangible effects (Tan 1991). A culture and social organization (including transnational social networks) that nourish entrepreneurship and capital accumulation have given the Chinese commercial advantages over indigenous peoples in Southeast Asia at least since the colonial era. These advantages provoke the animosity of fellow Indonesians. Soeharto's opening the country to foreign investment and the New Order's encouragement of big business brought new opportunities that Chinese investors and businesspeople have seized. Chinese businesses use Indonesian partners or front men, sometimes very highly placed politicians, or relatives of politicians, including Soeharto and his family (Robison 1986; Schwarz 1991b).[16] Popular antigovernment opposition is, therefore, often anti-Chinese as well (Suryadinata 1984). The 1984 incident in Tanjong Priok, for example, usually glossed as an Islamic riot with class overtones, mobilized people with slogans against Chinese and Christians.

On the other side of class politics, the Indonesian Chinese are also accused of sympathizing with the People's Republic of China and of being a source of communist infiltration. Attempts to recruit Indonesian Chinese into the PKI were largely unsuccessful (McVey 1965, 229) but it is widely thought that Chinese businessmen bankrolled the PKI in the 1950s and 1960s (Hindley 1964, 117), and the PKI in turn opposed discrimination against Chinese businesses in this era (Mortimer 1974, 154). Ethnic hostility toward Chinese is thus compounded by class animosities that work against them both up and down.

The Indonesian economy depends on Chinese business acumen, capital, and social networks; those who hold political power depend on income from Chinese businesses (Robison 1982, 142–43). The state thus protects Chinese interests, and toward this end, attempts to contain the general antipathy toward the Chinese by rendering them culturally invisible. Just as displaying the diversity of indigenous ethnic arts masks the cultural and political dominance of the Javanese, so too, hiding the artistic and cultural heritage of the Chinese, and even their names, aims to mask their economic dominance. Their numbers, their different physical appearance, their public economic niche, and sometimes their residential separation all limit Chinese invisibility. Sometimes, then, government officials must appeal outright (but still elliptically) for tolerance. In a speech before the National Youth Committee in celebration of Independence Day in 1990, Murdani warned that ethnic issues could destroy national unity. Without ever mentioning the word *Chinese,* he urged indigenous Indonesians to pull down the screens they had erected between themselves and "certain groups," and not to blame these groups for their success in the economic field, the only field in which Indonesians permitted them to play. "Forget this. Let's build the country together," Murdani concluded.[17]

Religion as Culture

The culture side of the Department of Education and Culture concerns itself with the preservation and promotion of traditional culture (again, in a delimited sense of arts and literature). This ministry has come to serve an important new function in recent years: it shelters those religions that have been defined outside of the officially designated *agama*. Bali succeeded in 1962 in having its religion designated as Hinduism, and as one of the recognized *agama* (Boon 1977, 214–18; Geertz 1973b), but subsequent efforts to have *kebatinan* (Javanese mysticism), or Kejawen (Javanism), or other local religious traditions granted legitimacy as *agama* have persistently failed (Atkinson 1983; cf., Weinstock 1981, 1987). These irregular religions have been categorized instead as *kepercayaan,* literally belief, but often connoting something like the English word *superstition.* "Belief," in the political discourse about religion, does not have the full authority that *agama* has. Sheltered under the umbrella of culture, however, "belief" has gained a legitimate, if secondary, place in the Indonesian order of things.

A series of "congresses" on Kebatinan (Mysticism) in the 1950s first lent bureaucratic form to the Kejawen tradition that has always been fragmented into small, autonomous groups of teachers and their followers. Efforts to organize the Kejawen tradition continued in the 1970s with the formation of the Joint Secretariat for Beliefs under a former minister of education. The generals around Soeharto were the moving force behind this new organization, created partly to balance Muslim power (Emmerson 1976, 237). In a speech Soeharto made before the national assembly in 1978, the Joint Secretariat for Beliefs was placed in the Department of Education and Culture, and a new organization was formed under it called the Association for the Experience of Belief in the Almighty God (Himpunan Penghayat Kepercayaan Terhadap Tuhan Yang Maha Esa). The leader of the Association, Zahid Hussein, is a close friend of Soeharto's. In 1981 representatives from several provinces attended the first national meeting to organize the Association for the Experience of Belief in the Almighty God.

A presidential decision of 1984 provided money for the Association to inventory and document the country's various "beliefs" and to educate Indonesians about this part of their heritage through television and other media. The Association also hoped to make such education part of the schools, but a proposal by the Department of Education and Culture to include comparative religion in the curriculum was stymied by Muslim opposition. The television and media propagation has proceeded as planned. Every two weeks a program appears on the government television network in which a Javanese teacher calmly and impassively extols the virtue of religious tolerance and the spiritual benefits of belief in the immanent and monistic Tuhan (God). The Association also publishes a glossy color magazine, *Sari Budaya Nusantara*. In one issue, Koenjaraningrat, Indonesia's premier anthropologist, wrote a piece called, "We Prefer to Boast about the Legacy of our Ancestors," with a full-page picture of a person from Irian Jaya in ceremonial dress. Another article title argued, "Javanese Culture Can Become the Basis for Strengthening National Understanding," while another discussed the problems of maintaining temples as national archaeological treasures. The Association is lobbying to have the first day of Sura, a mystically significant day in the Javanese calendar, recognized as a national holiday, and, toward this end, one article explained Sura's astrology and numerology.

The decision to house these irregular religions in the Department of Education and Culture is one of the "compromises" the government has made on issues of religion and diversity (Liddle 1988b, 30). While the Departemen Agama is thus mounting *dakwah* campaigns to convert those who do not yet have an *agama,* the Department of Education and Culture provides some traditionalist groups the wherewithal to hold out against the forces of organized religion. A missionary in Central Sulawesi was heard saying, "when the government promotes *adat* even for the tourists, it makes a lot of trouble for us" (Aragon 1991–92, 379). The Association provides an organizational center for almost 400 groups of all kinds that have not been given the status of *agama,* but it is clear from its own magazines and documents that it was formed not merely to protect these fringe religious groups in relation to the Muslim majority, but also to appease the ones lobbying for *agama* status. In this organization the government gains a loose, corporatist type of control over these otherwise free-floating groups.

Speeches and publications of the Association stress that belief in Tuhan is not an *agama,* and that it should not be compared to nor thought to compete with *agama.* Tuhan, a generic term for God, subsumes the particularistic names for God in all the *agama,* precisely parallel to the way *bangsa* (nation) subsumes *suku* (ethnic groups). The Association promotes the state's commitment both to *agama* and to "belief." To an important and influential minority that takes Islam for an exclusive faith, this organization does compete directly with religion. The television program appears competitive enough that some provinces have resisted showing it. Now that the symbolic markers of Muslim identity have become all the more salient in the context of a depoliticized Islam (Jones 1980), the absence of such markers in the literature and the broadcasts of the Association are conspicuous. To be sure, Hussein, the Association's head, is a *haji*, but the Arabic phrases that frame and pepper the public addresses of self-conscious Muslims are missing in his published speeches and in the televised lessons. The matronly teacher who sometimes gives these lessons wears her hair fully exposed, neatly contained by the traditional massive bun at the nape of her neck.

Despite its assertions that cultural beliefs do not compete with *agama*, the Association pushes the notion that *kepercayaan* can substitute in certain contexts in which the state requires an *agama* identity. Civil employees have sometimes been sworn into office using the Almighty God instead of Allah. The civil marriage issue has been the most persistently troublesome. In 1973 Muslims objected to eleven of the seventy-three articles of a "comprehensive and specifically secular" bill regulating marriage (Emmerson 1976, 229). Muslims opposed the option of civil marriage, as well as provisions that adopted children have the same rights as natural children, and that Muslim women could marry non-Muslim men (Kamal 1975). Editorials appeared in Jakarta newspapers, and Muslim youth staged a demonstration inside Parliament before a compromise was reached. The revised bill still provided that marriages would be legally valid if conducted according to the parties' *agama* or "belief." In fact, civil marriages blessed merely by "belief" have been difficult to implement in many specific instances when local officials have refused to recognize Kejawen or other local variants of religion as a legitimate basis for marriage.[18]

Keeping the Forces of Disorder in Balance

Wanting to create an indigenous national culture that will withstand foreign influences, both Eastern and Western, the government sponsors the retrieval, preservation, and invention of "traditional" arts. Although the aesthetics of some traditional costumes and dances run counter to some Muslim standards of dress and sexual comportment, artistic displays also attract tourist revenues, reinforce the saliency of cultural diversity and ethnicity over class, and, outside Java, contribute to a sense of autonomy from the Javanese-dominated center. The government's sponsorship of indigenous arts also deflects attention from Javanese political and numerical dominance, while reinforcing the image of Indonesia as a nation of many different *suku*, each with a distinctive and equally valuable heritage. The dazzle of dances and costumes also makes ethnicity seem more real than class interests. The Department of Education and Culture gives bureaucratic form to these goals.

Syncretic and tribal religions, rationalized as repositories of *cultural* treasures, now have a refuge in the department as well, partly offsetting the aggressive imperialism of the universalistic religions enshrined in the Departemen Agama. Sectarian rivalry, both within Islam and between Islam and other religions, is answered with a mantra of unitarian inclusiveness intoned by the Association for the Experience of Belief in the Almighty God. Indoctrination in Pancasila philosophy also proceeds more insistently and systematically than it once did.

But Indonesia must keep ethnicity, like religion, within bounds, or else risk regional secessions and anti-Chinese riots. Minorities of "isolated" ethnic groups and the Chinese face pressures to assimilate or Indonesianize. Chinese arts and culture are thus left out of the diversity quotient, ethnic identities have no *formal* status, and the extent to which ethnicity informally constrains opportunity is not an appropriate topic for public discussion.

The values of religious harmony, cultural diversity, and ethnic coexistence come readily to the fore when Indonesians talk about their country to outsiders. The national motto, Bhinneka Tunggal Ika, Various, yet One, proclaims that ethnic and religious differences rest beneath an overarching national identity. People sometimes tout the religious divisions in their own family to exemplify the ideal. An English language newspaper in Jakarta carried a story about a U.S. high school exchange student who was impressed when her guide explained that his mother was Hindu, his sister Catholic, and he was Muslim. "It's okay, we all have to get along," he assured her.[19] The government's challenge of keeping sectarian diversity benign parallels the everyday experience of many Indonesians who cope with religious pluralism within their families. Although people are highly conscious of ethnicity and religious diversity, the ideological commitment to tolerance prohibits their discussing these issues critically. Instances of intolerance, discrimination, and inequality may not become individual or group causes.

Unlike religion and ethnicity, which are bureaucratized through government ministries, ceremonially reinforced through ritual and artistic performances, and ideologically encompassed within the key value of Various, yet One, class differences and class politics remain undercognized. The New Order came to power by crushing organized communism, which remains as the nation's professed "enemy number one." The government's fears about a nonexistent communism express, I suspect, a vague class-based anxiety that affects the middle and upper classes in general (Vatikiotis 1990b, 1991). Considering the measures applied to suspected Communists, furthermore, it is not surprising that issues of inequality enter public discourse phrased only obliquely as problems of social justice or the communication gulf between leaders and "the people."

King depicted Indonesia in the late 1970s as a bureaucratic-authoritarian regime using repression, co-optation, and a network of corporatist organizations to control opposition (1982, 111). The combined effect of this corporatism, and of less systematic and less formalized concession granting to contradictory forces through a process Liddle (1987) terms *anticipated participation,* produces a centralized balancing act that resembles in its consequences, although not in its processes, political pluralism.[20] To the extent that a bureaucratic-authoritarian regime does resemble pluralism in its consequences, it must have some processes by which to discern what the dissatisfactions are and how deep and widespread the discontent about some topic is in order to grant the appropriate concessions, co-opt the right leaders, or apply sufficient (yet not excessive) repression.

The longevity of the New Order, the country's stability, and its economic growth all testify to Indonesia's success in this balancing act. But observers are concerned that the system has begun to tilt (Hefner 1990, 243). The executive branch in particular has become more and more isolated from criticism, and less able to admit the political impact of greed and corruption in the president's family (Wood 1990). Indonesian policymakers "are enmeshed in an expensive system of political control that is becoming increasingly infeasible and simultaneously generating pressures that require increasing control" (Hart 1986, 211).[21]

Notes

1. Bowen shows, however, that the ideological process is not totally controlled from above. Local actors, too, construct and interpret *gotong royong* such that its practice in the country's periphery is not always the ideal envisioned in the center. See also Warren 1990.

2. *Kompas,* 27 August 1990.

3. The weekly and daily flag ceremonies that I have seen in Indonesian school yards have gotten more elaborate and more militaristic over the last twenty years.

4. Anderson 1983; Bowen 1989; Robison 1986, 165.

5. At the university level, departments of anthropology, which had existed since the 1950s in literature divisions, were moved into the social sciences in the mid-1980s partly to focus the discipline's attention on issues of national integration and interethnic relations (Koentjaraningrat 1987).

6. Liddle (1988b) says that ethnic origin is not an impediment to success at the national level for bureaucrats and army officers. He feels this accounts for the absence of open ethnic or regionalist politics at the present.

7. *Kompas,* 25 August 1990.

8. *Kompas,* 25 August 1990.

9. During Taman Mini's construction in 1970 and 1971 critics protested that the expenditure on this park, a pet project of Soeharto's wife, was frivolous and showed blatant disregard for the country's widespread poverty (Robison 1986, 160–61)

10. See also Emmerson 1976, 247; Rodgers 1991, 93.

11. *Jakarta Post,* 7 July 1989.

12. *Sinar Indonesia Baru,* 11 September 1990. Published in Medan.

13. E.g., Atkinson 1989, xx; *Suara Pembaruan,* 31 July 1989; Tsing 1987, 201–2.

14. *Tempo,* 25 August 1990.

15. *Kompas,* 30 August 1990.

16. This relationship between Chinese businessmen and government leaders echoes a centuries-old pattern in which indigenous rulers have used Chinese or other foreign merchants as tax collectors, or offered protection to these merchants in exchange for economic support (Geertz 1980; Hall 1985, 236).

17. *Jakarta Post,* 16 August 1990.

18. *Editor,* 11 June 1988; *Tempo,* 8 July 1989.

19. *Jakarta Post,* 29 August 1990.

20. See also Schmitter 1974, 101–2.

21. See Yoon (1991) for the suggestion that racial animosity against Chinese is more of a threat to regime stability at this point than is class struggle, but that as other Indonesians increasingly join the entrepreneurial class, mitigating racial tensions, an "anticapitalist mood" may well be expected.

Chapter 7

Kinship in New Contexts

[26 July 1989. Jakarta. Interview with a Muslim man.] "Our values are changing, not simply the ideas and thoughts, but the feelings of people." He suggested that this is happening faster in the cities than in the highlands, and that it continues to happen. He used kissing as an example. Karo did not even know of this before World War II, and if they had known of it, would have found the whole prospect dirty and disgusting. Now they not only know of it, they *enjoy* it. He felt the world was moving toward a unity of *adat*, and he gave another example from the realm of food. Indonesians increasingly eat the bread, milk, and cheese that Europeans eat.

I responded that there will always be differences among people, of religion, of interests, and experiences. He nodded, adding that *adat* will change because people change. "God remains the same, but humans change," he said. We can become too fanatic about maintaining *adat*, for although *adat* changes, it will not be lost. To exemplify change he spoke of the relaxed interaction between fathers and daughters in the cities, while fathers and daughters in the village cannot walk together without feeling *mehangke* (ashamed). He went on to talk about Karo society traditionally being open (*terbuka*). Whole groups of outsiders, such as the Purba subclan, have been assimilated into Karo society, he observed. And he remarked how persons like me can be incorporated as "kin." This is not theater, he averred, it is real, and he contrasted this with Minangkabau society, which he judged as rather closed. [One of his two wives is a Minangkabau, the other a Karo woman.] He suggested, too, that Karo society is really more bilateral than patrilineal [he used those English terms], because the *bere-bere* link (mother's clan) is so important and that bond continues through the generations.

Kinship is essential to Karo ethnicity because the Karo conceptualization of themselves as a society rests on an imagined kinship order.[1] Acknowledged as a matter of metaphor and etiquette, rather than strictly genealogical and biological, Karo kinship is both conceptually finite, delimited by a five-clan patrilineal structure, and pragmatically open, welcoming of anyone who learns to command its rules and language. It remains, in highland villages, a hegemonic order. Anyone who lives there for any length of time—migrant

Javanese laborers, Chinese shopkeepers, non-Karo who marry in, anthropologists, and missionaries—is readily cloaked as a fictive kinsperson, given a clan name, and addressed with kin terms. This same openness and flexibility work to the advantage of Karo migrants, who look for "relatives" to help them in transition, and who forge whole new urban communities based on metaphoric extensions of kinship.

Discourse around the subject of *sumbang* (incest) and the Batak contrast with Malay show that the five-clan order definitive of Karo and other Batak was set contrastively against the bilateral, ego-centered kinship order of the Malay world. The Karo's patriliny and their asymmetrical affinal order represent a minority pattern in the predominantly bilateral environment of urban Indonesia. Many of the children of migrants growing up in that environment rather than in Karoland find the intricacies of the *anakberu-kalimbubu* relationship, and the involved kinship terms in which it is cast, somewhat arcane, especially as many of them do not command the Karo language. Ironically, the new multiethnic, urban environment kindles a sharp consciousness about Karo identity, but at the same time undermines the distinctive kinship elements through which that identity is constructed.

This chapter examines the ways Karo use kinship in highland and migrant settings, and the challenges that the conceptualized kinship order now faces. In particular, wealth differences and interethnic marriages strain the kinship system. Wealth deployed into weddings and other celebrations enhances the prestige of the sponsoring families, making visible their network of kin and metaphoric "kin." Wealth buys transportation, too, meaning that wealthier migrants can more easily stay in touch with highland relatives than can poorer migrants, but wealth differences also strain relations among kin, and wealthy migrants to the cities acquire tastes and desires that compete with the desire to sponsor big feasts.

Karo family life traditionally exhibited a distinctive affective tone, a product of cross-sex respect and avoidance rules that constrained expression and affection but also preempted conflict. The conceptual asymmetry of affinal relations and the wish to avoid "incest" against this affinal grain as well as within the patrilineal clans shaped these respect and avoidance behaviors. The *anakberu-kalimbubu* asymmetry is now undermined by the commodification of labor at urban feasts, diminishing the impact of a distinction between superiors who "just sit" and their *anakberu* who wait upon them. The conceptual framework of clans and asymmetrical alliances and the emotions and silences of family life that once mutually confirmed each other are being challenged. Both inheritance practices and women's changing use of names and titles hint that the constitutive patrilineal order is under some stress.

This realm of kinship underlying Karo ethnicity is fairly independent of state intervention. Both an intangible thing of relationships and conceptual designs and a reality constructed through a complex linguistic framework of kin terms, Karo kinship is not easily objectified for tourist consumption nor for inclusion in a national heritage. It is difficult for outsiders to see it at all, let alone understand it. Kinship reveals, in the Karo case, the forces of ethnic identity construction from the bottom-up. In spite of state rhetoric that subsumes ethnic identities under regional designations, Karo know themselves as participants in a society that is a bounded kinship order. Regardless of the challenges it faces now, this order still remains significant, both for the pragmatic uses to which people put kinship relations, and for the sense of community and meaning they gain from their relationships with others. Ethnicity is among the most salient of most Karo persons' identities because it draws meaning from a hegemonic, conceptual kinship order and from the small, repeated intimacies of domestic life.

Anakberu-Kalimbubu Relations and Interethnic Marriages

Strangers who have just forged a metaphoric kin tie sometimes speak as if clans were genealogical units and the relations between clans at the societal level were invariant (Kipp 1984b). For example, a man whose mother's clan is Ginting, meeting an older man of the Ginting clan, might suggest that the latter is a (classificatory) mother's brother, or he might say that the older man is his *kalimbubu*. These are polite fictions. Karo do not imagine that at the societal level their five clans are allied through marriage in an invariant order such that one clan always ranks at the top, and another at the bottom. They imagine, rather, that these five clans are linked to each other in a crisscrossing web of marriages. The directionality of marriages should not be reversed within one's closest circle of kin, but, at a little greater remove, people can often claim more than one way of being related, and are often in the position of being *anakberu* to someone by one genealogical route, *kalimbubu* by another. People will alternate as *kalimbubu* and *anakberu* at the same event if necessary in order to fulfill conflicting obligations (Kipp 1976, 76–79).

The *anakberu-kalimbubu* status relations provide highland Karo with a practical solution to the problems of mobilizing guests and labor for family celebrations. All of one's *kalimbubu* merit honor and deference, and, should they require labor at a harvest or at a feast, one must be willing to work as a servant or a go-between. In Payung village, for example, daily interaction with all co-villagers is carried out through kin terms of address, and when a wedding takes place, virtually every household receives an invitation to it. No one who attends does so as a mere neighbor, but each person is placed in some kinship category for purposes of assigning seating and other roles and for allocating work. For funerals, or *adat* events such as a legal discussion about inheritance, the *anakberu* of the host family can be organized to buy food, cook, serve, and clean up after a meal for a dozen people or for a thousand, as the occasion demands. At large festivities, the people mobilized to work will consist of many distant, metaphoric, or classificatory *anakberu*. The bulk of the services required for a feast are often carried out by people acting as *anakberu menteri,* meaning the *anakberu* of the *anakberu*. In effect this allows middle-aged and older people to delegate their responsibilities to younger people, their daughters and sons-in-law.

The urban setting transforms the logistics of feasting and, especially, the role of *anakberu*. For one thing, celebrations are far more expensive in the cities than in villages. Villages collectively own big drums for cooking rice, giant woks for stewing meat over open pit fires, and metal plates that can be loaned out to families hosting a feast. Most have a *los* (a shelter that residents may use for funerals and celebrations). In cities, party space and equipment must be rented. Party seating is often accomplished with rented folding chairs, the better to accommodate women's dress. (Both street-length Western-style dresses and the tightly wrapped sarongs of fancy *adat* costume make sitting on the floor difficult.) But most important of all, people hire catering services that provide the cooks as well as the servers and dishwashers. The shared effort and camaraderie of a group of *anakberu* cooking and serving together all day are gone, as well as the shared sense of having discharged one's obligations appropriately. For smaller events in cities, *anakberu* might be asked to cook something at their own homes and bring it to the event (for example, chicken for thirty people), but buffet serving obviates the need for that small army, carrying buckets and baskets of food, tea kettles, and plates, who serve hungry and impatient guests seated on mats in a village *los*.

The commodification of the labor at feasts reduces both the need for and the felt experience of being *anakberu,* and it reduces, too, the persistent, public demonstration of the *contrast* between *anakberu* and *kalimbubu*. The latter, as honored guests, "just sit," people say, while *anakberu* are "the tired ones." Today, all the guests at urban weddings "just sit" for the most part. When ceremonial labor can be purchased, the reciprocal bonds that bring people to work at feasts against the day when they must ask others to work at theirs begin to dissolve.

Within close families, too, people behave with each other according to these affinal status differences and sometimes use the terms *anakberu* and *kalimbubu* when speaking of their closest kin. A group conversing at a Sinulingga subclan meeting in Medan was discussing the *anakberu-kalimbubu* relationship and the obligation to honor one's *kalimbubu*. One man remarked that it was also very hard to deny any request that your *anakberu* might make, even for land. Here he spoke of *anakberu* as if in the generic, but it is specifically daughters (or sisters) who usually ask for land from their patrilineal families. Because of the pronounced affection parents and brothers often feel for their daughters and sisters, a woman who asks to use or inherit land is not easily refused (Portier and Slaats 1987). One older man ventured that this is why the term for a (man's) sister's child is *bere-bere,* a doubling of the word for give. The *kalimbubu* always *give* to the *anakberu,* he said.

The *anakberu-kalimbubu* asymmetry thus adds density to the already dense relations within close families, complicating them with associations of superiority and inferiority, the supernatural influence of blood on fertility and health, and mutual obligation (Singarimbun 1975). All the affection and familiarity, authority, resistance, and ambivalence that characterize intimate family life inform the meanings of the *anakberu-kalimbubu* relation, and are, in turn, informed by that relation. People talk about *kalimbubu* and feelings for their mother, for example, in the same breath (Kipp 1976, 81–83).

Throughout one's life, and regardless of gender or marital status, one regards one's mother's brothers and their lineal kin as *kalimbubu* superiors. These are the *kalimbubu* "by blood" (*si mada dareh*) or "by birth" (*si mupus*). Ideally, a man marries someone from this family, a girl related to him as *impal,* the closest representative of which is a mother's brother's daughter.[2] A marriage between *impal* repeats the direction of the alliance when a man's own father and mother married. But in practice, a man usually marries an unrelated woman whose parents and brothers are then regarded by him and his family as *kalimbubu iperdemui,* literally, *kalimbubu* by contact, or *kalimbubu* by marriage. At marriage, women take on the position of their husbands, becoming *anakberu* to their own brothers and parents. Correspondingly, a woman is herself *kalimbubu* to her husband's sister's family and later, to her own daughter and that daughter's marital family.

Affinity gains generational continuity in these asymmetrical alliances. Whether or not new marriages actually replicate the direction of parents' or grandparents' marriages, the sense of indebtedness to *kalimbubu,* and thus the obligation to honor them through the generations, continues. Marriage and funeral payments express this ideal, as well as the servings of rice handed out plate by plate in advance of the meals at these occasions (Kipp 1976, 1979). In most ceremonial moments, and certainly in most conversational referencing, *kalimbubu* are not differentiated by birth and marriage, however, nor by generation, but are simply lumped in speech as *kalimbubu.* In the ceremonial fiction of weddings, the new *kalimbubu* by marriage are courteously assimilated into the *kalimbubu* by birth, as if the marriage conformed to the ideal of alliance renewal. As a symbolic marker that each marriage is (post hoc) an *impal* marriage, one of the sections of the brideprice, called *ulu emas,* goes to the groom's mother's brothers, making them token fathers of the bride.

Karo often say that *impal* marriage was forced on young people in the past, and speak as if the marriage of *impal* was once the general practice rather than the rarity it is today. This is often read as a sign of *adat*'s decline. If not the general rule, it was probably more common in the past than it is at present. Karo newspapers from the 1920s decried the frequency of suicides committed by girls forced into marriages.[3] Young people have more mobility and more economic alternatives now than they did when life was tied almost exclusively to land.

Today the significant difference seems to be between marriages that result from spontaneous romances and marriages that are arranged by families. The latter are often termed *impal* marriages if there is the slightest basis for construing them as such (Kipp 1976, 100). The commonality, I think, is that no one expects an arranged union, whether of true *impal* or not, to be romantic (Kipp 1986a). These are pragmatic unions of convenience. In the 1950s a well-to-do man in the line of a raja family was widowed with eight children, including a newborn. His second wife described their marriage to me as an *impal* match, but in truth it had simply been arranged. She was more than twenty years his junior, herself an orphan, who had agreed to take on his large family, and who shared his Muslim religion. Real *impal* marriages, while rare, are not totally obsolete. A girl who was a toddler during my first field trip was herself a new mother when I visited Payung in 1990. She had married a close *impal* (a man who is nearer my age than hers) when he returned from working in Kalimantan and decided it was time to find a wife.

As long as both bride and groom are Karo, even marriages originating in romance and bringing together two stranger families are ceremonially and terminologically construed as *impal* marriages after the fact (Kipp 1976). But nowadays, more and more romances occur with non-Karo sweethearts encountered in school or the workplace. Many people worry about this. An ethnic newsletter, *Kamka*, carried two articles in the March 1989 issue that mentioned this concern. One, written by a young man from Kabanjahe, suggested that "tours" and "follow-up" contacts might bring Karo adolescents from cities and the highlands together. Another, written by a student, said that of twenty-three marriages of Karo students attending Gajah Mada University in Jogyakarta, 1984–88, twenty were to non-Karo spouses. As an antidote he suggested enhancing activities at the GBKP (Karo ethnic church) congregations in university towns.

Impal marriage, although statistically infrequent, remains an important component of an imagined kinship order. Most wedding preparations, therefore, include a preliminary procedure in which the groom and his family must gather in the home of their *kalimbubu*, perhaps the groom's own mother's brother, to apologize for not having married the *kalimbubu*'s daughter. In many cases, it is just a formality; in other cases, the mother's brother is deeply disappointed. A minister in the Karo church who married a woman from Menado described how his father had readily accepted his choice of a bride, but his mother's brother was so angry he did not speak to the couple until their first child was born.

The small family gathering, called a Forgiveness Asking (*Mindo Maaf*), reasserts the rule of *impal* marriage in its breach. Today these events take on a new bitterness when the chosen bride not only fails to meet the criterion of being an *impal*, but is increasingly likely not even to be a Karo.

[27 July 1990. Jakarta.] I went with S. to a Forgiveness Asking. A young man was anticipating marriage to someone other than his *impal*, and had to beg the forgiveness of his mother's brother, at whose house we gathered. Indeed, the fiancee and her relatives (none of whom were there) are from Menado. From what S. had told me earlier, I gathered that the boy's family was resigned to this interethnic marriage, but far from happy about it. Some forty to fifty people gathered in the living room of this upper-middle-class family. Most of the furniture, except a large television and VCR, had been moved out and mats placed wall to wall for the event. We began with a meal, served by the unmarried women relatives, some of whom were the host's own daughters. It was a religiously mixed gathering, with a haji there in the role of clan mate of the host, another man whom I know to be an active elder in the GBKP, and another who told me he was a Seventh Day Adventist. Thus, before we ate, there was no common prayer, but rather an announcement that we should pray individually.

Two or three men acted as *anakberu* representatives for each of the significant parties, the contrite groom and his family on one side, and on the other, the *kalimbubu* host whose honor had been diminished in the groom's choosing not to marry his daughter. There were the usual formalities, beginning with the question of what the meeting was all about. At first, everything was repeated twice, as the *anakberu* intermediaries had to relay to their respective *kalimbubu* what the other side had said (as if we were not all in hearing distance of each other). The groom's representatives said he had "made his own way," and that this had come about as a consequence of love (*cinta*), i.e., as something out of his control. The *kalimbubu* asked if this coming marriage were a matter of "force" or of "fear," or if either set of parents were pressuring them to marry. The groom's representatives phrased it as if he had performed *nangkih* (a stylized elopement) and was already living with his fiancee in her home. This brought sniggers and whispers from the women around me, who pointed out that this was backwards. In *nangkih,* the girl is supposed to elope to the *boy's* house. (People hinted *soto voce* that perhaps the bride was already pregnant.)

The groom's grandmother (father's mother, i.e., the host's mother) had arrived recently from the highlands to attend this event. Seated rather far from the center of the discussion, in the middle of the women, she began suddenly to "sing," performing that stylized wailing by which Karo women shape their grief into words set in minor tones. The room fell instantly silent, and people sat with eyes cast down as she continued. Many of her phrases ended with "O Turang!" the kin term used in reference for an opposite sex sibling, but used in address for lovers (Kipp 1986a). The lines of funeral laments and love songs often end in this vocative. I read her singing as grief for the failure of the brother-sister bond between her two children to be renewed in the next generation by the marriage of their children. "That's enough! That's enough!" people began to say, and she turned it off as suddenly as she had turned it on. I had the sense she had come to Jakarta for *this,* to "sing" her sorrow, regardless of how she really felt about her grandson's choice of a bride. The singing done, discussion continued as before.

The groom's family was asked to explain how it came to be that he fell in love with this woman. They responded that since his childhood they had tried to encourage him to marry his *impal,* but perhaps they had not done enough, they admitted. Now he lives in an apartment while attending college, and they cannot monitor his life. They did not know he was having this relationship with the girl.

Finally, the *kalimbubu* asked to speak directly to the groom, and to have him speak directly to them, dispensing with the intermediaries. The groom gave a lengthy response in Indonesian, although it was so humbly mumbled as to be totally inaudible. The haji, also speaking Indonesian directly to the young man, responded for the *kalimbubu*. Not only was the groom not marrying his *impal* (the haji was blunt), he was marrying outside his ethnic group, something not to be done lightly. The haji pointed out that the groom was not a Muslim, so he could not count on marrying again. This was a decision for life.

Other *kalimbubu* chimed in. They did not fear that their daughters would not "sell" (*lako*). They had wished for him to marry his *impal* only because they regretted the failure to renew the link. They feared that the young man would no longer come back to or attend to his *kalimbubu* [by birth]. The women of the *kalimbubu* were then asked if they had any further advice or objections. They did not, and the discussion returned to the intermediary mode again for the closing formalities.

The final resolution was simply the hope that God would bless the coming marriage. The family was resigning themselves to it as God's will. The groom's mother asked the *kalimbubu* to pray for this marriage. The event then dissolved with a common prayer led by the GBKP elder.

The hostess, a Javanese woman married to the groom's mother's brother, told me after the formalities ended that, of course, her husband had had to go through the same thing with his own mother's brother before her wedding. I had noticed that her husband had not been very vocal in the discussion, but then the hosts or primary parties in any formal or legal discussion usually take a back seat to the intermediaries who speak for them. In any case, this man was in no position to make his nephew grovel for breaking an ideal that he himself had broken. I thought, too, how his mother, the old woman who had wailed, must have come once as an apologetic sister to her own brother's house, asking forgiveness for not having brought up her son to marry his daughter. Her formulaic "O Turang!" surely evoked her failed reunion with her own brother long ago, as well as the failed reunion now of her own children.

Rude and raucous behavior around one's *kalimbubu* shows disrespect. Breaking wind around them is especially egregious, and infractions have, in legend, led people to leave their village or even to commit suicide. The requirement to honor one's *kalimbubu* is sanctioned by beliefs that fertility and well-being depend on being on good terms with them. Called poetically "the Visible God," *kalimbubu* wield a supernatural power through the mystical connection of "blood" between a woman and her parents and brothers. In 1989, a traditional healer in Kabanjahe told me how he treats illness induced by offending one's *kalimbubu*. Its symptoms may resemble those resulting from sorcery and poison, symptoms that resist diagnosis and treatment by Western-style medicine, he said.

Clearly these kinship ideas impinge on the realm Indonesians categorize as "belief," but long ago Karo Protestants rationalized honoring the *kalim-*

bubu as secular etiquette or kinship tradition, leaving out the supernatural sanctions. Children are still teased with the warning that if they do not honor their *kalimbubu*, corn will grow out of their nose, an imagery that makes adults laugh, but the idea that *kalimbubu* exercise godlike powers is not completely gone, even among those who have converted to an *agama*. Fertility problems especially elicit recourse to soliciting the blessing of one's *kalimbubu*.

> [5 October 1986. A conversation on the bus between Kabanjahe and Medan with a young couple, vegetable vendors, who live in Binjei.] They had been married over two years, and from their mention of various ministers, I gathered they were probably Protestants in the GBKP. They did not yet have any children, and they told me they had come to Kabanjahe to get some medicine [*tambar*] for this childlessness. I had learned that the woman's natal village was Kabanjahe, so I said, "Oh. You came to see your *kalimbubu* for this." The woman looked surprised that I had known that, and then said yes.

Only three months before this incident, I had sat in a bus going the opposite direction on the same route and had a similar conversation with a Christian, middle-school teacher and her husband. Having lost their first child soon after its birth, they were taking their second, a newborn, to seek the blessing of its *nini* (mother's parents, in this case). The live chicken they were bringing for this formal visit fluttered at our feet throughout the trip.

With or without supernatural sanctions, the ideal of honoring the *kalimbubu* remains strong among Karo in urban as well as village settings, and claims against that honor still carry weight.

> [September 1990. Payung Village.] A period of tension arose at a wedding when some distant *kalimbubu*, forming a circle to discuss and receive the payment called *ulu emas*, objected that they [had] been slighted. This payment goes to the groom's mother's brother primarily, but generally also to his other *kalimbubu* by birth, from whose families he should have selected his bride. The issue here was not the amount of money, but its manner of presentation. The groom's mother's mother's brothers, of the Pandia subclan, had been named second in the listing of the recipients after the groom's father's mother's brothers, of the Sitepu subclan. Perhaps as a consequence, they had been allotted smaller shares, but shares at this level are all minuscule. This was "only" a question of honor. The Pandia men claimed that their ancestors had given land to the groom's family (Bangun) in Payung, and that the order and division of the payments should recognize that gift. It took some fifteen minutes of voices raised in objection, with *anakberu* mediators

trying hard to apologize and rectify the gaffe, before the offended men were mollified.

Kinship and Wealth

If the *anakberu-kalimbubu* tie is losing its value in organizing labor, kinship remains pragmatic in urban settings in other ways. Urban dwellers board their nieces and nephews or their younger siblings from the highlands who are attending school. In one case, a man in Jakarta who had only one child himself, a daughter, was raising one of his brother's sons, partly as a favor to that brother, who had several other children and was a farmer. More commonly, older children attending a high school or young adults at a university will stay several years with urban kin. One man in Bandung apologized for the quiet behavior of a young man in his home, a "sister's child," who had arrived from the highlands only a week before, and still remained a little "confused." This man estimated that ten such children had stayed with him, coming and going over a period of a dozen years, while he had raised six children of his own. These visitors had not been paying boarders, he said; he had regarded them as his own children. In other cases, where the kinship tie is not very close, the live-in children do pay something for room and board or help with household labor, or both.

Giving relatives temporary shelter, helping them find jobs, and providing loans are, as far as I can see, characteristic of Karo families in all economic strata, but middle-class and wealthy Karo families face constant requests for aid and favors from their less well-to-do kin, both close and distant. A manufacturer of telecommunication and electrical cable in Jakarta, reputed to be the wealthiest Karo alive, helped his brother finance a collateral business that makes the wooden spools for his cable. Both men are training their children to take over their businesses. I knew two men who worked for the spool business, one of them a recent college graduate, the other of middle age who did not have a degree but had worked his way into a low-level management position. Both were only distant or classificatory kin of the two wealthy brothers, but had obtained their jobs through family connections, since all these men traced their origins to two neighboring highland villages.

The wealthy or well-positioned thus find that they have many "kin." Dreaded as their arrival may be, kin who come asking for favors also index one's success. Traditionally, village headmen and other leaders turned wealth into influence by marrying often and having many children, and by giving land to people whose gratitude made them "close" kin for some generations (Kipp 1976, 110–15; Kipp 1990, 121–27). Polygyny and land are no longer part of the equation, since the majority of the Karo are Christian, and now the wealthiest Karo with favors to dispense are those who live outside Karoland, working in business, the military, or the government.

More than simply an index of prosperity and success, having many kin is a valued end in itself, its own kind of wealth. For instance, in Kabanjahe a woman visited a working-class home two doors away where a man had just died. Returning, she gossiped to me and a shopkeeper across the street from her house that there was hardly anyone there paying respects, an embarrassing and pitiful situation. Families of limited wealth who have the will, the temperament, and the energy to work hard at other's feasts and to participate in public village life can gain the respect and "kinship" of their neighbors. The very poor, recluses, deviants, and troublemakers usually cannot mount the public ceremonies that confirm their worth as persons centered in a network of kin. In the Karo highlands, the prestige of financing a big funeral, wedding, or other celebration is not measured simply by the money spent, but by the number of people attending. If people gossip (exaggerating) that, on the day of the feast, "There was no one there at dawn to butcher, no one to carry water," the event has been judged a failure. Real outcasts find that not even their closest kin will rally for a public display of their social worth. In a highland village in 1990 a young man with a long history of thievery and adultery was stabbed to death in his sleep by an angry husband. The victim had been estranged from his neighbors and even his own mother, who now claimed not to have enough money to afford a proper funeral for him. The general tone of several discussions I heard about this murder was that the outlaw had met the fate he deserved.

Wealth has always been used to make and solidify kinship in Karo society, but it intersects with kinship in new ways for those who live outside Karoland. First, the more money one has, the more often one can return to visit highland kin or, if resident in Karoland, travel to see one's children and kin who live elsewhere. It takes a little over two days by bus, several hours by air, to travel from Medan to Jakarta. A working-class couple I knew in Jakarta had not been to Sumatra for several years; a small-business owner in Jakarta flew all four members of his family to Sumatra in 1990, and he told me he tries to get back every other year, although both his parents are dead; a businessman whose offices are in Medan and Jakarta flew back and forth almost continuously; in 1989 a father, grandfather, and brother accompanied a girl to the United States to settle her into a university, she returned home for summer vacation, and during the next school year her mother flew to the United States to visit her. If money cannot exactly buy family solidarity, it can at least buy the opportunities to forge it.

Second, money earned outside Karoland can sponsor funerals or reburials in new tombs or other ceremonies back in the home village, reasserting one's membership in that village and renewing one's kinship relations there, not to mention displaying one's wealth and success.[4]

[10 September 1990. Karoland.] Ros and I went to Batukarang today so I could take pictures of the tomb and statue I had heard about. It turned out to be a mausoleum with places for six sets of bones, two of which were so old there were no birth and death dates, and four others of men whose photographs had been incorporated in the grave markers. A substance like black marble encased the graves, and all were locked behind a metal cage. The statue itself, a chalky white figure of a man on a horse, stood on the roof, and below it, the ancestors' names were carved in stone. Ros estimated the structure cost 5 million rupiah. It was just recently inaugurated with a huge feast and celebration in August. She named those of our relatives who attended.

[11 September 1990. Medan.] Telling P. and E. about my recent visit to Batukarang, I asked why K., who lives in Jakarta, had decided to build the monument. P. said that K. had had a severe stroke from which he was expected to die some years ago, but he had instead lived to make a remarkable recovery. Perhaps this prompted him to do this for his ancestors. [He is also a devout Christian, however, and a generous benefactor of the Karo church.] They both pointed out that K. has not lived in Batukarang since 1951, and that there are few of his family left in the village. Being in the line of the *raja urung* [village confederation head], K. and most of his family were born advantaged, received an education, and thus left the village. P. suggested that the monument and the big party in its honor were to make K. known again in his village, and to get back in the good graces of people. Most of his other family celebrations, such as his children's weddings, had been held in Jakarta.

The *anakberu-kalimbubu* status distinction has, in theory, nothing to do with socioeconomic status differences. A wealthy or well-placed family necessarily encounters the situation of being the ritually inferior *anakberu* to families who are less wealthy or powerful than they are (Bangun 1981). This contradiction of status parameters, intrinsic to the Karo social order, operated in the past to the extent that village headmen or other leaders, who often had multiple wives, usually had greater wealth and power than their *kalimbubu*, but wealth differences were not as great then as they are now. Even today, living standards in highland villages are relatively uniform compared to the disparities one sees among urban Karo.

[14 July 1989. From an interview with two Jakarta professionals.] I asked about the effects of class. S. replied that in theory it should have no effect on Karo relations. He pointed out the relativistic quality of the *anakberu-kalimbubu* statuses, how we are *anakberu* to some families, and *kalimbubu* to others, and everyone plays both these roles at different times. But in practice, S. admitted, people who have less are *mehangke* (ashamed, respectful) to ask their wealthy kin to perform as *anakberu*. The same hinderance operates in the church, he observed. Again in theory, we are all the same before God. Those who have cars should invite those who do not have cars for rides to services, choir practices or meetings, but those who do not have cars feel *mehangke*. They simply say, "Forget it" (*nggo me*). B. added that it is not just a feeling of jealousy from those who have less, but that in fact the well to do also act uppity. He stressed that those who have less do not feel *mela* (shy or embarrassed), but rather *mehangke* (which connotes shame in the positive sense of respect or deference) toward the wealthy.

At the same time that wealth enables families to see each other despite great distances, and to affirm ceremonially their continuing kinship, it strains *anakberu-kalimbubu* relations and also the intimacy and goodwill between very close kin in very different economic circumstances. Differences of work, leisure activities, and religion separate the lived experiences of siblings and other close kin in new ways, and wealth differences in themselves can also create rough edges in these relationships. A poor woman in a village told me she does not often visit her brother in Medan, because she is afraid he will see her arrival as a request for help. Another, a woman who lives just outside Jakarta, explained she did not move back to Sumatra when her husband retired because her brother would feel bound to help them more if he saw their poverty relative to his circumstances. A young working-class couple in Jakarta (the man a construction worker, the woman a beautician) admitted that they, too, would rather not live in Sumatra, where their relatives would know firsthand how hard they have to struggle.

[26 July 1989. From an interview with a middle-aged Muslim man in Jakarta.] We had been talking about the demise of Karo Sada Kata, Jakarta's first and all-inclusive ethnic association. I asked if class differences had something to do with its dissolution. He mentioned differences of "profession" that come to separate people. He cited his brother, a business man, whose work he finds totally boring.

Likewise, that brother cares little for what *he* finds most interesting—politics. People get together, but they may have little in common anymore except their kinship relations, he pointed out.

Like the Sherpa, Karo interact with each other in a style that is at once egalitarian and competitive (Ortner 1989, 33–35). One woman reviled the Karo as jealous of each other's success, a feeling called *cian*. She ventured that this is why the Karo as a people fall behind other ethnic groups who cooperate to help each other. Hereditary rank was all but absent in traditional Karo society, so power and wealth differences emerged as a result of initiative, intelligence, luck, energy, allies, and might. Even in families with hereditary rights to a village headmanship, attaining the position was almost always the result of winning a struggle among agnates. Precisely because no one came into a position of prominence merely by birth, those who did ascend to power were widely admired and widely resented. Leaders saw as many enemies and contenders around them as kin and friends.

Traditionally, leaders' accumulation of wealth was also limited. The resources of wealthy men went into marrying many women, giving land to those who had none, and sponsoring feasts—all means of procuring or maintaining kin and allies, and all means by which economic advantage was converted into political power. Wealth is still convertible to political power, but the wealthiest people live in cities and are no longer anchored in a face-to-face Karo community. Furthermore, not all wealthy families care about political power within Karo society, so they are not as responsive to the community's claims on their wealth through feasting and other forms of largess. Above all, the differences in living standards between rich and poor is much greater than it ever was. Feelings of *cian* (resentment and envy) are kept at bay only with difficulty in these circumstances. These conditions strain a social order construed as a community of kin, and, as we will see later, also strain relations predicated on ethnicity or a common faith.

Patrilineal descent appears to lose some of its significance outside the highlands, partly an effect of wealth on women's identities, and partly a response to new *forms* of wealth. Inheritance of land, trees, and livestock was traditionally weighted strongly in favor of males, although women—as widows, daughters, and sisters—made successful claims to land as well (Portier and Slaats 1987; Slaats and Portier 1981). Males still retain this legal advantage with regard to land, but houses and household goods were never required to devolve patrilineally. Less and less Karo wealth is vested in land these days, being vested instead outside Karoland in bus companies, manufacturing, and such. Like houses and moveable goods of old, these new forms of wealth may as easily go to daughters as to sons.

Another hint of diminishing patrilineality involves women's names. Traditionally, women's names were prescriptively marked by gender. Every woman's name had to contain the word *beru* (written usually with the abbreviation, br.) between the given name and the clan name. My Karo name, for example, is Rita br. Purba. The term *beru* means "woman," so my name reads, "Rita, woman of Purba." My brother would be called simply Tomas Purba. In linguistic terms, women's names constituted a marked, men's an unmarked category. These naming conventions fit the reality that men were firmly identified with only one agnatic group, whereas women bridged two agnatic groups. The *beru* designation on women's names is not used consistently anymore in cities or even in secondary schools within Karoland. One increasingly hears young women state their clan names without it, implying perhaps a wish to make their names consonant with other Indonesian names, but also that identity is increasingly bilateral, the same for boys and girls.

While women bridge two agnatic lines, they also keep their natal clan names after marriage. Nowadays one hears wealthy urban women referred to with the title Nyonya (Ny.), Indonesian for Mrs. As in English usage, this title is used with a woman's husband's family name. This practice is far more frequent if the husband is wealthy or politically powerful than if the family is middle or working class. Women using the Ny. designation thus draw some of their husband's prestige or renown to themselves, a less strongly patrilineal (but no less patriarchal) practice than citing their natal clan names.

Weddings: Rituals of Kinship Revisited

[1 August 1989. Jakarta.] I joined a family to watch a videotape of a niece's wedding they had not been able to attend. It began with aerial views of Medan, the locale of the wedding, as the credits established the characters and the setting. The pictorial narrative began in the bride's home with a private prayer and hymn singing, led by the minister, before the couple got in a Mercedes to go to the church. Entering the church with "Here Comes the Bride" playing in the background, the couple was the center and focus of a conventional Christian wedding service in which the bride wore a white wedding dress. The sermon was in Indonesian, but the vows were in Karo, although the groom was Javanese. The tape continued the next day at the *adat* celebration in the Gedung Wanita Karo (Karo

Women's Building). For this, the bride and groom dressed in traditional garb, complete with rented gold jewelry around their heads and necks. Most of the guests, too, were dressed in traditional costume. Some guests ate their buffet meal seated in folding chairs and using spoons, while others sat on mats. The paying of the bride price, gift-giving, and advice speeches were all much more visible and audible than they are in real life, thanks to sound-recording equipment and tele-photo shots. Much of the advice (in this case of interethnic marriage) was about learning each other's *adat*. One man who encouraged this revealed himself to be a Toba who had married a Karo, and true to his own advice, he gave his whole speech in Karo. Most of the other speeches were in Indonesian, or else were translated into Indonesian for the benefit of the groom and his Javanese relatives.

Writing of highland Java, Hefner (1990) has noted that traditional feasting there has declined as people reorient their identities to a larger community and acquire new preferences that claim their economic resources. While Karo, too, have acquired compelling new desires for consumer goods, and many regard their children's education as a highest priority, I see little indica-tion that feasting and celebrations of kinship are declining. Both weddings and funerals are still subject to delayed observance while families marshal their resources. Couples whose parents cannot afford a wedding may marry without one, then a decade later (with their children in tow) sponsor their own wedding to "complete their *adat*" (*ndungi adatna*). Similarly, a parent or grandparent buried in an unmarked grave with a modest funeral may be unearthed, remourned, and reburied in a new tomb in the context of a big feast.

The obligation people feel to sponsor large weddings and funerals comes from different sources. First, elaborate ceremony is prompted from strong feelings for the child or parent whose life crisis defines the event. At this level, a ceremony expresses familial love and loyalty. Second, people feel an obligation to repay the community at large, including nonresident kin as well as neighbors—anyone who has fed and entertained them over the years at funerals and weddings. Third, ceremonies are still important barometers of a family's success and well-being, in a simple material sense as well as a social sense. These events redound to the prestige of the sponsors because they show the sponsors' wealth and generosity, the extensiveness of their social network, and the devotion of their *anakberu* and others who work at the event. Finally, in cities these events take on another significance, that of an ethnic display or ethnic celebration.

My dissertation, produced from fieldwork carried out in 1972–74, focused on weddings and funerals as rituals reflecting an ideology of kinship. Secular events for the most part, these rituals mark unavoidable transitions in lives and in families, bringing together kin divided by religious affiliation, by wealth, and by different life experiences in urban and highland settings, reaffirming people's commitment to each other as kin, and reaffirming an ideology of kinship that orders their view of themselves and their society. The whole wedding drama, I argued in my dissertation, downplays the ego-centric dimension of celebrating a specific marital union while creating an impression that collectivities of kin are the significant parties. Weddings depict an ideal fiction that the kin collectivities of the event were related previously as wife-giver and wife-receiver generations before this current match. In the early 1970s it was sometimes difficult to spot the bride and groom (who did not necessarily sit together), and to pick out their parents.[5] The sponsors played background roles in relation to the *anakberu* who spoke publicly and worked on their behalf. Today, weddings in cities and villages exhibit a greater focus on the bridal pair and the parents of the bride and groom than was true twenty years ago.

In 1990 I attended the wedding of a Payung family whose youngest child, a son, was getting married to a girl also from Payung. In 1973 I had attended the wedding of this family's oldest child, a daughter. Both were large weddings by village standards, the one in 1990 having well over 1,000 guests. Members of the groom's family, the sponsors, formed a double reception line to greet guests as they arrived and to help them find a place to sit, a feature that did not characterize the weddings of the early 1970s. Formerly, the presentation of standardized gifts (mattresses and pillows, kerosene lamps, a chicken, a bowl of raw rice with an egg on top) from specified categories of kin who receive parts of the bride-price was accompanied by brief words of advice or instruction, perhaps only a sentence or two, from the *anakberu* man who orchestrated the exchange. No one sitting farther than several feet away could ever hear the admonitions, which tended in any case to be brief and as standard as the gifts. ("Here is a lamp. Light it when your *kalimbubu* comes to visit.") This gift giving was done all at one time, the giftgivers forming one line directly across from those who took the gifts on behalf of the couple. The couple were, in fact, not even part of this activity, since their *anakberu* received the gifts for them while they waited somewhere in the wings.

Now rented microphones bring a new significance to speech making, and a new graphic element has been added, focusing attention on the bridal couple. The gift-giving categories stand up separately, not simply the two or three carrying the gifts for that category as before, but scores of people. Each group delegates a speaker to give advice and well wishes on its behalf. It is clear, furthermore, who receives the gifts and the advice, for the bridal couple themselves stand up together facing the speakers (or rest on a settee) throughout what is now a lengthy process. Other groups, defined by criteria other than kinship, such as colleagues from work or school, or friends from the church, also present gifts and speeches to the couple. Many of the gift-giving groups bestow a length of batik cloth, a *cabin*, symbolizing a baby-sling for the couple's future children. The bridal couple accumulates a stack of these, but they are not presented like the other gifts. The couple is momentarily wrapped together in each of the cloths, bride and groom holding the ends to form a common shawl around their shoulders while listening to the speech from the category of kin presenting it. This practice, a transformation of a ceremonial element practiced by the Toba Batak, who also wrap couples in blessing shawls, began to characterize highland weddings in the early 1980s, according to most people's memories. (One woman told me it had "always" been done this way.)

Celebrations that draw attention to a particular couple, a particular union, somewhat belie the ceremonial fiction of a timeless alliance between groups cemented by generations of intermarriage. Wedding anniversaries were, therefore, not marked traditionally. In 1990 a Golden Anniversary was celebrated in Tiganderket, a village not far from Payung.

[9 September 1990. Payung Village.] Rev. S. and an elder of the church in Kabanjahe stopped by here today on their way to Tiganderket for a Golden Wedding Anniversary celebration. S. said there was no *adat* to it, no making of payments, nothing really to discuss. There was going to be a *gendang* (musical ensemble) and traditional dancing, a little *adat* added to a party, he explained. He would represent the church there, for the event would have much to do with faith or belief (*kinitekken*), he explained. The elder thought maybe there was *some* historical basis in *adat* for this celebration, but the minister (who had worked six years in Australia as a campus chaplain for foreign students) said no, the idea of a golden anniversary was just an importation from Europe.

The invitation booklet for this event included a color photograph of the couple on the cover, and several pages inside describing the program. Like a wedding invitation, the family's kin were listed according to category. After a worship service in the church, a party was to be held in the village *los* (communal shelter). The pattern followed what happens at weddings: as people danced by kin category, one or more designated speakers orated on their behalf. The minister found the fusion of religion and *adat* in this event interesting. Instead of the *sukut* (sponsor's patrilineal kin) dancing first, for example, the first category was the GBKP congregation, which danced before any of the kin categories. A brief life history, sketched in the invitation, indicated that the sponsor had been active in the GBKP as an elder and in evangelization campaigns, and that he had been educated in middle schools and a technical school during the 1920s and 1930s. S., the presiding clergyman at the service, said the sponsor was not a rich man, "just average." But he must have encouraged his children in the church and in school also, for two of the eight have masters degrees, and two have engineering degrees. Three are elders in their church congregations. Only one remains resident in the village home.

In the 1970s weddings and funerals in highland villages made somewhat equal claims on people's ambitions and resources. People felt as obligated to sponsor big funerals as big weddings, mortgaging their property to do so in rare cases. As far as I can tell, this is still the case in highland villages. In the cities, however, weddings have far eclipsed funerals in importance. If an urban family sponsors a death festival of some kind, it is likely to be in the highland village, sometimes a reburial in connection with a new tomb there. People I asked could remember only one really big Karo funeral in Jakarta in the recent past—that of Lieutenant General Jamin Gintings, a former ambassador to Canada.

Large urban weddings far surpass the scale of any highland weddings that I have seen. Every stage of the process costs more and is more elaborate than a highland wedding. The prewedding dinners and *adat* discussions (termed *Ngembah Manok* and *Ngembah Belo Selambar*) also tend to be larger than is typical in the villages. In the 1970s simple stenciled invitations on thin paper were common for highland weddings. Today elaborate weddings in Jakarta have professionally printed invitations in a booklet format. Photographers produce video tape recordings of the whole event, beginning the tape with titles and credits over a music sound track, and editing days of activity into a short, narrative format. Still photographs, also professionally produced, wind up in large albums.

One measure of the new importance of weddings over funerals is the use of the *gendang,* the five-man orchestra that plays for traditional dancing. I attended virtually every wedding that was held in Payung village in 1972–74 and traveled to surrounding villages for weddings as I learned of these from friends who had been invited. I saw only one wedding during that time at which a *gendang* played for dancing, but then, as now, even modest village funerals required this expense. Dancing and simultaneous speechmaking take up several hours at funerals.[6] At large urban weddings, *gendang* sound routinely, and since there are no complete ensembles in Jakarta and other cities outside Medan, the musicians have to travel from Sumatra, bringing the cost to about 600,000 rupiah. In Jakarta in 1989 I met a *sarune* (oboe) player I had often seen in Karoland. He estimated that his group comes to Jakarta an average of six times a year, sometimes for weddings, and sometimes for dances sponsored by ethnic associations.

When a *gendang* is added to a wedding, it is incorporated into the gift giving and speech making. Instead of simply standing behind the speaker in the context of a gift presentation and speech, the categories of kin dance opposite the bride and groom and their parents, sometimes carrying their gifts on their heads while dancing. The tempo of the music tends to be serious and even somber to begin. Some speakers may then sing their words in the style typical of women in mourning. But the separate dances often end gaily, when the tempo picks up, and people may act a little rowdy, clown around, and enjoy the chance to show off their dancing skills.

The largest weddings in Jakarta are those in which both families are Karo, and both reside in Jakarta. When the daughter of a high government official in Jakarta married a man from Jakarta several years ago, friends told me, the guests numbered 3,000, the largest wedding they had ever attended. At the large wedding described below, the groom was from Medan, so not many of his kin made the trip to Jakarta for the celebration.

[26 August 1990. Jakarta.] After attending the GBKP church today, I went to a wedding. Someone told me that some 2,000 invitations had been sent, and a woman near me said she had never seen the Gedung Wanita (a meeting and party facility) so full. It was certainly one of the largest weddings I had ever attended. There was no *gendang*, however. The entire event was professionally videotaped. As we entered, we signed guest books, a new feature in my experience, and went through a reception line. The seating arrangements were posted in diagrams on the walls so that guests could easily locate where the kin category to which they belonged was seated. After going through the reception line, some guests proceeded directly up the carpeted aisle to a large stage where the bride and groom and their parents were seated in thronelike gold chairs with red velvet upholstery. I recalled the weddings I used to attend in Karoland where it was often difficult to *find* the bride and groom and their parents, and here they were playing king and queen for a day!

The body of the event consisted of advice giving and gift giving from various sets of kin, beginning with the groom's side before the meal, and continuing after with the bride's side. Categories of kin stood while one of them, designated to speak on their behalf, used the microphone. Despite the electronic equipment, the speeches could not be heard above the din of hundreds of conversations. Even the attentions of the bride and groom, who stood opposite the speakers, were often distracted by well-wishers or newcomers who came up to shake their hands.

Men walked among the guests seated on mats, handing out small rupiah notes, shares of the different sections of the bride-price. *Anakberu* also walked through the women's areas handing out the ingredients for chewing betel, the leaves and tobacco in premeasured portions in little plastic bags, but I did not see anyone chewing betel. Just outside the pavilion, under a tent cover, four buffet tables were spread with food that was constantly replenished by a staff of men in white coats. A man pushing an ice-cream cart provided small cones or dishes of ice cream, which many people sampled before the meal. Decorating the buffet area was a huge model of a boat. Most impressive of all, two enormous ice sculptures of the families' clan initials, *G* and *S*, stood at the end of the two center tables. Some guests ate their meals in rows of folding chairs, others wandered out into an adjacent courtyard and sat on steps or on the sides of flower beds.

Ceremonial displays of the past lasted only in memory. Today the video recording and albums of still photographs are not only a way of sharing the event with far-flung kin, but they also serve to enshrine the sponsor's display in the permanence of recorded sounds and pictures.

Not everyone approves of ostentation. A retired schoolteacher in Payung asked me in 1990 if there had been much "development" since my last visit (in 1986). When I replied no, he argued that it was because so much of people's money went into feasts, a "wasteful" activity that he supposed United States citizens did not engage in. The year before, in a Jakarta suburb, an English teacher had expressed a similar attitude. He told me that two of his siblings had lost their portions of the family land, one brother in order to finance a business, and one to finance his wedding to a Pakpak woman of high status. Education is more important than weddings, he thought. He also had little use for clan and village associations. They don't *do* anything, he pointed out, offering his idea about an alternative organization that would provide scholarships for deserving Karo students, then direct them to work in Karoland for a few years on development projects.

For most families, sponsoring big celebrations remains an important incentive for earning and saving (or borrowing) money. But the inflation of weddings in the cities means that only middle- and upper-class families can afford them there. Going through the legal and religious ceremonies that effect a marriage without having a large celebration, a couple will not have "completed their *adat.*" Even if working-class families could find the money for a celebration, they would not have the social network in the city from which to draw a large number of guests. As we will see in the following chapters, the participation of working-class families in ethnic associations and church congregations is limited by their resources. The urban poor cannot as easily maintain their links to the ethnic community that would attend their weddings as metaphorical kin.

An *adat* wedding in a city is also a self-conscious ethnic exhibition. A wedding in the Karo highlands these days will often bring several office colleagues or former classmates from Medan who are not Karo, but there are likely to be even more non-Karo guests at weddings held in Medan and Jakarta. Wedding costumes are one of the frequent markers of *adat* tradition in the national culture and tourist arenas. In the ethnology museum at Taman Mini, for example, behind glass display cases that take up half of one floor, male and female mannequin couples wear wedding garb from all over the archipelago. Dressing a bride in *tudung* with gold fringe and draping the wedding couple with elaborate rented jewelry of a specifically Karo design thus has quite a different effect in Jakarta than in highland villages (fig. 6). City weddings do not simply exhibit the sponsor's wealth and social success, they celebrate a particular cultural tradition.

Respect and Avoidance: The Affective Tones of Domestic Life

Singarimbun (1975) has described how a delimited bilateral circle of close kin operates in making decisions, and sharing common ceremonial expenses. Within this close circle, intimacy and the expression of affection are regulated and constrained in cross-sex relations. Standards of avoidance and respect shape the cross-sex relationships of parents with children, brothers with sisters, and persons with their parents-in-law and siblings-in-law in ways that are peculiarly Karo. Respect observances between relations in the primary family—brothers and sisters, mothers and sons, and fathers and daughters—restrict interaction in a number of ways. While these relatives might speak to each other, their behavior together strikes a Western observer as stiff and formal. A brother and sister should not be in the house alone together, for example, and affection is not expressed physically in any of these cross-sex, natal family relationships.

Between certain in-laws of the opposite gender (daughter's husband–wife's mother, son's wife–husband's father, husband's sister's husband–wife's brother's wife) there can be no direct conversation at all and no other kind of direct interaction such as the transfer of objects. Intermediaries must

Fig. 6. A bride, 1973

be used, and if there are no human ones at hand, any inanimate object becomes a surrogate go-between for relaying messages. Meeting each other on the path requires averting one's eyes. This degree of avoidance is termed *rebu*. Feelings of *mehangke* (shame, respect) are said to characterize both the respect relationships within the nuclear family as well as the *rebu* (avoidance) relationships between affines. *Rebu* relationships are sometimes glossed as *si mehangke* "those who feel *mehangke*" (Ginting 1986). When inadvertently broken by accident or in a thoughtless moment of anger, or when deliberately abrogated in the face of death, *rebu* is reinforced by strong emotions.

[30 June 1973. Payung Village.] During Bibi's terminal illness, her son-in-law, D., arrived at a point when we felt she was on the verge of death. People urged him to go to her deathbed and speak to her, which he did, even touching her then. This poignant moment brought the whole room to tears, and evoked a new peak of wailing. I asked one of Bibi's daughter's about *rebu* in this case. She said because Bibi was so sick, it no longer applied. . . . Some months later [13 November 1974], another daughter recalled that when Bibi was dying, all her sons-in-law, except one, broke *rebu* to speak to her. The one who had declined, even though those in attendance had encouraged him to speak to her, had not been on good terms with his mother-in-law, hearing that she talked negatively of him to others.

Avoidance rules mask or mute affect, whether positive or negative. Most of this woman's sons-in-law had acquired an admiration and affection for her from decades of frequent contact, albeit a contact restrained by the rules of avoidance. In the end, their respect or shame gave way to a flood of grief and the desire to say good-bye. On the other hand, the one son-in-law who chose to maintain avoidance to the end could not be publicly faulted for maintaining the socially correct posture.

Karo recognize their avoidance customs as unusual when compared to other Indonesians. One person suggested to me that *rebu* is a trait unique to the Karo, but this is not true. Other Batak have similar, if not as stringent, avoidances. Still, people seem to regard *rebu* as an *adat* watermark of sorts, as a badge of being Karo, so when the conversation turns to the topic of how *adat* is changing, *rebu* often heads the list. An article in an ethnic newsletter from Jakarta in 1980 entitled "Karo *adat* in Jakarta" mentions the declining observance of *rebu*. A seminar in Medan in 1989 drew Karo academics, journalists, and other scholars of custom to discuss both the former functions of avoidance in the close-packed, multifamily houses of the past, and the strains of keeping this custom in the present. The national news magazine

Tempo produced an article on the seminar, catching readers' attention with the humor and oddity of rules prohibiting talking to each other and of the expedience of using mute objects as intermediaries if no human ones were available (e.g., "O plate, please tell my mother-in-law that her grandchild has been born"). The seminar had explored thorny moral dilemmas, too, such as, should a man break *rebu* to rescue his mother-in-law from drowning? I have heard Karo in everyday conversations joke about the awkward situations that arise around these avoidance customs and wonder also at their functions, but many regard their threatened disappearance apprehensively as a sign of social and cultural decay.

But *rebu* is far from dead. My fieldnotes during 1972–74 contain many references to people saying that the *rebu* rules were increasingly broken, but also document many instances of avoidance in a highland setting: women jockeying with me to switch seats with them so they would not be close to a *turangku* (husband's sister's husband); friends scolding me for laughing at jokes made by someone I was supposed to avoid; or people being embarrassed to have said something vulgar within hearing of certain relatives. In the late 1980s I still observed men and women in urban church reception lines who would not shake hands with each other.

Ethnically mixed marriages strain these avoidance rules, and mixed marriages are more common among Karo who live outside Karoland than those who remain there. Marriage between Karo and non-Karo is occurring much more frequently today than twenty years ago, as a generation of Karo born in the cities reaches maturity.

[2 August 1989. Jakarta. Interview with a retired journalist.] We spoke of the increasing frequency of marriage to non-Karo. He said the positive aspect of this is that each can learn the other's *adat*. In fact, he said, they usually do not, and their home becomes generic Indonesian. "Ethnicity can be left behind," *suku banci tading* was the way he phrased it. He says *rebu* is still strong, however, and that he does not speak to his daughter-in-law, who is not a Karo. I mentioned greater intimacy also between fathers and daughters, brothers and sisters, and he agreed, saying that this, too, was a consequence of the [urban, ethnically mixed] environment.

In contrast to this, others told me that they did not keep *rebu* with a son-in-law or daughter-in-law of a different ethnic background. A Karo man living in Bandung and married to a Simalungun woman related in amazement that one of his sons-in-law, of Menado background, actually kisses his mother-in-law (the speaker's wife) affectionately. The non-Karo spouses, even if they know the rules and tactfully observe them, have not internalized the shame that indexes and reinforces *rebu* in village society.

[5 October 1986. Medan.] Riding the bus to Medan today, a woman talked with me about *rebu*. She knew a woman who had married a man from Germany. Upon being introduced to his Karo mother-in-law, the man put his hand on her, or perhaps took her hand. At any rate he touched her. They quickly explained to him that Karo do not do this. We have to honor our *kalimbubu*, the woman told me.

[27 July 1989. Jakarta.] At the Forgiveness Asking last night I noticed some *rebu* behavior between *turangku* (husband's sister's husband–wife's brother's wife). The hostess, a Javanese who is married to a Karo, needed to walk across the room for something. "I am not brave enough to go there. Accompany me," she said to her mother-in-law, a classic-looking Karo grandmother who had come to Jakarta only a few days before to attend this event. Putting down the brass tube in which she was pounding a betel quid, and adjusting her *tudung*, the older woman got up to escort the younger. I asked someone what was going on, and learned that the hostess did not want to walk past her *turangku* alone. The two women picked their way across the crowded room, the older woman keeping herself between her daughter-in-law and the man she was not "brave" enough to walk past.

Was this last incident an exaggerated or ceremonial observance of reserve that does not in fact characterize this Javanese woman's behavior in private settings? A beautiful woman, formerly a professional dancer, she had a fine sense of code switching. She insisted on speaking English with me, although she spoke to her mother-in-law and other kin in flawless Karo, and gave directions to her daughters in Indonesian. But even if theatrical in this instance rather than coming from an internalized sense of shame, her behavior acknowledged the continuing strength of *rebu* as expected behavior. My observations of people in private settings suggest that while some people are relaxing these avoidance restrictions, others are not, and the unevenness gives rise to uncertainty and discomfort at times. One young man in a village complained to me that he was uncomfortable with the way his elder *turangku*, a Toba woman who lived in Medan, spoke with him and insisted he respond.

Cross-sex respect relations within the nuclear family appear even more vulnerable to change in the urban setting than the avoidance rules between in-laws. The relations between brother and sister and between parents and their opposite-sex children in urban Karo families are considerably more intimate and casual than those in village Karoland. Certainly the father-daughter relationship is looser, as a couple of people mentioned to me and as I saw for myself. In Jakarta, a Karo man walks hand in hand with his twelve-year-old daughter at a beachside park, and later she plops on his lap and he rests his chin on her head as we talk. In Medan, two young women in their twenties tease their father and poke his ribs, or sit close to him while watching television. I have never seen this kind of affectionate ease between fathers and grown daughters in highland villages. A photo album of a well-to-do Jakarta family shows an adolescent brother and sister standing in arm during a vacation trip, a pose highlanders would find unseemly at best. Brother-sister reserve extends, in the villages, even to those who are classificatory brother and sister, for example, *turang impal,* cross-cousins of the sort forbidden to marry (mother's brother's son–father's sister's daughter). In a wealthy Jakarta home, I observed two *turang impal* watching television together sitting on a couch. One, a doctor's son in his late teens, had been raised in Medan, and his girl cousin, in her early twenties, was from Jakarta. The boy twisted a strand of her hair absentmindedly, and when he asked for a snack chip later, she stuck one in his mouth. This kind of physical familiarity would mortify cousins of this type in the village, who think of themselves as kinds of siblings.

People often rationalized *rebu* to me as if they, too, had read Fred Eggan's (1937) essay on Cheyenne and Arapaho kinship, saying that total avoidance prevents certain relatives from fighting. Certainly that is a consequence of these strictures, as the example of the son-in-law who would not speak to his mother-in-law even at her deathbed shows. But in cases where *rebu* and respect relations have eroded, fighting is less in evidence to me than simple affection and ease in relationships once marked by the tension of remaining constantly on guard. I suspect it is less discord than disorder that these rules guard against, specifically pertaining to a moral order as Karo define it.

Just as Jewish dietary laws reaffirm a cosmic moral order through the most mundane activities of preparing, eating, and avoiding certain foods (Douglas 1966), these avoidances between affines and limits on the interaction of close kin are persistent reminders within the lived experience of family life of an abstract kinship design. Most of the institutionally awkward relations are ones in which romance, if even thinkable, would either break the rule of clan exogamy or else reverse the directionality of a family's affinal relations.[7] These rules reflect how *sumbang,* "incest," is defined in Karo thinking, for it is only partly a matter of genealogical closeness; its definition rests, rather, on a societal order. Downcast eyes and stiff reserve between *turang* (brother-sister pairs) reaffirm the rule against "incestuous" marriage between *turang* who are strangers to each other, sharing merely the same clan name. The rule against speaking to *turangku* similarly reminds people that marital ties between families have a directionality with regard to gender: women from a family marry in one direction, men in another; that is, marriage is not a reciprocal relationship between families. Any kinsperson with whom one feels *mehangke* is someone with whom romance would be incestuous (cf., Murdock 1949, 273–77).

The respect and avoidance that give a distinct emotional tone to Karo home life and the imagined structures such as clans and affinal alliances reinforce each other as part of a total system. This system does not transplant well to the urban setting, where public life for the most part has nothing to do with the conceptual frames of clans and asymmetrical alliances, so even patriliny diminishes. Without these conceptual frames the onerous and clumsy separations within families begin to seem arbitrary rather than given. Conversely, without the recurrent downcast eyes, shufflings of position, and pregnant silences between kin, the abstract notions of clans and alliances also begin to seem arbitrary or fictional. Karo children growing up in cities can easily see that family and kinship work differently on television and in the families of their friends than what their parents tell them about *rebu, impal* marriage, and so on, but for these urban children, distinctively Karo kinship has little reality as a lived order or even a spoken framework. With this change, an interlocked system of kinship begins to come apart.

Conclusions

Karo ethnic identity rests on a sense of belonging defined by kinship. This sense is not just a generalized, shapeless assertion of relatedness, but comes from understanding a conceptual order built on presumptions of patrilineally distinct clans and asymmetrical marital exchanges. Such an order must be verbalized constantly to remain real; or it must be lived, acted out in some way. In highland villages kinship terms that distinguish mother's brothers and their children from father's brothers and their children, or, for example, that merge a man's mother's brother with that man's father-in-law, reify the Karo conceptual order in everyday conversations, as do the insistent inconveniences and formalities of respect and avoidance of certain close relationships, and the ceremonial display of some who work and others who "just sit" at ceremonial events. When wealthy kin can simply hire their own labor for feasts and poor families are reluctant to ask wealthy people to work as *anakberu* at theirs, *kalimbubu* and *anakberu* marital statuses seem less salient than socioeconomic statuses.

To the degree that life in ethnically mixed cities is rendering Karo kinship practices more bilateral, this conceptual kinship order—and the ethnic identity it defines—are threatened. Young people do not fully command the kinship terminology nor the rest of the language through which one negotiates a "kinship" link to a stranger.

[2 August 1989. Jakarta. From an interview with a retired journalist.] He began by saying that Karo have begun to preserve and promote their *adat*, and that it had started to revive. I pointed out the language issue. He agreed, then, that the situation is difficult. None of his six children (by the wife in this house) speak Karo, although they have been spoken to in that language enough to understand some of it. He says it is not always that they do not want to learn. One of his daughters in Bandung is very willing to learn Karo, but she gets little practice in a Sundanese/Indonesian environment. He agreed that without the language the culture is lost. In twenty-five years there might well be no Karo, he said, but with hard work he hoped parents could save that identity. [He used the English cognate *identitas.*]

When I mentioned encountering young people that did not know how to *ertutur* [negotiate a metaphoric kin relation], he agreed. They just make *impal* [marriageable cousin] of everyone. They do not recognize that *turang* [same clan], *bere-bere* [mother's clan], or *turang impal* [mother's brother's son–father's sister's daughter] are prohibited marriage classes, he said. In his father's day, the fact that two people had the same *bere-bere* was a real impediment, even if no genealogical connection could be traced between a couple. He said his parents had to run away to get married, because his father was of the Bangun clan and his mother's *bere-bere* was also Bangun [making them classificatory *turang impal*]. . . . He mentioned the rarity of divorce in the past as compared to today. In the past there was more polygyny, but not much divorce. You had to call your *anakberu* together to talk about it, and they would be reluctant. Indeed, they were supposed to talk you out of it. He guessed that although married couples often lived separately in those days, especially in polygynous situations, the actual rate of divorce was probably about one in one thousand.

We talked about whether young people really have the desire to cultivate *adat*. He said one problem is that until they are married, they are not adults, and would not be involved in *adat* discussions to learn how it is done. They would rather stay home and watch videos than sit through long formal discussions, he said.

Adolescents, and even young married couples, do not yet play active roles in *adat* discussions nor in organizing the activities around feasts. This is as true of the villages as of the cities. A man may begin to learn how to be a ceremonial go-between or speaker only when he is an adult approaching middle age. But in villages, young adults and even children hear conversations (often spirited ones) about *adat* negotiations, the logistics and failures of organizing feasts, and impending legal battles, as their elders anticipate and then rehash *adat* events in tea shops and on doorsteps. Children growing up in Jakarta hear such conversations much less often because they live in an ethnically diverse environment. Their only exposure to *adat* is what their parents tell them, and what they see from afar at ceremonial events. Missing more than just a cognitive understanding of Karo kinship, these young urbanites miss also the feelings and emotions that make their elders feel awkward around opposite sex siblings, and utterly speechless around certain in-laws. More and more young Karo people are marrying people of other ethnic groups.

For now, the glue of kinship and the benefits of modern transportation still hold Karo society together across the urban and rural contexts. Travel back and forth from city to village is literally constant. Weddings in both the highlands and the cities tend to be scheduled on weekends rather than in the middle of the week to avoid conflict with people's jobs. When I began to learn the Jakarta scene briefly in 1986, I, too, benefited from having "kin" there with whom to start. Spending several weeks in Jakarta in 1989 and 1990, and traveling briefly to Bandung, I was constantly running into people—at weddings, at church services, and in interviews—whom I had known or met in Kabanjahe, Medan, or highland villages. Experiencing this personal connectedness gave me a sense of Karo society as a society, one still retaining its boundedness across a diaspora.

Even for the wealthiest urbanites I met, who can shop in Singapore and educate their children abroad, their reference points have not shifted entirely to new national and international horizons. Their kin in the highlands or elsewhere, and the ethnic community in Jakarta, remain the communities where their success brings them the most renown and satisfaction. Benefactors of church and ethnic activities, and feastgivers on a new scale, some of these wealthy Karo are unofficial leaders in the urban "village" constructed around ethnic pride and ethnic politics.

Notes

1. Singarimbun's (1975) is the most comprehensive and useful account of Karo kinship.

2. This is a reciprocal term. A girl's closest *impal* is her father's sister's son.

3. *Tjermin Karo,* 28 June 1925; *Pandji Karo,* May 1929.

4. Cf., Bruner (1987) on Toba monuments.

5. A missionary attending a Karo wedding in 1910 was also impressed by the almost incidental role of the bridal couple (Bodaan 1910).

6. Rural villagers in the lowland region called Langkat, however, told me in 1983 that the pattern there was like the urban one; they hire the *gendang* for weddings more often than for funerals.

7. The exceptions are two: the respect relation of mother-son and the *rebu* between husband's father–son's wife.

Chapter 8

Ethnic Pride, Ethnic Politics

The Indonesian state attempts to muffle ethnic politics through an ethnically blind stance, declining to acknowledge ethnicity in its census and on its official identification cards. The historical and sociological roots of this position start with the opposition to colonial divide-and-rule tactics and with the fact that ethnicity is a potentially explosive element, given that two ethnic groups in particular, the Chinese and Javanese, command advantages that the hundreds of other peoples in the archipelago lack. *Sukuisme* (tribalism or ethnic partisanship) is thus one of those subjects (along with race, religion, and class) that is encoded and tabooed with the acronym SARA. On the other hand, the government needs Indonesia's traditional cultures to draw tourists, but also to reassure Indonesians themselves of an indigenous heritage that remains strong in the face of cultural imperialism from the West and the Islamic world.

Karo ethnicity is partly a product of this state context. The blessing of government officials, loftily phrased as a "foreword," often stands at the beginning of printed programs of artistic performances or in the publications that result from "seminars" about *adat* and culture. Government officials themselves may play a part in organizing such events, or they may be asked merely to express how this event or publication fits the patriotic goal of nourishing national culture. The ethnic impulse also spills over the designs and blessings of the state, however, springing from the very sources that the government's policies hope to control by ignoring. The Karo kinship order, for all its "openness," provides a clear insider/outsider conceptual boundary limned by the membership of five great clans. Karo construe all relations with each other as metaphoric kin relations. Ethnic solidarity draws much of its emotional power from this conceptual, familial order, and especially from the connotations of kin terms, used ubiquitously in extended fashion, through which Karo speakers learn initially about self and others. The familial connotations of Karo ethnicity, and the reward of community that it returns to some persons in the midst of the city's anonymity, also indicate why Karo rhetorically shield kinship and ethnicity from the corrosiveness of wealth differences and different communities of faith. In fact, as we will see, the ideals of communalistic rhetoric do not fully prevent wealth from shaping ethnic associations and the ethnic church.

Ethnic pride stems also from the kind of ethnic politics the state would like to ignore—from the competition for economic and symbolic spoils, and from perceived slights to honor or imputations of inferiority. Any specifically ethnic phenomenon turns out on closer inspection to have multiple meanings, but especially to be implicated in issues of power as well as pride. Urban migrants live in a setting where wealth and power differences are much greater than they are in Karo villages, and where, in offices and other public settings, gradations of power are finer and more immediate to everyday life than those in farming communities. Assertions of worth and honor based on ethnicity, assertions that, for the most part, middle-class, urban Karo make, must be seen in this context, that is, as defensive responses in a stratified society. But wealth and power also divide Karo from each other, separating even close kin by life-style and life-chances, and especially separating middle-class, urban Karo from their rural kin. Furthermore, the extent to which migrants can participate in ethnic displays, ethnic associations, and ethnic politics, including the politics of scholarship, depends on wealth.

[21 September 1986. Kabanjahe.] Yesterday I attended the grand opening of Universitas Karo Area (UKA). It was pretty grand, and fully as much a patriotic as an ethnic display. Rehearsals had gone on all the day before, and, by 8:30 in the morning, musicians and singers, and women and men in ceremonial dress were beginning to gather in an auditorium in a complex of buildings that belongs to the town and is the university's temporary headquarters. Military and police stood at crossroads to direct traffic, closing the roads around the building. Wreaths of flowers on tripods decorated the entry side of the auditorium, as well as the building directly across the yard from it. Around 9:15 A.M. a motorcade arrived carrying the VIPs, including an army lieutenant general and the district head, both accompanied by their wives. A *gendang* played at their arrival, and soon after, several hundred of the entering class, dressed alike in white shirts and black trousers or skirts, red ribbons in their hair, filed in amid loud cheers.

Inside the auditorium, more wreaths, potted plants, and a huge banner decorated the back of the stage. At the front near the podium were the usual pictures of Indonesia's President and Vice-President. The podium was draped with a Karo textile (*uis nipis*), and immediately in front of the stage was a series of upholstered chairs for dignitaries. Other guests sat behind them in rows of folding chairs, and behind the guests, the students.

After a unison singing of the national anthem, the lieutenant general came to the podium to lead us in a moment of silence for veterans and martyrs. The head of the Departemen Agama led us in prayer. He prayed aloud in Arabic, but told his audience (in this case majority Christian) to pray according to their own religion. A series of speakers took the podium in turn, including the Rector of the new university, the district head (Bupati) and his wife (she had chaired the committee that organized the new university), and local government officials. All these speeches began and ended with Islamic salutations (this was the first Muslim Karo ever to hold the office of Bupati), and all speeches were in Indonesian. Most speakers ended with a loud rendition of the Karo salutation, *mejuah-juah!*, sometimes shouted with a raised fist. The speeches expressed thanks to various persons or sectors of the community, exhorted the students to work hard, and hoped for success in the future. Especially, people hoped UKA would soon have its own campus and buildings. One speaker urged people not to blame the government for the recent drastic devaluation of the currency (45 percent), for Indonesia's economy was closely linked to the world economy. Others expressed wishes for the national elections scheduled for next year.

Interspersed among these speeches were a number of ceremonial presentations or graphic symbolizations. The lieutenant general and his wife were presented with a *uis nipis* cloth, for example. At one point the *gendang* played while the lieutenant general and other dignitaries danced, Karo-style, opposite other members of the audience. Two male students, dressed in black karate-style uniforms performed a new dance combining martial arts moves with traditional elements of choreography. The lieutenant general officially opened the university by pounding five solemn strikes on a gong. Two professional dancers performed a rendition of the classic Karo pop song *Piso Surit*. Students were represented in a couple of these displays: a boy and girl were publicly outfitted in jackets and scarves emblazoned with UKA's logo; four others knelt at the front with bowed heads as someone took a leafy branch, dipped it into water, and then sprinkled it over their proffered hands.

When the new district head assumed office a year before this opening, he met with village headmen and other leaders on the Plateau to determine what needs people perceived. A university, he told me, was one of the things people had asked for in these meetings. For decades, education has been a high priority with Karo families. Each university degree represents an entire family's achievement, memorialized in photographs and celebrated with big family meals. Each represents, also, a source of ethnic pride. Pictures of graduates and their parents often appear in ethnic newspapers. A thick book called *Who and Where Are the Merga si Lima Graduates?* was published in 1984. Organized by discipline, it lists hundreds of names and addresses (Ginting 1984).

The opening of a university in Karoland thus meant several different things. On a practical level, its location allows those who are already employed in Karoland a chance to attend a university. It also parallels the successful and highly visible Sisingamangaraja University in Medan, a Toba institution that stands as a monument to Toba identity. In 1986 I mentioned the new Karo university to a political scientist who studies Indonesia, and he said that local universities had sprouted up in many places recently. They were big money-makers for district heads, he said. Whether or not the Bupati profited from founding UKA, he took great pride in this accomplishment as he looked back on his term of office, which ended in 1990. I heard his farewell speech at the investiture of the new district head, and spoke with him personally at that time. He counted the university's founding as a personal and political victory, his and his wife's lasting contribution to the progress of the Karo people.

A university in Karoland with the word *Karo* in its name was an ethnic landmark, but ethnicity "happens," for the most part, outside of Karoland. Ethnic associations have no place in the highland villages, being urban inventions, springing from a sense of minorityhood and from a profound homesickness among those who live daily in isolation from other Karo. Ethnic newspapers, similarly, originate for the most part in migrant communities and circulate most systematically there. The very first Karo newspapers were printed in satellite communities around Medan. Those who are farthest from Karo culture as a lived, taken-for-granted milieu are those who must champion and cultivate it most deliberately.

The Batak Issue: What Is a Suku?

People in Jakarta seem not to hear me when I say "Karo"; they start talking instead about Batak. Twice in Jakarta, while I was trying to locate the houses of Karo families by using their clan names (Ginting and Sembiring), neighbors pointed me to their houses, saying something like, "Bataks, aren't they?"

[9 July 1989. Jakarta.] I asked the taxi driver, a Javanese, to take me to the GBKP church at Sumur Batu Raya, no. 8. I recalled from my visit here in 1986 that the address does not help much. You have to know how to find it in a maze of narrow residential streets, some of which are unmarked dead ends, and I did not remember well enough to direct him. The driver assured me that he knew how to get to this church, however, and perhaps to demonstrate that *he* well knew one Batak from another, proceeded on the way there to describe how the Karo are the most crude (*kasar*) of all the Batak. He took me instead to a HKBP, the Toba church, the giant spires of which are visible from Suprapto Street. At least it is in the general vicinity of Sumur Batu Raya, so getting another taxi near that church, and hoping for a local driver, I spent another twenty minutes driving around the neighborhood before we found the low, inconspicuous building that belongs to the GBKP. Deliberately unobtrusive in a predominantly Muslim neighborhood, it looks nothing like a church, yet houses the largest Karo congregation in Jakarta.

[28 August 1990. Jakarta.] In a conversation with several Karo friends, and the Sundanese wife of one of these, I brought up the observation that people in Jakarta do not distinguish Karo from Batak. One of the women, who is married to a Mandailing Batak, agreed, and then pointed out that it works the other way, too. Karo and other Batak in Sumatra have no idea about kinds of Javanese. The Sundanese woman smiled in agreement. Only when they come to Jakarta do they learn that there are Betawi, Sundanese, Javanese, and others. These are all just Javanese in Karo knowledge.

Because the Toba are so much more numerous than the other Batak peoples, and because they benefited from missionary schools and moved early into positions of prominence, they remain the most publicly visible. They use the single term *Batak* to refer to themselves and, further, regard a mythical Toba patriarch as the ancestor of all the other Batak peoples. The term *Batak* thus has two meanings. First, in ethnological discourse, it denotes a linguistic-cultural family that includes Toba, Karo, and other peoples. But Indonesian scholars often speak of this ethnological grouping as a *suku* (ethnic group). Koentjaraningrat, for example, writes about "Suku Batak."[1] Second, in everyday usage the single term *Batak* typically applies only to one of these peoples—the Toba.

[4 September 1986.] At the observance of Muharram in Tiga Panah's mosque yesterday, I chatted with the wife of a religion teacher. She and her husband were both from Kuta Cane (a large town between Karoland and Aceh). Her mother was Karo, although her father was Gayo. She said everyone in Kota Cane is Muslim, and that the town is an ethnic mixture of Karo, Alas, Gayo, and Acehnese. There are few Batak there, she said. When I pressed her to clarify this, she said, "Toba."

This dual meaning of *Batak* is the source of the controversy that Karo are not Batak. The metonymic process by which one part (Toba) has come to stand for the whole (Batak) means that outsiders frequently conflate Karo with Toba, a mistake that grates on Karo sensibilities. To say, thus, that Karo is a sub*suku* of Batak may imply only that Batak is the header subsuming several different categories, but alternately it suggests that Toba Batak is the header and the other kinds of Batak are derivatives or variants of that original source. In the latter sense, the Toba's origin story has become the template for how they and other Indonesians understand the category "Batak" (e.g., Rodgers 1990, 336). Those who wish to "de-Batak" the Karo want to establish, then, that Batak is not a *suku,* and that Karo is not a *sub*unit of anything. Karo society itself, rather, is a full-fledged *suku*—with a social order, a language, ceremonial costumes, and dances uniquely its own. In Taman Mini park, where diversity is represented for the most part as differences between government regions rather than between cultures or societies, I can only imagine the politics years ago behind the decision to represent the North Sumatra region with *two* oversized houses, one Toba and one Karo.

[3 August 1989. A trip to Taman Mini, Jakarta's cultural theme park.] The Karo house does have some display cases and antiques in it. Someone had told me (disapprovingly) that all the objects, including Malay things, had been moved into the Toba house next door. Certainly there is more to see in the Toba house than the Karo house—costumes, dioramas, a Malay bridal bower, and sample kitchens for Karo and Toba [although they had arranged the hearth wrong for Karo]. In both houses, Karo objects were usually labeled simply "Karo," but I saw one item in the Karo house that apparently had been labeled "Batak Karo," for the word *Batak* had been imperfectly covered up with white-out.

An article in an ethnic newspaper in 1985 with the headline, "It's a Small Matter, but one of Principle," describes the dismay of some Karo visitors to the Department of Tourism, Post, and Telecommunications in Jakarta where they saw a picture of a couple dressed in Karo ceremonial garb mislabeled as "Tapanuli Adat Clothing" (Tapanuli is a Toba designation). Such "small matters of principle" occur all the time. Mainstream newspaper articles about Karo, for example, often use the better-known Toba term for clan (*marga*) rather than the Karo cognate (*merga*).

In 1989 a group of men in Jakarta began to contest the appellation Batak as applied to the Karo. Led by an educator who holds a position in Golkar, the group also included a journalist/scholar and a retired politician. They organized a press conference on the topic, but were disappointed when only one paper in the mainstream press found the issue newsworthy. Nonetheless, members of the group wrote several articles that appeared in ethnic news-letters, and recruited two Karo academics (a linguist and an anthropologist) to write supportive articles as well. Especially, this group lobbied with the leadership of the GBKP to take the term *Batak* out of the church name. They wrote to Hendrik Neumann, youngest son of an early missionary to the Karo, to solicit his support of their efforts.

Some of this correspondence, along with previously published articles, was then published as a book, *Mengenal "Orang Karo"* (Concerning the "Karo people") (Bangun 1989). The Minister of Tourism, Post, and Tele-communications wrote the first of several forewords to the book by various officials. The importance of the publication, he wrote, rests on its contribution to cultural studies and its uses for tourism. A page with the eaglelike emblem of the Pancasila and a list of its five principles immediately follows this blessing of a high government official, and following that, a page is devoted to the preamble to the constitution of 1945. The patriotic flourishes introducing this publication were unusually elaborate, probably because the book represents, in fact, the kind of *sukuisme* the government opposes.

The body of the book begins with a reprinted piece by a Toba Batak poet and scholar, Sitor Situmorang, describing Toba clans depicted in a single, genealogical format and Toba principles of kinship. This is apparently placed first (and without editorial explanation) for contrast, because the next section explains that all Karo are kin by virtue of their clan connections, listing the Karo clan and subclan names, which are not the same as Toba names and cannot be placed in a genealogical format. More on the *anakberu-kalimbubu* relation follows. Establishing first the separate kinship orders of the two societies, the book goes on to marshal evidence from several angles— historical, linguistic, and cultural—behind the case that Karo are not a sub*suku* of Batak. One contributor, for example, makes the case that in the past, Batak was a religious designation in that people who converted to Islam ceased to be Batak. This religious identity (Batak) was misappropriated by the Dutch as an ethnic identity, entered written history, and has persisted.

The book *Mengenal "Orang Karo"* is careful not to make the case for Karo by denigrating Toba, nor by revealing the sense of competition the Karo feel with Toba. An academic member of this anti-Batak circle cautioned me that I could not write about ethnic antagonism in the age of Pancasila. But, he admitted, the animosity for Toba goes deep. He characterized the Toba as voracious eaters, loud, ill-behaved, and lazy. He felt that as long as Karo use the Batak designation at all, they will suffer by association with these character traits. The leader of the anti-Batak movement told me how he cringes when people greet him with "Horas!," the Toba salutation. Using polite speech (*kata tengteng*) so as not to reveal how greatly he is angered, he corrects people who say this or who call him a Batak. The Karo will never progress until they shed their image as Batak, he told me. It holds them back.

[2 August 1989. Jakarta. From an interview with a retired journalist.] I asked about the Batak issue. He began slowly and thoughtfully. The Karo did not write their own history, he said. It was not that they are not smart; they are master chess players, and invented the card game "Joker," which is played everywhere now. But they used their script only to record spells, medicines, and prayers, so to reconstruct their history they used (and still use) Dutch sources, which classified them as Batak on the basis of language and culture similarities. Karo have not been brave, either, about asserting their distinctiveness, he said. We are more refined than the Toba, who readily praise themselves and wear their identity proudly. As if this were the vision that haunted him, he told me about an area of the Simalungun region where virtually all the headmen are now Toba, and where the Simalungun language is being lost. He concluded that he has no problem with dropping the Batak designation. We cannot be unbending (*kaku*) but have to go with the times.

One person suggested that the new interest in separating Karo from Batak had come about after an inflammatory incident over what to name a forest preserve. Starting in 1985, some 900 million rupiah of government funds were allocated to build a new gateway, signs, and other amenities for a nature preserve located along the highway between Medan and Karoland. The rugged hills below the Plateau's escarpment are draped in a wonderful rain-forest vegetation. Articles about this forest in ethnic newspapers pointed to its key role in Medan's watershed, the variety of its flora and fauna, and thus its potential for education, the environment, and the tourist trade. The new gates, placed near the village of Toungkeh outside the town of Sibolangit, and sporting an arc with replicas of the traditional Karo roofs, stood ready to be inaugurated in 1988, but months went by while controversy brewed over an appropriate name.

The forest had been known as Taman Hutan Raya, shortened to Tahura. Its new name was supposed to "fit the identity of this area," according to one article in an ethnic newspaper. Proposals were received. One newspaper proposed the name "Soekarno-Hatta and Jamin Gintings," rationalizing this by citing brief visits the revolutionary heroes Soekarno and Hatta had paid to the region. The late Gintings was a Karo who achieved high positions in the military and the government. One student group in Medan argued to keep the old name. In connection with a marathon, a government official suggested the name "Super Semar," the nickname for the decree to eliminate the Indonesian Communist Party that Soeharto signed in 1966.[2]

The final straw, however, was a proposal by a wealthy Toba entrepreneur in Medan to name the forest Sisingamangaraja XII after the last Toba Batak raja, a legendary leader who opposed the Dutch colonialists to his death. On this basis the Toba have argued successfully to elevate Sisingamangaraja XII into an official national hero (Cunningham 1981). While he thus ranks among the heroes of the nation in Karo eyes, Sisingamangaraja XII does not represent a local or ethnic hero to them as he does to the Toba, so the suggestion to place his name over an archway at the edge of Karoland smacked of "colonization," as one GBPK minister put it. Without any official inauguration ceremony, the name Sisingamangaraja XII appeared mysteriously on a carved sign over the gateway. While contingents of lobbyists journeyed to Jakarta to meet with the leader of Golkar and the head of the Forestry Department to plead against the Sisingamangaraja name, vandals registered a more dramatic protest by removing the unwelcome sign and burning it. In the end, and in response to the protests, President Soeharto resolved the issue by choosing an ethnically neutral name, Bukit Barisan, the mountain range that runs along Sumatra's middle.

If the forest incident added fuel to the movement to de-Batak the Karo, even this did not galvanize everyone toward that position. The cause resonates most strongly with urban, educated Karo who constantly chafe at implied insults to their honor when people label them Batak in multiethnic settings. The advocates of this cause in Jakarta and other cities in Java all move in circles of the academic or political elite. The cause means little to peasant farmers on the plateau who live in a homogeneously Karo environment. One day in 1990, packed in the back of a micro pickup truck with a dozen or so women from villages along the road to Payung who were on their way to Kabanjahe's market, I heard a woman use the word *Batak* self-referentially in a conversation comparing me to themselves. Taking the imagined position of her interlocutor (me), she cast herself as Batak, perhaps like Karo in the past when speaking to missionaries or other outsiders and trying to connect with *their* categories. Then she substituted the word *Karo* in her next sentence.

But many well-educated urban Karo have not been persuaded by the movement either, and although they, too, refer to themselves as Karo rather than Batak, they see no need to change the name of the church and to rewrite culture history. A minister very high in the GBKP leadership suggested to me that those who shrink from the term *Batak* lack vision. The challenge, he thought, is to raise Indonesians' knowledge and estimation of the Batak. Karo academics in Medan in late 1990 indicated that the issue had died down in the past year, and that it had not had the effect the men in Jakarta had hoped. To these academics, the whole thing seemed to be a matter of politics rather than science, a product of Toba-Karo competition. The solution, according to one, was to raise the quality of Karo public figures, and raise more Karo into positions of prominence. A Jakarta man who prides himself on being a Marhaenist (socialist-populist) and an open dissident gave this view of culture history that shows an acquaintance with the scholarly literature:

[4 August 1989. Jakarta. Interview with a revolutionary era leader and politician.] Issues of religion and ethnicity are clearly not his bag; his attention is focused on national level politics. The Batak designation? He has no problem with it. This is an emotional issue for the movement's leader, he said, who feels it is a "fact" of history and culture. These, instead, were the facts as he knew them. The ultimate origins of Batak culture go back to the hill tribes of Indochina who migrated south and into the archipelago. Since then, Batak have been influenced by two additional sources. One was a migration from the Indian Ocean inland from Barus on the West Coast, up the rivers to Mt. Bukit. That is the origin of Toba and all other Batak, he said. In addition, Karo were also influenced by Indians and Malays coming in from the East Coast. In terms of culture and language, the Karo certainly are Batak, he said. If the Toba are too stupid to understand the relationship between the word *Batak* and the varieties thereof, that's their problem. "Let's not be stupid just because *they* are!"

Outside the big cities, in the smaller towns around the archipelago where Karo families are very few, ethnic antagonism with Toba is often put aside in the interests of friendship based on common ostracism and on kinship systems similar enough to forge fictive relations with ease. Richard Kipp's (1977, 1983) work on Karo pioneer farmers in lowland areas described the benefits of Toba-Karo friendships in a demanding, rural environment where Toba had settled first. My "niece" who lives in Bali told me in 1989 how closed and ethnocentric Balinese are, so proud of their religion and fearful that Christians will try to convert them. About fifteen Karo families live in Bali's capital of Den Pasar, but in her town, hers is the only Karo family. Her closest friends are thus among a small multidenominational group of Christians from various ethnic groups. With a Toba family her family has forged a metaphoric *senina* (agnatic) relationship. Likewise, in Banda Aceh I learned of only one clan association, in addition to an all-Karo group there, and that had formed between some Karo of the Ginting clan and some Toba, since some of the Ginting subclan names are the same as Toba *marga* names.

Ethnic Associations

Voluntary associations based on Karo identity exist in cities throughout the archipelago, from Banda Aceh to Biak.[3] If the number of Karo families in a town or city remains small, the group will be defined to encompass all of them, an all-Karo ethnic association. When the number of resident Karo grows, as it has in cities such as Jakarta, Bandung, and Medan, the unitary association begins to segment into smaller groups based on a range of other possible subcategories: clan or subclan, region or village of origin (or ward within a village), current neighborhood, students (or just students within certain faculties of a large university), and Karo religious minorities (Muslims and Catholics, for example).

[26 July 1989. Jakarta. From an interview with a middle-aged Muslim man.] I asked if he belonged to any groups by virtue of his clan (Tarigan). He said no, and that such groups have no use or benefit (*manfaat*). People in the same clan are not necessarily closer than people who are related as *anakberu-kalimbubu*, he pointed out. These clan associations do not help a family meet its common financial crises such as weddings and funerals. The clan associations are less effective now than groups based on village of origin, the reason being that the clan groups are (potentially) too large. The village groups are often built on close family or neighbor relationships that are *already there*, he stressed. He pointed out that Karo villages were not composed of single descent groups, but always had to have both *anakberu* and *kalimbubu* of the village founder. I added that the traditional houses were designed the same way; they were not for a single descent line. He said that an all encompassing organization such as Karo Sada Kata [the first Karo association in Jakarta] could no longer exist. There are too many Karo in Jakarta now.

Karo ethnic associations vary greatly in their formality of organization, size, purposes, and longevity. Some, perhaps most, exist as small, face-to-face mutual aid and social groups, meeting once a month or less often for a meal together, and for collecting a specified amount of money as an *arisan* (credit organization). Sometimes the *arisan* collections rotate among members on a regular basis; in other cases they insure members against specified misfortunes. One in Jakarta, for example, pays half of the airfare to Medan in the event of a parent's death. Some groups have other, quite particular

goals. An ethnic newsletter in recent years carried a notice about the formation of a club in Jakarta for Karo chess players, and I heard of a similar group
in Medan that aimed to play and preserve Karo music.

As any of these grow large, however, there is the tendency for them to
segment or dissolve. A few people suggested that clan-based organizations
were becoming less viable than village- or region-based groups. Three people
complained to me that none of these associations had much practical significance.

[4 August 1989. Jakarta. From an interview with a retired, nonconverted man.] I
began by asking about his participation in ethnic associations. He has no use for
them and belongs to none. They are always doomed to fail, he said, the reason
being that Karo society already has an organization, and it is kinship. Kinship is
complete (he added for stress, in English, "implicit"). In contrast, the associations
have no relationship to Karo life or Karo culture. For purposes of pleasure or for
arisan purposes, these groups were alright for others, he conceded, but he had no
need of them.

If Karo ethnic associations seem "doomed to fail," they seem equally doomed
to be tried. I do not know how many there are today, and counting them
would be difficult, since each is in some state of formation, activity, quies-
cence, or extinction. Ethnic newspapers regularly carry announcements that
new ones have formed; people speak about ones they joined in the past that
are now defunct. At their largest and most organized they encompass hundreds of members, have printed charters and membership lists, and hold
annual celebrations and traditional dances entertaining more than a thousand
people. At their smallest, they fade into bilateral kinship groups deriving
from a common grandparent (*sada nini*), a group of siblings and cousins who
meet periodically to share a meal and to visit.

Recruitment into all these groups is bilateral, in that families can belong
through a link from the male or the female half of a married couple. Clan or
subclan associations are properly referred to in print and other formal ways,
for example, not simply as the Tarigan clan group, but as "Tarigan and their
anakberu." *Anakberu* (wife-receiver) here designates the women of Tarigan
clan and the men who have married those women. When these clan associations meet, the *anakberu* members of the group carry out the work of serving
the meal and acting as intermediaries in the discussions, at least in theory,
just as they do in traditional kinship events such as weddings and funerals.
A man whose own subclan is Sibero, for example, might be among the most

active members of a Pandia subclan association because he is married to a Pandia woman. This also works fictively. I know a man in Jakarta of the Bukit subclan who participates as *anakberu* in the subclan association of Sembiring Depari. His wife is Javanese. Sembiring Depari is actually his mother's subclan, the subclan into which his wife was assimilated as a fictive mother's brother's daughter.

A number of factors limit the effective size of these associations and undermine their solidarity and continuity. Whether defined by village of origin, clan, neighborhood proximity, or, in smaller cities, simply by being Karo, these groups seldom attract all the people theoretically eligible to join. Of those who choose to join a group, some participate regularly and some only occasionally. People point out how busy their families are these days. Evenings and weekends provide limited time for activities of this sort, which compete with each other and with other recreational, social, and ceremonial events pressed into those same times. Most people have knowledge of many more groups that they are eligible to join than they have the time or resources for, so people choose which ones to commit themselves to, if any. They select groups in which they already have close friends or relatives, and in which they feel comfortable in terms of shared life-style, or groups to whose life-style they *aspire*. In some cases, not participating is a function of income. One man who belonged to a Ketaren subclan group in Jakarta estimated that about 150 were eligible to belong, but only 40 or so were active members. Those who are least active, he suggested, were those who have less. People who did not have cars expressed to me that their reason for not belonging to one group or another had to do with transportation difficulties. One Tarigan clan member told me he was not "able" to associate with the Tarigan group, the members of which were mostly very rich.

To give a sense of the variation, I provide examples of three groups, each based on somewhat different recruitment principles (see following sections). One draws people who originate from the same locale; one draws people of the same subclan; and one is circumscribed by a residential neighborhood in Jakarta. The subclan association, the only one organized on the kinship metaphor, shows most clearly how the kinship idiom benefits ethnic solidarity, but interaction among Karo anywhere is construed through such an idiom. All of these examples illustrate, too, how such groups manage religious pluralism, accommodating the foods and prayers such that religious divisions are not rendered impediments to membership. Each group is constituted and shaped by wealth differences, although these remain entirely implicit criteria for membership. In the first example, the group's composition includes some of the most wealthy and powerful Karo anywhere, along with some middle-class members, but meetings do not rotate to those whose homes are too small (or to people who would be embarrassed to host their wealthy friends), and contributions from the wealthiest subsidize the participation of less well-to-do families. Many who would be on the receiving end of these charities or inequities simply choose not to affiliate or participate in the group's events.

A Region-based Association: Jakarta, 1989

The area around Sibolangit is termed Sinuan Gambir (literally, those who plant gambier). An association of people originating from this area and living in Jakarta, called Persatuan Sinuan Gambir, has existed since 1982, and its membership list in 1989 numbered fifty-one families. Either the wife, the husband, or both spouses in a family came from the Sibolangit area. Judging from the name list, seven of the fifty-one families resulted from ethnically mixed marriages; in five of those, the husband was Karo, while in the other two, the wife was Karo. The membership list included each family's home address, and also the man's working address, the children's names, and the names of the man's and the woman's parents. Showing the patrilineal slant of Karo society and hinting at the ideals of asymmetrical alliance, the woman's parents were identified, *in reference to the man,* that is, as his *mama* and *mami,* terms that merge a man's mother's brother and mother's brother's wife with his parents-in-law.

Persatuan Sinuan Gambir's printed charter expresses the association's purposes as enhancing the familialness (*kekeluargaan*) and prosperity of its members. It operates as an *arisan* to help members who have suffered bad luck. The charter specifies further that the group is based on the Pancasila, but is nonreligious and nonpolitical. It goes on to set out the dues, terms of membership, and rules for election of officers.

This group meets every two months for a meal in one of the member's homes. Like many associations, it meets on Sunday afternoon, beginning just after church. The one meeting I attended began with people sitting down for casual conversation in gender-separate groupings. Roughly forty-five people were there, and of those very few were children or adolescents. The meeting was held in a spacious home in its family room. One corner of this room was faced with false rock holding niches of ferns and orchids and down which water flowed into a lighted fish pond. Men sat in chairs and on a large sectional couch, and after pulling on sarongs over their dresses, the women seated themselves on mats which had been spread on the floor. While a drink was served, the women perused several picture albums, one of which recorded a wedding and another, an award ceremony for the hostess's late husband, who had been a university professor. One woman received the *arisan* installments, which she entered in a ledger.

As with other kinds of associations, class strongly influences who belongs to this group and the extent of people's participation. Some of the members were probably wealthier than this hostess, and some were less well to do. The membership list gives the names of the wealthiest or most powerful members first. These included the widow of a lieutenant general, two men currently in high government positions, and some wealthy businessmen. The work addresses of members listed later in the book suggest many are small-business proprietors or minor bureaucrats. The man who invited me to attend was a proprietor of a small business. Hosting the Sinuan Gambir group ideally circulates among all the members, but in practice this man and some other members do not host it because their houses are too small. All those who attended this meeting arrived in automobiles. In fact, getting to this house, in a suburban location at Jakarta's far northern edge, would have been difficult using public transportation. Since members of the association live scattered all over the city, participation strongly favors those who own automobiles.

Before the meal, Rev. A. Sibero (who would become the head of the GBKP the next year) said grace. He resides in Medan and Kabanjahe, so is not a member of the Jakarta group. His family does originate from the Sibolangit area, however, and he happened to be in Jakarta that Sunday, as he often is, and attended the church where many of the members of this association attend. He was invited along for the meal. Only one family in this association is Muslim. The friend who invited me to this meeting had said with a gleam in his eye, "We will eat pork there," and sure enough, one of the dishes was *babi panggang,* the distinctive Karo dish made with fat pork in a sauce of blood, salt, and chilies. There was a wide variety of other foods as well, served buffet style around a kitchen table. In fact, it was one of the most sumptuous meals I have ever been served in an Indonesian home. The Muslim family, if they attended, would have had plenty to eat without the pork.

After the meal, there was a brief business meeting that was surprisingly formal, perhaps because of the presence that day of three "distinguished" guests, including me(!). We visitors were each asked to address the group. First to speak was a retired Bupati (district head) of an Irian Jaya district. He, too, resides in Medan, but was in Jakarta to see his two daughters, both of whom are married to very wealthy or well-placed men, and both of whom belong to this group. The second guest speaker was the church officer, who asked this group to help raise money for a church building to compete with a new mosque that had recently gone up in Tanjong Beringin, a village in the Sinuan Gambir area. Finally, I spoke, explaining who I was and what I was doing in Jakarta. The main topic of business concerned the plans to combine the next month's meeting with a picnic to celebrate the Independence Day holiday. Families would contribute 10,000 rupiah, it was decided, or as much as they could afford, in order to defray expenses for some group members. Having lasted about three hours, the meeting was over and people began to leave.

A Subclan Association: Medan, 1990

Members of the Sinulingga subclan who live in the Medan area have had an organized association for many years. At first it met every month, then it lapsed for awhile, and now is meeting once every three months. This association meets strictly for social purposes, with no *arisan* function, although each family contributes 3,000 rupiah to reimburse the host for the meal. At some special outing or event that would attract all the members and their families, it was estimated that about one hundred people would attend. At the meeting I attended, a regular meeting on a Sunday afternoon, about thirty-five adults were present. Aside from some babies and very small children, no young people attended. The group composition was primarily middle aged and middle class, except for three or four older people (including two women chewing betel) and two young couples with babies.

I attended with a woman originally from Menado who is married to a GBKP minister of the Sinulingga subclan. Her husband, who was unable to attend, dropped us off on his way to a meeting. Arriving at 3:00, we thought we would be a little late, but only five or six people had arrived before us. People trickled in gradually over a two hour period, and we joked about Indonesia's "rubber-time" concept. But women also offered the excuse that people were very busy these days. Weekends, especially, are times for weddings and other gatherings, and many people work on Saturdays. This busyness was the reason, they said, that the group had previously fizzled out, and was now down to a quarterly meeting schedule. People also spoke of transportation problems, citing the case of one family who lived as far away as Deli Tua, from which public transportation to this place would be difficult. Most of the members arrived by automobile or motorcycle.

We met in a home on the southern outskirts of Medan. Many Karo live in this area on the small roads that run off to either side of the main road connecting Medan to Karoland. This was a firmly middle-class home, roomy but with no elaborate decor. A spacious yard gave the house a suburban feel, and at the side of the house the hostess, a retired schoolteacher, maintained a large (probably commercial) orchid garden. One of her children works in Germany, and a son had recently returned home from attending college in the United States. The host family was devoutly Catholic, and the man had worked for the Catholic church before he retired. A framed photograph on the wall showed him and his wife shaking hands with the Pope during one of their trips to Europe.

When we first arrived and the numbers were small, men and women sat on the front porch on the upholstered furniture that had been moved outdoors to accommodate the meeting. We sipped cool drinks and made light conversation. One older man and woman, not married to each other, bantered in the form of a teasing argument that amused and entertained us. As more people began to arrive the women moved indoors to sit on mats that were spread wall to wall in the living room, and the men remained on the porch smoking and talking. For the women, the hostess passed around some hair ornaments and other costume jewelry she had recently brought back from Germany and which she was hoping to sell. After some bargaining, one woman, who is a merchant, bought a set of hair ornaments for 60,000 rupiah, fishing the cash from her brassiere.

Someone explained to me that this group was "the Sinulingga subclan and its *anakberu,*" and as the men came inside for the meal, people spoke the kind of pronouncements or directions one hears at a wedding or a gathering for a formal *adat* discussion: "*Kalimbubu* (wife-givers) sit against the wall, *anakberu* to the center!" In this case it meant that men of the Sinulingga subclan should sit against the wall, and men married to Sinulingga women, as *anakberu* inferiors, should sit toward the center. The whole *anakberu-kalimbubu* posturing did not much affect the women's interaction, however. Women had seated themselves in a shapeless grouping where they had talked and amused themselves for the previous couple of hours and where they remained for the meal. When the meal was served, there was again much ado about the *kalimbubu* helping themselves first to the buffet that had been set out in the kitchen, a slight nod to the traditional pattern at feasts or formal occasions in which *kalimbubu* could expect to remain seated and be served by their *anakberu,* who would then eat afterward. Here, all the men served themselves, the *kalimbubu* among them presumably going first, and then all the women rose to form a line without any regard to their different affinal statuses. The wife-giver–wife-receiver asymmetry had been transformed, in this buffet, into a simple gender division—men before women.

The man who said grace before the meal was of the Bangun subclan, so he must have been an *anakberu* in this Sinulingga grouping. Although he spoke aloud, and was himself a Protestant, he suggested each should pray also according to his or her own religion. Several Muslim families belong to this group, and there was no pork in the meal.

The business meeting was informal. For some time the group has been working on a genealogy project, but the person charged with the research has not completed the task. People discussed where and when the next gathering would take place, and whether it was time to elect a new chair and secretary. With that, the official business was over, and unstructured conversation resumed once more.

A Neighborhood-based Association: Jakarta, 1989

This group, an *arisan* that meets monthly, has no name and no published membership list. Its members live within walking distance from each other in a working-class neighborhood on Jakarta's east side. Here, simple houses with concrete floors and metal roofs rent for about 30,000 rupiah a month. The water piped into the houses has such a high saline content that water for cooking and drinking has to be bought separately from vendors who go door to door with tins on push carts. Open ditch sewers emit a predictable stench.

A meeting held on a weekday evening began just after dark. No one arrived by car, and in any case there would not have been a place to park in the little street. Although the core of the group was Karo, and the language of the event was primarily Karo, the ethnic composition was quite mixed. The host, a Muslim raised in central Aceh, could hardly speak Karo at all, and his wife was Javanese. Another family had joined by virtue of the woman being Karo, although her husband, who also attended, was Chinese. Another Karo woman was married to a Mandailing Batak. One of the women, probably the most well-to-do of the entire group, had been abandoned by her husband many years ago. Supporting her three children alone, at first by selling fish door to door, she had managed to acquire a shop, her own large house, and several rental houses from her profits. She came that evening accompanied by her cook, a Madurese woman who sat silently and rather glum-looking among the boisterous Karo women. Again, there were few older children or adolescents, although some small, dependent children attended. About thirty persons sat on floor mats in a long, narrow living room that had been emptied of furniture.

Most of the time was taken up with casual visiting and joking. The meal was preceded by a request that we each pray silently on our own, since it was a thoroughly mixed group of Muslims and Christians. One photograph on the wall depicted a son's recent circumcision celebration, and a portrait depicted a daughter dressed in a head veil pinned under her chin. Two young girls, apparently daughters of the host, served everyone or placed serving bowls around for people to pass. After the meal, money was collected to reimburse the host, and a woman acting as secretary entered the *arisan* installments in a ledger. There seemed to be no officers, no chair, and the "business" part of the meeting was quite informal. Persons spoke out as they wanted to, both men and women, and people talked loudly, making frequent jokes. Someone announced news of a member who was ill, and then the group planned how it would celebrate the Independence Day holiday. It decided to gather a little earlier in the afternoon to make *cimpa*, a typical Karo sweet made from rice flour and palm sugar, but otherwise to run the meal and the monthly meeting as usual.

While there were Karo associations in the Medan area as early as the 1920s, the earliest Karo ethnic associations outside North Sumatra of which I found any record go back only to the 1950s. The first one in Jakarta began in 1954 and called itself Karo Sada Kata (One word Karo). As the number of Karo in Jakarta grew, a second all-Karo group, Permaka (an acronym for Karo Society Association), appeared but was short lived. Families in Bandung also formed a group in the 1950s called Sada Perarih (One agreement), while in Yogyakarta, the Karo group called itself Sinuan Buluh (Those who plant bamboo). A group in Semarang, Keluarga Mbuah Page (Prosperous family), has existed since 1963. An all-Karo association called Persatuan Merga Si Lima (The five clan association) still exists in Banda Aceh. The chair of this group said about seventy-five households are on his list, although not all of these live in Banda and not all are regularly active. The group meets every month, rotating among six families whose houses are big enough to accommodate it. Karo students who attend high school or university in Banda, of which there are about one hundred, have their own group. Most of these students board with Karo families. Several years ago the adult group organized a big celebration and dance, bringing in Karo musicians for the event, and drawing Karo from all over Aceh. The chair of this group estimated that about 1,000 people attended.

One of the longest lived and most successful associations in Jakarta is composed of people from the highland village of Batukarang. Smaller associations of people from particular wards of this village or particular descent lines from there have also formed groups, but the whole village is the reference group for a yearly celebration termed *Ngerires*, Batukarang's name for the annual village celebration highlanders observe.[4] A stenciled letter sent in 1989 indicated that the Jakarta group was divided into thirteen sections for the purpose of organizing the event and for raising the millions of rupiah required. Each section, with a designated coordinator, was committed to giving a specified amount of money. The largest section, with forty families, had each family giving 10,000 rupiah for a total of 400,000 rupiah. The smallest section had only ten families, and was pledged to give 50,000 rupiah. The annual Jakarta *Ngerires* party usually entails importing musicians from Sumatra to provide dancing and, judging from newspaper reportage, attracts around two thousand people. A similar event sponsored by people from Berastagi has occurred for the past thirteen years.

Associations of Karo students have formed at universities throughout Indonesia. At Gajah Mada in Yogyakarta, one of the largest universities, there are about four hundred Karo students; at the University of Indonesia, about one hundred. In the latter case, only some forty of these participate regularly in the group's activities. These groups arise partly from the initiative of the students themselves, but usually receive assistance from local Karo families. These student groups usually aim explicitly to transmit Karo traditions, and implicitly, to encourage friendships and marriages with other Karo. The student associations work hardest at transmitting those traditions that have most to do with meeting and courting members of the opposite sex. They sponsor lessons in how to *ertutur*, that is, perform the formulaic interrogation by which two strangers discover their "kinship" relationship. Such groups also teach dancing, especially how to participate in *guro-guro aron*, a courtship dance in which boy-girl pairs alternately advance suggestively and then coyly retreat from each other. Traditionally, village youth organized *guro-guro aron* and invited people from surrounding villages. Today in urban settings, adults, working through associations, organize them.

The origins and activities of adult associations in various cities are often rationalized with reference to this goal of inculcating traditions in the young. A newspaper article about the founding of a Karo association in Riau in 1989 calling itself Merga si Lima stressed its role for adolescents, although its leaders and founders were adult men who worked in the area. Another newspaper report of the founding of a Jakarta organization of seventy families from the region called Kuta Gunung Si Ngalor Lau (near the town of Tiga Binanga) expressed its main purpose as introducing young people to Karo *adat* and providing the opportunity for them to *ertutur* (i.e., get acquainted) with each other.

Newspapers, Seminars, and Performances

Newspapers aimed specifically at a Karo readership (see fig. 7) first appeared in the 1920s. The first, *Sora Karo* (Karo voice) was published in the lowland town of Pancur Batu (then called Arnheimia) during 1923 and 1924. Its editor, Nereh Ginting, was also the leader of an ethnic association called Peserikatan Persadan Karo. Articles urged the importance of education and encouraged readers to convert to a modern religion, although favored neither Christianity nor Islam.

Feeling somewhat challenged by the appearance of this newspaper and the rising nationalism of those years, the missionaries began to publish *Merga*

Fig. 7. Ethnic newspapers

Si Lima in 1923. This was the most long-lived paper in this era, extending through the 1930s, undoubtedly because the mission covered its losses. ("Karo like to read, but they are reluctant to subscribe," a retired journalist commented.) *Merga Si Lima* used the Karo language exclusively, and one article argued for the importance of retaining Karo while people were also learning other languages. The newspaper included very little local news, but did include some national and international news with a decidedly colonial slant. One front page, for example, included a picture of Princess Juliana with her husband wishing her God's blessing on her birthday. Above all, the content was explicitly Christian—Bible lessons, exhortative essays, and church news. Two long articles in 1937 concerned agricultural lessons on how to plant potatoes and citrus trees.

Sendjata Batak (Batak weapon) appeared briefly in Kabanjahe under the editorship of Nurus Ginting Suka. Hendrik Vuurmans (1930), a missionary resident there at the time, characterized this Malay-language paper as "communistic." *Tjermin Karo* (Karo mirror) from the lowland town of Binjei was under the editorship of Mboelgah Sitepu. Appearing twice monthly for five months spanning 1924 and 1925, *Tjermin Karo* used Malay and Karo languages, but once printed a letter from a reader requesting that it publish mostly in Karo, since less than half the Karo people at that time understood Malay. Its motto was *Memajukan Bangsa dan Tanah Air*. In this era *bangsa* most often denoted ethnic group, so the motto would have translated To Advance Ethnic Group and Country. It remained neutral in its position on religion, carrying articles about Islam as well as Christian events, and even a long scholarly article by a Dutchman in Medan (W. H. M. Schadee) explaining Buddhism. It was not an avidly nationalist paper, but in 1925 it carried a series of pieces on the European plantations' violations of contracts with Karo villages over protected lands.

The indigenous press sputtered out for several years before reemerging in the form of *Pandji Karo* (Karo banner) in 1929. Under the leadership of G. Keliat, this paper's articles were all in Karo. It did not take a critical view of the colonial government. On the contrary, articles sometimes pointed to the benefits of Dutch rule and, as its predecessors had done, it promoted education and progress. This paper objectified Karo culture and language in a new, self-conscious way. Its motto encouraged people to cultivate their *adat*. Articles argued that preserving the Karo language was valuable, and one prescribed the proper way to go about arranging a marriage. One editorial encouraged people not to mortgage or sell their land. Another article provided a list of several *gendang* songs that had gone out of style and were seldom heard anymore, along with four that frequently were played at feasts in those days, urging people to use the old songs as well as the new. One contributor bemoaned the fact that friends in school and offices no longer bothered to *ertutur* (construct a kinship relationship). Apparently this paper did not survive very long.

During 1930 and 1931 *Bintang Karo* (Karo star) appeared in Kabanjahe under the editorship of Mahat Singarimbun. Most of its articles were in Indonesian, and it was explicitly nationalistic rather than ethnic in its focus, although one article in 1931 mentioned the jealousy Karo and Simalungun felt when seeing the success of Tapanuli Batak. The paper's editor in chief was not a Karo, and several Chinese were listed as contributors in the masthead. One of the main themes of this paper, as it remains to this day in Karo newspapers, was the importance of education. Apparently, however, the Karo press could not withstand the depression and the years of war and revolution that followed in the 1940s.

Terlong began in a stencil format in Medan in the 1950s, but later moved to Jakarta and assumed a magazine-style format in the 1960s. Most articles used Indonesian, although a few used Karo. The content mixed ethnic news, arts, and literature with national politics. It published political essays such as "Karoland Facing Confrontation," about the Malaysia-Indonesia tensions of that period, as well as news of ethnic clubs and associations, and of a Karo dormitory in Bandung. Short stories and a serialization of the first Karo-language novel (Synulta 1983) also appeared on its pages. (Synulta was on the editorial board.) Masri Singarimbun, who later attained a Ph.D. in anthropology, published his first book, *1,000 Perumpaman Karo* (1,000 Karo proverbs), here in serial form (1960). Articles about *adat* were also common in this magazine. While *Terlong* covers in the early 1960s sometimes showed a fascination with Western culture (Hollywood appeared on one cover, June Allyson on another), by 1964 *Terlong* took on an adamantly nationalistic visage. Covers depicted Sukarno and other heroes of the revolution, and one headline shouted, "Shatter Imperialism! Shatter Neocolonialism!" One essay from this period was called "Building a Socialistic Indonesian Society in Karo," and another discussed the Korean War.

Terlong apparently disappeared with the transition to the New Order, and a new magazine called *Piso Surit* replaced it.[5] The magazine evolved out of a stenciled newsletter of the Greater Jakarta Karo Students Association, calling itself *Buletin Makadjaya* (the association's acronym). This newsletter, beginning in 1970, published news from Karoland and news of Jakarta's ethnic association, Karo Sada Kata, along with essays and poems, usually in Indonesian. The first issue entitled *Piso Surit*, still in stencil format, appeared in 1971, and publication continued through 1979. In the mid-1970s the magazine lost its connection with the student group and became increasingly literary and folkloristic, although articles on *adat* and on politics continued along with some association news, announcements of births and deaths, and subscribers' addresses. One issue printed the recipe for *terites*, a signature Karo dish made from the green, partially digested grasses of a cow's stomach, and a later one gave the recipe for *tasak tiga*, another Karo culinary original. A humorous essay entitled "If Only . . ." once wished "if only there were no Karo who were embarrassed to speak Karo, or if there were no Betawi [Jakartans] who said, 'Horas lah!' [the Toba greeting] to us. . . ." In the late 1970s covers of *Piso Surit*, now a magazine, featured success stories about Karo men whose pictures appeared on several covers. These included a businessman, a politician, an academic, a retired brigadier general war veteran, and a movie star/karate champion.

Finally, in the 1980s, two newspaper-format publications, *Kamka* and *Simaka* appeared in Jakarta. *Simaka*, an acronym for the phrase Karo society communications, appeared from 1985 to 1989. *Kamka*, also an acronym meaning Karo society communications, was even more short-lived, beginning in 1987 and ceasing in 1989. Both were similar in focus and appearance, and both circulated outside Jakarta to Karo in Sumatra and elsewhere. Newsier and less literary than the magazines of the previous decade, *Simaka* began with a front-page masthead showing a picture of a traditional Karo house (or rice barn), and two Karo-language sayings, "Everything is fine for us," and "We are each other." Along the bottom of each front page, also in Karo, was the composite phrase encoding the kinship unity of the society: the Five Clans, the Eight Ways of Being Related, the Three Tied Together. Nevertheless, the paper was written largely in Indonesian. Like its predecessors, its articles covered association activities from all over Indonesia and spotlighted Karo achievers in many fields. News of Karoland, sometimes written by the district head himself, appeared, as did news of GBKP church activities, and to a lesser degree, activities of Karo Muslims and Catholics. Given the recent concern with interethnic marriage, this newspaper included a section called "So That We Can Get Acquainted," featuring pictures, ambitions, hobbies, and addresses of Karo adolescents hoping to meet friends who shared their interests. Advertisements—for bus companies, beauty salons, photographers, music supplies, traditional healers, caterers, and more—took up much of the back page and parts of other pages.

Like ethnic associations, ethnic newspapers start and then die, yet others arise in their place. By 1990, neither *Kamka* nor *Simaka* was being published, but there was talk of reviving *Piso Surit,* and I learned of one retired bureaucrat's hope to start a new paper called *Warga Si Lima* (Five members), which he envisions as blending ethnic and patriotic values. In Sumatra, meanwhile, a new paper called *Jambur* (Men's house) appeared in 1990. With a front page almost identical to *Simaka* in its use of the house motif and familiar sayings, it, too, includes a pen pal section called "Ask Our Relationship." Its content is more literary than *Simaka*'s, with some short stories and poems in Karo in addition to the usual news, *adat,* and editorial articles. While *Simaka,* published in Jakarta, circulated widely wherever Karo live in Indonesia, *Jambur,* published in Medan, is not yet well known in Jakarta. Finally, in 1990 I saw one issue of a paper called *Bina Citra,* which means building images, a multiethnic paper published in Medan. The majority of the staff listed in the masthead are Karo, and one article about Karo *adat* was even printed in the Karo language, but the paper is primarily in Indonesian and includes stories about other Batak peoples as well as Nias. Its motto is To Increase Education and Preserve National Culture, and a front-page article was called "The Younger Generation Lacks Consciousness of Culture." The front-page masthead is repeated on the back page, except that salutations of seven different Sumatran ethnic groups are placed along its bottom border.

Ethnic newspapers and magazines have played a variety of functions over the years. Beginning in the earliest papers of the 1920s and continuing to the present, these publications have encouraged education, not only in exhortative essays, but in picturing and headlining those who earn degrees. In 1988, *Simaka* listed individually all the Medan area college graduates, a list 1,000 names long. Persons who achieve Ph.D.'s or other advanced degrees regularly appear, photographed in the new cap and gown they have earned. Persons in any field who distinguish themselves are held up to inspire a new generation, and also for celebratory ends, as if their achievements reflect well on Karo society as a whole. These papers also index a new age and new ways of living, even as they caution about the need to preserve a tradition. Ironically, articles about preserving Karo language and culture are typically written in Indonesian. Above all, these newspapers have helped to bind a geographically dispersed society into a common communication network. Pictures of big weddings, announcements of deaths, and, in the past, listings of subscriber names and addresses served an important networking function. The recent focus on adolescent readers, especially the space provided for adolescent pen pals and introductions, shows the concern that more and more young people are marrying outside Karo society.

In addition to newspapers, publications of other kinds have been important in defining Karo identity in recent decades. Nalinta Ginting, a bookstore owner in Deli Tua just outside Medan, has published a series of pamphlets or handbook guides on matters of *adat*. With covers showing a traditional house or persons dressed in ceremonial costumes, these little "How to . . ." handbooks of about twenty pages instruct people on the various stages of getting married, or inaugurating a new house.[6] Some explain the outlines of Karo kinship. In a more detached, academic vein is a larger book on the customs and ceremonies of weddings (Bangun 1986a) widely available in ethnology sections of Indonesian bookstores. Two novels and a few novellas, all printed in the Karo language, are either out of print or poorly distributed and difficult to find (Barus 1988; Ginting 1984; Synulta 1978, 1983, 1984) as is Singarimbun's book of 1,000 Proverbs (1960). Some of these literary works have been serialized, some of them more than once, in ethnic newspapers. Historical and cultural analyses of Karo society, all of them in Indonesian, are more widely available than the literary works (Bangun 1986b; Prinst and Prinst 1984; Putro 1981; Sebayang 1986; Tamboen 1952). A fair number of Karo have read or heard the interpretations contained in these and the earlier Dutch works on which they draw. These books on culture, history, and origins are known to the educated elite, but also to a surprising number of others, providing most of what Karo know about their past (see fig. 8).

A new publisher, the Merga si Lima Foundation, based in Jakarta, published seven books in 1990: two general treatises on *adat* (Bangun 1990; Tarigan 1990a); lyrics of the songwriter Djaga Depari (Tarigan 1990b); and five collections of mythical short stories (Barus and Singarimbun 1990a, 1990b; Singarimbun and Barus 1990; Tarigan 1990c, 1990d). The authors, editors, or compilers of all these new works are academics or journalists working from a folkloristic sense of salvage. All live at far remove from the land and life that nurtured the literature and traditions they pursue. These books and those that preceded them freeze *adat*, history, and literature in a way that was not possible decades ago when Karo literacy was still very low.

Part of this same salvage tradition is a series of seminars on *adat*, some of which have also produced publications. The first of these seminars that I know of was held in Kabanjahe in 1958, apparently under the auspices of the local government head. Its resulting publication, a seventy-five-page stenciled book published by a bookstore in Kabanjahe, covers questions of origins and history, kinship, inheritance and tenure law, *gendang*, and ceremonies (Kongres Kebudayaan Karo 1958). I attended a similar event sponsored by the GBKP in 1983 that produced a much larger book of similar scope

Fig. 8. Ethnic scholarship

(GBKP, Moderamen 1983). An *adat* seminar with a forward-looking theme was held in Kabanjahe in September 1985 to discuss questions of adaptation, development, and change (Tarigan 1986). Two topically focused seminars, one on preserving the *adat* house (Warsani, Ginting, and Purba 1989) and another on avoidance customs, were held in Medan in 1989. All these seminars typically entail bringing back Karo scholars who live in Java, and both the one on houses and the one on change have included foreign anthropologists who happened to be in the Medan area for their own research.

Scholarly patronage has become a new way for people to use their wealth for socially esteemed ends. The Merga Si Lima Foundation, for example, which has recently commissioned and published the series of books on culture and literature cited above, draws contributions primarily from a relatively small number of wealthy Jakarta families. It paid some of the authors as well as all of the publication costs. Its charter also lists such goals as sponsoring seminars, lectures, discussions, and performances. It hopes to build a library containing everything ever published about the Karo. While the publications, seminars, and other events thus redound to a sense of ethnic pride, they also reflect the wealth, generosity, and ethnic loyalty of their sponsors.

Clearly, the *adat* seminar has become a tradition in its own right, but it is a tradition of the elite. Participation centers around an intellectual elite, while an economic and political elite serve as sponsors. The book resulting from the 1985 seminar on change, *Karo Culture and Life in the Present Age,* includes an appendix detailing how a delegation traveled to Jakarta and elsewhere to seek contributions to cover the seminar and publication expenses (Tarigan 1986). Another appendix gives a two-page organization chart of those who brought the seminar into being, including thirty-nine advisors, and yet another lists the planning committee's local structure. Each donor and his or her contribution are listed in another appendix. Of 5,672,000 rupiahs collected for this event, one man gave over half of it, and two others gave 500,000 rupiahs or more. The GBKP church was also listed with a 75,000 rupiah donation. The list of thirty-nine advisors, some of whom are listed among the primary sponsors, would be a good start for delineating just who are the elite in contemporary Karo society.

These scholarly or performative events can also become an arena for competition as well as cooperation. One academic, residing in Java, attended the seminar on avoidance in 1989 with his way paid to Medan by a wealthy patron, only to find that this marked him, in other participants' eyes, as part of that patron's "faction." Some of his fellow participants thus declined to hear his paper. Sometimes patrons envision scholarly projects of more narrowly personal value. One scholar told me he had been asked to research the genealogy of a wealthy family.

Seminars almost always include preliminary remarks by government officials of various kinds who express the importance of cultivating and preserving local cultures as a contribution to the nation's heritage. These remarks, and forewords written by other dignitaries, appear in the published results of the seminar. For example, the publication resulting from the seminar in 1985 included an endorsement by the governor of North Sumatra.

On 29 March 1989 a Karo Music and Culture Show took place in Jakarta at the Balai Sidang Senayan. The printed program included endorsements by no less than Indonesia's Minister of Education and Culture, the Governor of North Sumatra, and the Bupati of Karoland, men whose status reflects both the weight of the event and the connections of its organizing committee. The event was organized primarily by an ad hoc women's group calling itself Pernanden Merga si Lima (Mothers of the five clans, or Persima in shortened form), the leaders of which were from well-to-do families. Advertisements in the program, two of them in color, also helped defray some expenses. Tickets started at 3,000 rupiah and went as high as 100,000. The show included traditional music and dance (some 150 boys and girls were recruited into this production), a dramatization, a fashion show of clothing made from traditional textiles, and Karo pop music. The drama depicted a fictional scene from history: some salt haulers on their way to Karoland accidentally scare up an evil spirit in the forest through which they are passing, and, therefore, seek the help of a *guru* who instructs them to perform an *Erpangir ku Lau* (Hairwashing) ceremony as palliative. The well-organized committee that arranged this event assigned volunteers tasks such as working on tickets, transportation, decoration, promotion, documentation, and props and equipment. The committee members, wearing matching sarongs and pink *kebaya*, posed for a group picture at the event by a professional photographer. In the next month, April 1989, a similar event was held in Bandung, and, in June 1989, one took place in Medan.

Conclusions

Karo ethnic identity is no mere archaic survival, but rather, like any identity, "an on-going process, politically contested and historically unfinished" (Clifford 1988, 9). Nor is it possible to reduce this process to a single contest or a single impetus. One impetus, surely, is the quest for honor and worth in a world where there are competing standards of what constitutes worth, and where Karo are partly at the mercy of outsiders who have ideas about what certain identity labels (such as Batak, Karo, or Christian) mean. *Batak* probably began as a derogatory term and it remains so from Malay and Javanese perspectives. From the Karo perspective, the term *Batak* is further clouded by its association with Toba, and by the conflict and competition between Toba and Karo dating at least from the colonial period and continuing into the present.

On the whole, Karo society, both rural and urban, has fared relatively well since the colonial era began if one compares Karo by income and education with other ethnic groups in Indonesia. Education, wealth, success, and power are not evenly distributed, however, and it is not the poorest Karo who wave the ethnic banners, or who worry most about the Batak moniker. Ethnic pride and ethnic politics most concern those at the middle and top of Karo society, an elite that does not live in Karoland for the most part, although it keeps in frequent contact with kin and with activities there. Traditional pressures on the wealthy to be generous through feasting continue, but generosity has acquired some additional forms. One can become a benefactor of projects the ethnic community deems worthwhile—publications, seminars, performances, and projects of the ethnic church. Traditional largess was internal, limited to one's neighbors and kin within a rather small radius. The audience for ethnic displays is now society wide and also external to the Karo. Events and projects that bring Karo society into the view of outsiders also build "big-man" reputations inside the Karo community for those who sponsor and organize these projects.

What is the state's role in these processes shaping Karo identity? The requisite forewords by government or military officials in publications about *adat* and history, and the opening speeches by government officials at ethnic performances and displays, legitimate ethnic pride as patriotism. The more elaborate the display, the higher the officials who sanction the project. Thus the Karo Culture and Music night in Jakarta merits a comment from the Minister of Education and Culture, while a seminar in Kabanjahe will have only local officials of that ministry in attendance, and perhaps the district head or a military figure. The presence of these men of state legitimates cultivating and celebrating one's local tradition. Publications and performances on *adat* are rationalized as a contribution to preserving and shaping a viable, indigenous national culture even when, in the case of the publication aiming to de-Batak the Karo, the content is at the same time expressly ethnopolitical. The government's role in ethnic events resembles what political scientists term *corporatism*—a coaptation of groups that both legitimates and limits those groups' activities. In one sense, "groups" in this instance are only temporary, event-focused committees, but they are the government's point of articulation with or its handle on the unwieldy and unpredictable entity that is Karo society as an ethnic community.

The discourse about ethnicity must conform to certain unstated rules. Ethnic pride is acceptable; ethnic politics betray the ideal of national unity. One cannot speak publicly against other ethnic groups, intimate that competition between ethnic groups exists, or suggest that ethnicity negatively influences one's economic opportunities. When these negative aspects surface privately, people mention the ideals of the Pancasila for unity and harmony. Ethnic pride and ethnic feelings, while not exactly consonant with the nationalist ideology that guards against *sukuisme* (tribalism), have the scope to operate in the private sector as long as people's activities are merely social, such as the ethnic associations, or can be construed as preserving national culture, as in the seminars and performances. The ethnic newsletters perform both social and preservative functions, but, in the forest-naming incident and the Batak issue, exhibit frankly political functions that betray the competitive, conflictual side of ethnic politics. Perhaps because their circulation is limited to Karo, however, these papers do not attract the sanctions of the state.

The incident of naming the forest preserve enlightens us in another way about the workings of the larger ethnic community vis-à-vis the state. When the issue was important enough, emissaries converged in Jakarta to lobby the ethnic cause at the highest pinnacles of power. These lobbyists were successful in this instance, I suspect, because officials are sensitive to what Liddle terms *anticipated participation,* that is, the threat of violence or further outcry. Those in power at the center correctly read both the lobbying and the vandalism as a thermometer of how significant this symbolic issue was, and crafted a solution to avert an ethnic conflagration.

Notes

1. Usman Pelly, an anthropologist in Medan, writing about "Women in the Batak Cultural System," in a newspaper article in *Sinar Indonesia Baru* (October 1986) uses the term *sub-etnik* to refer to the different Batak peoples.
2. This would have been especially odd considering that Karoland was formerly a PKI stronghold and the Super Semar order to exterminate the communists brought months of terror to the area.
3. Cf., Bruner's work (1959, 1961, 1963, 1972a, 1972b, 1974) on Toba Batak associations in urban Indonesian settings.

4. If Payung Village is typical, these annual festivals were part of the rice cycle. *Ngerires* is named after the special food served at the Batukarang event, a peppery glutinous rice steamed in bamboo over outdoor cooking pits.

5. This name refers to a bird (named onomatopoeically after its own twitter), but also to a song by Djaga Depari that became a Karo pop classic.

6. See also Rodgers (1984) on the analogous phenomenon in Angkola Batak.

Chapter 9

Christianity, Ethnicity, and Class

Conversion to Islam in the precolonial period implied and often entailed a change in ethnic-political loyalty. Karo resisted Islam in the precolonial era despite incursions from their Acehnese and Malay neighbors. Similarly, in the colonial period, conversion to Christianity was widely viewed by Karo as a statement of loyalty to the Dutch. It retains that connotation for some non-Christians.

> [7 September 1973. Payung village. Conversation with a young Christian woman.] She recalled an incident that had happened when she was a child. Another little girl had asked if she was going to join a religion some day, and R. replied that she would become a Christian, thinking of an older married sister who lived in Medan and had become a Christian. The other little girl replied that she would be a Christian, too, but that her mother would surely be mad. When R. asked why, the friend explained that her mother had always told her that Christianity was brought by the Dutch, but Islam was here before that. Islam was not brought by humans, her friend had explained, but came from God, and was the belief of our ancestors.

The political entailments of Islam and then Christianity explain why Karo were not attracted to either of these world religions. By remaining "Batak," Karo retained a sense of political autonomy and cultural distinctiveness from their powerful Muslim neighbors. By not claiming the missionaries' religion, they registered their resistance to colonial domination.

Karo resisted the universalistic religions also because their traditional religion provided a sense of control, solace, and meaning. The uncentralized, diffuse, amoral supernatural powers of the traditional religion once reflected a political order of like dimensions (Kipp 1990, 121–36), but incorporation into the colonial polity changed Karo experiences of power. The amoral, fragmented powers of Perbegu no longer match people's experience of concentrated state power, of class stratification, and of moralistic nationalism. Since 1950 Karo have moved to the cities in great numbers. As they moved away from the smoking volcanoes and large trees associated with threatening spirits, away from the graves and shrines that housed ancestor bones and relics, these spirits and ancestors seemed less and less real or relevant (Kipp 1986b). The traditional religion was an integral part of a total way of life that no longer exists. The migrants' experiences in new social orders and their expanded worldview raised new questions of meaning and morality, and the universalistic religions increasingly provided the answers.

In today's postcolonial cities, maintaining the traditional religion is not a viable option, for reasons both political and spiritual. Indonesia's nationalist ideology equates *agama* with good citizenship and modernity. Especially, the government deems religious citizens as more immune to social ills such as communism (Cohen 1992, 29). The seances, rain callings, hairwashings, and spirit shrines of village life would appear hopelessly backward and old-fashioned in the cities, but also slightly rebellious. Pancasila ideology denigrates all traditional religions, while giving legitimacy to a variety of modern religions.

Indonesian independence and Pancasila ideology have thus changed the political connotations of what conversion to Christianity or Islam means. With the Dutch out of the power equation, Karo who opted for Christianity could retain their distinctiveness from the Muslim majority, maintaining their cultural autonomy while being guaranteed legitimacy as national citizens. A majority of the Karo today identify themselves with Christianity—a minority faith in the national context. In this sense, religious faith continues to serve as an ethnic flag, even if religion no longer clearly defines or delimits what *Karo* and *Batak* mean.

Wealth differences challenge communities of faith, as they do communities based on kinship and ethnicity. This is nowhere more obvious than in the Gereja Batak Karo Protestan (GBKP), the Karo Batak Protestant church, not only the largest single religious body in Karo society, but the largest organization of any kind under which Karo unite or have ever united. The GBKP has long faced competition from other Christian groups, most noticeably from Pentecostal groups. The GBKP's effective style of organization and its ability to capitalize on the talents and philanthropy of its wealthy and well-educated leaders are both its great strengths and its Achilles' heel. Poorer Karo, especially, find the bureaucratic character of the church spiritually dry, so turn instead to more emotional styles of Christianity for their religious needs.

The Ethnic Church: Gereja Batak Karo Protestan

When the GBKP was formed in 1941 it claimed only 5,000 members, a small minority of the population.[1] The mission from which it emerged had begun in 1890, but conversions were slow, Karo explain now, because of Christianity's association with the colonial masters. The chaos of the war years, first the Japanese occupation and then the fight for independence, fostered uncertainty and fear for many Christian Karo. One former mission teacher recalls destroying a photograph of himself in company of some missionaries, fearing that during the Revolution people would take this as evidence of his siding with the Dutch.[2] There were, in fact, few casualties of Karo Christians on account of suspected Dutch sympathies.

The missionaries had given their indigenous teachers and evangelists little chance to learn about the administrative work of running a church. Karo Christians were not allowed to attend discussions of budgets and personnel, for example, nor allowed to see records of such discussions. They probably had little sense of record keeping, of the conflicts and power struggles among the missionaries and within the mission organization, and little understanding of how the missionaries arrived at the decisions they did. The missionaries to the Karo had also been slow to train indigenous workers for the ministry. Evangelists and religious teachers led Sunday services, but were not allowed to perform marriages and administer communion. Nonetheless, when the Europeans were interned by the Japanese in 1942, the indigenous workers took over management of the mission. Two formative synods of the GBKP were held in 1941 and 1943. Two young men who were studying for the ministry at Sipoholon at the time became the first ordained ministers of the new church. With independence, the GBKP reestablished relations with the mission organization in Holland, but maintained an independent status. Some strain apparently continues to mark relationships with the Dutch: in recent years, the church has received more attention and help from German rather than Dutch sources, and none of several foreign workers with the GBKP in 1986 were Dutch.

As the oldest Christian community among the Karo, and as the largest single religious body in Karoland, the GBKP is the establishment church. Compared to any other religious organization there, it commands a wealth of property, owning about thirty-five church buildings in Karoland alone, and running twenty-seven government-accredited schools from primary through high school. The GBKP has long maintained an orphanage at Suka-makmur, and it recently opened a special education facility in Kabanjahe. A two-story office building was completed in Kabanjahe in 1987 near a conference complex for holding seminars and courses. The church maintains a similar conference center, used especially for women's activities, in Berastagi. In the 1980s the GBKP opened a dormitory to accommodate sixty high school and college students who attend various institutions in Medan. The church publishes a quarterly magazine, along with music and other literature for church activities, and runs a bookstore in Kabanjahe. Most of the funding for this and for the church's activities comes from internal collections rather than external sources of aid, but the church leadership continually seeks and receives government and international funds for building and for other projects.

[20 July 1983. Kabanjahe.] On Monday I arrived at the Moderamen office, the organizational center of the GBKP, to find Pdt. Ginting Suka, the head of the church, making last minute preparations for his trip to Vancouver for the World Council of Churches meeting. He was preparing a grant proposal to be sent to the Netherlands, and asked me to help him with the English. He was working on a letter of rationale to accompany the budget. He dictated the letter in Karo, I translated it into English. (He tried first in Indonesian, but switched to Karo at my request. He said he *thinks* of such things in Indonesian.) His grantsmanship was clear. He told me he could not ask for money simply to evangelize without also saying the church was going to do something about development, so the letter included a paragraph about courses in nutrition and animal husbandry, and about building water supply systems in villages.

The GBKP has been working with local government officials to persuade them to help with the preparations for the 100-year anniversary celebration of the GBKP (seven years away, in 1990). Yesterday A. and I traveled in a GBKP landrover with several men from the Moderamen to a ribbon-cutting ceremony in Buluh Hawar, site of the first mission post, to celebrate the opening of a new road and bridges into this rugged, back-woods region. Delegates from the office of the Governor of North Sumatra were there, and also the Bupati of Deli-Serdang, where Buluh Hawar is located. These and other government dignitaries were feted with choir songs and a meal. A *gendang* played for dancing, and the dignitaries received traditional Karo cloths. Numerous speeches interlaced these presentations and performances, and we went to view the grave of Sara Tampenawas, a Minahassa woman who died in service to the mission in 1892.

While celebrating the government's completion of a road part of the way to Buluh Hawar, this ceremony also aimed to spur the government to complete the road in anticipation of the GBKP's 100-year anniversary. Citing the expected arrival in Buluh Hawar of international visitors for this event, speakers also sought government funds for refurbishing the grave monument and the church.

Organization is one of the GBKP's great strengths, both internal organization, and its links to powerful outside parties. The GBKP was one of the first members of the Dewan Gereja-Gereja Indonesia, a national-level body of the World Council of Churches. There are some fifty members of this national body (now called the Perkesatuan Gereja-Gereja Indonesia, or PGI), and in 1986 representatives of the several North Sumatra churches in this group met at the GBKP conference center in Berastagi to talk about ecumenical efforts in evangelization. The GBKP has ties with several other church or mission organizations based in Europe and America, and it cooperates in a district-level ecumenical group of nine member churches.

Internally, the GBKP is a highly centralized body, yet one that involves a large number of people in leadership at the local congregational level. The whole church is represented in the Synode (synod), which meets only every five years. Meetings of the Synode make decisions on a one-person, one-vote basis, and members pride themselves on the egalitarian nature of these meetings. The working heart of the church, its real power center, remains in Kabanjahe, at the offices of the Moderamen. A handful of Moderamen officers, with a staff of twenty-three people, supervises the placement of personnel, education and other services, publications, and the financial affairs of the church. At the next level, the church is divided into eleven regional *Klasis* (districts). Karoland has three Klasis, the Medan area, two. The Klasis centered in Jakarta includes not only the twelve congregations in that city, but six others throughout Java. Congregations are not autonomous with regard to their pastors, but must take whomever the Synode assigns to them, or do without if there is none. Communications from the Synode, Klasis, or Moderamen are announced after Sunday services. A constant round of seminars, conferences, training courses, meetings, and programs of other kinds involve all ages and all sectors of the church.

Women's activities have especially flowered in recent years. A women's organization called Moria has existed for about forty years, descended from sewing clubs for women and girls in the Dutch era, when missionary wives taught home economics as well as religious study. Since 1978 a German woman has been working with the Moria organization, encouraging women (who make up as much as two-thirds of the congregation in many places) to be more assertive in their roles in the church. Moria groups meet weekly for a devotional, and at special conferences members learn new songs, produce dramas and entertainments, learn how to make instructional materials and visual aids for Sunday schools, how to lead Bible study groups, and how to form rotating credit organizations. In the larger churches, Moria groups also form choirs.

Another German woman has been working during the same period to develop the Sunday school and other programs for children. Both Moria and the Sunday schools use a set of regularly published instructional materials. The word puzzles, cartoon figures, and bright art that enliven the larger GBKP Sunday schools contrast with the spare Indonesian schoolrooms where children spend their weekdays, and where instructional materials are usually limited to a blackboard, paper and pencils, and small paperback books. Congregations in cities devote special effort to interest teenagers in activities such as choirs and social outings.

Small groups of adults within each congregation meet weekly in homes for prayer and study meetings called *perpulungen jabu-jabu* (family gatherings). Like Moria meetings, these devotionals proceed from published lessons that specify scripture readings for the week and provide discussion leaders with guidelines. Participants share their insights and interpretations of the verses. Women's groups and the family devotionals always include prayers, songs, and a collection. The host or hostess also serves drinks and a snack. Some GBKP members thus attend three services a week—Sunday, family gathering, and either a Moria or a youth choir practice. Other activities happen erratically. For example, the congregation or the *perpulungen jabu-jabu* groups organize visits to the homes of the sick or bereaved to pray and sing with them and offer support. In a highland village, I once accompanied a church group hoping to reconcile a quarrel between a husband and wife.

These weekly discussions, starting with a Bible passage, working through its exegesis, and moving into its moral implications, were thoroughly familiar to me, having been raised in a Protestant environment, but such events are like nothing in the Karo tradition. The traditional religion is ritual-focused rather than text-focused, and morality is only implicitly embedded within this religion rather than explicitly and continually drawn up for examination. Above all, the traditional religion was not singled out *as* religion, but was one strand in a social fabric that encompassed a whole, relatively homogeneous, residential community.

Community, even in highland villages, is much more complex these days than it used to be. This new religion, thoroughly rationalized as such, provides signposts for individuals who have to think their way through moral dilemmas in a world where neighbors follow other religious signposts and other cultural traditions, and where community is not based on common residence.

[19 July 1989. Bandung, West Java.] I attended a Moria meeting with the minister and his wife. There are several neighborhood-based Moria sections in this city, but today's meeting was a regularly scheduled gathering of representatives from all the sections. The event started at 3:15 in the afternoon and ended three hours later. Some thirty women sat in a ring around the edges of a large room that had been spread with mats. The house was very spacious, and also had a good-sized yard. Everyone arrived in cars, although many had shared rides rather than driven themselves.

The reading for the week was from Nehemiah, some verses about honesty that the hostess read aloud. Representative speakers from each section, introduced by the minister's wife, began the discussion by reflecting aloud on the verses, and then the minister spoke, and I was asked to say something. After this formal beginning, the discussion opened into a more conversational format, and the talk was lively. How do you reconcile the value of honesty with the danger of hurting people's feelings or inciting arguments? Should you tell someone when you think her jewelry and makeup are overdone? Does your husband have to know how much you paid for your new sarong? I was struck by how well several of the women spoke, and by how entertaining and yet serious the discussion was. People raised difficult ethical situations, and the group considered what would be right in that instance, comic relief intruding now and then into our moral quests.

At some point, the discussion got into economic issues. The question was why more women do not come to the Moria meetings. They mentioned how people used to think nothing of walking some distance; now everyone expects to ride. People say, "If I had a car, I would come to church," but is that a valid excuse? As for Moria, some women are frank about not wanting to foot the bill for the snacks and drinks. (And perhaps do not have houses that can hold a gathering of thirty people.)

Like the Dutch tradition that spawned it, the GBKP emphasizes the requirement for education in its leaders. *Pendeta* (Karo, *pandita*), ministers, have to have a university education and four years of seminary. Presently there are about 100 ordained ministers, or about one for every 2,000 church members, but also an additional 35 evangelists and teachers, both men and women, who are not required to have the full university and seminary training. Many of the smaller, rural congregations do not have a resident minister, but use visiting ministers, or else one of the congregation elders presents a sermon using a text and guidelines issued from the Synode. In all locales,

GBKP ministers use the same sermon guidelines, so the content of sermons on any Sunday is similar throughout GBKP congregations. While there is no official restriction on ordaining women, all the ministers are men. In fact, two ministers who are leading officers in the Moderamen are married to ordained ministers of the Menado church, but a nepotism ruling has prevented their wives from serving the GBKP as clergy. Both these women remain active in teaching and other activities, however.

The tone of GBKP services is reverent and staid, orderly, controlled, and relatively hierarchical. Pendeta wear vestments when they preach, and carry out a liturgy that begins with a reminder of sin and the need to ask forgiveness, includes a unison credo such as the Apostles' Creed, and a unison Lord's Prayer. The content of sermons tends to emphasize issues of faith and morality rather than hell and condemnation. The pendeta remains an elevated figure, beneath which a corps of elders and deacons—male and female—helps with the vestments, takes collections, and makes announcements. The service and the announcements have a scripted quality. Very little is impromptu. Many of the larger churches hold two Sunday morning services—at 8:00 and 10:00. The greater popularity of the early one stems from the fact that in this age, when schools and offices regulate people's weekly schedule, Sunday has become the favorite day for weddings and other family celebrations. People can thus attend an early service and also meet these obligations.

The larger churches support choirs, either youth groups or women's groups, that perform in the services. The GBKP has published a new hymnal to consolidate an old one with some addenda published separately at various times. The original GBKP hymns were about fifty in number, and through the years addenda have quadrupled that amount. The older songs from the Dutch tradition are invariably sung at a pace that strikes a Westerner as grindingly slow. Some of the newer songs, many from American Christian traditions, are sung somewhat faster, and have tended to replace the older hymns. One pendeta and his wife remarked how you could date someone's entry in the church by whether they knew the original fifty hymns, as some of the newer members know only the ones in the addenda. The new hymnal cover has a picture of a Karo drum and oboe (*sarune*) superimposed over a cross, showing how far thinking has come since the use of the *gendang*, prior to 1966, was prohibited to GBKP members (GBKP, Team Penelitian 1976).[3] A church musician in Jakarta who has studied in Germany has begun to compose some new hymns that follow chord progressions of traditional Karo songs. Ironically, the mission first introduced the Karo to the aesthetics of

Western music (Kipp 1990, 164); now the GBKP wants to introduce Karo music into the church.

Like the other churches or religious groups in Karo society, the GBKP benefited from the G30S aftermath of terror. Mass conversions and baptisms took place throughout Karoland in the period 1965–70. In 1966 the GBKP had 33,240 members, in 1968 it listed 77,294, and by 1970 was up to 100,000 (Grothaus 1970). As reported elsewhere in Indonesia, this flight to religion was not an uncoordinated, grassroots response by people hoping to dupe the authorities into thinking their religiosity precluded attraction to communism. Indeed, the authorities themselves helped effect these mass conversions. The Indonesian Council of Churches organized the evangelization team in the Karo area, which was headed by the commander of the North Sumatra military and the Governor of North Sumatra. Some 1,500 lay Christians made up the "team," which consisted of full choirs and brass bands (Pederson 1970, 190). The Council and the GBKP then organized follow-up visits to consolidate people's decisions. None of these mass baptisms were spur-of-the-moment reactions, since the GBKP requires candidates to study for one year prior to baptism. In recent years, too, again benefiting from the political climate that has pushed more and more Karo to join one of the official religions, the GBKP has grown in numbers and strength. Evangelization trips today sometimes give out medicine as an aid to attracting an audience. The educational and social services of the GBKP also probably have some recruitment value. Teams of young people have been organized now and then to carry out special projects such as building public latrines or water systems in villages. In 1989 the church claimed over 205,000 members (in 559 congregations), less than half of which lived in Karoland proper (GBKP, Panitia Jubileum 100 Tahun 1990).

The GBKP is an explicitly ethnic church, and this is its source of attraction for many Karo.

[28 March 1974. Medan. Conversation with a Christian academic.] We talked about the Karo becoming Christian. He said it was harder to get people to be Christian in the highlands than in the cities. If Karo go to the cities, they will join the church. Karo are timid (*percik-cik*). Afraid to face things alone, they look for other Karo in the city, and the place they find them is at the [GBKP] church. That is why the old religion dies in the cities. Karo are ashamed (*mela*) to hold seances in the cities, and yet also afraid to live on their own. This is what impels people into the church.

The GBKP follows a deliberate policy to establish new congregations in cities or urban neighborhoods with only a handful of resident Karo in place, hoping that the group will attract new migrants as they arrive and that the congregation will grow from the initial kernel. A minister who studied and worked in Yogyakarta many years said that students and others came to the GBKP meetings in that university city who had not before been in the church or been particularly active. Homesick students or migrants, hungry for the company of those who speak their own language, find attending the GBKP a kind of homecoming. The church in Yogyakarta also organized cultural performance evenings featuring traditional music and dance. In the cities, the GBKP became a magnet for migrant Karo, a place where Karo was spoken and where one could count on finding friends and kin. Thus, in the postwar period, the church's fastest growth was not in Karoland itself, but in the Medan area and, later, in Jakarta.

In the highlands, almost all services and songs are in the Karo language, including those in Sunday school. The Bible, hymns, and some other church literature are available in the Karo language. In 1983 the New Testament was issued in a modern translation using "everyday" Karo language, and in 1987 a new translation of the whole Bible was published (Pustaka Si Badia 1987). The original translation of the Bible into Karo, first completed by the missionary Neumann decades ago, contains many anachronisms that people no longer understand. Hoping to keep the Karo language vital in the face of constant seepage from Malay, Neumann purposefully selected glosses for difficult concepts from archaic or rare Karo lexemes, even if it meant giving their meanings a new twist. But Indonesian (Malay) vocabulary has continued to displace Karo words or to supplement Karo vocabulary. The new translation reflects these changes. Just as the modern English translation of the Bible has never replaced the King James version in the hearts of many English speakers, Karo remark that the new version, for all its clarity, does not sound quite as "holy" as the old.

Christian adults have often told me that they always pray in Karo, since no second language feels as satisfying for this purpose. But many of these people now have children whose command of Karo is rudimentary at best. In Medan and Jakarta congregations, Sunday schools are held in Indonesian, otherwise the message would be lost on the students, and one Sunday in each month the sermon is in Indonesian as well. Even so, finding Christian services in Indonesian for their children has been one incentive for some GBKP families to move their membership to other churches.

What is the use of an ethnic church for those who have lost their ethnicity?

I posed that question to a GBKP minister in the middle of a conversation about how young people in the cities do not understand Karo language and culture. He pointed out the many ecumenical connections of the GBKP, indicating that should the day ever come when ethnicity did not constitute a meaningful basis for a church, the way was being paved for joining with other churches into some new kind of grouping. Church leaders are well aware of the paradox of the ethnic church in the city—that it draws the first-generation migrants, but that it speaks only with difficulty to the second generation. The diminishing cultural markers in the urban context explain the ethnic church's sponsorship of the *adat* seminar I attended in 1983, its encouraging the composition of hymns with traditional melodies, and its other efforts to cultivate traditional arts and customs. The magazine of the church, *Maranatha*, often contains articles on Karo culture or *adat*, and on reconciling Christian faith with *adat* practice (see fig. 9).

The GBKP also continues to grow in the cities, and in the outer corners of Karoland that have been relatively isolated in the past. There, where children still learn Karo as a first language and many older people still have an imperfect command of Indonesian, the fact that the GBKP operates in the Karo language is a big advantage over other Christian groups, most of which evangelize in Indonesian. A Medan newspaper in 1983 carried an article and photograph describing the baptism of 140 people from the village of Juhar who were entering the GBKP. Another pioneer region for the church remains the backwoods regions of Deli-Serdang and Langkat, lowland areas where the Dutch missionaries worried about the inroads of Islam into areas predominantly Karo and where the GBKP has faced the same geographical and political impediments that stymied the missionaries in this region.

More than straddling a linguistically and culturally divided society, a society both urban and rural, the GBKP straddles an increasingly class-stratified society. Two ministers in Jakarta, speaking with me after a Sunday service in the oldest Karo congregation in the city, admitted that many Karo do not attend the GBKP services because they are not comfortable about the wealth differences that mark members of the congregation, or because not having an automobile makes transportation difficult, and they hate to ask others for rides. The common bond pulling people to the GBKP is ethnicity, a bond that brings together people whose daily lives are separated by neighborhood, income, and life-style. Wealth differences among Karo can be ignored in weekday life, but on Sunday, some people arrive at the urban churches in chauffeured Mercedes, while others arrive in pedicabs.

Authority in the GBKP exacerbates these wealth differences. Leadership

Fig. 9. Publications of the ethnic church

positions in local congregations tend to go to those who are well-educated, wealthy, or politically powerful. In highland villages, this means that elders and deacons, elected positions within each congregation, are often teachers or other government employees. These men and women have the best educations in the village, and also enjoy the benefits of a salary in addition to their farming income. In the Jakarta congregation mentioned above, several of the deacons and elders are people who constitute a society-wide elite, whose names would be known to Karo everywhere. Leaders of functional groups within the church follow the same pattern. The woman who heads the Moria organization for the Java Klasis is the widow of Jamin Gintings, and the woman who heads the Moria in Sumatra is married to the head of the church and is herself an ordained minister. This correlation of leadership with wealth and education is only a tendency; any group of congregation or Moria leaders will usually contain some men and women of average or even poor means.

The requirements of dressing as a church leader can also be financially burdensome, especially for women. Moria choirs wear matching sarongs and blouses, and fix their hair in a gigantic false bun low on the head, the formal style for women that is pan-Indonesian. Installing these hairpieces, complete with jeweled combs and decorative pins, requires a trip to the hairdresser for many women (especially if they have short hair that has to appear as if pulled back in a bun), and the close-fitting, see-through lace blouses require an expensive brassiere that extends to the waist. Tightly wrapped sarongs and dress-up slippers limit locomotion to mincing steps. Climbing in and out of public transportation in the cities is almost impossible in this dress costume. Women in the Medan churches, if elected to the position of elder, are expected to dress in this "traditional" (i.e., Indonesian) style every Sunday. A woman elder married to a Medan doctor arrives at church in her family's automobile, but she complained, nonetheless, that the requirement for elders to dress this way was *kolot* (old-fashioned). The Jakarta congregations do not require traditional dress of women elders, but since wealth differences in these congregations are often great, and since elders and deacons often perform tasks or make announcements in front of the congregation, pride about their clothing probably restrains some poorer members from assuming leadership roles.

Like the ethnic newspapers, the ethnic church encourages and celebrates the accomplishments of individuals who succeed. In turn, the church benefits from those achievements by tapping these people as leaders and benefactors. In 1990 I attended a *perpulungen jabu-jabu* in Medan in a university neighborhood. One of the members of that group was a candidate for a dean's position, and one woman prayed that if it be God's will, this man might attain that position. "We are but a small people," she said in her prayer, as if this man's achievements and ambitions were all the more remarkable for his ethnic origins. In 1981, when Atar Sibero became the Director General of Area Development, a division with the Department of the Interior, his congregation in Jakarta held a special thanksgiving service in midweek. In 1990, when the Jakarta Klasis was anticipating building a new church and offices, Sibero was on the fund-raising committee and spoke at the ground breaking. The chair of that committee, who also spoke at the ceremony, was a wealthy manufacturer. In the same year, Sibero chaired the committee for the GBKP's 100th anniversary celebration.

Committees for planning and raising the funds for buildings or events are inevitably headed by community or society elites. This fund-raising tactic of forefronting wealthy or prominent men and women as leaders is, of course, a common strategy of philanthropy everywhere. In many cases their membership on these committees is largely honorary, although they may be asked to give a speech at the ground breaking or at the event for which funds were raised. Their names appear in the published programs or in letters requesting funds, and they contribute a disproportionate share of the donations that are collected, although the legwork and administrative organization of a fund drive or of a planning committee comes from the Moderamen or the clergy on the Klasis staff.

In April 1990 the GBKP marked its 100th anniversary with several days of celebration. This event, the Jubileum, was by all accounts (I did not personally witness this event) a remarkable display of ethnicity and power. If any single occasion has ever drawn more Karo together in one place, I do not know of it, and no one I asked could name any. The celebration of a pointedly ethnic church, the Jubileum drew attention to Karo ethnic identity and proclaimed a common history, specifically the historical event of the founding of a mission. But the Jubileum also demonstrated the power, organization, and resources of the largest institution in Karo society. Of some 600,000 to 800,000 Karo, over 200,000 are GBKP members. Estimates are that 100,000 people converged for the Jubileum, including planeloads that flew from Jakarta and elsewhere.

Planning and fund-raising began a full decade in advance. During the entire Jubileum year, celebrations marked all levels of the church, as congregations and functional groups mounted their own commemorative moments. (I attended one of these congregation-based celebrations in the lowland village of Namo Rambe in September 1990.) The original plans to hold the all-GBKP celebration in Buluh Hawar did not work out, probably because of the logistics of getting in and out of that village. Instead, special grounds were constructed at Sukamakmur, located just off the main road between Medan and Karoland, about an hour's drive from the city, where the GBKP orphanage is located. The landscaped grounds of the orphanage formed the entryway, land was purchased and cleared about a half mile behind the orphanage, and a road was constructed to the site. Temporary pavilions for sheltered seating, kiosks to sell commemorative souvenirs (a calendar, a decorative plate, a trophy, and buttons), and a stage were erected there, and for a lasting monument, a large statue of several figures raising a cross. Carved below the statue is the Jubileum motto, Here am I Lord, use me. Now left standing in the middle of nothing, this statue will remain to decorate a conference center, or perhaps a museum, according to current plans. Nearby is a proposed retirement community, and its first houses were under construction in 1990. Contests, an auction, and sales of commemorative items helped raise funds in addition to the collections taken in church services. Some donors gave enormous contributions. Both the statue and a new archway at the entrance on the highway were financed by the same benefactor, a wealthy Jakarta businessman.

One of the high points, according to those who recounted the event for me, was a theatrical production depicting the founding and early years of the mission. Professional actors from Jakarta were contracted to perform this two-hour drama that took place on the first day of the three-day event, drawing an estimated 20,000 people. Present for the main event two days later were the usual government dignitaries, as well as European and American missionaries who had had some association with the church since Independence. Despite the planning and preparation, the Jubileum committee was not prepared for the 100,000 who arrived for that ceremony. Stories people told me about the event described failed attempts to rendezvous with family members, or to get close to the kiosks and the stage because of the press of the crowds. Cars were parked along the highway for miles, meaning that people had to walk that distance to the site, and then walk the half mile to the ceremonial field along a rough, gravel road, a physical hardship for women choir members, mummified in tight sarongs and long-line brassieres and teetering on small-heeled slippers.

For all its grandeur and size, the Jubileum did not unite all Karo in a moment of ceremonial solidarity. Muslims and Hindu Karo were not there, nor were the Catholics and other Karo Christians who do not belong to the GBKP. Those trying to purge Karo identity of the Batak label were also not happy about the event, although the leader of this movement is a GBKP member. The GBKP institutionalizes the Batak designation and brings it constantly into prominence, so the movement has lobbied forcefully for the church to reconstruct its title without the word *Batak* in it. The GBKP leadership, after deliberating about the issue, decided for now to keep the church's name intact. Blaming the Dutch for pasting the Batak moniker on the Karo in the first place, one leader of this movement was chagrined that the *mission*'s founding rather than the church's birth was the focus of this anniversary. He would date the church's anniversaries from 1941, he said, when the first synod of the independent church came in to being, not from 1890 when the Dutch missionaries began their work.

Pentecostals and Other Christians

As everywhere else, Protestants in Karoland are split into numerous denominations. In 1986 the Protestant section of the Departemen Agama in Kabanjahe listed twenty Protestant organizations operating in Kabupaten Karo. Two of these are other ethnic churches ministering to the Simelungun (6,541 members) and Toba Batak (5,523 members) who live in Karoland. Adventists had a following of over 2,000 in 1986, and the Methodists, many of whom are Chinese, about the same number. Eleven of the twenty churches fall into the Pentecostal grouping. The smallest of these Pentecostal groups had only 30 members, another had only 100. The Protestant section of the Departemen Agama staff in Kabanjahe told me that in the interest of "quality," Indonesia was no longer allowing the formation of new Protestant churches. At that time, there were about 380 different Christian churches in Indonesia listed with the Departemen Agama, more than there are ethnic groups.

The largest Pentecostal group in Karoland, with 9,012 members in 1986, is the Gereja Pantekosta di Indonesia (GPdI). This church has existed in Indonesia since 1921, and in Karoland since 1931. Two American evangelists from a Seattle organization called Bethel Temple had first attempted to evangelize in Bali, but, when the Dutch expelled them from there, they set up a training school for evangelists in Surabaya. The growth of the church in Indonesia far outstripped the size of the home church, the GPdI now claiming some 2 million Indonesians as members.

As a result of his contact with some Dutch evangelicals, Johannes Purba, a Karo man, studied at the Pentecostal training school in Surabaya and returned to Karoland in 1931 to establish a church. He sometimes used a *gendang* to attract people to his sermons, and after people had danced, he would preach, sometimes in the light of a big bonfire. At first, the new church attracted those who were for the most part not committed to any religion. In recent years, there has been also some defection from the GBKP into this and other Pentecostal groups. The GPdI, as the oldest and largest Pentecostal group, is now something of the establishment church within the Pentecostal cluster, and many of the smaller sects have broken away from it.

Pentecostalism's views of spiritual authority and ecclesiastical order invite fractioning. Opposite by design from churches such as the GBKP, the GPdI is intentionally weak in matters of organization, fearing that bureaucracy saps the spiritual energy of the church. Requirements are kept to a minimum. Thus, there are no particular educational requirements for ministers, although there are recognized levels depending on experience—helper, apprentice, and minister (*pendeta*). Ministers receive no salary from the central church; on the other hand, they maintain their freedom to live and work where they want rather than where the church directs them. The central organization does provide literature and hymnals. Most of its literature is in Indonesian, in keeping with its pan-Indonesian membership, but services in Karo villages are in Karo, and there are also some songs in Karo. The Pentecostal groups have formed their own ecumenical group, the Dewan Pantekosta Indonesia, although two Pentecostal groups belong to the Protestant Council of Churches (PGI).

In Karoland, the most successful of the churches that have split off from the GPdI is the Gereja Sidang Rohulkudus Indonesia (GSRI), which means Church of the Assembly of the Holy Ghost of Indonesia. Despite its name, it is a Karo-led and Karo-dominated church, claiming 6,541 members in Karoland and about 14,000 members in all North Sumatra, most of whom live in Medan or its surroundings. The GSRI was founded by T. G. Munte, who as a young boy was educated in mission schools. He recalls that in those days he was cynical about all religions, suspecting that they were among the devices the colonialists used to keep people from revolting. In 1941 he attended some Pentecostal services, had a religious experience, and then joined the Pentecostal church. Soon after this, he married the sister of Johannes Purba, the man who brought Pentecostalism to the Karo. In 1948 he switched to another Pentecostal sect, Sidang Jemaat Allah, which still exists in Karoland but has less than 1,000 members. His move at this time was prompted by an American Assembly of God evangelist, Ray Arthur Busby, who with his wife ran a theology school in Medan in which Munte and his wife became students. Munte was not baptized until 1951, however, by Ray

Jackson, who like Busby and the founders of Indonesian Pentecostalism, was also from Seattle.

In 1959 Munte decided to break from Sidang Jemaat Allah and form his own church, the GSRI. He admits that his secession did not stem from differences of doctrine or procedure and that as far as that goes his church is very similar to other Pentecostal groups. He felt that some members of the GPdI resented the leadership of the church by U.S. citizens. Munte himself no doubt resented this leadership, and he judges that the shattering of the Pentecostal churches in general comes mainly from the fact that some people do not want to be led by others.

Inside the GSRI church in Kabanjahe, an imposingly large and strikingly blue building, the ceiling is very high, and there is a balcony that was never completed and is not regularly used. Several hundred people gather in this large auditorium for two services on Sunday and one on Tuesday evening. Services last as long as four hours. They begin with prayers and singing and then members of the audience are invited to stand up and "witness," or to express a need of some kind. A sermon is preached for about an hour, then the rest of the service is given over to prayer, which results in the "baptism by fire" of the Holy Ghost. The audience sits on the floor on mats, and people raise both hands with palms facing outward. As the congregation prays aloud, each speaking singularly but all together, some begin to be entered by the Holy Ghost and to make a high singing sound. Others begin to speak in tongues, many begin to cry, and a few fall down stiffly in trance. This goes on for an indefinite time, with the intensity of the sound and of the emotions rising and falling in waves. When the momentum seems spent, the minister directing the service brings it to a close with a song and a prayer.

Participants stress that going through this "baptism" makes them feel very happy afterwards. Some speak of being embarrassed when they first saw this, or thinking that friends doing it were crazy, but once having experienced it themselves, they have no more hesitation. Speaking in tongues, which neither the speaker nor the listeners understand, is taken as a powerful evidence of the presence of the Holy Ghost. Sometimes speakers also prophesy, and in these cases, the Holy Ghost speaks through the person's regular voice using conventional language. Sometimes the messages are quite general, such as, "many people in this church will be saved on the final day," and sometimes more specific, such as suggesting that someone should become a minister.

When asked how their church differs from others, people explain that some churches have baptism with water, but theirs has baptism by the Holy

Ghost. As for contrasts with other Pentecostal groups, GSRI pastors aver that theirs is the only church that is led by the Holy Ghost rather than by mere humans. My questions were often answered with the uncertain response that only the Holy Ghost knows or decides such a thing. An apprentice preacher does not know if he will someday become a pastor or not—that depends on the Holy Ghost. It is impossible to say how long a service will last, since it is the Holy Ghost who decides when the "baptism by fire" is over. Members told me that their long services attest to their depth of faith compared to other Christians. In other churches, people just go through a routine attendance and want to go home as soon as possible. The pastors of the church suggest that while the GSRI is smaller than some others in Karoland, a higher percentage of its members attend faithfully.

The GSRI stresses personal faith and salvation, having no concern with social action of the sort that the GBKP or the Catholics perform—in education and development, for example. Rather, the focus is on the depth and satisfaction of the personal religious experience, the happiness this creates in one's life, and the promise of heaven after death. I saw the same framed print in the office of the GSRI in Kabanjahe and in the Medan home of Rev. Munte: a Bosch-like drawing of "The Broad and Narrow Paths" (trans. from Dutch), with rich and merry people headed on a broad path toward a distant inferno, and on a difficult, hardly visible path leading to a palatial heaven, a few serious souls. One evangelist in this church spoke to me about the "room" in heaven with his name on it in a way that made me imagine a literal room. The ecstacy of the baptism by fire, he said, gives a small foretaste of the heaven's joys.

The GSRI is a very text-oriented church as well. Among the many ministers and leaders of all faiths I interviewed, the GSRI ministers were the most apt to authorize their statements with chapter and verse citations from the Bible. While Jesus is certainly not absent from the songs and sermons, the emphasis is clearly on the Holy Spirit aspect of the Trinity. When Jesus died and rose to Heaven, someone explained to me, then the Holy Ghost was sent as his replacement in the world to become the main way for humans to achieve contact with God.

One GSRI evangelist observed that the church attracts those who are not very well-off. Rich people think they cannot afford the time for the long services, he pointed out. He said few office workers or educated people make up the church's following, not even moderately successful merchants. The congregation is mostly poor farmers. Munte and other ministers also say that many people are attracted to the church because they are suffering from illnesses that have not been successfully treated by conventional medicine. These ministers often recount miraculous healing of high blood pressure or TB in their own life histories, and a woman told me that she and her husband joined after he was healed of emphysema. "People told us that if we went and *believed,* that he would be cured, so I suggested we go," she remembered. "When he was cured, we wanted to witness about it after that." These healings are instantaneous, not requiring laying on of hands or any special action. They simply happen in the course of the service, apparently during the baptism by fire.

Religious ecstacy offers a momentary escape from weekday lives made difficult by poverty and illness, and it promises a greater happiness in the Hereafter. People who are almost totally powerless gain a momentary feeling of power and importance, having been a vessel for the very Spirit of God. This church meets the spiritual needs of many Karo who do not feel at home in the mainstream churches. Munte says he never wanted to draw people away from the other churches, but rather to attract the heathens (*kafir*) who belonged to no church, and most of the church's growth has actually come from this source. There are some striking parallels between the "baptism by fire" of the GSRI church and the spirit possession of traditional Karo religion that might have made it especially attractive to Perbegu. But there are a number of people, some of them ministers, who have come to the GSRI as a spiritual haven after a long search that has taken them from one church to another. Speaking from the experience of having shopped around, they declare that there is no other church that gives so much satisfaction and in which the power of the Holy Ghost is more evident.

Karo who live in urban areas, and who have some history of association with the GBKP or the Catholic church, are also attracted to Pentecostal churches. In 1989 I attended a service of the Gereja Bethel Indonesia in Jakarta, a congregation called Mawar Saron, where an estimated 10,000 people attend five services on Sundays, the earliest service beginning at 6:00 A.M. The atmosphere was upbeat and participatory like other Pentecostal services, but also highly orchestrated like the glossy televangelism of the United States. Clearly, too, this church is not afraid of organization, operating a well-oiled, social services machine that wins the loyalty of people facing difficulties of various kinds. The church uses a rented hall with 2,000 padded folding chairs, but is raising money for a round, modern-style building that exists for now as an architect's model and is designed to seat 10,000 worshipers.

[6 August 1989. Jakarta.] I attended Mawar Saron with Nd. L., her husband, their son, and a college-age niece. All retain their membership in the GBKP, and still attend those services some Sundays. One of Nd. L.'s brothers is an elder in a GBKP congregation near Medan, and very active in synodal affairs, but a younger brother has left the GBKP altogether to serve as a full time evangelist in the Gereja Bethel, although he has had no education for the role. We arrived for the 8:30 service as people were leaving from the early service. By their appearances, people coming and going from the church looked to be working class or middle class, a thoroughly mixed group of people from all ethnic backgrounds. The parking lot was full, and eventually every seat in the auditorium was filled.

As people entered, each received a twelve-page color newsletter that is distributed weekly at Bethel churches throughout Indonesia. Each also received a "prayer request form" to fill out, five lines where people may list problems for which they request prayers. Nearly everyone filled these out, and they were later passed in just before the collection and placed in a large glass box near the pulpit. A picture from the visitors' brochure showed "morning prayer each day from 5:00 to 6:00," with three men praying over the box, one kneeling on all fours with his hands resting directly on the prayer request forms. Little envelopes, passed out just before the collection, provided a place for offerings in response to answered prayers and private vows.

A band consisting of guitar, drums, keyboard, trumpet, and violin played the hymns. There were no hymnals. The words to the songs (without music) were thrown up on a screen by an overhead projector. The simple tunes were repeated and repeated. Three song leaders, a man who looked Indian, a woman who looked Chinese, and a man who was of indigenous Indonesian stock, used microphones in front of the band, and another song leader/director led the singing from the pulpit. Two groups of three teenage girls, one at each side of the stage, used their arms, hands, and tambourines to perform routines with each song. Everyone on the stage wore black or white. All of the song leaders, band members, ushers, and collectors wore black pants or skirts with a white long-sleeved shirt and small black tie. The minister wore a black suit, and the assistant who introduced him and made announcements wore a white suit. Only the tambourine corps wore a little color in the form of red, navy, and yellow cummerbunds that matched the streamers attached to their tambourines. Their blouses and skirts were all white.

The music was fast and catchy, and many people clapped their hands. Others sang with both arms raised high, sometimes swaying, and sometimes with heads thrown back as if beseeching the heavens. One of the often repeated theme songs had a phrase about lifting a hand to God. Prayers were not generally tearful. As the leader prayed aloud through the microphone, the congregation prayed aloud, too, each person's individual prayers making up a collective din. There was no common confession of faith, doxology, or Lord's Prayer, but the first scripture reading was led by the minister as a common reading.

The primary minister, Jacob Nahuway, was on a tour to Korea, Japan, and Hawaii, so his assistant, Samuel Yao presented the sermon. His message, about family harmony, was full of common stereotypes (men are strong, women are weak; men's character is like the buffalo, women's like the butterfly), but he was a very accomplished speaker who kept his audience's attention with engaging stories, examples from his life or ministerial practice, and even impersonations. His listeners laughed often. At the end, communion was offered to each person at his or her seat, recipients raising their little squares of white bread and tiny glasses of grape soda first to heaven. Visitors there for the first time were asked to stand (there were about twenty of us), and we were given a brochure on the church, and asked to fill out slips with our name and address so that we could be contacted at home.

The woman who had invited me to this service suggested that most of the people attracted to this church are people with problems of one kind or another. Another woman, an elder in a GBKP congregation, suggested also that the Bethel church tends to attract people who are already Christian, and who have suffered an illness, a divorce, a failed business, or some other tragedy. Another loyal GBKP member admitted that her church did not offer the social amenities of the Bethel church, and that the GBKP could well follow its example in sick visitation. Brochures depict the service orientation of the church, showing a woman talking with a man in a "consultation" (*konsultasi*) service. A photograph of a minister on the telephone is captioned, "telephone service 24 hours." In the sermon described above, the minister had said that of ten people he sees for *konsultasi,* eight of them have family problems of some sort. Every Friday there is a healing service with prayers and laying on of hands for those who are sick.

The friend who took me to the service said that she and her husband had begun to come to this church in 1984 when her husband was suffering from a severe illness. People came from the church to visit him in the hospital and prayed for him. She said she had no resentment toward the GBKP, but she pointed out that their ministers do not do *konsultasi,* and if you are in the hospital a month, they might come to see you only once. She also found the Bethel service more satisfying than the GBKP service, and said she feels that she gets an answer to her prayers and problems in this church. But there are not many other Karo in this congregation, she admitted, perhaps twenty others in addition to her family.

The brochure of the Bethel church says that its leader, Pdt. Jacob Nahuway, has an M.A. from Seoul, Korea, where he was inspired by the congregation of the Rev. Paul Cho, purportedly the largest single congregation in the world, claiming 500,000 members in 1975. Returning to Indonesia in 1978, burning with the ambition to build a similar congregation, he started in 1979 with about 30 members. By 1982, 900 people attended on Sundays, accommodated in two services; by 1989, the Mawar Saron congregation had climbed to 10,000 worshipers.

Although Catholicism came to the Indies in the 1500s with Portuguese interests, it faced certain restrictions in the Dutch period that were lifted only in the 1930s. In 1936 Alpidius van Dijnhoven, a Catholic missionary, began living at Seribudolok in the Simelungun region, and in 1938 he was joined by a Pastor Hamers, who lived at Sidikalang. Some Karo living in these towns were attracted to their teachings. One of these, Ngambung Sitepu from Sukajulu in southern Karoland, asked van Dijnhoven to come to his village and teach the new religion. Van Dijnhoven did so, using Sitepu's house in which to gather an audience. Eventually, several people joined his church, and not long afterward, they constructed a building that served both as church and as a three-year primary school. Its two teachers were non-Karo from Haranggaul. Activities were disrupted during the war years, when van Dijnhoven and other Westerners were interned by the Japanese. In 1948 van Dijnhoven and another priest, Maximus Brans, worked out of Berastagi, building on the progress that had begun before the war, and setting up a parish organization in Kabanjahe. Also in this year several young Karo men were sent to Pematang Siantar at the church's expense, returning to become teachers and congregation helpers.

Van Dijnhoven left in 1949, but Brans was then joined by Pastor Lukas Renders. Services were first held in Kabanjahe with ten families, but the church gradually attracted more and more followers. A Catholic division of the Departemen Agama was installed in Kabanjahe in 1950. In 1952 there was a mass baptism of forty-two persons. Students continued to be sent away for education, primarily as teachers and nurses. Relatively few men were attracted to the clergy because of the requirement for celibacy, but in the first thirty years of its history in Karoland the Catholic church recruited 124 Karo girls to become nuns. In contrast, only four Karo men have become priests and two have become missionary friars, and all of these have been stationed elsewhere. Since 1970 the pastors who have worked in Karoland have been primarily Indonesian rather than European.

In 1986 the Roman Catholic Church claimed 32,577 members in Karoland, or some 13.87 percent of the population. This is the second largest Christian group after the GBKP. There are only three priests serving in this territory, one of whom is at Kabanjahe, while the other two travel around to the 130 or so congregations on the plateau, visiting each every three or four months if possible. Church elders lead Sunday services in the absence of the pastor.

The church operates an impressive range of services and facilities from a complex in Kabanjahe. In addition to a house and office for the priest, there is a large church building, an accredited primary school and middle school, and a dorm for nuns. A medical center adjoins this complex. There are some sixty church-owned buildings throughout the rest of Karoland, including a kindergarten, six more primary schools, three additional middle schools, and a high school. A dorm for Catholic students operates in Berastagi. Since 1969 the church has also run an Institute of Agricultural Practice that gives advice and sponsors short courses. It has also carried out irrigation and water supply projects in one village.

It is no secret that its wealth and facilities have attracted many to the Catholic church. One woman who had been a student in a Catholic school told me that her teachers asked if she wanted to continue her education, and when she said she wanted to be a nurse, she was given her choice of schools. She picked Bandung, and later returned to Karoland as a public health nurse. Her husband, who teaches at one of the Catholic schools in Kabanjahe, and was among the first group of boys sent away to train as teachers, said that Karo look for proof (*bukti*), not just words and promises, so he followed Catholicism because of its educational and material benefits.

Conclusions

The definitive criteria for being Karo and Batak no longer rest on a religious contrast, but the strength and success of the ethnic church show that ethnicity is not totally dissociated from issues of religion either. In a Muslim nation, a majority of the Karo have chosen to be Christian, and the largest religious body in Karo society, the GBKP, is an explicitly ethnic church. That church, while still experiencing growth, has also experienced attrition in recent decades. The GBKP's attraction is diminished for the children of urban Karo who do not use Karo as a first language, and some urban families, especially ethnically mixed ones, elect other Protestant churches where Indonesian is the medium. Even the clergy in the GBKP can, in theory, accept the possibility that there will someday be no need for an explicitly ethnic church.

"There are no classes in Karo. Everyone is the same," said the man in the

Protestant section of Kabanjahe's Departemen Agama when I asked whether denomination was correlated with class. When Christianity was introduced to the Karo, theirs was a relatively homogeneous, unstratified, agrarian society. Today, Karo society is increasingly urban and wealth-stratified. The fissures among Karo Protestants, like those among Western Protestants, have begun to form along familiar class lines and socioeconomic coordinates. A vegetable vendor on Medan's outskirts, a university professor, a highland farmer, an office worker in Bandung—these people may be united by a common ideology of kinship and feeling for their origins, but they live very different lives. Aside from the fact that ill feelings of envy and pride on one side and haughtiness on the other can destroy a community of faith, that community also succumbs to the differentiation of experience that provokes different religious needs and responses in different people. The peasants and urban poor in the GSRI are not "satisfied" by what they feel is the spiritually dry atmosphere of the GBKP. The educated, middle-class Catholics and GBKP loyalists, for their part, find the hand clapping, crying, and trancing of the Pentecostals excessive and irreverent. It is difficult to imagine that any one church could satisfy the various needs that this range of Christian variants suggests.

The government's legitimation of Christianity as one of the state religions benefits Karo Christians, who in turn embrace the Pancasila as a shield of their minority status in a Muslim country. The Indonesian Christian minority is a visible segment of the middle class, one that includes many Indonesians of Chinese descent as well as educators, bureaucrats, lawyers, and doctors of diverse ethnic backgrounds who represent the legacy of colonial mission schools. Christians are thus widespread throughout the archipelago, and well-placed if not great in number. The secrecy about recent national statistics of religious identity probably aims to disguise the growing share of Christianity compared to the other religions. Christians' presence, power, and growth challenge Muslim tolerance and challenge the state to fulfill its Pancasila ideals. These ideals can be used to justify the use of force against Muslim radicals, and the limitation of Islam's influence in the economic and social policies of the country, an influence about which the armed forces in particular seems apprehensive (Schwarz 1992a). Throughout the country as a whole, Christian enclaves such as the Karo thus function much as the Dutch imagined they would, as "buffers" between Muslims, checkering what would otherwise appear as an almost uniformly Muslim terrain, although religious pluralism *within* Islam is still more significant than Christianity's effect in dampening the power of Muslim activists.

Notes

1. Total Karo population was around 180,000 by 1936, by one missionary's estimate, making the 5,000 Christians around 3 percent of the total (J. van Muylwijk 1939).

2. Interview with Pdt. Ngantan Ginting Munte, 19 July 1983.

3. Some traditional music is said to have an almost irresistible power to evoke trance. In addition, making music itself involves relations with spirits, since musicians are thought to gain their talents and knowledge from spiritual familiars, *jinujung*.

Chapter 10

Muslim Karo

Christianity and the traditionalist/modernist split within Islam fracture Islamic unity in Indonesia, but so does ethnicity. Religious communities of Muslims in Karoland segment along ethnic lines. Given the association in the past between conversion to Islam and ethnic assimilation, it is not surprising that Karo Muslims pay special attention to rationalizing the consonance of Islam with Karo *adat,* especially with principles of kin and family.

Muslims perceive Islam as more egalitarian than Christianity, and in Karoland, wealth differences, such as they are, do not sift Muslims into different mosques the way Christian denominations mirror socioeconomic dimensions. Ethnicity does play such a role, however. No more oblivious to power and wealth differences than their Christian neighbors, Karo Muslim communities are hierarchical along a patron-client pattern rather than a class pattern. Coordinating and unifying the *umat* (the community of all believers) above the patron-client cells and across the ethnic divisions is the arm of the state, specifically the Departemen Agama, the master patron of all the Islamic groups.

The History of Islam in Karoland

Bordered on north and east by Muslims for several centuries, Karo have been drawn to Islam in small numbers for some time. This resulted in ethnic assimilation along the East Coast as Muslim Karo became Malay. No record exists of active proselytization from the East Coast into Karo areas, but there were always political and economic incentives for conversions in the coastal lowlands. This was especially true for men who aspired to positions of leadership, since the political hierarchy culminated in the office of the sultan, and those who held positions under him were expected to be Muslim. Headmen of the larger villages in Deli and Serdang were often Muslim in the early twentieth century (Neumann 1901, 179–81). In one small village, Neumann reported, all the people including the headman had begun to study for baptism, with the notable exception of the headman's son who was in line for his position (1907).

The relationship with the Muslim world toward the North was somewhat different. Local legends describe traveling *da'i* (missionaries) bringing the message of Islam to the Karo Plateau. Martadi (n.d.) cites a manuscript called "Keris Bawar Aceh" that gives the following account, drawn here in summary:

> The Sultan of Perlak, Makhdun Johan Berdault Syair Nuuri, had a nephew (brother's son) named Adi Genali. He was the first raja of Kerajaan Islam-Lingga, and he had three sons. He held a circumcision ceremony for these sons. One of them, whose name was Sibayak Lingga Kebal Nohor, had a foreskin that proved too thick for the circumciser's knife, and the operation failed. Adi Genali was embarrassed at this, and at the fact that his son might have used magic to accomplish this invulnerability, so he sent Sibayak Lingga Kebal Nohor to Karoland. He and his retinue, which included an *ulama,* stopped several places en route, but finally arrived in Karoland and established the current village of Lingga. The *ulama* was called Tengku Datuk. He died and was buried at Mbalbal Petarum, where to this day the raising of pigs is prohibited.

While this story suggests how Muslim influences might have arrived in Karoland, the Sibayak's failure to succumb to the circumciser's knife may also express the Karo's resistance to Islam.

Similar legends about the reign of Iskandar Muda (1607–1636), Aceh's most illustrious sultan, suggest other lines of influence. In an attempt to expand his territory and spread Islam, Iskandar Muda created relations with Karo leaders, four of whom he appointed *raja* or *sibayak* over clusters of villages.[1] Legends about these foundings vary in the details and also over the question of which was first (Tamboen 1952). Here is a sample.

> Iskandar sent a delegation to Karoland, led by Tuan Kita. In this group was a *mubalig* named Tengku Muhammad Amin, later known as Tengku Lau Bahun. At this time, Karoland was suffering from drought, a plague of caterpillars, a small pox epidemic, and continual warfare between villages. At Lau Bahun Lingga, they called the various headmen of Karoland to a meeting. This place is known now as Tiga Raja. Tuan Kita had brought a water buffalo called Jagad Manggaluta, and the headmen were each asked to ride the buffalo. Whenever the buffalo stretched himself out as if carrying a great weight, the man he was carrying was to be *raja*. The Sibayak of Kabanjahe, Pa Mbelgah Purba, who was of stout build, got on, but the buffalo seemed not to feel his weight at all.[2] Then the Sibayak of Lingga, who

was a small man, mounted. Tuan Kita had spoken to him secretly beforehand and told him that when he mounted the buffalo he should stick its back with a needle. The Sibayak of Lingga did this, and the animal stiffened and lowered his back as if he felt a great weight. Thus, the Sibayak of Lingga became the first *raja*. After Tuan Kita left, Tengku Muhammed Amin stayed behind to help the people. (Martadi n.d.)

Martadi suggests that stories of the buffalo trial were a tactic for legitimating this new level of leadership that was without precedent in Karo society.[3] Before this, leaders on the Karo Plateau had seldom amounted to more than villagewide suzerains, and, likewise, these four *raja* could not sustain their power. In the twentieth century, the Dutch revived these four defunct *rajadoms* for administrative purposes and added a fifth.

Martadi surveys the many legends of early contacts with Aceh, most of which are merely rudimentary accounts of the itineraries of merchants or holy men. For example, around 1870, three Acehnese selling cattle traveled from Aceh Tenggara to Gurukenayan, where they were killed. An army officer from Aceh came to investigate, much to the fear of the local people. Another account involves one Tengku Tambak Malim, who came to Bintang Meriah bringing a flag with Arabic letters on it and also a letter in "Arab-Malayu" (Jawi script). He became ill, died, and was buried at a place between Bintang Meriah and Perbesi, where his grave is still honored today. The letter and flag are reputed still to exist in the possession of a man in Jakarta. Martadi concludes that the combined weight of these and other stories, cursory and partly mythical as they are, suggests erratic Aceh-Karo contacts in the precolonial era. Despite the formal relationships with Aceh that may have existed at one time, Martadi guesses that Muslim merchants may well have been the most important channel of Islam in Karoland as they often were elsewhere.

The Acehnese enjoyed a reputation among the Karo as formidable fighters, especially because some were reputed to have knowledge of supernatural powers of invulnerability (like Adi Genali's son who could not be cut by the circumciser's knife). Muslims in Karoland say that in the past people were often attracted to Islam because of such *ilmu* (knowledge). Converts hoped to learn the prayers and spells conferring invulnerability or effecting cures. It is not surprising, then, that Arabic prayer phrases, especially the word *bismillah* (in the name of God), also found their way into some Karo spells. The following story, combining the theme of merchant transmission and the lure of *ilmu*, is told of a man who lived in Kabanjahe as late as the 1930s.

There was a cake seller named Pakih Majid Sikumbang. After selling his cakes in Lingga one day, he could not get his customers to pay. When he returned to Kabanjahe, his wife, Habibah Tanjung, berated him for coming home without the money. The next day, he returned to Lingga with more cakes. Some people paid in the normal way, but some mocked him, proffering their payments by holding the coins between their toes. He stood calmly while (through the will of Allah) the coins came to him without his having to reach for them. Those who had tried to pay with their feet fell down and died on the spot, and others who saw this ran away in fear. "Don't run off," Pakih Majid Sikumbang shouted. "You haven't paid for the cakes yet!" People were in such a hurry to get away, someone's sarong fell off and he didn't even stop to pick it up. Later, some people got sick, so they came to visit the cake seller in Kabanjahe, paying their debts and apologizing for their behavior. Some asked to study his *ilmu*, but he simply told them to join Islam, and he taught them the Islamic prayers. (Martadi n.d.)

On the whole, the occasional merchants, holy men, and political envoys who carried Islam into Karoland made very few converts, perhaps because conversion might have suggested cultural or political submission to Aceh. The rugged terrain that restricted intercourse between Karoland and other areas made this resistance easier. To this day, it is far easier to reach Banda Aceh via Medan and up the coast than to forge directly from Karoland through the highlands. For the most part, the Karo Plateau remained a far hinterland to Aceh. The Sultans of Aceh could neither control, interfere with, nor easily reward highland headmen, who thus saw little gain for themselves in becoming Muslim.

Most Acehnese influences in Karoland appear to have come via Kota Cane, a town in Aceh Tenggara. Tiga Binanga, along the road between Kabanjahe and Kota Cane, is one of the oldest Muslim areas on the Karo Plateau, and Tiga Beringin, a small village nearby with about twenty-five households, is entirely Muslim. According to local lore, the founder of Tiga Beringin was Juan Tarigan. Tarigan lived at a village called Kuala, where his father had married. His father, who died in 1890, had embraced Islam while on a trip to Aceh, but Tarigan did not enter the faith as a result of that. He was won to Islam only after debating three days and nights with an Acehnese man named Tengku Muda. His conversion caused something of an uproar among his relatives, specifically his *kalimbubu* in Kuala, so in 1901 Tarigan established the new village of Tiga Beringin, where his descendants live today. He held *pengajian* (Qur'an recitation and religious instruction) at his home, and brought teachers from Aceh now and then. His sons all walked to Kota Cane, some one hundred kilometers away, to receive religious instruction, and returned to proselytize in Karoland. Eventually, a *madrasah* (religious school) was erected in Tiga Beringin, and this little village became a center from which *dakwah* was carried out in surrounding villages, sometimes using a *gendang*, martial arts shows, and tests of strength and invulnerability to attract an audience. Tarigan, for example, is said to have been able to hold a red-hot knife and once to have uprooted a banana tree bare-handed. Tiga Beringin became an important center for Islam in Karoland, and this little village continues to produce leaders for the growing community of Karo Muslims.

The Karo largely resisted Islam despite at least one cultural factor that might have eased its acceptance: they had an indigenous practice of penile surgery. Called *ikacip-kacipi,* this practice is always translated into Indonesian with the word *sunat,* which means circumcision, but the operation simply split the foreskin without removing it, so was technically a form of superincision (Tarigan 1990a). The verb *ngkacip* means to pinch or squeeze something. In the method of superincision most frequently used, a sharp blade of grass or a quill was inserted beneath the foreskin and bound in place for several days until the skin was severed. At the bathing place, older boys would tease the little boys whose foreskins were still intact, saying that they smelled bad. Boys performed the operation on themselves in private and without ceremony or fanfare, usually in early adolescence.[4] The custom is apparently dying out, however, which Singarimbun attributes partly to the fact that in towns and cities people now bathe in private bathrooms, so boys do not face the constant pressure to perform this painful operation on themselves.[5]

In the colonial period the construction of roads opened Karoland to migrants and merchants from other areas. Christian Toba Batak moved to Karoland to take teaching and office jobs, but migrants also came from elsewhere, especially merchants and other entrepreneurs, and these were likely to be Muslim. Reflecting this influx of Muslim migrants, small mosques were built in Kabanjahe and Berastagi in the 1920s, structures still in use today. A Minangkabau mattress merchant, St. Aminuddin Djambak, is especially remembered from this era. He peddled his mattresses from a base in Berastagi, and carried out *dakwah* in the process. In 1930 an organization called Al Jamiatul Washliyah (or Alwashliyah) was established in Medan, and branches of this were later established in Berastagi (1933) and Kabanjahe (1937). In the 1930s a significant community of Minangkabau began to form in Kabanjahe, establishing a chapter of Muhammadiyah there in 1936. For the most part, these Muslim migrants and the religious communities they founded did not attract many Karo, and none of the leaders of these local chapters were Karo.

The disruptions of the Japanese occupation and later the revolution brought additional Karo into Islam. As elsewhere in Indonesia, the Japanese treated Islam more favorably than the Dutch had, and in Karoland the Alwashliyah group in particular seems to have benefited from Japanese attention. The Japanese turned Muslim boy scout groups organized through Muhammadiyah and Alwashliyah into quasi-military organizations. With the proclamation of independence in 1945, these groups became known as Lasykar Hizbullah Sabilillah, and helped Republican troops disarm the Japanese and police the area.

During the revolution, people burned their villages and fled, many leaving Karoland altogether and escaping to Aceh Tenggara, where they remained several months to a year. There, in this period of stress and privation remembered as *mengongsi,* some refugees converted to Islam. One of these, M. M. Ibrahim Sembiring from Tiganderket, was among a small group of men from Payung County who joined Islam at this time. After the war, he and others returned home to found Muslim groups in their villages. One man who had inherited the position of *raja* in 1943 fled his home in 1947, then joined the army fighting for independence and converted to Islam. (His teacher was Sulaiman Tarigan, son of the founder of Tiga Beringin, and later the first head of the Departemen Agama in Kabanjahe.) This *raja* expressed his motive to convert as if it were insurance against becoming a victim of the revolution. In areas adjacent to Karoland, indigenous rulers who had benefited from cooperation with the Dutch were deposed and killed in a bloody social revolution (Reid 1979). Karo raja and leaders were deposed but generally not killed, and this particular *raja* went on to hold civil service positions in the new Republic and to become a Golkar loyalist. In his later years he performed the *haj* (pilgrimage to Mecca) and has emerged as a leader in the Islamic community in Karoland.

The Republic's Departemen Agama has boosted the Islamic presence in Karoland. The district's office dates from 1946 and was first headed by Sulaiman Tarigan, who counted the number of Muslims in Kabupaten Karo at around 5,000 in 1950, but most of these were not ethnic Karo. Sulaiman Tarigan recruited Abd. Salem Tarigan, then at Kota Cane, to work with him, and after the former's death in 1961, Salem Tarigan assumed leadership of the office. During the 1950s, *dakwah* groups from Medan targeted Karoland as an area where a majority still practiced the traditional religion. Hamka lectured in Karoland during one of these campaigns, and Berastagi was the site of an Islamic Congress (Al Ittihadiyah) in 1952. Student groups in particular made *dakwah* tours during the fasting month, and *madrasah* were founded in Kabanjahe and Berastagi during the 1950s. As a result of these efforts and events, the number of Karo converts began slowly to increase.

The years following G30S and the change to the New Order government stimulated still larger numbers of Karo to join Islam. The atmosphere in Karoland (an area of high PKI involvement) and in Medan during this time was painfully tense. Faculty members at the University of North Sumatra organized groups of male students to sleep at their homes in the evenings to guard against being hauled out in the middle of night. People feared both anti-Communist reprisals and Communist retaliation, and no one was sure whom to trust. In Karoland, as elsewhere, many of the reprisals against suspected Communists were led by Muslim groups.

In early October 1965, just after the abortive coup, several Islamic leaders from Karoland went to Medan to consult with people there, and then returned to organize youth groups such as Kesatuan Aksi Pemuda Pelajar Indonesia (KAPPI) whose purpose was to round up PKI members. As reported elsewhere in Indonesia, during their raids on offices and homes they supposedly found hit lists of people who were to be killed when the Communists came to power, and several Islamic leaders were said to be on these lists. PKI suspects were interned temporarily in a school building in Kabanjahe. Both the Governor of North Sumatra and the Bupati of Karoland (who were both Karo) were implicated in PKI involvement and later removed from office. A non-Karo, and a leader in the Muslim community in Karoland, Baharuddin Siregar was then appointed Bupati. After some time, Siregar organized a meeting at a sports field in Kabanjahe to announce the dissolution of all PKI related groups. Following this, an Islamic service was held on the grounds of the Bupati's office. KAPPI held an anniversary celebration in Kabanjahe's Gedung Nasional in 1967. The leader at this event, Zaidan Ginting, was a prominent local Muslim who had headed KAPPI and led some of the other groups that routed out Communist suspects. As he was leaving this event, he was shot by a young man named Johan, later identified as a member of the Gerakan Pemuda Kristen Indonesia (Christian youth movement of Indonesia). Ginting did not die, but was left permanently disabled.

As the rounding up of suspected Communists occurred, no one wanted to be placed in that category. Thus, during the years immediately following G30S, converts swelled the ranks of all the religions, including Islam. A mass conversion of 1,500 people was celebrated in Kabanjahe in 1968. The number of Muslims in Karoland increased from 24,150 in 1966 to 31,775 in

1970, not as dramatically as the growth in Christianity during this same period, but still a significant increase. Undoubtedly, many who signed up as Muslims during this period, like those who took shelter in Christianity, were little more than nominal converts, but with time, a nominal identity can result in a new spiritual life. The terror of the post-G30S era is a memory now, but the New Order has not slackened its campaign against communism, nor its insistence that having an *agama* befits national loyalty. Some people have recently activated or reactivated religious commitments they once made in this postcoup era.

Karoland still remains an area with one of the highest figures of people who as yet are not registered under any *agama,* and has increasingly become the objective for Muslim groups in Medan that carry out various kinds of *dakwah* activities.[6] The different groups do not necessarily reflect differences of practice and dogma, and to make the most of these various efforts, a coordinating board (Badan Koordinasi Da'wah Islam) was formed in 1983 at the behest of a new leader in Kabanjahe's Departemen Agama. This body was conceived as a central information center for the *dakwah* groups in order to prevent overlapping and duplication. The board hoped to send new *dakwah* groups or workers to build on the activities of those that had worked before. This board has not lived up to its design, and Islamic proselytization remains somewhat uncentralized. The Departemen Agama itself keeps tabs on the groups and the persons carrying out *dakwah* in Karoland, however, and performs some of the functions envisioned for the Badan Koordinasi.

Dakwah methods range from one-night rallies in villages carried out by groups of Muslim students during the fasting month to solitary *da'i* (missionaries) who reside in a village and work in the surrounding territory. Other *da'i* reside for a time in the larger towns, making overnight trips out to villages. In 1983 there were twelve such *da'i* resident in Karoland, none of whom were Karo. These resident *da'i* are all young men and are sent to the area as bachelors, marriage into a local family being part of their method of building a base of converts. *Dakwah* trips to other villages organized by Muslims resident in Karoland also take place.

As a result of these efforts, as well as the persistent political incentives to have an *agama* and the natural increase in the families that joined Islam from the turn of the century to the Revolution, the number of Muslims in Karoland has grown markedly in the 1980s. Recent figures from the Departemen Agama on the number of Muslims in Karoland indicated 41,873 in 1983, which climbed to 52,234 by 1985. Newspapers have carried reports of mass conversions: 700 at Kabanjahe in 1982, 98 at Naman in 1980, 145 in Langkat in 1978, a group of 30 Karo youths in Jakarta, and so on (Aqib 1985). These mass *syahadatkan* (confessions) are formal affairs in which the participants publicly confess Islam and are registered as members of the *umat* (community of Muslims). Departemen Agama officials and other important visitors usually attend these ceremonies.

The growth of Islam in Karoland has benefited, too, from financial contributions of the *dakwah* groups listed above, and from funds from all levels of the government. Government funds have gone into the construction of new mosques and the maintenance of old ones. Bowen (1991) points out that the Indonesian term for development especially connotes *building*. New mosques have mushroomed all over Karoland in recent years. In 1983, there were fifty-nine mosques; in 1985, seventy-five. Most of these are small, even rudimentary, like the houses and little shops that comprise the villages in which they are located. The mosques of Kabanjahe and Berastagi are correspondingly more elaborate. Officials of the Departemen Agama in Kabanjahe told me that a new mosque is not necessarily a product of an Islamic congregation but rather a "first step" in *dakwah*. It becomes a center for Islamic activities and a meeting place that itself attracts a growing community.

Finally, the visibility of Islam in Karoland was enhanced in 1985, when the new Bupati was appointed, the first Karo Muslim to hold the office. His ties with the Departemen Agama were stronger than those of his Christian predecessors, and his religious identity was apparent every time he spoke in an official capacity and addressed his audience with the Islamic greeting that prefaces public speeches, "Assalamu'alaikum . . ."

Religious Education

Some Muslim leaders expressed to me the worry that the money going into all the new buildings might be better spent to support teachers and leaders for the new converts and fledgling congregations. What happens to the masses who convert to Islam in the dramatic public ceremonies, or to those who at one time or another have professed an allegiance to Islam? Many of them live in surroundings where there is very little opportunity for deepening their knowledge of Islam. Similarly, the hit-and-run *dakwah* groups do not provide a continuing supportive environment for those they may attract to Islam, and many Muslim leaders in Karoland worry about competition, duplication, and wasted efforts among the various *dakwah* groups.

The Departemen Agama, with central offices in Kabanjahe and smaller offices throughout the district, organizes Islam to a degree that it does not organize Christianity. Islam dominates the Departemen at the national level, and this is true also at the district and county levels in Karoland, where Islam is actually the minority religion. The go-between for all religious groups and the government, the Departemen maintains a corporatist influence over Christians as well, but the ecclesiastical structure of churches buffers this influence. The top-heaviness of Islam in the Departemen, as well as the *umat*'s lack of centralization, gives the Departemen great visibility in local Islam. The Muslim office in the Departemen supervises and registers the weddings of Muslims, manages the deployment of Muslim teachers in the public schools, funnels government funds into mosque repair and construction, and keeps some tabs on *dakwah* activities. One section of the Islamic office within the Departemen helps facilitate making the *haj*. In 1986 the work program for the Muslim section of the Departemen in Kabupaten Karo (the other sections' work programs were similar to it) began, not with specifically religious goals, but with the goals of helping the *umat* to practice the Pancasila and the Constitution of 1945, and to crush those religious groups that shatter unity. Further, the office hoped to dispel the notion that the Pancasila somehow conflicted with religion, and to assure Muslims that the government's requirement that all organizations adopt the Pancasila as their sole foundation did not restrict the freedom of religious organizations.

Karo Muslims who live in the larger towns in Karoland may participate in a community of believers large enough to provide social services such as kindergartens and birthing clinics. They can send their children to learn to read the Qur'an at the mosque, or to attend a *madrasah* rather than a public school. The percentage of Muslims in villages varies greatly, from hardly any in some villages (such as Barusjahe) to as many as 50 percent in others (e.g., Perbesi, Gurukenayan). Children of Muslim families in Payung, for example, where there are some 150 Muslims out of a population of 1,452, do not have much opportunity for religious education. They learn what they can by accompanying their parents to weekly *pengajian* and to ceremonial events, but most do not study to read the Qur'an.

There are twenty-seven *madrasah* throughout Karoland, most of these concentrated in the two largest towns. These religious schools combine both religion and general subjects in their curriculum, but devote more time to religion than do the public schools. Because their curriculum does not fit government standards, they are administered by the Departemen Agama rather than the Department of Education and Culture. Their fees are generally less than those of the public schools, and their teachers receive a lower salary than public school teachers. The religious schools are a kind of alternate track in that students who have been educated at primary and middle school levels in *madrasah* cannot easily switch to a government high school and university because of their background. Thus, even devout Muslim families who aspire eventually to educate their children in the government university system send their children to government schools or to government-standard religious schools. In Kabanjahe, a primary and a middle school run by Muham-madiyah, for example, uses the government's curriculum. Some families send their children to government schools, then arrange religious lessons through private teachers or group arrangements of other types. In Karoland there are no *pesantren* (schools where children board for an extended period of exclusively religious study), but some parents send their children to *pesantren* elsewhere. South Tapanuli and Kota Cane have long been places where Karo Muslims sent their children.

Religious education involves moral instruction, instruction in ritual prac-tice, and learning about the contents of the Qur'an and Hadith. A great deal of time is spent learning to "read" (I = "baca" or K = "oge") the Qur'an in Arabic. The youngest primary school children begin to learn Arabic script and the pronunciation of the letters. By the third grade, if they have attended a *madrasah* or had private instruction, many are thus very capable of "read-ing" verses from the Qur'an. While some explanation or translation of the verses is usually given, the emphasis is on pronouncing the words correctly rather than understanding their meaning. It is, in fact, a recitation more than a reading, and a recitation with the quality of singing, for the words are not uttered in normal speaking intonation.[7] People who become Muslims as adults, without the childhood education in Qur'an reading, do not usually acquire the skill, but they memorize as much Arabic as they can by ear and with the aid of Latin transcriptions. Those who receive Islamic education as children can usually recognize a great many Arabic words and can pronounce a reading, but admit that when they "read" the Qur'an they do not understand all of it. "Can you read Arabic?" I once asked the teacher at a *madrasah*. "No, but I can read the Qur'an," he answered. A prominent Muslim figure from Medan was addressing a group of Muslims in Berastagi, counseling them to learn what they could and not feel ashamed if their knowledge was still limited. "Even if we do not understand the meaning of the words," he said. "When we hear the Qur'an we feel content [*senang*]. That is the evi-dence of faith."

Pengajian Groups: Cells of the Umat

Aside from the Friday service that Muslim males are obligated to attend, the heart of organized religious life for adults centers around study groups called *pengajian*. These sometimes meet as mixed-gender groups, but more often as groups of women or groups of men separately. They are especially important in the religious life of women, who generally do not go to the mosque on Fridays. Most groups meet weekly, but others only every other week, often gathering at members' homes on a rotating basis. They can be as large as fifty to sixty members. In small Karo villages, the *pengajian* group includes all the resident Muslims, including people of other ethnic groups who have married in, or Javanese sharecroppers living in the vicinity. In the larger towns of Karoland, physical proximity or neighborhood influences their composition somewhat, but other factors—notably ethnicity and patronage—influence who joins what group.

Some *pengajian* groups are formed by or form around powerful men. For example, a large group at Berastagi was formed at the behest of a relatively well-to-do man who is a former headman and has occupied other positions of leadership. In Kabanjahe another group formed around the figure of a traditional *raja*, or *sibayak*, who recently retired from the district legislature and is active in Golkar. His followers are almost exclusively Karo. Similarly, the Muhammadiyah group in Kabanjahe is almost exclusively an organization of Minangkabau. Its leader is a successful restaurateur who has lived in Kabanjahe since the 1930s and prides himself on his goodwill with leaders in the Christian community and on his renown even among non-Muslims. Like many other leaders of *pengajian* clusters, he is also a *haji*. These clusters form the effective social blocs through which the *umat* as a whole operates. For example, when the Bupati and his wife decided to organize a "Cleaning and Greening" of the road into Kabanjahe, representatives of the *pengajian* groups were invited to a meeting at the Departemen Agama where they made decisions about how to carry out the communal workday and committed their groups to send a certain number of persons. *Pengajian* groups thus represent spheres of influence as well as spheres of ethnic and neighborhood community, forming around certain influential leaders.

As elsewhere in Indonesia, Karoland's Muhammadiyah group is marked by a modernist, social services approach (Peacock 1978). In Kabanjahe it runs a kindergarten that has a van to pick up and drop off its students and a government-accredited primary school and junior high, and it has recently built an impressive new mosque and birthing clinic. Its *pengajian* are conducted entirely in Indonesian, and the fifty or so women who attend the women's *pengajian* crowd themselves into the little desks of a second-grade classroom behind the mosque for their weekly meeting. They are almost entirely non-Karo. Asked about the differences of belief or practice that separate this group from others, its members denied that there are any. Other Muslims in Kabanjahe explained to me, however, that Muhammadiyah teaches a different manner of carrying out *sembahyang* (divine services). The Muhammadiyah group uses a set of Arabic phrases more abbreviated than the ones used by the more traditional Muslim groups. There have been times when the Muhammadiyah group has not participated at public, holiday *sembahyang* (such as on Hari Raya) over this difference. Thus, both ethnicity and disagreements about ritual practice sometimes separate the Muhammadiyah group from other segments of the *umat* in Karoland. The *pengajian* group for Muhammadiyah women does not undertake the hypnotic chanting nor the Arabic recitation of the two Karo groups I describe in the following sections. *Pengajian Asijijah* has the ritually spare tone of a Protestant study group.

[19 September 1986. Kabanjahe. *Pengajian Aisjijah.*] A young woman who reads the Qur'an well has been asked to do a reading. The audience listens as she reads for some five minutes or so, but there are no coordinated chants or responsive recitations. The teacher, a Malay man who heads the religious court (Pengadilan Agama), speaks on the subject, "What is Islam?" Using a blackboard for emphasis, he explains Islam as submission. The universe submits to Allah. The lawlike regularity of the heavenly bodies, the inevitable consequences of gravity, the inevitable developmental sequence of our bodies from birth, through growth, decline, and death—all of these demonstrate the universe's submission to the laws of God. Only humans have the capacity *not* to submit to Allah. Not only does submission mean carrying out what Allah has commanded, such as avoiding certain things and performing certain actions, but also accepting whatever happens to us. Does our business bring in 5,000 rupiahs one day and only 2,000 the next? Not to complain. When we stub our toe, do we curse the children who left the stone there, or wonder why no one else had stumbled in this way? Ideally, we should smile and go on, accepting our injury as an opportunity to submit to Allah's will. The sermon or lecture ended with a prayer, and the *pengajian* was over.

The content of *pengajian* sessions varies between and within groups. Furthermore, the teachers or leaders of these sessions are not the men who form their power centers, for the latter are not necessarily especially learned in Islam. Rather, the group leader recruits a teacher or teachers who can read the Qur'an and instruct followers concerning ritual practice, belief, and morality. A description of three of these groups and their meetings gives a flavor for the content of religious life among Muslims in Karoland. While they resemble the Christian family devotionals or prayer meetings, they are different in relying much less on discussion (*diskusi*) than on a pedagogical format that gives center place to the authority of the teacher. For ethnographic examples, I use two groups that are explicitly ethnic in focus.

In these Karo *pengajian,* the efforts to reconcile Islam with Karo identity are obvious. A group of Karo Muslims in Berastagi is held together by a former headman of that town. Once also a leader of a Perbegu revivalist group called Persadaan Merga si Lima (see the next chapter), he abandoned that organization and during the last three years has been the pivot of this Muslim group. The very name of the group, *Pengajian Merga si Lima,* says it is a specifically Karo organization. The Karo language is the prevalent medium of conversation and teaching, and according to the group's leaders, it encourages new Karo converts to see their *adat* and their religion as "one path."

Men and women meet separately, the men weekly in the evenings, the women in the afternoons. I attended the women's section of *Pengajian Merga si Lima* meetings several times in 1986. The woman who teaches the women's section has taught in *madrasah* for several years, and before that studied four years at a *pesantren* (religious boarding school) in Tapanuli Selatan. She lives in Medan, where she practices as a *patah tulen,* a traditional bonesetter, but her husband's family lives in Berastagi. A gifted speaker who knows how to use self-parody for humorous effect, she also has a good command of Arabic and has recently made the *haj.*

[October 1986. Berastagi. *Pengajian Merga si Lima.*] The leader begins the women's meetings with about forty minutes of "responsive reading" (to borrow a Christian equivalent), in which she gives a sentence and then the group responds, all in Arabic.[8] The leader reads from Arabic, but most follow her in a book of Latin-script transcriptions. Some simply work from memory. Sometimes, other women take over the role of the leader, as if spontaneously, and the primary leader joins the group as respondent. Toward the end, the group chants "Laillahallah" for five minutes or more, eyes closed, heads bobbing up and down and side to side in a metered rhythm as a kind of meditation. This sequence ends in a prayer, with a leader and group responses of "amin."

A break for tea and snacks, a collection, and announcements follow. The teacher then talks for some thirty to forty minutes, sometimes expounding a verse from the Qur'an, sometimes giving moral instruction. She is one of the few women who wears a hat that covers her hair at all times, and she admonishes her listeners to do likewise, because only a woman's husband should see her hair, which is like a woman's breasts in its erotic potential. Women should dress modestly, she says, because when women dress attractively such that men desire them, then they are the cause of men's sinning. She counsels her listeners to keep the five daily prayers, a ten-minute ritual that takes only an hour out of one's day. She says we must accept what God has sent as our fate, and not get angry with our husbands.

For variation, one session of this group met in a mosque. There were no refreshments, but being in the mosque, the group took the opportunity to perform the afternoon prayer together, wearing their white *telkong* (a prayer hood that covers the head and upper body, leaving the face exposed), which the women had brought along for the occasion. Another session was given over wholly to the teacher's telling of her recent trip to Mecca. She gave a chronological account that began with what it felt like to board the plane in Medan and continue to pray and recite verses all the way to Mecca. She spoke for an hour and a half, sometime crying as she remembered her emotions along the way, sometimes digressing to refresh her audience's knowledge about the stories from the Qur'an and Hadith that illuminate the places and objects along the pilgrimage, sometimes turning her experiences on the trip into homilies and didactic lessons, sometimes giving her audience ethnographic background on the foods, customs, and ways of the Arabs and the incomparable thrill of sharing a religious experience with persons of various races and origins. Her listeners were attentive and empathetic. Arriving at the *Ka'ba,* the peak moment of the pilgrimage, she said she had to pray in Karo, the language that comes from her heart, or else she would not have felt satisfied.

The *Pengajian Merga si Lima* women planned a third-anniversary celebration. For weeks they talked about it, anticipating something both definitively Karo and yet also religious. The women talked about a feast meal, wearing *ose* (traditional dress costume), and hiring a *gendang* for dancing. Many women in this group had made matching Malay-style dresses, however, and wanted to wear those. The event itself turned out not to be the ethnic celebration people had envisioned, apparently because Departemen Agama officials and non-Karo Muslim leaders in Berastagi would not agree to it. It was instead simply a set of speeches and a sermon, held on the veranda of a large mosque just outside the town. The *pengajian* organizer's wife arrived wearing a *tudung,* but she removed it halfway through and put on a Muslim-style cap. Other than a Qur'an recitation by a woman, and another woman who served as moderator, the speakers were all men, including the head of the Departemen Agama from Kabanjahe, a *mubalig* from Medan, who gave a sermon of about an hour's length, another Berastagi Muslim leader who was not a Karo, and the Karo man who is the acknowledged organizer of this *pengajian* group. Other women's *pengajian* groups in Berastagi attended, but only a handful of men. There was no music, and instead of a feast, only tea and *cimpa* (rice-flour snacks) were served.

One of the leaders of Berastagi Muslims, a non-Karo, spoke with me as we gathered on the lawn for this event, and I began to see why the ethnic celebration the women wanted would not have pleased him. A feast would have been wasteful, he said, complaining to me confidentially that these Karo women were poorly educated about Islam. The women were disappointed that they were not able to carry out their celebration as they had originally hoped. As we walked home afterward, they groused about the meager food and the event's lifeless character. Because of all the non-Karo guests, not even the language of the event had marked it as ethnically Karo.

[12 September 1986. Kabanjahe. *Pengajian Muslimin Karo.*] This group meets twice monthly in the home of Haji Sibayak Suka. It is a mixed-sex group but, as in any public context, males and females sit on opposite sides of the room. A man acting as moderator opens the meeting. He speaks briefly on the fact that the rhythm of our heartbeats seems to voice a repeated, "Allah, Allah, Allah," and that one position of the arms in *sembahyang* (worship service)—arms folded with hand gripping the wrist—allows us to feel our pulse and hear that refrain.

He turns the floor over to the Haji, who speaks for some fifteen minutes on the necessity of maintaining Karo kinship norms. Using the encapsulating phrases of the kinship ideology—*Merga si Lima, Tutur si Waloh, Rakut si Telu* (The five clans, the eight relations, three tied together)—he dwells especially on the latter, referring to the interdependence of the different roles of the *anakberu, senina,* and *kalimbubu.* He compares these three categories of kin to parts of the body. The *kalimbubu* is the head, the *senina* is the torso or trunk, and the *anakberu* are the limbs. He uses traditional phrases that make a similar equation: *kalimbubu si embus takalta* (the *kalimbubu* who make our heads hard [referring to the closing of a baby's fontanel]); *anakberu si latih* (the *anakberu* are the ones who get tired, i.e., carry out the work of a feast); and another word for *senina* is *sembuyak* (those of a common womb). The ethic encoded in these kin categories should not be lost, he urges, bemoaning the fact that young people nowadays sometimes speak disrespectfully to their *mama* (mother's brother), and people are not as strict about keeping the avoidance rules between in-laws. *Adat* and *agama* are "one path," (*sedalanen*) he avers, and Karo Muslims have to cultivate both.

The moderator gives the religious teacher twenty-five minutes. He leads the group through a kind of responsive reading of an Arabic passage. Most seem to follow from memory, some more sure of the words than others, and a few follow along from a book. His lesson, given in Indonesian although he is a Karo, uses a teaching style that sounds as if it is aimed at children, but is in fact a favorite device of Indonesian teachers at all levels. Often, he utters only the first syllable of the last word of a sentence. The audience is expected to say the last word as a fill-in-the-blank exercise, but since the correct response is often the most simple concept and is more than obvious from the context, this is less a conceptual test than a pedagogical device to encourage audience participation. He teaches us how to pronounce Allah after the Arabic fashion so that we do not sound like Indonesian Christians, who sometimes use the word *Allah* for God. He demonstrates the proper angle of the back when bending during *sembahyang,* and other details of the ritual.

After this, the moderator takes over. Tea is served, a collection taken, announcements made, and newcomers asked to tell something about themselves. Following a prayer led by a man, and punctuated with unison *amin* between sentences, the meeting ends.

Marking Muslim Identity

Aside from their participation in Muslim religious activities, the everyday life of most Karo Muslims in Karoland is little different from that of other Karo. Muslim households are marked by the persistent greeting, "*as-salamu'alaikum,*" that each person entering the house, even a child returning home from school, utters at the doorstep. Those in the house, or the person being greeted, respond with "*allaikumsalam.*" This Arabic salutation and response ("Peace be with you" and "With you also peace") are not usually exchanged between people unless both are members of the *umat.* That is, it is not a greeting for humans in general, but in Karoland, at least, marks Muslim identity and community. As an identity marker, it occasioned an awkward moment when the new Karo University was inaugurated in the fall of 1986. The major speakers were Muslim—the Bupati, a Lieutenant General, the Rector of the University, and the Bupati's wife. All of these began their speeches with the Arabic greeting. The Christian majority who made up the audience were uncertain whether to respond with the Arabic or not. Some did, some were silent, and afterward Christian friends said they had felt uncomfortable at these moments.

The calls to prayer, now broadcast on loudspeakers throughout the day from neighborhood mosques, and in the evening on television, remind Muslims of their duty and remind others of the Muslims' presence. The first call sounds at around 4:30 in the morning. Only a minority of Karo Muslims observe all five *salat* (daily prayers).[9] More regularly, people perform the evening *salat,* called *maghrib.* In general, more men than women carry out this pillar, and more old people than young. Those who are retired or beyond the age when work and small children demand much of their time can more easily work this observance into their day than younger people.

During Ramadan, the fasting month, Muslims are required to abstain from food and drink during the daylight hours. For the minority who keep this pillar of the faith, this means altering one's daily schedule to keep daylight activities to a minimum and to eat large meals at night and in the early morning to sustain one through the day. This is also the month of the most intense *dakwah* activities. The great relief at the end of this month of fasting culminates in the celebration of Hari Raya Idul Fitri, the biggest holiday of the Muslim year. This is both a family and community holiday in that Muslims who live outside Karoland return to visit their parents and family, and people express solidarity with a wider circle of kin and neighbors. Families prepare special snacks and invite kin and neighbors to visit. One receives guests and also makes the rounds of other's houses. Within the *umat,* people use these visits to make formal apologies to their teachers, elders, and other superiors, kissing their hands to beg forgiveness for any slights of the past year. But Christians and others are also invited to visit during this period just for the sociality of the season.

Throughout the Muslim world in recent decades, women's dress has become an important badge of Muslim identity. Except on definitively Muslim occasions, most Karo Muslim women do not dress differently from non-Muslim women, and Muslim women's notions of modesty are not markedly different from those of Karo women in general.[10] Deliberately Muslim costume consists of a Malay-style long skirt and matching long-sleeved top that disguises the waistline, reaching below the hips. Most women wear this when going to *pengajian* or some other function with Muslims, even if not necessarily a religious function. If a woman attends a meeting at the Departemen Agama, for example, perhaps representing her *pengajian* group, she dresses as a Muslim. For special occasions, girls or women in the same study group have these two-piece dresses made in matching colors. Only a few Karo women dress in this Malay style consistently, and those who do also wear caps completely covering their hair, adding a shear headscarf over that in public. Some Muslim women wear a cap most of the time, even at home, but with Western-style dresses that expose their legs. Many women, even at *pengajian,* and wearing Malay dress, put only a thin headscarf on their heads. Girls attending *madrasah* wear uniforms of long skirts, long-sleeved blouses, and a headscarf (some pin these tightly under their chins, others wear them so casually that they persistently fall off), but then switch to knee-length skirts or pants after school. Basically, women dress as Muslims when attending events demarcated as Muslim events, and at other times dress like their neighbors.

Pork eating, the age-old marker of Batak from Malay, now separates Muslim Karo from other Karo. When Muslims speak about the hindrances to Karo converting to Islam, they speak obliquely of pig raising rather than pork eating. That is, they speak as if Karo farmers raise pigs, so would be reluctant to give up this source of household income. This is perhaps a delicate way of getting around the reality that, whether they raise pigs or not, Karo enjoy eating pork, not to mention an occasional dog, which is also forbidden according to Islam. Pork was traditionally the most common food of feasts, the menu of the general or average funeral or wedding meal. Chicken or goat is considered the minimal comestible for a feast, cow or buffalo the most luxurious. Today Muslim relatives and guests who attend a feast where pork is served have to have separate food prepared, or else go without meat to accompany the rice, which would be an embarrassment for the host. As more and more persons convert to Islam, families increasingly slaughter a cow or buffalo at feasts to save the effort of cooking two different meat dishes. Thus, religious pluralism has been one of the forces behind a progressive inflation in the cost of feasts. Aside from feasts, pork is also available in Karo restaurants where *babi panggang* is billed as the major fare. This is cubes of roasted pork, served with a salty hot sauce made from the pig's blood. (Karo make a sauce from chicken blood as well, and blood is also a forbidden food for Muslims.) A few restaurants in Kabanjahe offer dog meat, which is viewed as an especially male food. Having to give up pork and, to a lesser extent, blood and dog meat still makes Islam unattractive to some Karo, but Karo Muslims now find it easier to avoid pork than they did in the past, when their numbers were so small that feastgivers and relatives did not adjust menus for them.

Like Christian Karo, Muslim Karo try to reconcile their religion and their *adat* to make these "one path." In large measure, this is possible. Like Christians, they are supposed to forsake all participation in ancestor propitiation and interaction with other spirits. Also like Christians, Muslims are not expected to alter their style or standards of interaction with kin. On the contrary, Karo Muslims whom I know embrace the specifically Karo elements of social organization—avoidance between in-laws, clan exogamy, respect for the *kalimbubu*, and a value on *impal* marriage. The old association of Islam with incest, as the Karo broadly define it, still taints the perception of Islam for many non-Muslim Karo, but if one asks Muslim Karo whether persons in the same clan may marry, they will vehemently deny this. As good Muslims, someone told me, people are enjoined to obey whatever norms are appropriate for their society, as well as religious rules.

Theoretically, Muslim law conflicts with the Karo's *adat* law at some points, for example, in inheritance and marital law. Islam gives female children shares of an estate half the size of their brothers' shares. Karo inheritance of land, at least in ideal terms, is patrilineal. In fact, there were always rules for breaking the patrilineal rule, and women often do receive land as inheritance. In any case, the religious court (Pengadilan Agama) in Karoland (and elsewhere in Indonesia) hears almost exclusively divorce cases, and almost never inheritance cases. Karo Muslims appear to follow *adat* law in inheritance, and when there is a dispute, to use the traditional form of deliberation (*runggu*) between a family's *kalimbubu* and *anakberu*. Only if unresolved there do cases proceed to a higher court, but like the disputes of Christians, these appeals go to the state courts (Pengadilan Negeri) rather than the religious courts.

Christians often dismiss Islamic propagandists and the conversions they produce as insincere. In fact, *da'i* and other teachers emphasize that it is not difficult to become a Muslim, pointing to the short confession of faith one has to memorize, and the positive things one has to do rather than the prohibitions. GBKP members contrast this with the year of study that precedes baptism. Christians feel that people are attracted to Islam because they can keep attending ancestor seances and performing *erpangir* and other traditional rituals. Others accuse that people become Muslim because they want to get ahead in their jobs (*naik pangkat*).

This negative perception is, at best, only partly true, overlooking and underestimating the degree of commitment and faith that many Karo Muslims display. In the past, certainly, many Karo who claimed to be Muslim lived in predominantly non-Muslim villages, had little chance to learn about Islam, and little social support for practicing their faith. Unlike the Christian communities, too, in which elders and congregations monitor members' behavior and expel those who persistently follow Perbegu or blatantly controvert moral rules, the *umat* takes a less formal approach to membership: a person is a Muslim who claims to be one. Christians thus complain that the number of

Muslims is inflated, because no one is ever taken off their rolls. Indeed, many who carry out the rituals of the traditional religion, including many who claim to be *guru* of various kinds, also say they are Muslim. But a commitment to Islam that begins with little more than a memorized confession of faith can become a gradually deepening commitment under the right circumstances. Those circumstances can be as diverse as the political pressure to exhibit religious devotion, the influence of religious teachers and leaders, the encouragement from a devout relative, or a move to a majority Muslim environment. Having once made a decision to become a Muslim, persons may only gradually and after some years begin to find out what that means and to alter their lives accordingly.

Karo Muslims seem little affected by the currents of religious and political change that have made such an impact in the Islamic world elsewhere in recent decades. The discussions about the role of Islam in political life that Jakarta intellectuals have pursued in recent years make hardly a dent in Karo thinking. Likewise, there is not a strong youth movement such as that which swept through educated young Muslims in Malaysia and elsewhere in Indonesia. The divisions that separate Muslims elsewhere into fundamentalists, modernists, and traditionalists are not particularly evident in Karoland. Muhammadiyah members do indeed speak of the necessity to return to fundamentals (*pokok*), but the fact that few Karo belong to this organization has less to do with their ideological disagreement on that point than with ethnic boundaries. Many of the more educated members of Muhammadiyah decry the divisions within the Muslim community, seeing them as petty differences of ritual practice, ethnicity, or political loyalty, when in fact, they point out, there is agreement (or at least no disagreement) on the larger issues—the nature of Islam, its sources of authority, and its place in politics and human life.

Perhaps Islam in Karoland looks more uniform than it does elsewhere because of its minority and newcomer status. Many older people who converted to Islam as adults have very little knowledge of the religion. Struggling to memorize the minimal rules, prayers, and recitations, they are in no position to reflect on intellectual or ideological alternatives within the faith, nor even to question the details of ritual practice. The fire of the Muslim movement elsewhere has been the fire of resurgence, renewal, revival, and reform among persons nominally if not actively Muslim. *Dakwah* in most other areas is aimed mainly at Muslims themselves. In contrast, Karoland is an area where *dakwah* still means primarily winning new converts, so the impetus and movement come not from an impetus for reform, but from the energy of a religious community emerging for the first time.

Conclusions

What happens to Karo Muslims in the cities? Ethnic associations drawing Karo Muslims together do exist in Medan and Jakarta, some of them student organizations, but I was unable to trace any of these. I learned of two *pengajian* groups in Medan of mostly Karo participants. Two men who had been suggested to me as leaders of Jakarta groups indicated that their groups were momentarily defunct. Karo Muslims have the advantage of being readily assimilable into local religious communities wherever they migrate within Indonesia. Since most other Indonesians are Muslims, the religious factor is also less inhibiting for young Karo Muslims who contemplate interethnic marriage than it is for Karo Christians. To the extent that Karo Muslims more frequently marry non-Karo,[11] this contributes to the loss of Karo ethnic markers. If Karo Muslims in the cities continue to seek community as Karo, they join ethnic associations pointed toward that end in which religious differences are held to be irrelevant. In the urban setting, then, religious community and ethnic community are generally dissociated for Karo Muslims in a way that is not true of Karo Christians, or at least not GBKP Christians.

In the homeland, however, ethnicity and religious community are still very closely associated since, in the larger towns, the *umat* segments into ethnic clusters. Both of the explicitly Karo *pengajian* groups I knew were formed precisely to harmonize Islam with Karo culture and language, teaching through the medium of the Karo language, and rationalizing Islam as compatible with a Karo identity. Indexing the success of this rethinking, Karo Muslims increasingly use their clan names with impunity. Membership in a clan is perhaps *the* elemental characteristic of Karo ethnic identity, since Karo think of their society as a community of kin organized through clans. In the past, converts to Islam who became Malay in the Karo lowlands, or those who remained on the Plateau, often elided their clan names. The pioneer Muslims from the village of Tiga Beringin did not use their clan names, for example, although two of their descendants, a man who works in Kabanjahe's Departemen Agama and a politician in Jakarta, proudly name themselves Tarigan and even rename the founding ancestor as such. Many Karo Muslims in Karoland and elsewhere, like their Christian counterparts, embrace both their faith and their ethnicity as central, but separable, parts of themselves.

Finally, segmentation of the *umat* does not follow the class pattern that is beginning to characterize Protestant denominations in Karo society. A Muslim academic suggested to me that Islam was philosophically more egalitarian than Christianity, but wondered if perhaps the Dutch had simply imparted Christianity in a hierarchical style. The missionaries' attention to rank, he thought, had impeded their success among Karo for whom "raja means nothing." Authority and equality in Karo Muslim and Christian communities are actually mixed and complex. Some *pengajian* clusters form around influential men, showing how hierarchy, if not class, does work within the Karo *umat:* the believers segment into patron-client cells. The GBKP and the Catholic church are both highly centralized bodies, and the GBKP may be further described as elitist, but the GBKP's study groups promote participants sharing their understanding through *diskusi.* In contrast, the *umat* is not strongly hierarchical in its totality, but Muslim study groups rely more heavily on the authority of teachers and leaders than on egalitarian discussions.

Notes

The first section of this chapter draws heavily from Sejarah Masuk dan Perkembangan Agama Islam di Tanah Karo Simalem, a book manuscript by Drs. Martadi E., kindly loaned to me by the author.

1. The term *sibayak* (literally, rich one in Karo, or fat one in Indonesian) is a Karo title for an influential man; the term *raja* connotes that a leader is Muslim.

2. Pa Mbelgah Purba was an important leader at the end of the nineteenth and early twentieth centuries, not when this story purports to occur, in the seventeenth century.

3. These stories compare well with Bowen's (1991) accounts of legends about the founding of Gayo domains. Legitimacy derived from the authority of an outside source of power—as well as trickery—appear in Gayo stories, too. In Karo stories the trickery often implies a legitimacy derived from being smart.

4. This compares closely with what Robert Levy (1973) describes for Tahiti.

5. *Sinar Indonesia Baru,* 27 September 1986. Published in Medan.

6. Some of the organizations that currently or in recent years have worked in Karoland include: Dewan Da'Wah Islam Pembangunan (DDII), Pelaksana Pembian Pembangunan Islam (P3I), Yayasan Perjalanan Haji Indonesia, Yayasan Baitul Makmur Medan, Persatuan Perwiridan Keluarga Tapanuli Selatan, Majelis Dakwah Islam (MDI), Rabillah Alam Islam Permakilan Indonesia (coordinated through the Departemen Agama), Pengajian Sarjana Muslim Karo di Medan, Perserikatan Muhammadiyah, Arisma, and Alyam'ijah Al Washliyah.

7. A Karo woman who had made the *haj* related how she had seen an Arab in Mecca sitting and reading the Qur'an silently, "as we would read a comic book," she said with amazement.

8. The group used a book titled *Surat Yaasin Takhtin Tahlil Berma'na.*

9. *Salat* is usually translated as prayer, but there is another word, *do'a*, meaning to petition or communicate with God, which perhaps better corresponds to Christian notions of prayer. *Salat* is a set of motions, postures, and specified phrases that aims to focus one's mind on Allah five times a day, acknowledging one's submission.

10. Older Karo women of any faith wear sarongs that reach to the ankles and *kebaya* with long sleeves. Middle-aged and younger women, especially in towns and cities, wear dresses or skirts and blouses, but add a sarong over these when necessary for sitting on the floor.

11. I did not gather statistics on this, but it is my impression that interethnic marriage is more common for Karo Muslims than Christians.

Chapter 11

The Traditional Religion: Hinduism?

The traditional Karo religion has no good name. One widely used term for it, *Perbegu,* may have originated as an epithet used by Christians (Steedly 1989, 27). *Begu* means ghost, and the term *perbegu* (one who has or uses ghosts) suggests a method of sorcery based on commanding giant ghosts for malevolent purposes. Christians and Muslims persistently name the various kinds of spirits of the traditional religion as *setan* (evil spirits), although some *begu,* notably ancestral spirits (*begu jabu*), are primarily benevolent and protective, and most other spirits are merely amoral, or else alternately beneficial and threatening (Kipp 1990, 128–33). With Pancasila nationalism, the term *Perbegu* has acquired other negative connotations as well, indicating backward or, at best, stubborn people. Christians term them *tertutup* (closed). Perbegu holdouts are *belum beragama* (people who do not yet have a religion). In the early 1970s and 1980s I sometimes heard adherents call this religion Agama si Pemena, the First Agama (or just Pemena), but as discourse about the concept of *agama* has tightened its definition (chap. 5), many people are now reluctant to use this name.

Whether or not *Perbegu* began as a pejorative term, it probably began as a name for something assumed to be analogous to Islam or Christianity—a set of beliefs and practices that had some kind of systemic coherence and that could be conceptually isolated from other aspects of life. In the 1920s and 1930s the missionaries organized native evangelists and teachers into discussion groups to determine what aspects of Karo life and practice contradicted Christian principles. Hoping to insulate the Karo from the cultural influence of surrounding Muslim peoples, the missionaries wanted to keep as much of Karo *adat* in place as they could, while prohibiting whatever contradicted Christianity. It turned out that beliefs about spirits and supernatural powers were interwoven with virtually every activity—laced throughout the agricultural cycle, linked to political and personal power, inextricable from relations with family, kin, and neighbors, and central to ideas about the etiology of disease. Christians set to work on the difficult task of separating issues of faith (*kinitekken*) from *adat*. Whatever coherence the traditional religion might have had in the era of its hegemony, the coherence it has now comes mainly as a system of negative correspondences or points of conflict with Christianity and Islam.

The range and variety of supernatural beings and powers indicate how the traditional religion pervaded all aspects of Karo life. *Begu jabu* (ancestral spirits) are the focus of family cults that, at the lowest level and most frequently, unite households. At higher levels and much less frequently, patrilineal descent groups of three or four generations' depth may coalesce, perhaps to rebury ancestral bones. Families put plates of food and other offerings aside for the spirits during weddings and other life crises, during illness or other dangers, in the fields at planting rituals, and during the village's annual festival (*kerja tahun*). Offerings can be placed on graves, or set on top of a wardrobe in the corner of the room. Any ancestor who died a violent death, or died in childbirth, falls in the category of powerful, vengeful beings who "died in one day" (*mate sada wari*). Spirit mediums are the vehicle through which family spirits can stay in contact with their living kin and descendants at seances in which the ghosts are "brought home" (*perumah begu*). Seances follow soon after burials, or can be done anytime, often in connection with a vow.

Giant ghosts (*begu ganjang*) are basically malevolent spirits who strike randomly, but also can be sent to carry out the bidding of humans, especially to defend property against theft. A variety of other spirits (*keramat*) associated with any unusual formation such as hot springs, mountain peaks, or spooky forests may bring illness on hapless passersby, but can also be propitiated by anyone in search of protection and power. Village communities once maintained shrines for *keramat* in the vicinity, refurbishing these regularly during the annual festival and as necessary to avert potential illness or casualties of warfare. These or other nameless spirits might possess ordinary villagers as well as *guru* during trances brought on by certain songs of the *gendang*. Families pay homage to spirits of the earth (Beraspati Taneh) and rice (Beru Dayang) in the season of the annual festival, timed in relation to the rice cycle. Personal spirit familiars (*jinujung*) empower people as spirit mediums, healers, and other ritual practitioners, and explain even the mystery of musical talent, for *gendang* players are said to have their abilities by virtue of *jinujung*. Impersonal supernatural sanctions operate within kin and community relations. The anger or offense of one's *kalimbubu* (wife-givers) is enough to bring illness or bad luck without their having to utter a curse or spell to that effect, and parents merge at their death into the ancestors from whom one requests blessings. Finally, supernatural powers rise up to kill those who dare to lie under oath, a powerful incentive to speak the truth in claims of crime and conflict.

Those who still carry out the hairwashings, seances, rain callings, and rice rituals are now a beleaguered minority. Family offerings for ancestors, shrines erected in newly planted rice fields, or a hairwashing for medicinal purposes can be performed privately (fig. 10). At this individual level, Perbegu practices remain viable even in religiously plural villages, but it is increasingly hard to find a critical mass to support villagewide rituals, except perhaps in remote areas of Karoland. The decline in community ritual observances was evident in the colonial period, however, even before significant numbers of Karo had converted to one of the world religions (Steedly 1989, 56–57). While seances, curing rituals, and hairwashings are still sponsored by some families, these events ideally draw on the participation of a wide circle of the sponsor's kin, and specific ritual roles are often tied to specific kin-role obligations. It is hardly possible to find families anymore in which these duties would not conflict with some relatives' identities as Christian or Muslim. For this reason, Perbegu ritual sponsors draw on distant or metaphoric kin to carry out ritual acts that in the past would have been carried out by close kin.

Perbegu has virtually no visibility in the cities. Certainly some Karo who live in cities continue to believe in ancestors and other kinds of spirits, and they may continue private devotions to these. Steedly (1989) describes a rotating credit association of petty traders, the core of which consisted of several female *guru* who shared their monthly credit pool to sponsor hairwashing ceremonies to please their spirit familiars. Notably, these women could not rely on kin participation in these ritual activities. I, too, learned of three Karo *guru* in Jakarta's Cililitan area, women and men who earned extra income by treating the afflictions of Javanese and members of other ethnic groups as well as Karo. What is left of the traditional Karo religion is merely fragments, a "privatized cult of healing," in Steedly's terms (1989, 30), that the government and the organized religious communities define as "belief," or superstition, outside both the legitimate spheres of *adat* and *agama.* Many Karo appear to keep neither the rituals of Perbegu, nor the requirements of any *agama,* and this, too, was noted by missionaries in the colonial era (e.g., Neumann 1907). The one avowedly Perbegu man I interviewed in Jakarta prided himself on being a political dissident. He was not interested in talking to me about Perbegu as a faith or way of life; religion seemed unimportant to him. But he made it clear that at least he would not stoop to being a "nominal" Christian or Muslim just because it was politically expedient.

Fig. 10. A spirit medium at work

Traditionalists, rejecting all of the five religions the state recognizes, defy the order the state wishes to impose. They are, therefore, disorderly and relatively disorganized compared to the practitioners of *agama*. Like colonial rulers who found it difficult to administer uncentralized peoples, the Indonesian state is suspicious of people whose religious life does not fit hierarchical, bureaucratic structures. These people are not easily co-opted and monitored. One solution has been to redefine their religions as "belief" and "culture" and to give them a place under the Department of Education and Culture. The state legitimates the traditional practices through this bureaucratic arm while attempting to undermine them with another, the Departemen Agama. While this definitional repositioning provides Karo traditionalists with the space to resist conversion, it also preempts the argument that traditionalist practices are legitimate as *agama,* and gives the state a structure for monitoring people thought to be among the most vulnerable to communism.

Organized Perbegu

Following the abortive coup in 1965, when thousands in Karoland rushed to join the organized religions, a movement started in Berastagi to organize Perbegu (Steedly 1989, 60–62). Calling itself the Association of the Five Clans (Persadaan Merga si Lima), it aimed to promote and preserve *adat* in this chaotic period of reprisals against communists, and to protect Karo who did not belong to an *agama*. One account suggests that this group was also prompted by a tragic flood and mudslide that killed ten people. A woman dreamed that the spirits of Mount Sibayak and other surrounding *keramat* were angry at being neglected by so many people and at the general unlawfulness of the times. The group sought to connect once more with these spirits, and to revive and protect Karo *adat* from further decay.[1] Its main ritual event was an annual hairwashing ceremony directed to the spirits of Mount Sibayak, the steaming volcano that overlooks Berastagi. The trances that accompanied these events led the Christians to label this group Perodakodak, after the *gendang* song that induces such trance. While the movement spread to other villages and even to the cities, and its annual hairwashing drew thousands of participants at its peak, it had fizzled by the mid-1970s.

It became clear that the traditional religion, even if placed in some kind of bureaucratic framework, would not be granted *agama* status, so some practitioners sought and found protection in two organizational shelters: they declared themselves a Hindu variant, or they redefined their practices as *culture* and joined groups organized under the Department of Education and Culture. In fact, these are not exclusive options, and many who call themselves Hindu may also belong to one or more "cultural" groups as well. One of the latter groups is called Himpunan Penghayat Kepercayaan Terhadap Tuhan Yang Maha Esa (HPKTYME), an organization centered in Jakarta that produces televised broadcasts appearing every two weeks on the state network (see chap. 6). The head of the culture section of the Kabanjahe office of the Department of Education and Culture said that in addition to Kabanjahe, there were four other branches of this organization in Karoland. Since it is a *cultural* phenomenon, he stressed, it does not conflict with *agama,* and members may have various religious identities.

I sought out the leader of the Kabanjahe chapter of the HPKTYME in 1986. I found him in a small, dark, and cluttered stall in the market, where he rented space for his sewing machine and took in clothing for alterations and repair.

[4 October and 20 October 1986. Kabanjahe. Interviews with a "cultural" group leader.] I asked about the goals and activities of the HPKTYME group and the history of his participation. From his evasive answers, I gathered that there were no organized activities. He does receive magazines and other literature from the Jakarta office, and he had attended one of the three national congresses this group has held, and to which representatives from some 500 different "cultural" groups from all over Indonesia were invited. He received a small salary (5,000 rupiah monthly) to organize and promote belief in the Absolute God, but he complained that it was not enough. Around 1980 he used to hold weekly meetings in a big *adat* house in the village of Sinaman. Playing a tape of *keteng-keteng* music (a percussion ensemble), he would perform his mantra. Having stopped even this, he was chided by the Level I leader in Medan, a Javanese man, who blamed him for not doing more.

Throughout our conversations, he spoke mostly in Indonesian, although he apologized for that. Several times he broke, as if involuntarily, into an unintelligible mantra, moving his hands above his head, then clasping them in a praying position, now clenching his fists, and always speaking in a rapid, spit-fire style. He said he would be glad to teach me his mantra and I could tape-record it if I wanted, but that really there are many ways to reach Tuhan Yang Maha Esa (the Absolute God). Some go through Jesus, some through Muhammad. He described his own mantra method as "direct." He admitted that his mantra is not traditional, in a strict sense. Traditional Karo *guru* lacked the knowledge of this direct access, but their associations with ancestor spirits, those who died in one day, and *keramat,* were certainly indirect means, because all spirits submit (*tunduk*) to the Absolute

One. He said that as with traditional Karo *guru,* his mantra comes from his throat [the traditional locus of spirit voices]. Because his body is "pure," the spirits that enter him come from everywhere—India, China, Sisingamangaraja (the Toba hero)—not just locally.

Still, he described his group as "preserving the culture of our ancestors," in accord with government ideals, citing President Soeharto on this point. He stressed that this organization was not an *agama.* Rather, it concerns only belief (*kepercayaan*). The Karo ideals of honoring the *kalimbubu* are of this sort, too. If we do not honor our *kalimbubu,* he said, Tuhan Yang Maha Esa is displeased with us.

Also under the Department of Education and Culture is an organization called Persatuan Pengobatan Tradisionil (Traditional healers union), and has existed since about 1980. This group is specific to Karo society. I interviewed the leader of it in his home in Kabanjahe, from which he runs a rice mill and where he receives patients.

[15 October 1986. Kabanjahe. Interview with traditional healer and his wife.] The organization he leads aims to professionalize the healing arts. The group has over 400 members, he said, with over twenty different kinds of specialties. Members live in Karoland and adjacent lowland areas, and *guru* who do not join, he suspects, are evil practitioners, those who own a giant ghost and fear its retribution if they join. After "testing" the knowledge of a professed *guru* who comes asking to join the group, the leader issues him or her a membership card signed by government officials that constitutes a kind of license. His membership list also functions, at least theoretically, as a referral device: he can match up people's infirmities with an appropriate specialist. Finally, the group maintains the right to sanction anyone who contravenes ethical standards, such as charging too much. (During the interview, a young man who worked for him in the mill and suffered periodic epileptic attacks said he felt an attack coming on, and asked for a preventative treatment. The treatment—based on pressure and massage—proceeded as we talked.)

Healers' powers come from various sources, he explained. Some healers get their power from *jinujung* (spirit familiars), but one can also simply study the techniques. His own power comes from Dibata (God), he said. Merely shaking hands with someone, he can feel the "energy" (his term) from their palm, and can tell the state of their health. (He pronounced me healthy.) Noting that healing is clearly connected to issues of faith or belief, and seeing a picture of Jesus on his wall, I raised the question of religion. Healers are of all different religions, he said. (A devout Muslim teacher I knew also carries a card from this organization.) He admitted that some Christians and Muslims were reluctant to use his services, but that others, especially after exhausting conventional medical treatments, sought his services. As for his own religious affiliation, he said he was a Protestant.

The Department of Education and Culture umbrella also includes Balai Pustaka Merga si Lima, which some describe as a descendent or perhaps a remnant of the Berastagi-based revitalization group dating from the 1960s. It seemed not to be active in 1986, but the head of the culture section of the Department of Education and Culture in Kabanjahe showed me the charter for still another group posted on his office wall for which he was listed as the head. The Lembaga Kebudayaan Merga Si Lima (The five clans culture institute) was just forming at that time. Its charter claimed its purpose to be nonpolitical, and further that its goals were to enhance belief in the Absolute God, and to strengthen nationalism consonant with the constitution and the Pancasila.

These groups organized under the Department of Education and Culture achieve many different political ends. First, they shelter religious practices (and practitioners) that do not fall under the rubric of *agama*. This mitigates or softens the dictum that requires all Indonesians to profess a limited number of acceptable *agama,* conceding something to those who resist. Second, they provide the government with a means to monitor resistance to its pressures to profess an *agama,* and to maintain contact with sectors of the society thought to be most ripe for communist propaganda. Finally, the HPKTYME group at the national level counters the extremism of reformist Islam, and its activities in Karoland and elsewhere provide Kejawen (Javanism) with a base of allies that spans the archipelago.

Hindu Karo

Bali's "internal conversion" is well known among scholars of Indonesia (Geertz 1973b). Under the political pressure to have an *agama,* and for more subtle issues of honor in a world turned "modern," the Balinese reinvented their religion as Hinduism. In a practical sense, this has meant that Balinese practices now enjoy the status of a fully legitimate *agama*. In a religious sense, this turn to Hinduism has meant a new "rationalization" of Balinese religion. Leadership and organization were bureaucratized and centralized, and scholars looked anew to the textual tradition of classical Hinduism to learn about it, holding themselves true to the identity they had taken on.

Some Perbegu followers found a model in Bali, although they may have found it too late. Karo claims to Indic ancestry are no more farfetched than those of many other Southeast Asian peoples. The argument was set out most extensively in a book called *Karo Dari Jaman ke Jaman* (Karo from age to age) (Putro 1981), which has had a fairly wide distribution. Whether they embrace the Hindu religious label for themselves or not, many Karo can point to their indigenous script, to clan names such as Berahmana, and cremation as traces of an Indic past. Just as Bali's Hinduism exhibits many variations from the Indian model, the reasoning goes, other forms of Hinduism found elsewhere in the archipelago will also have taken on locally distinct faces in response to years of change in isolation. By this reasoning, the Karo traditional religion is one of these Hindu variants.

More than providing a model, the Balinese have actively facilitated Karo and other people's efforts to become Hindu, forging communication with local men who step forward as leaders of this movement, and providing them literature and advice, as well as some funds for construction of temples. An organization called Parisada Hindu Dharma handles the proselytization and organization of Hinduism outside Bali as well as the reform and standardization of Hinduism within Bali (Boon 1977, 217; Hefner 1985, 252ff.). The Medan area is home to a fairly large Indian population dating from the colonial period and centered in an ethnic neighborhood, Kampong Keling. But the Hindu Karo have shown more affinity with the Balinese than the Indian variety of Hinduism. They are especially repelled by the self-mortification of the Indians (who, until it was outlawed, votively skewered their cheeks, for example). Struggles over leadership and cultural incompatibilities of other sorts may also have turned the Karo to the Balinese rather than the Indians for leadership.

For some Hindu Karo with whom I spoke, there was little pretense that their new label had in any way influenced their ritual practice or their beliefs. One elderly man told me that Hindu and Pemena were the same, except that Pemena had had no *surat* (holy writ). Naming themselves Hindu had been simply a pragmatic solution to keeping their traditional religion while also meeting political expediencies.

[10 September 1986. Kabanjahe. Head of the Departemen Agama.] Examining department statistics for past years, I noted the sudden appearance in 1984–85 of 5,000 Hindus in Kabupaten Karo, when previous years had listed none under the Hindu category. He said there had just not been any data gathered under that category before. I asked if some of these 5,000 were not actually Perbegu adherents. He said he could not say that. The department recognizes only certain official *agama*, he explained. If people say they are [Hindu], then they are. He has no ability to judge otherwise, he said, and he refused to speculate on the topic.

Despite the presence of some 5,000 declared Hindus in Kabupaten Karo, the Departemen Agama has no Hindu section. In 1989 I learned that some fifty students were studying in Medan to be Hindu religion teachers for the public schools, and the Departemen Agama will eventually be responsible for placing them. The Departemen had allocated money to Hindus, with a million rupiahs budgeted for the construction of buildings.

There are apparently two main clusters of Hindus in Karoland, both of them in Tiga Binanga County, one centered round the village of Bintang Meriah and another around Perbesi. A newspaper report of a "holiday" worship service in Perbesi in 1986 estimated that 10,000 people had attended this event that included Karo cultural elements such as a *guro-guro aron* dance and professional singers as well as a hairwashing ceremony.[2] The head of Parisada Hindu Dharma in Kabupaten Karo in 1986 was Lemba Ginting, originally from the town of Tiga Binanga but now resident in Kabanjahe. He estimated that some 50,000 Karo, in Karoland, Medan, and adjacent districts, had taken on the Hindu designation. This has all transpired since 1977, when the option to affiliate as Hindu became legally possible for Karo.

Like some Balinese pedants, a few Hindu Karo have made a concerted effort to learn about Hinduism in its classic sense, and to reinterpret their traditional practices in a new light. One of these was Sempaten Sinulingga, a retired primary school principal who lived in the village of Bintang Meriah.

[6 November 1986. Bintang Meriah. Interview with Hindu group leader.] Once a GBKP member, Sinulingga decided to leave that church after an accident and several illnesses had befallen him. In 1982 a Karo who teaches at the Medan Hindu teacher's school gave him some literature about Balinese Hinduism, and Sinulingga went on to organize and lead the Hindu Karo movement in Bintang Meriah. Balinese officials sent him a collection of several of the Hindu classics, most of them translated into Indonesian by Gede Pudja. He was proud of his small library on the subject that he guessed surpassed that of any other Hindu Karo. He kept it in a glass cabinet and used the books at meetings in his home every other week. He described these meetings as *sembahyang* (worship or prayer services) explaining the etymology of this Indonesian word from the terms *sembah* (to worship) and *nenek moyang* (ancestors). At these meetings, someone read from one of his books, and then the group discussed it. I asked if, like Muslims, members attempt to memorize Sanskrit passages. Sinulingga's wife (Nd. Bahtera) said there was little point in memorizing a language no one understood. The point is to understand, she said.

The group has an official-looking stamp linking it to the national Parisada organization, the levels of which parallel levels of the government. It read, "Parisada Hindu Dharma, Tingkat II, Kab. Karo," with a swastika design but no obvious

Karo symbols. To join his group, Sinulingga told me, members "sanctified themselves" with a hairwashing ceremony. It was not necessary for leaders of the organization from outside to witness it. Sinulingga cast himself as the lowest-level leader in the Parisada organization, one who teaches and administrates. A second-tier leader is called *finandita*, a ceremonial officiant, and the highest ranking spiritual leaders, marked by their abstaining from meat consumption, are termed *pendeta*. There are no Karo at this level, he said. In 1985 he attended a conference in Medan that drew several Balinese religious leaders.

What is the relationship between Pemena and Hindu, I asked Sinulingga. In the beginning, he said, Karo were Hindu, but they did not have a book. One Nabi Bhrgu arrived, leaving behind books on bark (*pustaka*). Hindu influences in Indonesia came first to Karo, he said, then to the other Batak peoples, to Palembang, and finally to Java and Bali. Bali was last, and there also some books were left. He stressed that the Karo were not attempting to copy Indian and Balinese religion, but would remain Hindu *Karo* always. The religion of Hindu Karo is mostly about *dibata* (God or gods?), and *nenek moyang*, he said. If there had been no ancestors, none of us would be here, and the *nenek moyang* show us the way to God. Ancestors are good and do not disturb humans, but there are also bad spirits, called *setan*, of many different kinds and levels. God created these, too, to show humans good by having an opposite against which to compare it. I asked about *dibata ni idah* (the visible god), i.e., the *kalimbubu*. He responded that they have a holy character for a household, and are protective of it. If angered, "the rice will not bear fruit," it is said, but this also can be fixed with apologies.

With Hinduism of any sort there are five cardinal beliefs, Sinulingga continued. One is belief in *Sang Hyang Widhi*, the Absolute God. Two is *atna*, which he understood as ancestral spirits. Three is the law of *karma phala*, which he explained as cause and effect, or you reap what you sow. "If we plant rice, we get rice, not corn." The fourth belief is *samsara* (reincarnation). "We come back again in one of our grandchildren, if not our looks, then our voice or our talents." And the fifth belief is *maksa*, which he translated as heaven (*sorga*).

In 1986 the Hindu community in Bintang Meriah and two nearby communities had recently built a *pura* (a shrine for receiving offerings) located several kilometers away in Tanjong Pula. Balinese consultants helped design it. At its base rest figures that look like dogs with marbles for eyes, but were described to me as *singa* (lions). Elephants, geese, and a snake are stacked in sequence. By 1990 a second *pura*, plus a meeting hall (*balai*), had been completed just outside Bintang Meriah. A Balinese-style stepped gate leads into a yard containing these buildings. This *pura* has two figures of the winged Garuda, and still more *naga* (snakes). On the day I visited it in 1990 another kind of offering shrine, called *cibal-*

cibalen, stood there too. Karo traditionalists construct these triangular platforms, made of perishable split bamboo on stilt legs, and leave them in place after a ritual to decay in the elements (see fig. 10). Remnants of the offering still remained on this one.

When I returned to Bintang Meriah in 1990 Sinulingga had died. Nd. Bahtera recounted that she had held a funeral seance for him, hiring a well-known spirit medium who is also an officer in the local Hindu chapter. Returning to speak through the medium, Sinulingga had advised his children, all sons, to live as he had lived, not to use their educations simply for self-aggrandizement, but to accomplish good. His sons had all graduated from college, in fact, and one was working in a Jakarta bank, another as an engineer in Kalimantan. None of them are Hindu, apparently, but one has converted to the Catholic church, one to a Protestant faith.

Sinulingga's family pattern may well foretell the future of Hindu Karo. While the same ten families in Bintang Meriah continued to come to worship and discussion sessions twice in the lunar month, and another man in the village had taken Sinulingga's place as leader, the group had not grown in the four years between 1986 and 1990. In 1986 I had learned that the group's membership was primarily older people, except for a few younger married couples. The group had attracted no adolescents to its teachings.

There are no Hindu Karo in Jakarta, as far as I could determine, but the Medan area does have some.

[26 September 1986. Medan. Interview with a former leader of Parisada Hindu Dharma (Karo).] It turns out that he had had a falling out of some kind with Parisada, and no longer functioned officially in the organization, but he had once traveled to Bali at Parisada's expense to investigate Balinese Hinduism and return to explain it to other Karo. He works as a traditional healer, running a clinic out of his home where patients can stay. He specializes in tumors.

He entered into a long explanation on the cultural and historical connections of Karo and India, citing cognate terms in Sanskrit and Karo, and tracing the line of cultural influence from Srivijaya (near Palembang) to Baros (on the West Coast) to Karo. He pointed to the triadic congruence of the Toba Batak's *dalihan na tolu* (the triangular hearth stones that hold the cooking pots) with the triangular dormers that grace Karo roofs, and the triumvirate *kalimbubu, anakberu,* and *senina* (agnates), with the Brahma, Vishnu, and Siva triune. Virtually in the same breath, he was quite frank about the political pressures after G30S to have a religion, and he knew that many Karo who cared little for these historical and cultural rationales had taken the Hindu option.

Again, the religious affiliations of the families of Hindu Karo hint that this variant faces an uncertain future. This man's own father is an elder in the GBKP, and his wife and children affiliate with that church as well. A picture of the Last Supper adorns his living room wall, and he told me that his family takes its turn along with others in hosting the weekly prayer meetings of the GBKP.

Conclusion

Issues of identity revolving around the meaning of kinship, religion, and custom are far from settled from the perspective of those who cling tenaciously to the traditional religion, whether they label themselves Hindus, or proudly resist any *agama* designation (Steedly 1989). They do not buy the argument put forth most explicitly by the GBKP (e.g., GBKP, Moderamen 1983; Surbakti 1986), but also in the Muslim *pengajian* groups, that one can extract religion out of the totality of *adat* such that being a Christian or Muslim does not mean one is rejecting Karo tradition. Can *adat* and *agama* be separated, I asked a former leader of the Hindu Karo community. He denied this vehemently, moving into an impassioned complaint that so many Karo these days were abandoning their clan names, were ashamed of their origins, and spoke freely and coarsely with their *mama* (mother's brother).

The people who continue to practice the traditional rituals, who know the *turi-turin* (stories) that root Karo *adat* in the past, those who can find no solace or meaning in the new *agama* are left, in Steedly's terms, "hanging without a rope." They cannot accept the national rhetoric about what it means to be modern (*moderen*); they cannot execute rituals that depend on the participation of a village congregation or a congregation of kin, for both villages and kin networks are hopelessly plural. They are left with only the shell of a ritual tradition. Their insistence that *adat* cannot be segregated from issues of belief and ritual practice is drowned out by other voices, louder and more numerous, insisting that Muslims and Christians have not abandoned *adat*, reconstructing that term in a new way that implies a secular body of custom and practice not to be confused with superstitious "beliefs" or religious faith.

The traditionalists are losing the contest over what Karo identity means, and as the word contest implies, this is a power struggle. The traditionalists constitute a minority, but more importantly, they are an unorganized minority. Uniting under the banner of Hinduism has perhaps allayed some of the worst pressures to convert to other religions, but it has not succeeded in drawing the traditionalists into an effective structure that could hold its own against the Muslims, who benefit from Departemen Agama patronage, or the Christians, who inherited a bureaucratic legacy and a material estate from the missionaries.

The traditionalist stance is the stance of the poor and uneducated. No traditionalists, not even Hindu Karo, have positions in Jakarta circles. In contrast, Muslim Karo politicians or Christian businessmen and bureaucrats link homeland and migrant communities, pour wealth earned at the nation's center back to the Karo periphery, and come back to display their wealth and their faith in their home villages. At least two Hindu Karo leaders whom I met might be termed middle class, or lower middle class. One of these, Sempaten Sinulingga, perhaps true to his background as a teacher, was not content simply to adopt Hinduism as a name. For him, it represented a standard to which he was trying to educate himself and others. More typical of the traditionalists, at least in the urban Medan context, are the failed gambler, the petty vegetable dealers, and aging *guru* that Steedly describes. I came to suspect that many of the rank and file of those who declared themselves Hindu were *guru,* female healers and spirit mediums, supplementing their income by managing the ritual needs of other traditionalists, both Hindu and non-Hindu. In the cities, of course, *guru* benefit from reputations that transcend ethnic boundaries, drawing patients who are Chinese, Javanese, and Tamil, as well as Karo (Yoshida 1992). Given their visibility as ritual healers and impresarios, these men and women may especially need the political protection of the Hindu label, or else feel they have to abandon their medical-ritual practice and the income supplement that it brings.

Notes

1. The former leader of this group denied that it had been in conflict with *agama* in any way, citing his own identity as a Muslim at that time. He saw it as an issue of preserving *adat,* but admitted that many people did see it as counter to their religious commitments, and he attributed its ultimate failure to this.

2. *Sinar Indonesia Baru,* 24 October 1986. Published in Medan.

Chapter 12

The Secularization of Karo Identities

Religious pluralism seems to matter very little in Karo life, at least in public settings. Since kinship networks are wide, they invariably include persons of different faiths, but at a wedding or funeral, for example, everyone accepts similar standards of interaction as kin. Whether at a large private feast or a public community gathering, people expect religious pluralism and accommodate it. Speakers announce that people should pray according to their own religion, even if someone then proceeds to offer the public prayer as a Christian or Muslim. Pork is served much less often than beef these days at feasts or, if it is served, an alternate meat course will be prepared for Muslim relatives. A thesis from an Islamic Institute in Medan begins with the hypothesis that Karo kinship contributes to religious tolerance, describes the "family hegemony" that characterizes Karo society, and concludes that kinship *adat* has greater weight here than *agama* (Hasbi 1979–80).

Religious pluralism creates problems only in the most private circle of family life. Parents, family, and religious leaders all counsel young people not to marry someone of another faith. In fact, interfaith marriages, in the sense of partners who retain different faiths, are illegal (Cohen 1992; Pompe 1988). Either the bride or groom must convert to the other's religion, and interfaith marriages are a growing "problem" in Indonesia. Like other Indonesians, Karo presume that most often the bride will convert, but this is not inevitably the case. In one family where a young man from a Christian family decided to marry a Muslim girl and convert to Islam, some of his relatives were so upset they threatened to boycott the wedding. The pressure to change religion in the interest of family unity may also come from parents, children, or siblings. One man explained that when his two children were growing up, he decided to enter Islam. His daughter was then attending a Catholic church, while his son had become a Muslim through the attention of a Muslim uncle. The father decided the family should all take the same religion, so the daughter, who said she was not really committed to Catholicism, decided to become Muslim then as well.

Some families are, nonetheless, split with regard to religious affiliation. One student at an Islamic Institute in Medan described her own conversion to Islam as a result of a *dakwah* group from Medan that came to her village in 1980. She converted despite the fact that her father is an elder in the Protestant church and a religion teacher in the schools. Her mother converted to Islam as well, but then after a short time, under pressure from her husband, rejoined the Protestants (Sitepu 1984). In this account (a thesis) Erlina Sitepu judges that people's reluctance to separate themselves from their kin impedes the rate of conversions to Islam among the Karo.

Marriages between persons of different faith, and conflicts among close kin, are thus the primary point of religious tension in this pluralistic society. Both Christians and Muslims, as people who follow an *agama,* accept similar implicit rules about insulating kinship behavior from religious conflict, but this is more difficult for traditionalists for whom religious obligations and kinship obligations are not easily separable.

[September 1973. Payung Village.] I was talking with Nini L., a Perbegu woman who also practices as a *guru* occasionally. She was telling me about a relative who had died a Christian, although his wife was not Christian. One son was Christian, two were not. His burial went according to "Christian *adat,*" she said, but then his widow and the two non-Christian sons decided to have a seance and call the man's soul back, keeping their plans secret from the Christian son. When this son learned of the plans, he stormed out of the house in anger. At the seance, a *keteng-keteng* (percussion ensemble) played, and sure enough, the soul of the deceased came back to speak to his family with much insight (*mesingteng*). Many Christians, after they die, have been called in seances like that, Nini L. related, as if it were a little triumph, the fact that Christian souls, too, could be "brought home" in this way.

A seance is a public event, or at least a family event that requires cooperation from an extended network of kin. A Christian son who fails to sit before the medium to converse with his deceased father creates a conspicuous absence. Private rites, however, even in religiously plural families, often present no problems. In one family, a mother remains a firm traditionalist, despite her children's conversion to Christianity. When her daughter married, she attended the church wedding as the occasion required, but later no one in the family objected to her preparing an offering for the ancestors and depositing it on top of a wardrobe in the house.

Not all Karo accept the premise that kinship and culture can be secularized. Traditionalists are least likely to accept this premise. Those who are well educated, and who are among the middle class or who aspire to be, as well as Christians and Muslims, do accept it. Isolating religion from kinship protects the basis of community, not simply among people who are actually kin, but also because Karo use kinship metaphorically both for pragmatic purposes and for the satisfactions intrinsic to sociality.

Just as Karo rhetorically and ideologically elevate kinship solidarity above religious differences, they also proclaim that kinship bonds transcend wealth differences. The kinship order rests on hierarchical affinal relations, but not a hierarchy based on material wealth and power. In fact, kinship statuses of superior *kalimbubu* and inferior *anakberu* may contradict other kinds of hierarchies (Bangun 1981). The ideology of kinship that ties all Karo to each other, and through which Karo construct their ethnic identity, obscures the significance of emergent class distinctions.

Although Karo society could well be described as classless as late as the colonial era, heritable differences of wealth began to emerge at that time. The Dutch granted land to leaders and showed a special interest in educating the sons of headmen. After the revolution, these sons of headmen or of *sibayak* were among the first Karo to benefit from urban migration, and today the sons of colonial-era leaders are found disproportionately among the Karo elite. Those who were educated and worked in salaried positions in the colonial era impressed their children with the value of education. Heritable advantages and disadvantages carry greater weight than before, but there are also new ways to rationalize success and failure. The Karo's passion for gambling, their quests for magical knowledge and for spiritual helpers, and sometimes their resignation to an impersonal fate continually frustrated the missionaries, who wanted them to see success linked to diligence and discipline rather than amoral, quixotic forces. Now successful Karo like to see their achievements as a measure of moral worth, overlooking, sometimes, the significance of simple luck, especially the luck of having been born into certain families.

[22 July 1989. Jakarta. Interview with a wealthy businessman, S., and his wife.] We discussed the tendency for education to run in families. S.'s father was one of the first to come to Jakarta for education, returning to work as a medic in Kabanjahe. He sent all of his sons to school. S. went into the military, but retired young to start his own business. Mrs. S.'s father, a Bupati, also educated all his children. Two of Mrs. S.'s brothers became doctors, one became a teacher. Both Mrs. S and her sister (whose husband occupies a high position in one of the government ministries) married well.

S.'s father's brothers were not as successful. Their children now come asking S. for help—money to buy prescriptions, for example, or for a job in his company. He has also provided funds for some of them to attend school. Some of these have then dropped out of the typing or accounting programs he funded. Others, upon getting a job, buy a car and hire a driver the first thing, trying to act like big men. He despairs of trying to help those who do not have ability or who are lazy. He pointed to his own work schedule, leaving the house at 8:00 every day, and often not returning until 8:00 in the evening, implying that if these relatives worked like that, they would not be poor.

In the past, wealthy men expended their resources through feasting and multiple marriages, although they retained enough for sumptuary markers of their status—heirlooms, jewelry, and funeral displays. Now, both the absolute and relative differences of rich and poor are far greater than they were in the past. The types and values of sumptuary markers have expanded, but wealth differences also influence the diet, health care, and educations of people's children in ways that were not true of rich and poor in precolonial Karoland. Wealthy headmen or leaders once lived in the midst of kin whom they saw daily in face-to-face encounters, and who also pressed them for loans of rice, money, and land. Today, the most wealthy Karo live in ethnically mixed urban neighborhoods, their large houses encased in guarded compounds, where kin who want to borrow must come to visit. Living with a wealthy family in Jakarta in 1989, I found that my close friends who were of working-class status would not stop by for me there, suggesting I come instead to their homes. They did not want to give the impression of coming for a handout.

With incorporation into the colonial state, Karo began to gain a new sense of ethnic identity. The missionaries, carving out territories along linguistic lines, demarcated Karo from Simalungun as well as Toba Batak. Only after independence did many Karo accept the religion the missionaries had brought. Conversion revised the religious marker between Batak and Malay from heathen/Muslim to Christian/Muslim, and Christianity remains to some extent an ethnic flag, but the old isomorphism of ethnic and religious identities was beginning to come apart even in the colonial era. Competition between Karo and Toba in the ethnically heterogeneous towns of Karoland, especially within the Christian fold, further etched the distinctions *within* the Batak category (and between Christians), forging a sense of specifically Karo identity and heightening the value of the kinship order that unites Karo as Karo. Incidents and struggles since then, most recently over naming a forest preserve, continue to sustain this contrast to the point where some Karo elite have begun to disavow the Batak label altogether.

At the same time that wealth differences and ethnic consciousness began to emerge, Karo were beginning to define religion as a separate sphere of experience in response to Christian missionary activities and, later, conversions to Islam. Kinship was made over as disenchanted custom, enabling Karo to assert an ethnic commonality overriding their religious differences. Religion was relegated to a new private sphere. Within this private sphere, moreover, a significant number of Karo of all faiths are noticeably devout and studious, nourishing their religiosity in new ways. The missionaries often complained that Karo missed a feeling for the spiritual, being preoccupied instead with making money, eating well, and staying healthy. These goals remain important for most Karo families, but so does the practice of their faith. The routine grace before meals in Christian families, the worn Bibles I see people thumbing in prayer meetings, the Haji who never fails to respond to the call to prayer, his wife who studies to read the Qur'an with a tutor, the Hindu teacher who studies the Bhagavad-gita, the woman who blows red saliva on the "face" of the rice spirit as medicine against the cruel harvest, tearful Pentecostals with hands raised to heaven—these images bespeak the richness of Karo spirituality today. Just as Karo are more self-consciously Karo than they were in their precolonial past, they are also more self-consciously religious than they were when religion was not visibly demarcated from the rest of their lives. As is the case everywhere, too, there are merely nominal adherents of all faiths, people who are more attuned to the politics or practicalities of everyday life than the mysteries of the spirit.

Indonesia: Jousting with Secular Individualism

Government officials in Indonesia often assert that theirs is neither a religious state, nor a secular one. The government's rejection of the secular label contrasts with its neighbor Singapore, which openly terms itself secular, and where new Shared Values (analogous to Indonesia's Pancasila) contain no mention of God.[1] In contrast, the Indonesian government sees itself a champion and patron of religion (in certain modern and politically quiescent forms) rather than simply indifferent to it. Newspaper editorials or reports of speeches further spread the word that secularism is a Western malady, and Islamic scholars elsewhere concur that secularism and relativism are peculiar to the Western world (Al-Attas 1978).

Anthropologists and area-studies specialists of other sorts often wrangle with the problem of applying generalizations wrought from the study of Western history to non-Western settings. The myth of evolutionary inevitabilities may blind our comprehension of cultural uniqueness and historical contingency, but other myths may blind us as well. Adding to the analyst's dilemma, Indonesians often *assert* that their culture and their values are not those of the West, implying that their future will also be different. Indonesians imagine Westerners as individualistic and "free" in comparison to themselves, unconnected by family bonds and unmoved by societal sanctions. Heider (1991, 109) lists individualism versus social embeddedness as one of the prominent themes of Indonesian commercial films. Movies depict interaction rather than characters' inner states, and promote the sanctity of the family group over the desires of the individual.

The florescence of capitalism in New Order Indonesia has not occurred because people embrace capitalism as an ideal nor the individualism that accompanies it.

> It seems to me highly significant, incidentally, that in the rhetoric of the Suharto [*sic*] government, the term 'capitalist' is still a dirty word. Indonesia's ideology, whether one defines it formally as Pancasila or realistically as anti-communism, extols few of the central pillars of capitalism, if any. It excoriates 'free fight liberalism,' individualism, acquisitiveness, private property rights, uncontrolled individual initiative, independence of government 'guidance' or regulation, free speech and a free press, unconstrained reliance on market forces and even 'the rule of law' in the sense that we in the West think of it. (Mackie 1990b, 108–9)

J. A. C. Mackie discusses Soeharto's patronage of the village cooperative program, despite its many failures, because of his strong commitment to the idea of collectives. Whether Soeharto believes in collective ideals himself, he understands very well what Indonesians want to believe about themselves.

Ideologies do shape policies and popular values, but they also mask social realities. Any Westerner who has ever tried to stand in line at the free-for-all of a postal counter or other public service quickly perceives that, in this kind of arena, Indonesians are far more individualistic than they think. A growing compartmentalization does mark Indonesian life, as it marks other societies of the modern world. Can this fail to affect, finally, the values and identities, the sense of self, of those who live in this new kind of compartmentalized social order? The Indonesian posturing against the evils of "individualism" speaks partly to the lived reality of a growing private sphere in an urbanized world where life is segmented into context-specific roles.

Secularism, like any other ism, can become an ideology, "a new closed world-view which functions very much like a new religion" (Cox 1965, 21). Most Indonesians would shrink from secularism in this sense of a deliberate stance of godlessness. Nor is the world entirely disenchanted for most Indonesians, who continue to interpret their lives in religious terms.[2] While it may be true, then, that secularism is rare in Indonesia, as it is in other Southeast Asian countries (Clammer 1984), secularization is the order of the day.

The term *secularization* has been used for so many different processes, however, that some scholars have argued it has no further use in sociological inquiry (Martin 1978). Even those who see some value in the term admit that it has attained a "mythical" status, signifying a universal or inevitable process of technological progress and corresponding moral decline that may describe only the Western trajectory (Glasner 1977). Leaving aside a judgment about whether this is progress or decline, I use the term here not to suggest the disenchantment of the world and the demise of religiosity, but rather to name the splintering of life that accompanies urbanization and industrialization wherever they occur (ibid., 60).

The literature on secularization points to a process by which both social institutions and individual loyalties grow specialized, autonomous, and differentiated over time (Fenn 1970; Luckmann 1967). Religion becomes encased in tailored organizations, but is practiced as a private matter of choice. Rather than life losing its "ultimate significance," it comes to have "a plurality of systems of ultimate significance" (Fenn 1970). The ultimately significant may derive also from family life, politics, or even sports. This is true for any society, of course, but family, politics, sports, religion, and so on, operate more or less independently in specialized spheres in those societies marked by what Durkheim called organic solidarity. "What were originally total life values become part-time norms" (Luckmann 1967, 39).

Secularization, in this sense of compartmentalization, arises as a product of the sheer "social density" of large heterogeneous societies (Durkheim [1933] 1964).[3] More than simply heterogeneous, large societies are also hierarchical, with centralized polities and a citizenry that is wealth-stratified. In Indonesia, heterogeneity abets hierarchy, enhancing the center's ability to maintain control. Crosscutting diversities of religion and ethnicity, each of which alone challenges the unity of the nation, together benefit the power of state. Here, where diversities intersect, diminishing each other's impact, managing diversity has been more effective than repressing it. The management techniques that the Indonesian state has used include an ideology that encompasses diversity, organizational shuffling to permit co-optation and surveillance of religions, and a sensitivity to "anticipated participation" (meaning criticism and protest) from any constituency.

Indonesia's policies on culture and religion appear straightforwardly about culture and religion, specifically, about controlling Islam and forestalling ethnic or regional secession. The dangers these divisions pose to national integration are obvious to everyone: that hatred of the Chinese will erupt into rioting; that Aceh, Irian Jaya, Timor, or other edges of the country will attempt to claim their own domain; that the "normative piety" of some Muslims will be imposed forcefully on other Muslims or even non-Muslims.

Pancasila ideology aims most obviously to quell religious politics. The first pillar of the Pancasila transcends religious differences with reference to an Almighty God that presumably all Indonesians can acknowledge. Eschewing the stance of a secular state, the government aims to mollify those who might still wish for a thoroughly Islamic state. Through the Departemen Agama, furthermore, the government gains a measure of corporatist influence over all religious communities, but most significantly, over Islam. Religions that do not fit the definitions of the Departemen Agama are redefined as "culture," and shuffled into the Department of Education and Culture.

Official pronouncements to the contrary, a plurality of institutionalized religions and, in Indonesia's case, of officially sanctioned *agama,* suggests a necessarily secular environment (see Yinger 1967). Policies on religion carve out *agama* as an institutional sphere purified of secular "culture" and (superstitious) "belief." The government favors and finances these conceptually bounded *agama,* encouraging Christianity and Islam to displace the traditional religions, the practice of which always spills haphazardly into matters of culture and politics, opening the possibility that religious revivals may stoke the fires of ethnic resistance. Christianity and Islam, universal religions that cut across ethnic groups, have also grown stronger in relation to each other. Belonging to one of the official religions says nothing, supposedly, about one's ethnic identity or culture. One can be Christian and still be Javanese or a Muslim and still be a Batak. Extracting "culture" from the rationalized *agama* and protecting several religions of state invites religious pluralism within ethnic blocs.

The Pancasila does not refer directly to ethnicity, being a statement of values that ideally transcend it. But the national motto—Various, yet One or Out of Diversity, Unity—is widely understood to speak primarily to ethnic diversity. The motto does not imply assimilation so much as coexistence. While the education side of the Department of Education and Culture promulgates the superordinate, unifying Pancasila philosophy throughout all levels of the public schools and the civil service, the culture side of the same ministry promulgates the maintenance of ethnic differences at the benign level of dress costumes, marriage rites, songs, dances, handicrafts, and traditional houses. Cultivating and displaying the ethnic arts does not compete with loyalty to the nation (except if one is Chinese). On the contrary, local arts speak to the creation of a genuinely indigenous national culture, symbolically reasserting the break with colonial domination. In addition, the wealth and variety of the nation's arts and cultures lure the wealth of foreign tourists and stimulate the domestic tourist industry.

To the extent that ethnic consciousness diminishes religious unity, and religion pluralizes ethnic groups, policies promoting culture and religion are also about each other. What is more, both are also about class, or precisely, about keeping class out of sight. Because Indonesia so seldom fit the parameters of class as these appeared in Western history, even some Marxist scholars were drawn instead to the concept of *aliran,* social categories based on religious style (Mackie 1990a, 73, 91).[4] Whether working on Java or elsewhere, scholars drew their analytical frames from those categories that Indonesians themselves use and act upon, and class is not typically one of them (Kahn 1982).

> Class analysis has been strangely absent from the large corpus of foreign and domestic writing about Indonesian society and politics. The problems of writing about a social formation which embraces diversity as its national motto are bound to create difficulties for a western-derived theoretical and political outlook. . . . And yet, for all the clear, saturating influences of regional, ethnic and religious alliances, and the organizational imperatives of party and military politics, Indonesian politics since independence has had a remarkable focus on class concerns. Whatever else the events of 1965 were about, they fundamentally involved the liquidation of the human and organizational basis of the most overt class-based political force in the country, and the foundation of a state pursuing profoundly different class interests. (Tanter and Young 1990, 7)

The state's promotion of traditional arts and the patronage of religion magnify the visibility of ethnicity and religion, while class interests remain unseen.

From its very beginning, the New Order has been quite open about promoting religion as an antidote to godless communism. Whether or not godliness actually does lessen class consciousness, both Marx and the leaders of Indonesia think that it does. Religious antagonisms between Javanist Muslims apparently prevented rural *elites* from cooperating in their class interests in the pre-1965 era in East Java (Hefner 1990, 207). Occasionally, someone even views the balance of religion and class from the opposite vantage, suggesting that the government regards a growing class awareness as a palliative against the threat of radical Islam (e.g., Hart 1986, 210; Vatikiotis 1991, 32), or against racial outbursts against Indonesian Chinese (Yoon 1991).

In contrast, promoting the traditional arts is usually not analyzed in class terms, as if the ethnic entities to which these arts draw the mind do not affect people's perception of class issues. Nonetheless, scholars as often find ethnic divisions foiling class consciousness as religiousness. Mackie, for example, suggests that the lack of middle-class consciousness in Indonesia has to do with the fact that so many in this class are ethnically Chinese (1990b, 99). Javanese laborers in Sumatra's plantation belt continue to speak of "we" Javanese, and "they" in various ethnic categories, rather than speaking of economic commonalities that unite some Batak with some Javanese (Stoler 1985, 196–97).

The accusation that colonial states reigned through divide-and-conquer tactics is widespread in the postcolonial world, and Indonesians often see this tactic in the actions of their former colonial rulers, the Dutch. They do not suggest that their government uses similar tactics in the present, but the structural differences between colonial and postcolonial states are perhaps more apparent than real (Vail 1989, 2; Washbrook 1990). Michael Hechter (1975) suggests that even England's relationship to its Celtic fringe has been one of "internal colonialism," with a dominant core draining labor from an ethnically distinct periphery and selling manufactured goods to it. Economically, Indonesia's core is Jakarta, rather than Java-Bali as a whole (Drake 1989, 214–15), so ethnicity does not correlate in this case with a neat core-periphery model. Rather, state policies in Indonesia balance a complex mix of class interests, ethnic tensions, and religious politics.

To suggest that the government actively cultivates religion and culture to offset each other and to counteract class evokes the familiar image of the *dhalang* (Javanese master puppeteer), an image that has been applied to Indonesian politics many times. Imagining social engineering of this sort attributes more control to the state than it actually has. But observers of

Indonesia generally would not dispute these elements: the government promotes *agama;* it supports the traditional arts; it proclaims communism its "enemy number one." The suggestion that the state maintains control by keeping competing forces at a standoff fits also a common judgment about Soeharto and his remarkable staying power, and about the nature of pluralism in the Indonesian polity. Liddle, among others, has suggested that one of Indonesia's unique characteristics is "Soeharto's extraordinary skill in responding to the demands (or, rather, in anticipating them, since there are few mechanisms for direct participation) of threatening constituencies" (1990, 57). If this balancing act is not predesigned, it is at the very least a consequence of policies directed toward specific problems and constituencies that cancel each other out.

The *dhalang* imagery implies, too, that the masses are helpless puppets. However, the Karo situation reminds us that these "puppets" can assent or resist, mock or misunderstand. They can also use nationalist ideologies for their own rhetorical and practical ends.[5] One example of this is how the movement to de-Batak the Karo could use an acceptable national ideal—preserving traditional culture—to clothe an old ethnic rivalry. Hegemonic ideologies may come from the top down or from the center out, but are also resisted at the bottom, reconstructed and reinterpreted at the peripheries.

The state's policies and propaganda succeed to the extent that they match the needs and interests of people like the Karo, but "the Karo" are no longer a monolithic entity, if indeed they ever were. Some elements of the government's policies succeed because they coincide with what some Karo want and feel, in particular those Karo who are financially successful, well-placed, and who exercise leadership in the ethnic community. Not all Karo, especially those who live in highland villages, feel the need to join ethnic associations, sponsor "cultural" evenings, and study *adat*. Though not all have become devout, the government's patronage of *agama* matches a widespread and deeply felt religiosity among many Karo Christians and Muslims. The government's promotion of traditional arts matches a keenly felt sense of ethnic pride and a need for roots among urban or other transplanted Karo. The government's castigation of communism matches a nervousness about wealth differences among people who speak of and to each other as kin. Compartmentalizing religion and ethnicity from each other, and protecting both these communalistic spheres from the corrosive effects of wealth differences, Karo move among different roles, relationships, and identities with a sense of their priorities. Religious differences do not overcome ethnic solidarity; ethnic pride does not overcome national patriotism; and class issues remain, at least for now, concealed behind communities of faith and an ideology of kinship and ethnic solidarity.

Notes

1. Reported in *Mirror*, 15 March 1991. Published by Singapore's Ministry of Information and the Arts.

2. This suggests why Indonesian narratives and experiences so often prove refractory to historical and anthropological interpretation. See Steedly 1989 on Karo narratives that resist our making sense of them.

3. The historical path of secularization (in any of its senses) is not everywhere the same (Meland 1966; Wilson 1987). The specific shapes and relations of religion and the secular are not the same either, even among Western societies. Organized religion and personal religiosity differ significantly in places such as Poland, Britain, and the United States.

4. The *aliran* concept applies at best and only to Java, there evoking three basic social divisions: *abangan* (animistic Muslim peasants), *priyayi* (mystical elites or bureaucrats), and *santri* (devout Muslims).

5. See Warren (1990) for a discussion of this with reference to Bali; and Bowen (1986) with reference to Aceh.

Glossary and Abbreviations

abangan	Nominal Javanese Muslim
adat	Customary law, or sacred tradition
agama	An organized, world religion
aliran	Social category based on religion
anakberu	The inferior wife-receivers; families into which daughters marry
arisan	Rotating credit group
babi panggang	Roast pork
bere-bere	Mother's clan; also a man's sister's children
bupati	District head
dakwah	Muslim renewal or proselytizing
dhalang	Javanese puppeteer
dar al-Islam	The world of Islam
datuk (or datu)	Chief or big man in the Karo lowlands who is Muslim
DPR	Dewan Perwakilan Raykat, House of People's Representatives
erpangir ku lau	Ritual hairwashing
GBKP	Gereja Batak Karo Protestan, Karo Batak Protestant Church
gendang	Traditional Karo musical ensemble
Golkar	Golongan Karya, the goverment party
GSRI	Gereja Sidang Rohulkudus Indonesia, Church of the Assembly of the Holy Ghost of Indonesia
G30S	Gerakan Tigapuluh September, the September 30th Movement
guro-guro aron	Courtship dance
guru	Ritual specialist or healer
haji	A person who has made the pilgrimage to Mecca
HKBP	Huria Kristen Batak Protestan, the (Toba) Batak Christian Protestant church
impal	Marriageable cousin; mother's brother's daughter or father's sister's son
jinujung	Spirit familiar
kabupaten	Government district
kalimbubu	The superior wife-givers; families into which sons marry
kebaya	Woman's blouse
kepercayaan	Belief, often contrasted with *agama*

keramat	Nature spirit
madrasah	Islamic religious school
mehangke	Shame, respect
merga	Clan
Merga si Lima	The Five Clans; Karo society
Moderamen	The organizational center of the GBKP
mubalig	Muslim preacher
nenek moyang	Ancestors
Pancasila	Indonesia's national philosophy: belief in the Almighty God, humanism, nationalism, democracy, and social justice
pandita	Minister (Indonesian, *pendeta*)
patah tulan	Bonesetter
pengajian	Qur'an recitation and religion instruction
Perbegu	Traditional Karo religion, or a practitioner of it
perpulugen jabu-jabu	Family devotionals in the GBKP
pesantren	A boarding school for Islamic study
PKI	Partai Komunis Indonesia, the Indonesian Communist Party
pura	Hindu shrine
rebu	Formal avoidance behavior
rupiah	Valued between 1,600 and 1,700 to the U.S. dollar for most of this research period
santri	Devout Muslim
SARA	Abbreviating the tabooed topics, *suku, agama, ras, antar gologan:* ethnicity, religion, race, and class
sarune	Oboe
sembahyang	Worship service
senina	Patrilineal kin; sibling of the same sex
sibayak	Chief or bigman, especially in the Karo Highlands
suku	Ethnic group
sukuisme	Tribalism
sumbang	Incest
tudung	Woman's headwrap
turang	Sibling of the opposite sex
turang impal	Sibling-like cousin of the opposite sex; ♂ father's sister's daughter or ♀ mother's brother's son
turangku	Husband's sister's husband and wife's brother's wife
UKA	Universitas Karo Area, Karo Area University
ulama	Muslim religious scholar
ulu emas	Section of the bride-price paid to the groom's mother's brothers
umat	The community of Muslims

References

Abdullah, Taufik. 1981. The sociocultural scene in Indonesia. In *Trends in Indonesia, II,* ed. Leo Suryadinata and Sharon Siddique, 65–76. Singapore: Singapore University Press.

Acciaioli, Greg. 1985. Culture as art: From practice to spectacle in Indonesia. *Canberra Anthropology* 8 (1 and 2): 148–72.

Ackerman, Susan E., and Raymond L. M. Lee. 1988. *Heaven in Transition: Non-Muslim Religious Innovation and Ethnic Identity in Malaysia.* Honolulu: University of Hawaii Press.

Adams, Kathleen M. 1990. Cultural commoditization in Tana Toraja, Indonesia. *Cultural Survival Quarterly* 14 (1): 31–34.

Al-Attas, Syed M. al. Naquib. 1978. *Islam and Secularism.* Kuala Lumpur: ABIM.

Alavi, Hamza. 1972. The state in postcolonial societies: Pakistan and Bangladesh. *New Left Review,* no. 74: 59–82.

Anderson, Benedict O'G. 1983. *Imagined Communities.* London: Verso.

Anderson, John. 1971. *Mission to the East Coast of Sumatra in 1823.* Kuala Lumpur: Oxford University Press.

Andrain, Charles F. 1988. *Political Change in the Third World.* London: Allen and Unwin.

Apter, David. 1968. Government. In *International Encyclopedia of the Social Sciences,* vol. 6., ed. David L. Sills, 214–30. New York: Macmillan and Free Press.

Aqib, Zainal. 1985. *Gelombang Masuk Islam.* Surabaya: Bina Ilmu.

Aragon, Lorraine V. 1991–92. Revised rituals in Central Sulawesi: The maintenance of traditional cosmological concepts in the face of allegiance to world religion. *Anthropological Forum* 6:371–84.

Arens, W. 1979. *The Man-Eating Myth.* New York: Oxford University Press.

Atkinson, Jane Monnig. 1983. Religions in dialogue: The construction of an Indonesian minority religion. *American Ethnologist* 10:684–96.

———. 1989. *The Art and Politics of Wana Shamanship.* Berkeley: University of California Press.

Awanohara, Susumu. 1984. A first warning shot. *Far Eastern Economic Review* 27 (September): 14–15.

———. 1985. The Islam factor: Indonesian politics. *Far Eastern Economic Review* 24 (January): 26–31.

Aznam, Suhaini. 1992. Counting the cost of Timor. *Far Eastern Economic Review* 2 (April): 34, 36.

Babcock, Timothy. 1989. *Kampung Jawa Tondano: Religion and Cultural Identity.* Jogjakarta: Gadjah Mada University Press.

Badan Perencanaan Pembangunan Daerah. 1985. *Buku Pintar Daerah Tingkat II Karo 1985.* Kabanjahe: Bappeda.

Bangun, Payung. 1981. Pelapisan Sosial di Kabanjahe. Ph.D. diss., Universitas Indonesia.

Bangun, Roberto, ed. 1989. *Mengenal "Orang Karo."* Jakarta: Yayasan Pendidikan Bangun.

Bangun, Teridah. 1986a. *Adat dan Upacara Perkawinan Masyarakat Batak Karo.* Jakarta: Kesaint Blanc.

———. 1986b. *Manusia Batak Karo.* Jakarta: Inti Idayu Press.

———. 1986c. Perseketuan orang Batak Karo di daerah perantauan. In *Seminar Kebudayaan Karo dan Kehidupan Masa Kini,* ed. Sarjani Tarigan, 192–210. Medan: Publisher unknown.

———. 1990. *Penelitian dan Pencatatan Adat Istiadat Karo.* Jakarta: Yayasan Merga si Lima.

Banton, Michael P. 1977. *Rational Choice: A Theory of Racial and Ethnic Relations.* Bristol: SSRC Research Unit on Ethnic Relations.

Barnett, Steve, and Martin G. Silverman. 1979. *Ideology and Everyday Life.* Ann Arbor: University of Michigan Press.

Barth, Fredrik, ed. 1969. *Ethnic Groups and Boundaries.* Boston: Little, Brown and Company.

———. 1984. Problems in conceptualizing cultural pluralism, with illustrations from Sahar, Oman. In *The Prospects for Plural Societies,* ed. David Maybury-Lewis, 77–87. 1982 Proceedings of the American Ethnological Society. Washington, D.C.: American Ethnological Society.

Barus, Ngukumi. 1988. *Petimbang Karo.* Medan: Ulamin Kisat.

Barus, Ngukumi, and Masri Singarimbun. 1990a. *Beru Ginting Pase.* Jakarta: Yayasan Merga si Lima.

———. 1990b. *Telu Turi-turin Si Adi.* Jakarta: Yayasan Merga si Lima.

Basham, Richard. 1983. National racial policies and university education in Malaysia. In *Culture, Ethnicity and Identity: Current Issues in Research,* ed. William C. McCready, 57–77. New York: Academic Press.

Becker, David. 1987a. Development, democracy and dependency in Latin America: A postimperialist view. In *Postimperialism: International Capitalism and Development in the Late Twentieth Century,* ed. David G. Becker, Jeff Frieden, Sayre P. Schatz, and Richard L. Sklar, 41–62. Boulder, Colo.: Lynne Rienner.

———. 1987b. Postimperialism: A first quarterly report. In *Postimperialism: International Capitalism and Development in the Late Twentieth Century,* ed. David G. Becker, Jeff Frieden, Sayre P. Schatz, and Richard L. Sklar, 203–25. Boulder, Colo.: Lynne Rienner.

Becker, David G., Jeff Frieden, Sayre P. Schatz, and Richard L. Sklar. 1987. *Postimperialism: International Capitalism and Development in the Late Twentieth Century.* Boulder, Colo.: Lynne Rienner.

Bell, Daniel. 1975. Ethnicity and social change. In *Ethnicity, Theory and Experience,* ed. N. Glazer and D. P. Moynihan, 141–74. Cambridge: Harvard University Press.

Benda, Harry J. 1958. *The Crescent and the Rising Sun: Indonesian Islam under the Japanese Occupation, 1942–1945*. The Hague: van Hoeve.

Benjamin, Geoffrey. 1976. The cultural logic of Singapore's "multiracialism." In *Singapore: Society in Transition*, ed. Riaz Hassan, 115–33. Kuala Lumpur: Oxford University Press.

Bennett, John W., ed. 1975. *The New Ethnicity: Perspectives from Ethnology*. 1973 Proceedings of the American Ethnological Society. St. Paul: West Publishing Company.

Bentley, G. Carter. 1987. Ethnicity and practice. *Comparative Studies in Society and History* 29:24–55.

Bevervoorde, K. Th. Engelbert. 1892. En bezoek aan de Bataksche Hoogvlakte. *Bijdragen tot de Taal- Land-en Volkenkunde* 41:609–21.

Beyer, Ulrich. 1982. *Und Viele Wurden Hinzugetan: Karo-Batak-Kirche: Mission und Wachstum*. Wuppertal: Vereinigten Evangelisch Mission.

Biro Pusat Statistik. 1984. *Indonesia 1984*. Biro Pusat Statistik: Jakarta.

Block, Fred. 1987. *Revising State Theory: Essays in Politics and Postindustrialism*. Philadelphia: Temple University Press.

Blu, Karen. 1980. *The Lumbee Problem*. Cambridge: Cambridge University Press.

Bodaan, Laurens. 1910. Uit het volkleven der Karo-Bataks. *Maandberichten Nederlands Zendelinggenootschap*, no. 6:91–93.

Boland, B. J. [1971] 1982. *The Struggle of Islam in Modern Indonesia*. The Hague: Martinus Nijhoff.

Boon, James A. 1977. *The Anthropological Romance of Bali 1597–1972*. Cambridge: Cambridge University Press.

Booth, Anne, and Peter McCawley. 1981. *The Indonesian Economy During the Soeharto Era*. Kuala Lumpur: Oxford University Press.

Booth, Anne, and R. M. Sundrum. 1981. Income distribution. In *The Indonesian Economy During the Soeharto Era*, ed. Anne Booth and Peter McCawley, 181–217. Kuala Lumpur: Oxford University Press.

Bottomore, Thomas B. 1966. *Classes in Modern Society*. New York: Pantheon.

Boulding, Elise. 1979. Ethnic separatism and world development. In *Research in Social Movements, Conflicts and Change*, vol. 2, ed. Louis Kreisberg, 259–81. Greenwich, Conn.: JAI Press.

Bowen, John R. 1986. On the political construction of tradition: Gotong royong in Indonesia. *Journal of Asian Studies* 45:545–61.

———. 1989. Poetic duels and political change in the Gayo Highlands of Sumatra. *American Anthropologist* 91:25–40.

———. 1991. *Sumatran Politics and Poetics*. New Haven: Yale University Press.

Boyd, Robert, and Peter J. Richerson. 1987. The evolution of ethnic markers. *Cultural Anthropology* 2:65–79.

Breuilly, John. 1982. *Nationalism and the State*. Manchester: Manchester University Press.

Briskin, Linda. 1990. Identity politics and the hierarchy of oppression: A comment. *Feminist Review* 35:102–8.

Bronson, Bennet. 1977. Exchange at the upstream and downstream ends: Notes toward a functional model of the coastal state in Southeast Asia. In *Economic Exchange and Social Interaction in Southeast Asia*, ed. Karl Hutterer, 39–52. Ann Arbor: University of Michigan Center for South and Southeast Asian Studies.

Brown, Iem. 1987. Contemporary Indonesian Buddhism and Monotheism. *Journal of Southeast Asian Studies* 18:108–17.

Bruner, Edward M. 1959. Kinship organization among the urban Batak of Sumatra. *Transactions of the New York Academy of Sciences* 22:118–25.

———. 1961. Urbanization and ethnic identity in North Sumatra. *American Anthropologist* 63 (3): 508–21.

———. 1963. Medan: The role of kinship in an Indonesian city. In *Pacific Port Towns and Cities*, ed. Alexander Spoehr, 418–26. Honolulu: Bishop Museum Press.

———. 1972a. Kin and non-kin. In *Urban Anthropology*, ed. A. Southall, 373–92. London: Oxford University Press.

———. 1972b. Batak ethnic associations in three Indonesian cities. *Southwestern Journal of Anthropology* 28 (3): 207–29.

———. 1974. The expression of ethnicity in Indonesia. In *Urban Ethnicity*, ed. Abner Cohen, 251–80. London: Tavistock.

———. 1987. Megaliths, migration and the segmented self. In *Cultures and Societies of North Sumatra*, ed. Rainer Carle, 133–49. Veröffentlichungen des Seminars für Indonesische und Südeespraeken der Universitat Hamburg, vol. 19. Berlin: Dietrich Reimer Verlag.

Buckley, Charles Burton. 1984. *An Anecdotal History of Old Towns in Singapore*. Singapore: Oxford.

Butler, Judith. 1990. *Gender Trouble: Feminism and the Subversion of Identity*. New York: Routledge.

Callinicos, Alex. 1976. *Althusser's Marxism*. London: Pluto Press.

Carnoy, Martin. 1984. *The State and Political Theory*. Princeton: Princeton University Press.

Cederoth, Sven. 1981. *The Spell of the Ancestors and the Power of Mekkah: A Sasak Community in Lombok*. Göteborg, Sweden: Acta Universitatis Gothoburgensis.

Centers, Richard. 1949. *The Psychology of Social Classes: A Study of Class Consciousness*. New York: Russell and Russell.

Chalmers, Ian. 1991. Indonesia 1991: Democratization and social forces. *Southeast Asian Affairs 1991* 17:107–21. Singapore: Institute of Southeast Asian Studies.

Chan, Wing-Tsit, ed. 1963. *A Source Book in Chinese Philosophy*. Princeton: Princeton University Press.

Ch'en, Kenneth. 1964. *Buddhism in China: A Historical Survey*. Princeton: Princeton University Press.

Clammer, John. 1984. Secularization and religious change in contemporary Asia. *Southeast Asian Journal of Social Sciences* 12 (1): 49–58.

Clifford, James. 1988. *The Predicament of Culture*. Cambridge: Harvard University Press.

Cohen, Abner. 1969. *Custom and Politics in Urban Africa*. Berkeley: University of California Press.

————. 1981. Variables in ethnicity. In *Ethnic Change*, ed. Charles Keyes, 307–31. Seattle: University of Washington Press.

Cohen, Margot. 1992. To Mecca with love. *Far Eastern Economic Review* 9 (April): 28–29.

Cohen, Ronald. 1978. Ethnicity: Problem and focus in anthropology. *Annual Review of Anthropology* 7:379–403.

Coleman, James S. 1956. Social cleavage and religious conflict. *Journal of Social Issues* 12 (3): 44–56.

Collier, David. 1979. *The New Authoritarianism in Latin America*. Princeton: Princeton University Press.

Comaroff, Jean, and John Comaroff. 1991. *Of Revelation and Revolution*, vol. 1. Chicago: University of Chicago Press.

Cortesão, Armando, trans. and ed. 1944. *The Suma Oriental of Tome Pires*. London: Haklyut Society.

Cox, Harvey. 1965. *The Secular City*. New York: Macmillan.

Crais, Clifton C. 1992. *White Supremacy and Black Resistance in Pre-Industrial South Africa*. Cambridge: Cambridge University Press.

Crouch, Harold. 1978. *The Army and Politics in Indonesia*. Ithaca: Cornell University Press.

Cunningham, Clark E. 1958. *The Postwar Migration of the Toba-Bataks to East Sumatra*. New Haven: Southeast Asia Studies, Yale University Press.

————. 1981. Celebrating a Toba-Batak national hero: The 1979 events for Sisingamanagraja XII. Paper presented at symposium, Cultures and Societies of North Sumatra, Hamburg, 25–27 November.

Dahl, Robert A. 1956. *A Preface to Democratic Theory*. Chicago: University of Chicago Press.

————. 1982. *Dilemmas of Pluralist Democracy: Autonomy versus Control*. New Haven: Yale University Press.

————. 1986. *Democracy, Liberty and Equality*. Oslo: Norwegian University Press.

Dahrendorf, Ralf. 1959. *Class and Class Conflict in Industrial Society*. Stanford: Stanford University Press.

Dalton, Bill. 1977. *Indonesia Handbook*. Franklin Village, Mich.: Moon Publications.

Darmaputera, Eka. 1988. *Pancasila and the Search for Identity and Modernity in Indonesian Society: A Cultural and Ethical Analysis*. Leiden: E. J. Brill.

Davis, Gloria. 1979. What is modern Indonesian culture? An epilogue and example. In *What is Modern Indonesian Culture?* ed. Gloria Davis, 307–18. Athens: Ohio University Center for International Studies.

de Haan, C. 1870. Verslag van eene reis in de Battaklanden. *Batavishe Genootschap van Kunst en Wetenschappen* 38:1–57.

de Haan, F. 1897. Een oud bericht aangaande de Batta's. *Tijdschrift voor Taal-Land-en Volkenkunde* 34:647–48.

Dentan, Robert K. 1975. If there were no Malays, who would the Semai be? *Contributions to Asian Studies* 7:50–64.

Despres, Leo A. 1975a. *Ethnicity and Resource Competition in Plural Society*. The Hague: Mouton.

―――. 1975b. Toward a theory of ethnic phenomena. In *Ethnicity and Resource Competition in Plural Society*, ed. Leo A. Despres, 185–207. The Hague: Mouton.

―――. 1984. Ethnicity: What data and theory portend for plural societies. In *The Prospects for Plural Societies*, ed. David Maybury-Lewis, 7–29. 1982 Proceedings American Ethnological Society. Washington, D.C.: American Ethnological Society.

Deutsch, Karl, and William Foltz. 1963. *Nation-Building*. New York: Atherton Press.

Dick, Howard W. 1990. Further reflections on the middle class. In *The Politics of Middle Class Indonesia*, ed. Richard Tanter and Kenneth Young, 63–70. Australia: Centre of Southeast Asian Studies, Monash University Press.

Dion, Marc. 1970. Sumatra through Portuguese eyes: Excerpts from João de Barros: Decadas de Asia. *Indonesia* 9:129–62.

Djajadiningrat, Hoesein. 1934. *Atjetsch-Nederlandsch Woordenboek*. Batavia: Landsdrukkerij.

Dobbin, Christine. 1974. Islamic revivalism in Minangkabau at the turn of the nineteenth century. *Modern Asian Studies* 8:319–56.

―――. 1977. Economic change in Minangkabau as a factor in the rise of the Padri Movement, 1784–1830. *Indonesia* 23:1–38.

―――. 1983. *Islamic Revivalism in a Changing Peasant Economy: Central Sumatra, 1784–1847*. London: Curzon Press.

Douglas, Mary. 1966. *Purity and Danger*. London: Routledge and Kegan Paul.

Drakard, Jane. 1986. Ideological adaptation on a Malay frontier. *Journal of Southeast Asian Studies* 17 (1): 39–57.

―――. 1990. *A Malay Frontier: Unity and Duality in a Sumatran Kingdom*. Ithaca: Cornell University Southeast Asia Program.

Drake, Christine. 1989. *National Integration in Indonesia*. Honolulu: University of Hawaii Press.

Dreyfus, Hubert L., and Paul Rabinow. 1983. *Michel Foucault: Beyond Structuralism and Hermeneutics*. Chicago: University of Chicago Press.

Drummond, Lee. 1983. Review of *Ethnic Identity: Strategies of Diversity*, by Anya Peterson Royce. *American Ethnologist* 10:802–3.

Durkheim, Emile. [1933] 1964. *The Division of Labor in Society*. New York: Macmillan.

Echols, John M., and Hassan Shadily. 1961. *An Indonesian-English Dictionary*. Ithaca: Cornell University Press.

Eder, James F. 1987. *On the Road to Tribal Extinction: Depopulation, Deculturation, and Maladaptation Among the Batak of the Philippines*. Berkeley: University of California Press.

Eggan, Fred. 1937. The Cheyenne and Arapaho kinship system. In *Social Anthropology of North American Tribes*, ed. Fred Eggan, 79–80. Chicago: University of Chicago Press.

Ehrenreich, Barbara. 1989. *Fear of Falling: The Inner Life of the Middle Class*. New York: Harper.

Emmerson, Donald K. 1976. *Indonesia's Elite: Political Culture and Cultural Politics*. Ithaca: Cornell University Press.

———. 1983. Understanding the New Order: Bureaucratic pluralism in Indonesia. *Asian Survey* 23:1220–41.

———. 1987–88. Invisible Indonesia. *Foreign Affairs* 66 (2): 368–87.

———. 1991. Diversity, democracy, and the "lessons" of Soviet failure: Western hopes, Asian cases. *Pacific Review* 4:1–12.

Engels, Frederick. 1972. *Origin of the Family, Private Property and the State*. New York: International Publishers.

Enloe, Cynthia Holden. 1973. *Ethnic Conflict and Political Development: An Analytic Study*. Boston: Little Brown.

Epstein, Arnold L. 1967. Urbanization and social change in Africa. *Current Anthropology* 8:275–95.

———. 1978. *Ethos and Identity: Three Studies in Ethnicity*. London: Tavistock.

Errington, J. Joseph. 1984. Self and self-conduct among the Javanese *priyayi* elite. *American Ethnologist* 11:275–90.

———. 1985. *Language and Social Change in Java*. Monographs in International Studies, Southeast Asia Series, no. 65. Athens: Ohio University Center for International Studies.

Errington, Shelly. 1983. Embodied *sumange'* in Luwu. *Journal of Asian Studies* 42:545–70.

Feith, Herbert. 1962. *The Decline of Constitutional Democracy in Indonesia*. Ithaca: Cornell University Press.

Feith, Herbert, and Lance Castles. 1970. *Indonesian Political Thinking 1945–1965*. Ithaca: Cornell University Press.

Fenn, Richard K. 1969. The secularization of values. *Journal for the Scientific Study of Religion* 8:112–24.

———. 1970. The process of secularization: A post-Parsonian view. *Journal for the Scientific Study of Religion* 9 (2): 117–36.

Fenton, Steve. 1987. Ethnicity beyond compare. *British Journal of Sociology* 38:277–82.

Foltz, William. 1963. Building the newest nations: Short-run strategies and long-run problems. In *Nation-Building*, ed. Karl Deutsch, 117–31. New York: Atherton.

Foucault, Michel. 1977. *Discipline and Punish: The Birth of the Prison*. New York: Vintage.

Fryer, Donald W., and James C. Jackson. 1977. *Indonesia*. London: Ernest Benn Limited.

GBKP, Moderamen. 1983. *Adat Istiadat Karo*. Makalah Seminar Adat Istiadat Karo. 31 August to 3 September 1983. Berastagi: GBKP.

GBKP, Panitia Jubileum 100 Tahun. 1990. *Selamat Jubileum 100 Tahun GBKP*. Kabanjahe: GBKP.

GBKP, Team Penelitian. 1976. *Benih Yang Tumbuh 4: Gereja Batak Karo Protestan*. Jakarta: Dewan Gereja-gereja di Indonesia.

Geertz, Clifford. 1960. *The Religion of Java*. Glencoe, Ill.: Free Press.

———. 1963. Primordial sentiments and civil politics in new states. In *Old Societies and New States*, ed. Clifford Geertz, 105–57. New York: Free Press.

———. 1973a. Person, time, and conduct in Bali. In *The Interpretation of Cultures*, by Clifford Geertz, 360–411. New York: Basic Books.

————. 1973b. "Internal conversion" in contemporary Bali. In *The Interpretation of Cultures*, by Clifford Geertz, 170–89. New York: Basic Books.

————. 1980. *Negara: Theatre State in Nineteenth-Century Bali*. Princeton: Princeton University Press.

————. [1974] 1983. "From the native's point of view": On the nature of anthropological understanding. In *The Pleasures of Anthropology*, ed. Morris Freilich, 58–73. New York: Mentor.

————. 1984. Distinguished lecture: Anti anti-relativism. *American Anthropologist* 86:263–78.

Gellner, Ernest. 1983. *Nations and Nationalism*. Ithaca: Cornell University Press.

George, Kenneth Martin. 1989. The Singing from the Headwaters: The Headhunting Rituals of an Upland Sulawesi Community. Ph.D. diss., University of Michigan.

Gerini, Gerolamo E. 1909. *Researches on Ptolemy's Geography of Eastern Asia, Further India and the Indo-Malay Archipelago*. London: Royal Asiatic Society and Royal Geographical Society.

Giddens, Anthony. 1982. Class structuration and class consciousness. In *Classes, Power, and Conflict*, ed. Anthony Giddens and David Held, 157–74. Berkeley: University of California Press.

————. 1984. *The Constitution of Society: Outline of the Theory of Structuration*. Berkeley: University of California Press.

————. 1991. *Modernity and Self Identity: Self and Society in the Late Modern Age*. Stanford: Stanford University Press.

Gietzelt, D. 1989. The Indonesianization of West Papua. *Oceania* 59:201–21.

Ginting, Berita. 1984. *Siapa dan Dimana Sarjana-Sarjana Merga si Lima*. Jakarta.

Ginting, Juara Rimantha. 1986. "Pandangan tentang gangguan Jiwa dan penanggulangannja secara tradisional pada masyarakat Karo." Ph.D. diss., Universitas Sumatera Utara.

————. 1989a. Rumah adat Karo milik dunia. *Waspada* 17 (June): 5.

————. 1989b. Pelestarian rumah adat Karo, untuk apa? *Waspada* 11 (July): 4.

Ginting, Meneth, and Ruth Daroesman. 1982. An economic survey of North Sumatra. *Bulletin of Indonesian Economic Studies* 18:52–83.

Ginting, Nalinta. 1984. *Turi-turin Beru Rengga Kuning*. Deli Tua: Toko Buku Kobe.

Glasner, Peter. 1977. *The Sociology of Secularization: A Critique of a Concept*. London: Routledge and Kegan Paul.

Glazer, Nathan, and Daniel P. Moynihan, eds. 1975. *Ethnicity: Theory and Experience*. Cambridge: Harvard University Press.

Goffman, Erving. 1956. The nature of deference and demeanor. *American Anthropologist* 58:473–502.

————. 1974. On face-work: An analysis of ritual elements in social interaction. In *Language, Culture and Society*, ed. Ben G. Blount, 224–49. Cambridge, Mass.: Winthrop.

Goldstein, Carl. 1990. Brand warfare. *Far Eastern Economic Review* 15 (November): 68–70.

Gonda, Jan. 1973. *Sanskrit in Indonesia*. New Delhi: International Academy of Indian Culture.

Goulet, Denis. 1983. *Mexico: Development Strategy for the Future*. Notre Dame: Notre Dame University Press.

Goyder, John C. 1983. Ethnicity and class identity: The case of French- and English-speaking Canadians. *Ethnic and Racial Studies* 6:72–89.

Gramsci, Antonio. 1957. *The Modern Prince and Other Writings*. New York: International Publishers.

————. 1971. *Selections from the Prison Notebooks of Antonio Gramsci*, ed. Quintin Hoare and Geoffrey Nowell Smith. New York: International Publishers.

Greenberg, Stanley. 1987. *Legitimating the Illegitimate*. Berkeley: University of California Press.

Gregory, Richard. 1987. *The Oxford Companion to the Mind*. Oxford: Oxford University Press.

Grothaus, Werner. 1970. 80 Jahre Karobatakkirche. *In die Welt für die Welt* 6 (8–9): 1–11.

Gusfield, Joseph. 1962. Mass society and extremist politics. *American Sociological Review* 27 (1): 19–30, 211–46.

Habermas, Jurgen. 1975. *Legitimation Crisis*. Boston: Beacon.

Halewijn, E. A. 1876. Geographische en ethnographische gegevens betreffevde het rijk van Deli. *Tijdschrift voor Indische Taal-, Land-, en Volkenkunde* 23:147–58.

Hall, Kenneth R. 1977. The coming of Islam to the archipelago: A re-assessment. In *Economic Exchange and Social Interaction in Southeast Asia*, ed. Karl L. Hutterer, 213–31. Michigan Papers on South and Southeast Asia, no. 13. Ann Arbor: Center for South and Southeast Asian Studies.

————. 1985. *Maritime Trade and State Development in Early Southeast Asia*. Honolulu: University of Hawaii Press.

Hamilton, Alexander. 1930. *A New Account of the East Indies*. London: Argonaut Press.

Hamilton, Nora. 1982. *The Limits of State Autonomy: Post-Revolutionary Mexico*. Princeton: Princeton University Press.

Handleman, Don. 1977. The organization of ethnicity. *Ethnic Groups* 1:187–200.

Harris, Grace Gredys. 1989. Concepts of individual, self, and person in description and analysis. *American Anthropologist* 91:599–612.

Harris, John, ed. 1764. *Voyages and Travels*. 2 vols. London.

Hart, Gillian. 1986. *Power, Labor, and Livelihood: Processes of Change in Rural Java*. Berkeley: University of California Press.

Hasbi, H. 1979–80. *Hegemonitas Kelurga dan Keagaman Beragama dalam Masyarakat Batak Karo*. Medan: Institut Agama Islam Nasional.

Hassan, Irene, Nurhadan Halud, Seymour Ashley, and Lois Ashley. 1975. *Tausug English Dictionary*. Manila: Summer Institute of Linguistics.

Hechter, Michael. 1975. *Internal Colonialism*. Berkeley: University of California Press.

Hefner, Robert. 1985. *Hindu Javanese*. Princeton: Princeton University Press.

————. 1987. Islamizing Java? Religion and politics in rural East Java. *Journal of Asian Studies* 46:533–54.

————. 1990. *The Political Economy of Mountain Java: An Interpretive History*. Berkeley: University of California Press.

Heider, Karl G. 1991. *Indonesian Cinema: National Culture on Screen*. Honolulu: University of Hawaii Press.

Helm, June, ed. 1967. *Essays on the Problem of the Tribe: Proceedings of the American Ethnological Society*. Seattle: University of Washington Press.

Higham, Charles. 1989. *The Archaeology of Mainland Southeast Asia*. Cambridge: Cambridge University Press.

Hindley, Donald. 1964. *The Communist Party of Indonesia, 1951–1963*. Berkeley: University of California Press.

Hirschman, Albert O. 1979. The turn to authoritarianism in Latin America and the search for its economic determinants. In *The New Authoritarianism in Latin America*, ed. David Collier, 61–98. Princeton: Princeton University Press.

Hirth, F., and W. W. Rockhill. 1911. *Chau Ju-Kua: His work on the Chinese and Arab Trade in the Twelfth and Thirteenth Centuries Entitled Chu-fan-chi*. St. Petersburg: Printing Office of the Imperial Academy of Sciences.

Hobsbawm, Eric, and Terence Ranger, eds. 1983. *The Invention of Tradition*. Cambridge: Cambridge University Press.

Horowitz, Donald. 1985. *Ethnic Groups in Conflict*. Berkeley: University of California Press.

Hostetter, Clyde H. 1988. The days of the scorpion. *Griffith Observer*, March, 6–19.

Howell, Signe. 1989. *Society and Cosmos*. Chicago: University of Chicago Press.

Huntington, Samuel P., and Joan M. Nelson. 1976. *No Easy Choice: Political Participation in Developing Countries*. Cambridge: Harvard University Press.

Hutchinson, John. 1987. Cultural nationalism, elite mobility and nation-building: communitarian politics in Northern Ireland. *British Journal of Sociology* 38:482–501.

Ibrahim, Ahmad, Sharon Siddique, and Yasmin Hussain. 1985. *Readings on Islam in Southeast Asia*. Singapore: Institute for Southeast Asian Studies.

Indonesia Editors. 1992. Current data on the Indonesian military elite July 1, 1989–January 1, 1992. *Indonesia* 53:95–136.

Ismail, Mohamed Yusoff. 1987. Buddhism and ethnicity: The case of the Siamese of Kelantan. *Sojourn* 2:231–54.

Jackman, Mary R., and Robert W. Jackman. 1984. *Class Awareness in the United States*. Berkeley: University of California Press.

Jackson, Karl D., and Luciana W. Pye, eds. 1978. *Political Power and Communications in Indonesia*. Berkeley: University of California Press.

Jakubowics, A. 1984. State and ethnicity: Multi-culturalism as ideology. In *Ethnic Politics in Australia*, ed. J. Jupp, 14–28. London: Allen and Unwin.

Jay, Robert. 1963. *Religion and Politics in Rural Central Java*. New Haven: Yale University Press.

Jayawardena, Chandra. 1980. Culture and ethnicity in Guyana and Fiji. *Man* 15: 430–50.

Jaylani, Tedjaningsih. 1959. Islamic marriage law in Indonesia. M.A. thesis, McGill University.

Jessop, Bob. 1985. *Nicos Poutlantzas: Marxist Theory and Political Strategy*. New York: St. Martin's Press.

Jiobu, Robert M. 1988. Ethnic hegemony and the Japanese of California. *American Sociological Review* 53:353–67.

Jones, Sidney R. 1980. "It can't happen here." A post-Khomeini look at Indonesian Islam. *Asian Survey* 20 (3): 311–23.

———. 1984. The contraction and expansion of the umat and the role of the Nahdatul Ulama in Indonesia. *Indonesia* 38:1–20.

Juynboll, Theodor W. 1925. *Handleiding tot de Kennis van de Mohammedaansche Wet.* Leiden: Brill.

Kahn, Joel S. 1982. Ideology and social structure in Indonesia. In *Interpreting Indonesian Culture: Thirteen Contributions to the Debate,* ed. Benedict Anderson and Audrey Kahin, 92–103. Ithaca: Cornell University Press.

Kamal, Mohammad Hassan. 1975. Contemporary Muslim religio-political thought in Indonesia: The response to "new order modernization." Ph.D. diss., Columbia University.

———. 1982. *Muslim Intellectual Responses to New Order Modernization in Indonesia.* Kuala Lumpur: Dewan Bahasa dan Pustaka.

Kariel, Henry S. 1968. Pluralism. In *The International Encyclopedia of the Social Sciences,* ed. David Sills, vol. 12, 164–69.

Kartomihardjo, Soeseno. 1979. Code switching in East Java. In *What is Modern Indonesian Culture?* ed. Gloria Davis, 55–68. Athens: Ohio University Center for International Studies.

Kayal, Philip. 1973. Religion and assimilation: Catholic "Syrians" in America. *International Migration Review* 7:409–26.

Keeler, Ward. 1987. *Javanese Shadow Plays, Javanese Selves.* Princeton: Princeton University Press.

Keesing, Roger M., and Robert Tonkinson, eds. 1982. Reinventing traditional culture: The politics of kastom in island Melanesia. *Mankind* 13(4).

Kern, Hendrik. 1903. Dravidische volksnamen op Sumatra. *Bijdragen tot de Taal-Land- en Volkenkunde* 7 (1): 358–62.

Keuning, Johannes. 1953–54. Toba-Bataks en Mandailing-Bataks: Hun culturele samenhang en daadwerkelijke antagonism. *Indonesia* 7:156–73.

Keyes, Charles. 1976. Towards a new formulation of the concept of ethnic group. *Ethnicity* 3:202–13.

———. 1979. *Ethnic Adaptation and Identity: The Karen on the Thai Frontier with Burma.* Philadelphia: Institute for the Study of Human Issues.

———. 1981. *Ethnic Change.* Seattle: University of Washington Press.

King, Dwight Y. 1978. Social mobilization, associational life, interest intermediation, and political cleavage in Indonesia. Ph.D. diss., University of Chicago.

———. 1982. Indonesia's New Order as a bureaucratic polity, a neopatrimonial regime or a bureaucratic-authoritarian regime: What difference does it make? In *Interpreting Indonesian Politics: Thirteen Contributions to the Debate,* ed. Benedict Anderson and Audrey Kahin, 104–16. Ithaca: Cornell University Press.

Kipp, Richard D. 1977. Adaptive strategy in a migrant community: The extension of Karo Batak kinship networks. In *Cultural-Ecological Perspectives on Southeast Asia,* ed. William Wood, 165–73. Athens: Ohio University Center for International Studies.

———. 1983. Fictive kinship and changing ethnicity among Karo and Toba migrants. In *Beyond Samosir,* ed. Rita Smith Kipp and Richard D. Kipp, 147–55. Athens: Ohio University Center for International Studies.

Kipp, Rita Smith. 1976. The ideology of kinship in Karo Batak ritual. Ph.D. diss., University of Pittsburgh.

———. 1979. The thread of three colors. In *Art, Ritual and Society in Indonesia,* ed. E. M. Bruner and J. O. Becker, 62–95. Athens: Ohio University Center for International Studies.

———. 1984a. The Karo Batak of Sumatra revisited. *Explorer's Journal* 62:120–25.

———. 1984b. Terms for kith and kin. *American Anthropologist* 86:905–26.

———. 1986a. Terms of endearment: Karo Batak lovers as siblings. *American Ethnologist* 13:632–45.

———. 1986b. Karo Batak rice rituals then and now. In *Cultures and Societies of North Sumatra,* ed. Rainer Carle, 253–73. Veröffentlichungen des Seminars für Indonesische und Südeespraeken der Universität Hamburg, vol. 19. Berlin: Dietrich Reimer Verlag.

———. 1990. *The Early Years of a Dutch Colonial Mission: The Karo Field.* Ann Arbor: University of Michigan Press.

Kipp, Rita Smith, and Richard D. Kipp, eds. 1983. *Beyond Samosir: Recent Studies of the Batak Peoples of Sumatra.* Athens: Ohio University Center for International Studies.

Kipp, Rita Smith, and Susan Rodgers, eds. 1987. *Indonesian Religions in Transition.* Tucson: University of Arizona Press.

Klesner, Joe. 1990. Electoral processes and regime liberalization: Brazil and Mexico compared. Paper presented at the annual meeting of the American Political Science Association.

Kligman, Gail. 1988. *The Wedding of the Dead: Ritual, Poetics, and Popular Culture in Transylvania.* Berkeley: University of California Press.

Koentjaraningrat. 1987. Anthropology in Indonesia. *Journal of Southeast Asian Studies* 18:217–34.

Kondo, Dorinne K. 1990. *Crafting Selves.* Chicago: University of Chicago Press.

Kongress Kebudayaan Karo. 1958. *Sedjarah Kebudayaan Karo.* Kabanjahe: Toko Bukit Mbelin Gunana.

Krause, Lawrence B., Koh Ai Tee, and Lee (Tsao) Yuan. 1987. *The Singapore Economy Reconsidered.* Singapore: Institute of Southeast Asian Studies.

Kuipers, Joel C. 1991. *Power in Performance.* Philadelphia: University of Pennsylvania Press.

Kuper, Leo. 1969. Ethnic and racial pluralism: Some aspects of polarization and depluralization. In *Pluralism in Africa,* ed. Leo Kuper and M. G. Smith, 459–87. Berkeley: University of California Press.

Laitin, David. 1986. *Hegemony and Culture.* Chicago: University of Chicago Press.

———. 1991. The national uprisings in the Soviet Union. *World Politics* 44:138–77.

Lal, Barbara B. 1983. Perspectives on ethnicity: Old wine in new bottles. *Ethnic and Racial Studies* 6:154–73.

Lasch, Christopher. 1979. *The Culture of Narcissism.* New York: Norton.

Latuihamallo, P. D. 1968. Missionology and politics. *Southeast Asian Journal of Theology* 10:99–131.

Layne, Linda. 1989. The dialogics of tribal self-representation in Jordan. *American Ethnologist* 16:24–39.

Leach, Edmund. 1954. *Political Systems of Highland Burma.* Boston: Beacon Press.

———. 1961. The structural implications of matrilateral cross-cousin marriage. In *Rethinking Anthropology,* ed. E. R. Leach, 54–104. London: University of London Press.

Lee, Raymond. 1988. Patterns of religious tension in Malaysia. *Asian Survey* 28 (4): 400–418.

Lehman, F. K. 1979. Who are the Karen, and if so, why? Karen ethnohistory and a formal theory of ethnicity. In *Ethnic Adaptation and Identity,* ed. Charles F. Keyes, 215–53. Philadelphia: Institute for the Study of Human Issues.

Lessa, William A., and Evon Z. Vogt, eds. 1965. *Reader in Comparative Religion.* New York: Harper and Row.

Lev, Daniel. 1972. *Islamic Courts in Indonesia.* Berkeley: University of California Press.

Levine, Daniel H. 1986. Religion and politics in comparative and historical perspective. *Comparative Politics* 19:95–122.

Lévi-Strauss, C. 1969. *The Elementary Structures of Kinship.* Boston: Beacon Press.

Levy, Robert. 1973. *Tahitians: Mind and Experience in the Society Islands.* Chicago: University of Chicago Press.

Liddle, R. William. 1970. *Ethnicity, Party, and National Integration.* New Haven: Yale University Press.

———. 1985. Soeharto's Indonesia: Personal rule and political institutions. *Pacific Affairs* 58:68–90.

———. 1987. The Politics of shared growth: Some Indonesian cases. *Comparative Politics* 19:127–46.

———. 1988a. Indonesia in 1987: The New Order at the height of its power. *Asian Survey* 28:180–91.

———. 1988b. *Politics and Culture in Indonesia.* Ann Arbor: University of Michigan Press.

———. 1989a. Development or democracy. *Far Eastern Economic Review* 9 (November): 22–23.

———. 1989b. The relative autonomy of the third world politician: Soeharto and Indonesian economic development in comparative perspective. Paper presented at the annual meeting of the American Political Science Association.

———. 1990. Indonesia is Indonesia. In *Politics of Middle Class Indonesia,* ed. Richard Tanter and Kenneth Young, 53–58. Australia: Centre of Southeast Asian Studies, Monash University Press.

Light, Ivan. 1981. Ethnic succession. In *Ethnic Change,* ed. Charles Keyes, 54–86. Seattle: University of Washington Press.

Lijphart, Arend. 1968. *The Politics of Accommodation: Pluralism and Democracy in the Netherlands.* Berkeley: University of California Press.

———. 1977. *Democracy in Plural Societies.* New Haven: Yale University Press.

Linnekin, Jocelyn, and Lin Poyer, eds. 1990. *Cultural Identity and Ethnicity in the Pacific.* Honolulu: University of Hawaii Press.

Linz, Juan. 1975. Totalitarian and authoritarian regimes. In *Handbook of Political Science.* Vol. 3, *Macropolitical Theory,* ed. Fred I. Greenstein and Nelson W. Polsby, 175–411. Reading, Mass.: Addison-Wesley.

Little, Kenneth. 1957. The role of voluntary associations in West African urbanization. *American Anthropologist* 59:579–96.

Loeb, Edwin. [1935] 1972. *Sumatra: Its History and People.* London: Oxford University Press.

Long, Litt Wong. 1986. Muslim Chinese in Malaysia. Paper prepared for a sociology seminar, National University of Singapore, 8 July.

Luckmann, Thomas. 1967. *The Invisible Religion: The Problem of Religion in Modern Society.* New York: Macmillan.

Macdonell, Arthur A. 1954. *A Practical Sanskrit Dictionary.* London: Oxford University Press.

MacIntyre, Alasdair. 1967. *Secularization and Moral Change.* London: Oxford University Press.

McKay, J. 1982. Exploratory synthesis of primordial and mobilizationist approaches to ethnic phenomena. *Ethnic and Racial Studies* 5:395–420.

Mackie, J. A. C. 1976. *The Chinese in Indonesia.* Honolulu: University of Hawaii Press.

————. 1990a. Property and power in Indonesia. In *Politics of Middle Class Indonesia,* ed. Richard Tanter and Kenneth Young, 71–95. Australia: Centre for Southeast Asian Studies, Monash University Press.

————. 1990b. Money and the middle class. In *The Politics of Middle Class Indonesia,* ed. Richard Tanter and Kenneth Young, 96–122. Australia: Centre for Southeast Asian Studies, Monash University Press.

McKinnon, Edmund Edwards. 1984. Kota Cina: Its context and meaning in the trade of Southeast Asia in the twelfth to fourteenth centuries. Ph.D. diss., Cornell University.

————. 1987. New light on the Indianization of the Karo Batak. In *Cultures and Societies of North Sumatra,* ed. Rainer Carle, 81–110. Veröffentlichungen des Seminars für Indonesische und Südeesprakekn der Universität Hamburg, vol. 19. Berlin: Dietrich Reimer Verlag.

McVey, Ruth. 1965. *The Rise of Indonesian Communism.* Ithaca: Cornell University Press.

————. 1970. Nationalism, Islam, and Marxism: The management of ideological conflict in Indonesia. In *Nationalism, Islam, and Marxism,* by Soekarno, 1–33. Modern Indonesia Project Translation Series. Ithaca: Cornell University Southeast Asia Program.

————. 1982. The Beamtenstaat in Indonesia. In *Interpreting Indonesian Politics: Thirteen Contributions to the Debate,* ed. Benedict Anderson and Audrey Kahin, 84–91. Ithaca: Cornell University Press.

————. 1983. Faith as the outsider: Islam in Indonesian politics. In *Islam in the Political Process,* ed. James Piscatori, 199–225. Cambridge: Cambridge University Press.

Madan, T. N. 1984. Coping with ethnic diversity: A South Asian perspective. In *The Prospects for Plural Societies,* ed. David Maybury-Lewis, 136–45. 1982 Proceedings of the American Ethnological Society. Washington, D.C.: American Ethnological Society.

Madjid, Nurcholish. 1979. The issue of modernization among Muslims in Indonesia: From a participant's point of view. In *What is Modern Indonesian Culture?* ed. Gloria Davis, 143–55. Athens: Ohio University Center for Southeast Asian Studies.

———. 1989. *Islam, Kemodernan dan Keindonesiaan.* Bandung: Mizan.

Mahasin, Aswab. 1990. The Santri middle class: An insider's view. In *The Politics of Middle Class Indonesia,* ed. Richard Tanter and Kenneth Young, 138–44. Australia: Centre of Southeast Asian Studies, Monash University Press.

Maine, Henry Sumner. [1884] 1970. *Ancient Law.* Reprint of tenth edition. Gloucester: Peter Smith.

Malloy, James M. 1970. Authoritarianism and corporatism in Latin America: the modal pattern. In *Authoritarianism and Corporatism in Latin America,* ed. James M. Malloy, 3–19. Pittsburgh: University of Pittsburgh Press.

Marcus, George E., and Michael M. J. Fischer. 1986. *Anthropology as Cultural Critique.* Chicago: University of Chicago Press.

Markoff, John, and Daniel Regan. 1986. Religion, the state and political legitimacy in the world's constitutions. In *Church-State Relations,* ed. Thomas Robbins and Roland Robertson, 161–82. New York: Transaction Books.

Marsden, William. 1966. *The History of Sumatra.* Kuala Lumpur: Oxford University Press.

Martadi, E. n.d. Sejarah Masuk dan Perkembangan Agama Islam di Taneh Karo Simalem. Typescript.

Martin, David. 1978. *A General Theory of Secularization.* New York: Harper and Row.

———. 1990. *Tongues of Fire.* Oxford: Basil Blackwell.

Marwick, Arthur. 1980. *Class: Image and Reality in Britain, France and the USA Since 1930.* New York: Oxford University Press.

Maybury-Lewis, David. 1984a. Conclusion: Living in Leviathan: Ethnic groups and the state. In *The Prospects for Plural Societies,* ed. David Maybury-Lewis, 220–31. 1982 Proceedings of the American Ethnological Society. Washington, D.C.: American Ethnological Society.

———. 1984b. Introduction: Alternatives to extinction. In *The Prospects for Plural Societies,* ed. David Maybury-Lewis, 1–6. 1982 Proceedings of the American Ethnological Society. Washington, D.C.: American Ethnological Society.

Mazrui, Ali A. 1969. Pluralism and national integration. In *Pluralism in Africa,* ed. Leo Kuper and M. G. Smith, 333–50. Berkeley: University of California Press.

Mead, George Herbert. 1934. *Mind, Self and Society from the Perspective of a Social Behaviorist.* Chicago: University of Chicago Press.

Meland, Bernard Eugene. 1966. *The Secularization of Modern Culture.* New York: Oxford University Press.

Miksic, John N. 1979. Archaeology, trade and society in Northeast Sumatra. Ph.D. diss., Cornell University.

Miliband, Ralph. 1969. *The State in Capitalist Society*. New York: Basic Books.

———. 1972. Reply to Nicos Poulantzas. In *Ideology in Social Science*, ed. Robin Blackburn, 253–62. London: Fontana.

Milner, Anthony. 1977. The Malay Raja: A study of Malay political culture in East Sumatra and the Malay Peninsula in the early nineteenth century. Ph.D. diss., Cornell University.

———. 1982. *Kerajaan: Malay Political Culture on the Eve of Colonial Rule*. Tucson: Association for Asian Studies, University of Arizona Press.

———. 1986. Malay local history: An introduction. *Journal of Southeast Asian Studies* 17 (1): 1–4.

Milner, Anthony C., E. Edwards McKinnon, and Tengku Luckman Sinar. 1978. A note on Aru and Kota Cina. *Indonesia* 26:1–42.

Mines, Mattison. 1988. Conceptualizing the person. *American Anthropologist* 90: 568–79.

Mintz, Malcolm. 1971. *Bikol Dictionary*. Honolulu: University of Hawaii Press.

Mitchell, J. Clyde. 1956. *The Kalela Dance: Aspects of Social Relationship among Urban Africans in Northern Rhodesia*. The Rhodes-Livingstone Papers, no. 27. Manchester: Manchester University Press.

———. 1960. Tribalism and the plural society. In *Black Africa*, ed. John Middleton, 257–69. London: Macmillan.

Mol, Hans. 1976. *Identity and the Sacred: A Sketch for a New Social Scientific Theory of Religion*. Oxford: Blackwell.

———. 1978. *Identity and Religion: International, Cross-Cultural Approaches*. Beverly Hills: Sage.

Mortimer, Rex. 1974. *Indonesian Communism under Sukarno*. Ithaca: Cornell University Press.

———. 1982. Class, social cleavage and Indonesian communism. In *Interpreting Indonesian Politics: Thirteen Contributions to the Debate*, ed. Benedict Anderson and Audrey Kahin, 54–83. Ithaca: Cornell University Southeast Asia Program.

Mudzhar, H. M. Atho. 1985. Mesjid dan bakul keramat: Konflik dan intigrasi dalam masyarakat Bugis Amparita. In *Agama dan Realitas Sosial*, ed. Mukhlis dan K. Robinson, 1–90. Indonesia: Universitas Hasanuddin.

Mukhlis, and Kathryn Robinson. 1985. *Agama dan Realitas Sosial*. Indonesia: Universitas Hasanuddin.

Mulkhan, A. Munir. 1989. *Perubahan Perilaku Politik dan Polarisasi Umat Islam 1965–1987*. Jakarta: Rajawali Pers.

Murdock, George Peter. 1949. *Social Structure*. New York: Macmillan.

Nagata, Judith. 1981. In defense of ethnic boundaries: The changing myths and charters of Malay identity. In *Ethnic Change*, ed. Charles Keyes, 87–116. Seattle: University of Washington Press.

———. 1984. Particularism and universalism in religious and ethnic identities: Malay, Islam and other cases. In *The Prospects for Plural Societies*, ed. David Maybury-Lewis, 121–35. 1982 Proceedings of the American Ethnological Society. Washington, D.C.: American Ethnological Society.

Naim, Sahibi. 1983. *Kerukunan Antar Umat Beragama*. Jakarta: Gunung Agung.

Nash, Manning. 1989. *The Cauldron of Ethnicity in the Modern World.* Chicago: University of Chicago Press.

Nasir, Anwar. 1987. Hi tech, low yield. *Far Eastern Economic Review* 11 (June): 110–11.

Neumann, J. H. 1901. Uit een brief van Br. Neumann. *Maandberichten Nederlands Zendelinggenootschap* 11:179–81.

———. 1907. Ressort Sibolangit: Het jaar 1906. *Mededeelingen Nederlands Zendelinggenootschap* 51:59–71.

———. 1922. Zending en school in Deli. *Mededeelingen Nederlands Zendelinggenootschap* 66:58–67.

———. 1926. Bijdragen tot de geschiedenis der Karo-Batak stammen. *Bijdragen tot de Taal- Land- en Volkenkunde* 82:1–36.

Niebuhr, H. Richard. 1954. *The Social Sources of Denominationalism.* New York: Henry Holt.

Nielson, Francois. 1985. Toward a theory of ethnic solidarity in modern societies. *American Sociological Review* 50:133–49.

Noer, Deliar. 1978. *Administration of Islam in Indonesia.* Cornell University Modern Indonesia Project, no. 58. Ithaca: Cornell University.

Norton, Anne. 1988. *Reflections on Political Identity.* Baltimore: Johns Hopkins University Press.

Norton, R. 1983. Ethnicity, "ethnicity" and culture theory. *Man* 18:190–91.

———. 1984. Ethnicity and class: A conceptual note with reference to the politics of post-colonial societies. *Ethnic and Racial Studies* 7:426–34.

Nottingham, Elizabeth K. 1971. *Religion: A Sociological View.* New York: Random House.

Obeyesekere, Gananath. 1992. *The Apotheosis of Captain Cook: European Myth-Making in the Pacific.* Princeton: Princeton University Press.

O'Brien, Jan. 1986. Towards a reconstitution of ethnicity: Capitalist expansion and cultural dynamics in Sudan. *American Anthropologist* 88:898–907.

O'Connor, James. 1973. *The Fiscal Crisis of the State.* New York: St. Martin's Press.

———. 1974. *The Corporations and the State: Essays in the Theory of Capitalism and Imperialism.* New York: Harper and Row.

O'Donnell, Guillermo A. 1977. Corporatism and the question of the state. In *Authoritarianism and Corporatism in Latin America,* ed. James M. Malloy, 49–87. Pittsburgh: University of Pittsburgh Press.

Ortner, Sherry. 1989. *High Religion.* Princeton: Princeton University Press.

Osman-Rani, Hassan. 1990. Economic development and ethnic integration: The Malaysian experience. *Sojourn* 5 (1): 1–34.

Parker, Richard. 1972. *The Myth of the Middle Class.* New York: Harper.

Parkin, Harry. 1978. *Batak Fruit of Hindu Thought.* Madras: Christian Literature Society.

Patterson, Horace O. 1977. *Ethnic Chauvinism: The Reactionary Impulse.* New York: Stein and Day.

Peacock, James L. 1973. *Indonesia: An Anthropological Perspective.* Pacific Palisades, Calif.: Goodyear Publishing.

————. 1978. *Purifying the Faith: The Muhammadijah Movement in Indonesian Islam*. Menlo Park, Calif.: Benjamin/Cummings.

Pederson, Paul. 1970. *Batak Blood and Protestant Soul: The Development of National Batak Churches in North Sumatra*. Grand Rapids, Mich.: Eerdmans.

Pelzer, Karl. 1978. *Planter and Peasant: Colonial Policy and the Agrarian Struggle in East Sumatra, 1863–1847*. The Hague: Nijhoff.

Penny, David H., and Masri Singarimbun. 1967. Economic activity among the Karo Batak of Indonesia: A case study of economic change. *Bulletin of Indonesian Economic Studies* 6:31–65.

Philibert, Jean-Marc. 1986. The politics of tradition: Toward a generic culture in Vanuatu. *Mankind* 16:1–12.

Pluvier, Jan. 1978. *Indonesia: Kolonialisme, Onafhankelijkheid, Neo-Kolonialisme*. Nijmegen: Socialistise Uitgeverij.

Poerwadarminta, W. J. S. 1976. *Kamus Umum Bahasa Indonesia*. Jakarta: Balai Pustaka.

Poggi, Gianfranco. 1978. *The Development of the Modern State*. Stanford: Stanford University Press.

Polo, Marco. 1929. *The Book of Ser Marco Polo*. Trans., ed., and notes by Sir Henry Yule. 3d. ed. London: John Murray.

Pompe, S. 1988. Mixed marriages in Indonesia: Some comments on the law and literature. *Bijdragen tot de Taal-, Land-en Volkenkunde* 144:259–75.

Portier, M. Karen, and Herman Slaats. 1987. Women and the division of parental land in Karo society. In *Cultures and Societies of North Sumatra*, ed. Rainer Carle, 303–8. Veröffentlichungen des Seminars für Indonesische und Südeespraeken der Universität Hamburg, vol. 19. Berlin: Dietrich Reimer Verlag.

Poulantzas, Nicos. 1972. The problem of the capitalist state. In *Ideology in Social Science*, ed. Robin Blackburn, 238–53. Glasgow: Fontana.

————. 1974. *Political Power and Social Classes*. London: New Left Books.

Premdas, Ralph R. 1985. The Organisasi Papua Merdeka in Irian Jaya. *Asian Survey* 25 (October): 1055–74.

Prinst, Darwan, and Darwin Prinst. 1984. *Sejarah dan Kebudayaan Karo*. Jakarta: Yrama.

Purdy, Susan S. 1982. The civil religion thesis as it applies to a pluralistic society: Pancasila democracy in Indonesia (1945–1965). *Journal of International Affairs*. 36:307–16.

Pustaka si Badia. 1987. Jakarta: Lembaga Alkitab Indonesia.

Putro, Brahma. 1981. *Karo Dari Jaman ke Jaman*. Medan: Yayasan Massa.

Raffles, Sophia. 1830. *Memoir of the Life and Public Services of Sir Thomas Stanford Raffles, F.R.S. etc., Particularly in the Government of Java, 1811–1816, and of Bencoolen and its Dependencies, 1817–1824; With Details of the Commerce and Resources of the Eastern Archipelago and Selections from his Correspondence*. London: John Murray.

Rais, Amin. 1983. Kata pengantur. In *Beberapa Pandangan tentang Pemerintahan Islam*, ed. Salem Azzam, 1–31. Bandung: Mizan.

Rambo, A. Terry, Kathleen Gillogly, and Karl L. Hutterer, eds. 1988. *Ethnic Diversity and the Control of Natural Resources in Southeast Asia*. Michigan Papers on South and Southeast Asian Studies, no. 32. Ann Arbor: Center for South and Southeast Asian Studies.

Reid, Anthony. 1970. Early Chinese migration into North Sumatra. In *Studies in the Social History of China and Southeast Asia*, ed. Jerome Cheu and N. Tarling, 289–320. Cambridge: Cambridge University Press.

———. 1979. *The Blood of the People: Revolution and the End of Traditional Rule in Northern Sumatra*. Kuala Lumpur: Oxford University Press.

Richmond, Anthony H. 1984. Ethnic nationalism and post-industrialism. *Ethnic and Racial Studies* 7:4–18.

Ricklefs, Merle C. 1981. *A History of Modern Indonesia*. Bloomington: Indiana University Press.

Robison, Richard. 1982. Culture, politics, and economy in the political history of the New Order. In *Interpreting Indonesian Politics: Thirteen Contributions to the Debate*, ed. Benedict Anderson and Audrey Kahin, 131–48. Ithaca: Cornell University Press.

———. 1986. *Indonesia: The Rise of Capital*. Australia: Allen and Unwin.

———. 1988. Authoritarian states, capital-owning classes, and the politics of newly industrializing countries: The case of Indonesia. *World Politics* 41, no. 1 (October): 52–74.

Rodgers, Susan. 1979. Advice to the newlyweds: Spirok Batak wedding speeches— adat or art? In *Art, Ritual, and Society in Indonesia*, ed. Edward M. Bruner and Judith Becker, 30–61. Athens: Ohio University Center for International Studies.

———. 1981. *Adat, Islam and Christianity in a Batak Homeland*. Athens: Ohio University Center for International Studies.

———. 1983. Political oratory in a modernizing Southern Batak Homeland. In *Beyond Samosir: Recent Studies of the Batak Peoples of Sumatra*, ed. Rita Smith Kipp and Richard D. Kipp, 21–52. Athens: Ohio University Center for International Studies.

———. 1984. Orality, literacy and Batak concepts of marriage alliance. *Journal of Anthropological Research* 40:433–50.

———. 1986. Batak tape cassette kinship: Constructing kinship through the Indonesian national mass media. *American Ethnologist* 13:23–42.

———. 1987. City newspapers in the creation of a Batak political heritage. In *Cultures and Societies of North Sumatra*, ed. Rainer Carle, 189–220. Veröffentlichungen des Seminars für Indonesische und Südseespracken der Universität Hamburg, vol. 19. Berlin: Dietrich Reimer Verlag.

———. 1990. The symbolic representation of women in a changing Batak culture. In *Power and Difference: Gender in Island Southeast Asia*, ed. Jane Monnig Atkinson and Shelly Errington, 307–44. Stanford: Stanford University Press.

———. 1991. The ethnic culture page in Medan journalism. *Indonesia* 51:84–103.

Rogers, Marvin. 1982. Patterns of change in a rural Malay community: Sungai Raya revisited. *Asian Survey* 22 (8): 757–77.

———. 1988. Depoliticization of Indonesia's political parties: Attaining military stability. *Armed Forces and Society* 14:247–72.

Rosenau, Pauline Marie. 1992. *Post-Modernism and the Social Sciences*. Princeton: Princeton University Press.

Rothschild, Joseph. 1981. *Ethnopolitics: A Conceptual Framework*. New York: Columbia University Press.

Royce, Anya Peterson. 1982. *Ethnic Identity: Strategies of Diversity*. Bloomington: Indiana University Press.

Schadee, W. H. M. 1918. *Geschiedenis van Sumatra's Oostkust*. Mededeeling, no. 2. Amsterdam: Oostkust van Sumatra Instituut.

Schmitter, Philippe C. 1974. Still the century of corporatism? *Review of Politics* 36:85–131.

Schwarz, Adam. 1990. Commercial break. *Far Eastern Economic Review* 21 (June): 74–75.

———. 1991a. Piece of the action. *Far Eastern Economic Review* 2 (May): 39–41.

———. 1991b. Empire of the son. *Far Eastern Economic Review* 14 (March): 46–49.

———. 1992a. Islam and democracy. *Far Eastern Economic Review* 19 (March): 32.

———. 1992b. Strains of Growth. *Far Eastern Economic Review* 2 (April): 33.

Scott, James C. 1977. Protest and profanation: Agrarian revolt and the little tradition. *Theory and Society* 4:1–33; 211–46.

———. 1985. *Weapons of the Weak: Everyday Forms of Peasant Resistance*. New Haven: Yale University Press.

Sebayang, R. K. 1986. *Sejarah Sebayang Mergana*. Medan: R. K. Sebayang.

Seligson, Mitchell A. 1987. Democratization in Latin America: The current cycle. In *Authoritarians and Democrats: Regime Transition in Latin America*, ed. James M. Malloy and Mitchell A. Seligson, 3–11. Pittsburgh: University of Pittsburgh Press.

Sennett, Richard, and Jonathan Cobb. 1972. *The Hidden Injuries of Class*. New York: Vintage Books.

Sherman, D. George. 1990. *Rice, Rupees, and Ritual*. Stanford: Stanford University Press.

Shibutani, Tamotsu, and K. Kwan. 1965. *Ethnic Stratification: A Comparative Approach*. New York: Macmillan.

Shils, Edward. 1957. Primordial, personal, sacred and civil ties. *British Journal of Sociology* 8:130–45.

Shinn, Rinn-Sup. 1983. Government and Politics. In *Indonesia, A Country Study*, ed. Frederica M. Bunge, 177–217. Washington, D.C.: U.S. Government Publications Office.

Shweder, Richard H., and Edmund J. Bourne. 1984. Does the concept of the person vary? In *Culture Theory*, Richard A. Shweder and Robert A. Levine, 158–99. Cambridge: Cambridge University Press.

Siddique, Sharon. 1990. The phenomenology of ethnicity: A Singapore case-study. *Sojourn* 5 (1): 35–62.

Singarimbun, Masri. 1960. *1000 Perumpaman Karo*. Medan: Ulih Saber.

———. 1975. *Kinship, Descent and Alliance Among the Karo Batak*. Berkeley: University of California Press.

Singarimbun, Masri, and Ngukumi Barus. 1990. *Beru Dayang Jile-jile*. Jakarta: Yayasan Merga si Lima.

Sitepu, Bujur. 1978. *Mengenal Kebudayaan Karo*. Indonesia: Sigurunggurung.

Sitepu, Erlina. 1984. Problematika Masyarakat Islam dalam Menanggulangi Keluarga

Muallaf di Desa Sukanalu, Kecematan Barusjahe, Kabupaten Karo. Master's thesis. Medan: Institut Agama Islam Nasional.

Situmorang, Sitor. 1987. The position of the Si Singamanga-rajas from Pakkara in relation to the three main *marga*-groups: Borbor, Lontung, and Sumba. In *Cultures and Societies of North Sumatra,* ed. Rainer Carle, 221–33. Veröffentlichungen des Seminars für Indonesische und Südeespraeken der Universität Hamburg, vol.19. Berlin: Dietrich Reimer Verlag.

Sjamsuddin, Nazaruddin. 1989. *Integrasi Politik di Indonesia.* Jakarta: Gramedia.

Sklar, Richard. 1987. Postimperialism: A class analysis of multinational corporate expansion. In *Postimperialism,* David G. Becker, Jeff Frieden, Sayre P. Schatz, and Richard L. Sklar, 19–40. Boulder, Colo.: Lynn Reinner.

Skocpol, Theda. 1985. Bringing the state back in: Strategies of analysis in current research. In *Bringing the State Back In,* Peter Evans, Dietrich Rueschemeyer, and Theda Skocpol, 3–37. New York: Cambridge University Press.

Slaats, Herman M. C., and M. Karen Portier. 1981. *Grondenrecht en Zijn Verwerkelijking in de Karo Batakse Dorpssamenleving.* Nijmegen: Publikaties over Volksrecht, Katholieke Universisteit.

Smit, Gezinus. 1911. De kweekschool te Raya. *Maandberichten Nederlands Zendelinggenootschap,* special issue, 22–28.

Smith, Anthony D. 1983. *State and Nation in the Third World.* New York: St. Martin's Press.

———. 1984. Ethnic persistence and national transformation. *British Journal of Sociology* 35:452–61.

Smith, Michael G. 1969. Institutional and political conditions of pluralism. In *Pluralism in Africa,* ed. Leo Kuper and M. G. Smith, 27–65. Berkeley: University of California Press.

———. 1984. The nature and variety of plural units. In *The Prospects for Plural Societies,* ed. David Maybury-Lewis, 146–86. 1982 Proceedings of the American Ethnological Society. Washington, D.C.: American Ethnological Society.

Smith, Timothy. 1978. Religion and ethnicity in America. *American Historical Review* 83:1155–85.

Southall, Aiden. 1976. Nuer and Dinka are people: Ecology, ethnicity, and logical possibility. *Man* 11 (4): 463–91.

Spies, O. 1961. Mahr. In *Shorter Encyclopedia of Islam,* ed. H. A. R. Gibb and J. H. Kramer, 314–15. Leiden: Brill.

Steedly, Mary Margaret. 1989. Hanging without a rope: The politics of representation in colonial and post-colonial Karoland. Ph.D. diss., University of Michigan.

Stoler, Ann Laura. 1985. *Capitalism and Confrontation in Sumatra's Plantation Belt, 1870–1979.* New Haven: Yale University Press.

Strathern, Marilyn. 1988. *The Gender of the Gift.* Berkeley: University of California Press.

Sturrock, John, ed. 1979. *Structuralism and Since: From Lévi-Strauss to Derrida.* Oxford: Oxford University Press.

Su, Chung-Jen. 1967. Places in Southeast Asia, the Middle East, and Africa visited by Cheng Ho and his companions A.D. 1405–1433. In *Symposium on Historical,*

Archaeological and Linguistic Studies, ed. F. S. Drake, 198–211. Hong Kong: Hong Kong University Press.

Surbakti, A. R. 1986. Jambur budaya adat istiadat Karo. *Maranatha,* no. 2, Tahun 1, July.

Suryadinata, Leo. 1984. *Dilema Minoritas Tionghoa.* Jakarta: Grafiti Pers.

―――. 1986. *Cukong* in the New Order. Paper prepared for a political science seminar, National University of Singapore, 14 August. Typescript.

Suryohidiprojo, Sayidiman. 1990. Jatidiri dan kebudayaan bangsa. *Kompas,* 9 August.

Sutrisno, Slamet. 1983. *Sedikit Tentang Strategi Kebudayaan Nasional Indonesia.* Yogyakarta: Liberty.

Swift, Ann. 1989. *The Road to Madiun: The Indonesian Communist Uprising of 1948.* Cornell Modern Indonesia Project, Monograph Series, no. 69. Ithaca: Cornell University Southeast Asia Program.

Synulta, Er. 1978. *Ale-ale Uis Gara.* Medan: Djembatan Emas.

―――. 1983. *Surat Ukat.* Medan: Ulamin Kisat.

―――. 1984. *Luak Gurila Nari,* Vols. 1 and 2. Medan: Ulamin Kisat.

Tainter, Joseph A. 1988. *The Collapse of Complex Societies.* Cambridge: Cambridge University Press.

Talens, Jan P. 1916. De gedachtenisviering te Kabanjabe (Hoogvlakte Deli). *Maandberichten Nederlands Zendelinggenootshcap* 3:33–39.

Tambiah, Stanley. 1989. Ethnic conflict in the world today. *American Ethnologist* 16:335–49.

Tamboen, P. 1952. *Adat-Istiadat Karo.* Jakarta: Balai Pustaka.

Tamney, Joseph, and Riaz Hassan. 1987. *Religious Switching in Singapore: A Study of Religious Mobility.* Australia: Flinders University Press.

Tampenawas, Richard. 1894. Een en ander uit de aanteekeningen van R. Tampenawas, te Pernangenen. *Mededeelingen Nederlands Zendelinggenootschap* 38:227–46.

Tan, Mély G. 1991. The social and cultural dimensions of the role of ethnic Chinese in Indonesian Society. In *Indonesia* (special issue). The Role of the Indonesian Chinese in Shaping Modern Indonesian Life, ed. Virginia M. Barker, 111–25. Ithaca: Cornell University Southeast Asia Program.

Tanter, Richard, and Kenneth Young. 1990. *The Politics of Middle Class Indonesia.* Australia: Centre of Southeast Asian Studies, Monash University Press.

Tarigan, Henry Gunter. 1990a. Sunat tradisional pada masyarakat Karo. In *Perecikan Budaya Karo,* by Henry Gunter Tarigan, 173–78. Jakarta: Yayasan Merga si Lima.

―――. 1990b. *Perecikan Budaya Karo.* Jakarta: Yayasan Merga si Lima.

―――. 1990c. *Piso Surit.* Jakarta: Yayasan Merga si Lima.

―――. 1990d. *Tedeh-tedeh Perukuren.* Jakarta: Yayasan Merga si Lima.

―――. 1990e. *Turi-turin Beru Ginting Sope Mbelin.* Jakarta: Yayasan Merga si Lima.

Tarigan, Sarjani, ed. 1986. *Seminar Kebudayaan Karo dan Kehidupan Masa Kini.* Medan: unknown publisher.

Taylor, Charles. 1989. *Sources of the Self: The Making of Modern Identity.* Cambridge: Harvard University Press.

Thomas, Nicholas. 1992. The inversion of tradition. *American Ethnologist* 19:213–32.

Thompson, John L. 1983. The plural society approach to class and ethnic mobilization. *Ethnic and Racial Studies* 6:127–53.

Thompson, Kenneth. 1986. *Beliefs and Ideology.* Sussex: Ellis Horwood Limited.

Thomson, Alan. 1968. The churches of Java in the aftermath of the 30th of September Movement. *Journal of Southeast Asian Theology* 9:7–19.

Tibbets, G. R. 1971. *Arab Navigation in the Indian Ocean Before the Coming of the Portuguese.* London: Royal Asiatic Society.

Turnbull, Constance M. 1977. *A History of Singapore 1819–1975.* Kuala Lumpur: Oxford University Press.

Tsing, Anna Lowenhaupt. 1987. A rhetoric of centers in a religion of the periphery. In *Indonesian Religions in Transition,* ed. Rita Smith Kipp and Susan Rodgers, 187–210. Tucson: University of Arizona Press.

Utrecht, Ernst. 1978. Religion and social protest in Indonesia. *Social Compass* 25:395–418.

Vail, Leroy, ed. 1989. *The Creation of Tribalism in Southern Africa.* Berkeley: University of California Press.

van den Berg, Engelberts J. 1908. De zending op de Karo-Hoogvlakte in 1907. *Mededeelingen Nederlands Zendelinggenootschap.* 52:67–79.

Van den Berghe, Pierre. 1975. Ethnicity and class in Highland Peru. In *Ethnicity and Resource Competition in Plural Society,* ed. Leo A. Despres, 71–85. The Hague: Mouton.

———. 1981. *The Ethnic Phenomenon.* New York: Elsevier.

van der Kroef, Justus M. 1976. National security, defense strategy and foreign policy perceptions in Indonesia. *Orbis* 20, no. 2 (Summer): 461–96.

———. 1985. "Petrus": Patterns of Prophylactic Murder in Indonesia. *Asian Survey* 25 (7): 745–59.

van Dijk, C. 1981. *Rebellion under the Banner of Islam: The Darul Islam in Indonesia.* The Hague: Nijhoff.

van Muylwijk, Jan. 1939. De Karo-Batak-Zending, Ms. Nederlands Zendeling-genootschap.

van Nieuwenhuijze, C. A. O. 1958. *Aspects of Islam in Post-Colonial Indonesia.* The Hague: Van Hoeve Ltd.

Vatikiotis, Michael. 1988. Reviving the red threat. *Far Eastern Economic Review* 9 (June): 27.

———. 1989a. Wider jurisdiction. *Far Eastern Economic Review* 8 (June): 40–41.

———. 1989b. Call to the faithful. *Far Eastern Economic Review* 14 (December): 34.

———. 1990a. Practical piety. *Far Eastern Economic Review* 14 (June): 26–32.

———. 1990b. Ancient enmities. *Far Eastern Economic Review* 28 (June): 12–13.

———. 1990c. Glasnost or 100 flowers. *Far Eastern Economic Review* 18 (October): 23–24.

———. 1990d. Muffling the Monitor. *Far Eastern Economic Review* 15 (November): 23–24.

———. 1991. Discreet charms? *Far Eastern Economic Review* 21 (March): 30–32.

Vatikiotis, Michael, and Mike Fonte. 1990. Rustle of ghosts. *Far Eastern Economic Review* 2 (August): 18–19.

Vincent, Joan. 1974. The structuring of ethnicity. *Human Organization* 33 (4): 375–79.

Volkman, Toby Alice. 1984. Great performances: Toraja cultural identity in the 1970s. *American Ethnologist* 11 (1): 152–69.

———. 1985. *Feasts of Honor: Ritual and Change in the Toraja Highlands.* Champaign-Urbana: University of Illinois Press.

———. 1990. Visions and revisions: Toraja culture and the tourist gaze. *American Ethnologist* 17:91–110.

von der Mehden, Fred R. 1986. Islamic Revival in Malaysia and Indonesia. *Muslim World* 76:219–33.

Voorhoeven, Petrus. 1961. *A Catalogue of the Batak Manuscripts [Chester Beatty Library].* Dublin: H. Figgis.

Vuurmans, Hendrik. 1930. De pers in het Karo-Batakland. *Mededeelingen Nederlands Zendelinggenootschap* 74:328–45.

Wagner, Roy. 1975. *The Invention of Tradition.* Englewood Heights, N.J.: Prentice-Hall.

Wallerstein, Immanual. 1960. Ethnicity and national integration. *Cahiers de'etudes Africaines* 1 (3): 129–39.

———. 1974. The rise and future demise of the world capitalist system. *Comparative Studies in Society and History* 16:387–415.

Warren, Carol. 1990. Rhetoric and Resistance: Popular Political Culture in Bali. *Anthropological Forum* 6 (2): 191–205.

Warsani, Irmawati Suprapto, Juara Rimantha Ginting, and Jonni Purba, eds. 1989. *Pelestarian Rumah Adat Karo, Laporan Seminar.* Medan: Universitas Sumatera Utara.

Washbrook, David. 1990. South Asia, the world system, and world capitalism. *Journal of Asian Studies* 49:479–505.

Weatherbee, Donald. 1985. Indonesia: The Pancasila State. *Southeast Asian Affairs* 133–51.

———. 1986. Indonesia in 1985: Chills and Thaws. *Asian Survey* 26:141–49.

Weatherford, J. McIver. 1981. *Tribes on the Hill.* New York: Rawson, Wade.

Weber, Max. 1961. Ethnic Groups. In *Theories of Society: Foundations of Modern Sociological Theory,* vol. 1, ed. Talcott Parsons et al., 305–9. New York: Free Press.

———. 1964. *The Theory of Social and Economic Organization.* Trans. A. M. Henderson and Talcott Parsons. New York: Free Press.

———. 1978. *Economy and Society.* Vol. 1. Ed. Guenther Roth and Claus Wittich. Berkeley: University of California Press.

Wee, Vivienne. 1985. Melayu: Hierarchies of being in Riau. Ph.D. diss., Australian National University.

———. 1988. Material dependence and symbolic independence: Constructions of Melayu ethnicity in Island Riau, Indonesia. In *Ethnic Diversity and the Control of Natural Resources in Southeast Asia,* ed. A. Terry Rambo, Kathleen Gillogly, and

Karl Hutterer, 197–226. Michigan Papers on South and Southeast Asian Studies, no. 32. Ann Arbor: Center for South and Southeast Asian Studies.

Weinstock, Joseph A. 1981. Kaharingan: Borneo's "oldest religion" becomes Indonesia's newest religion. *Borneo Research Bulletin* 13:47–48.

———. 1987. Kaharingan: life and death in Southern Borneo. In *Indonesian Religions in Transition*, ed. Rita Smith Kipp and Susan Rodgers, 71–97. Tucson: University of Arizona Press.

Weissbrod, Lilly. 1983. Religion as national identity in a secular society. *Review of Religion Research* 24:188–205.

Westenberg, Carl J. 1892. Aanteekeningen omtrent de godsdienstige begrippen der Karo-Bataks. *Bijdragen tot de Taal-, Land-, en Volkenkunde* 5:208–53.

Wijngaarden, Jan K. 1894. De zending onder de Karau-Bataks (Deli). *Mededeelingen Nederlands Zendelinggenootschap* 38:62–85.

Williams, Brackette F. 1989. A class act: Anthropology and the race to nation across ethnic terrain. *Annual Review of Anthropology* 18:401–44.

Williams, Raymond. 1977. *Marxism and Literature*. Oxford: Oxford University Press.

Willis, Avery. 1977. *Indonesian Revival: Why Two Million Came to Christ*. South Pasadena: William Cary Library.

Wilson, Bryan. 1976. *Contemporary Transformations of Religion*. Oxford: Clarendon Press.

———. 1987. Secularization. In *The Encyclopedia of Religion*, ed. Mircea Eliade, 159–65. New York: Macmillan.

Winzeler, Robert L. 1988. Ethnic groups and control of natural resources in Kelantan, Malaysia. In *Ethnic Diversity and Control of Natural Resources in Southeast Asia*, ed. A. Terry Rambo, Kathleen Gillogly, and Karl L. Hutterer, 83–98. Michigan Papers on South and Southeast Asia, no. 32. Ann Arbor: Center for South and Southeast Asian Studies.

Wolf, Eric. 1982. *Europe and the Peoples Without History*. Berkeley: University of California Press.

Wolff, John U. 1972. *A Dictionary of Cebuano, Visayan*. Ithaca: Cornell University Press.

Wolters, O. W. 1970. *The Fall of Srivijaya in Malay History*. Ithaca: Cornell University Press.

———. 1975. Landfall on the Palembang Coast in medieval times. *Indonesia* 20:1–57.

Wood, Perry L. 1990. Indonesia: Seeking to preserve stability amidst change. Paper presented at the thirty-ninth annual meeting of the Midwest Conference on Asian Affairs, Bloomington, Indiana, 1 November.

Woodward, Mark. 1989. *Islam in Java: Normative Piety and Mysticism in the Sultanate of Yogyakarta*. Tucson: Association for Asian Studies and University of Arizona Press.

Worsley, Peter. 1984. *The Three Worlds: Culture and World Development*. London: Weidenfeld and Nicholson.

Yengoyan, Aram. 1988. Hierarchy and the social order: Mandaya ethnic relations in Southeast Mindanao, Philippines. In *Ethnic Diversity and the Control of Natural*

Resources in Southeast Asia, ed. A. Terry Rambo, Kathleen Gillogly, and Karl L. Hutterer, 173–94. Michigan Papers on South and Southeast Asian Studies, no. 32. Ann Arbor: Center for South and Southeast Asian Studies.

Yinger, Milton. 1957. *Religion, Society and the Individual: An Introduction to the Study of Religion.* New York: Macmillan.

———. 1967. Pluralism, Religion, and Secularism. *Journal for the Scientific Study of Religion* 6 (1): 15–28.

Yoon, Hwan Shin. 1991. The role of elites in creating capitalist hegemony in post-oil boom Indonesia. In *Indonesia* (special issue). The Role of the Indonesian Chinese in Shaping Modern Indonesian Life, ed. Virginia M. Barker, 127–43. Ithaca: Cornell University Southeast Asia Program.

Yoshida, Masanori. 1992. Folk Healers in Multi-Ethnic Settings: The Case of Tebing Tinggi, North Sumatra, Indonesia. *Man and Culture in Oceania* 8:59–88.

Young, Crawford. 1983. The temple of ethnicity. *World Politics* 35 (4): 652–62.

Zoetmulder, Petrus J. 1982. *Old Javanese-English Dictionary.* The Hague: Nijhoff.

Index

Abangan, 102n.5
Abdullah, Taufik, 97, 98, 113
Acciaioli, Greg, 112
Aceh, 16, 47, 49, 92, 95
Acehnese, 28, 31
Ackerman, Susan E., 75, 76, 84n.22
Adams, Kathleen M., 110, 111
Adat, 125, 146, 155, 178, 243; books on, 182; and Christianity, 143, 239–40; debate around meaning of, 251; and ethnic associations, 176; and Islam, 215, 228, 230, 233–34; seminars on, 157, 182–85
Agama, 109; at Taman Mini, 110; definition of, 90, 103n.11, 118, 239, 243; pressures to adopt, 115, 190
Al-Attas, Syed M. al. Naquib, 257
Alavai, Hamza, 71n.12, 84
Alienation, 8, 9, 12
Aliran, defined, 264n. 4
Althusser, Louis, 72
Anakberu-kalimbubu relations, 33–34, 126, 129, 142, 163, 167, 250; in clan associations, 168; and interethnic marriage, 31, 37–38, 127–33; mentioned 190, 240; roles within, 128, 146, 230, 234; and wealth differences, 137–38, 154; women in, 129, 173. *See also* Asymmetrical alliance; Kinship
Anderson, John, 26, 28, 30–32, 42, 44, 58, 72, 75, 84n.14, 122n.4
Andrain, Charles F., 80
Angkola, 39n.18, 41, 112–13, 188n.6
Anthropology, 122–23, 123n.5
Anticipated participation, 80, 187

Apter, David, 84n.19
Aqib, Zainal, 223
Arabic, 225
Aragon, Lorraine V., 119
Archaeological sites, 111
Arens, W., 25
Arisan. *See* Credit organizations
Arts, traditional, 74, 112–13. *See also* Dance
Aru, 16
ASEAN, 110
Association for the Experience of the Belief in the Almighty God (HPKTYME), 120
Asymmetrical alliance, 153, 170. *See also* Anakberu-kalimbubu relations; Marriage, of cross-cousins
Atkinson, Jane Monnig, 118, 123n.13
Avoidance, 126, 147–53
Awanohara, Susumu, 91, 92, 108
Aznam, Suhaini, 92, 115

Babcock, Timothy, 20
Badui, 116
Balai Pustaka Merga si Lima, 246
Balinese, 166, 247–48
Bangsa, shift in meaning of, 65n.16. *See also* Nationalism; Suku
Bangun, Payung, 137, 255
Bangun, Roberto, 163
Bangun, Teridah, 63, 182
Banton, Michael, 20
Barnett, Steve, 8, 13n.5
Barth, Fredrik, 19, 84n.17
Basham, Richard, 75

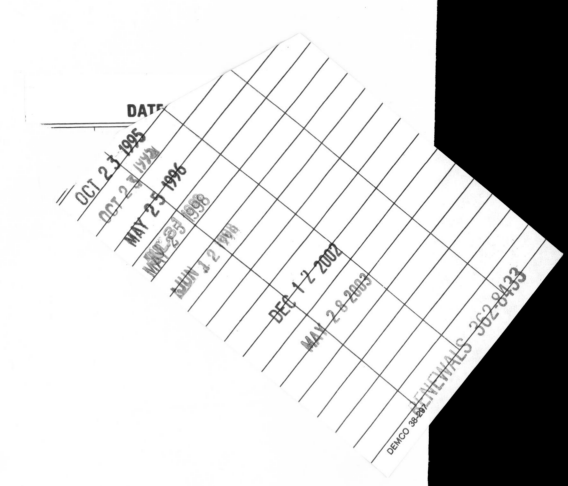